STUDIES OF LATIN AMERICAN SOCIETIES

D0727946

STUDIES
OF LATIN AMERICAN
SOCIETIES

———◆———

T. Lynn Smith

ANCHOR BOOKS
Doubleday & Company, Inc.
Garden City, New York

The Anchor Books edition is the first publication
of STUDIES OF LATIN AMERICAN SOCIETIES

Anchor Books edition: 1970

Dedicated to

LOWRY NELSON, CARL C. TAYLOR, and CARLE C. ZIMMERMAN

Lifelong Friends

Who led the way in the pragmatic study of societies in

Latin America

ACKNOWLEDGMENTS

Mr. Blaine Stevenson assisted in the preparation of copy for the printer and in the compilation of the bibliography, and Mrs. Diane Miller typed portions of the manuscript for this book.

Contents

Introduction

DURING THE 1960s sociological study of the societies and cultures of Latin America has been burgeoning in the universities and colleges of the United States. This is part and parcel of the increasing maturity of sociology as a scientific discipline, the decreasing provincialism on the part of those professionally engaged in the field, and the greater emphasis now being placed on cross-cultural studies in general. This change is signified by rapidly increasing numbers of professionally trained men and women who are doing research on various aspects of society in Spanish American countries and in Brazil; by more and more graduate students in sociology who are taking Latin American subjects for their theses and dissertations; by the enlarged enrollments of Latin American graduate students in the social science departments in the universities of the United States; and, most important of all, by the upsurge in the number of sociology departments that offer one or more courses dealing with societies and cultures in the southern portions of the Western Hemisphere.

Parallel with these important developments is the increased extent to which sociologists are collaborating with men and women in anthropology, economics, geography, history, political science, and the romance languages in interdisciplinary courses, institutes, lecture series, and other academic activities of one kind or another. In short, since 1960 sociology has been overcoming the lethargy which long characterized it (in comparison with several of the other social sciences) in everything related to the general comparative study of societies and cultures, and those of Latin America, in particular.

Presently there is a dearth of organized, systematized materials readily available to those students who enroll in the sociology courses dealing with Latin American societies or in the sociological parts of the interdisciplinary courses that focus attention upon the Spanish American and Portuguese portions of the Americas. Likewise, those teaching Latin American courses in the other social sciences find it difficult to find up-to-date materials on the population, the social structure and social institutions, and sociocultural changes and development for use as supplementary readings by the members of their classes. For this reason, after some urging by former students who now are responsible for many of the courses dealing with Latin American societies and cultures, and by other friends and associates throughout the United States, I decided to organize this small volume. It is made up of selections from the various titles I have published as a result of my efforts to apply the scientific method and the comparative approach in sociological studies of Latin American societies. It is hoped that such a book will prove especially useful to such groups as the following: (1) the students and instructors who are engaged in the engrossing study of societies and cultures in the richly varied Latin American countries; (2) those in the disciplines most closely related to sociology who need sociological materials for use as supplementary reading; (3) thousands of men and women actively engaged in work in Latin America (members of the Peace Corps, those employed by the United States Information Service, the ones on assignments by the U. S. Agency for International Development, missionaries of many denominations, and so on); and (4) those in the general public who want comprehensive information about the people, societies, and cultures in the immense area that lies to the south of the Rio Grande.

Frequently I have been asked by potential users of this book how I became interested in the sociological study of Latin American societies and about my various activities in connection with those studies. Therefore, brief responses to these queries are given here.

My first visit to Mexico marked the beginning of a sustained endeavor to apply a genuine comparative method in the scientific study of the societies of the United States and those of the various Latin American countries. By such a comparative method I understood how a sociologist can analyze the various features of two or more cultures or societies, using one and the same frame of reference, employing exactly the same methods of observation and analysis, and (to the extent possible) doing the work at the same time.

The more important of my professional activities related to Latin America prior to 1950 are mentioned in Selection Number 1. Subsequently a widely varied set of endeavors and experiences has characterized my work, and contributed to the fund of knowledge about Latin America that I have been able to attain. Probably the most important of these was the opportunity to work with graduate students from various parts of Latin America, the United States, and elsewhere, who were preparing themselves to work professionally with Latin American societies and cultures. Especially valuable in this connection has been the daily interchanges with the graduate students who worked under my direction in planning and executing their researches and writing their theses and dissertations.

The close associations and friendships formed in this manner led to a continuous exchange of publications with many persons in all parts of the Americas, and has produced a flow of materials to me (letters, clippings from newspapers, reprints of articles, monographs, books, copies of laws and decrees, reports of the census and other statistical offices, and so on). They also have led to many lengthy and serious conversations with former students (on the occasions of their visits to their old alma mater, and while I was in various parts of Latin America) in which perceptive, active, and highly informed young professionals briefed their former teacher on social problems, changes, trends, and developments in their respective countries. Rather intimately interwoven with all of this are the activities and aftermaths of the numerous commissions, conferences, committees, seminars, short courses, and work as adviser to the governments of Brazil and Colombia, in which I have participated, and through which lasting friendships were formed with Latin Americans interested in the social sciences in all of the countries. Many of the most useful reference works I have used in my various studies were obtained through the exchanges of publications which resulted from this line of activities.

Other experiences of the utmost importance in facilitating my observation of the structure and functioning of society in

Latin America occurred during extended periods in which I
have taught at various universities in Brazil, Chile, Colombia,
Mexico, and Venezuela. Indeed, I know of no better way of
having one's attention directed to the critical facts, those
which make or break the validity of any hypotheses he may
be entertaining, than by presenting his ideas in Spanish or
Portuguese to groups of students and young governmental
officials on their home grounds.

Finally, a series of research projects organized and conducted in a systematic manner have supplied much of the
data for the studies included in this compilation. These include the survey of Tabio, from which an extract is published as Selection Number 11, demographic studies of all the
Latin American countries (begun initially with the assistance
of a fellowship from the John Simon Guggenheim Memorial
Foundation), and work on colonization and settlement along
the eastern slope of the Andes from Venezuela to Bolivia
(also made possible by a five-year fellowship from that
Foundation).

The selections included in this volume were chosen to some
extent for the purpose of giving a fairly broad view of how
Latin American societies are organized and how they function.
Except for the extract from the survey of Tabio, none of them
report upon the results of my studies of specific communities
or of society in miniature. If some of the readers wonder if
the Brazilian and Colombian societies may not be stressed too
much, I can merely indicate that major parts of the time
spent has been upon studies of the organization of life and
labor in those two countries.

To a considerable extent, however, both my own use of
time, and the emphasis upon those countries in the selections
is deliberate. Brazil, or Portuguese America in its entirety,
occupies far more than one-third of all the territory within
the twenty Latin American countries, and has slightly more
than one third of the total population of Latin America; and
Colombia, third most populous of the Spanish American
countries, is almost as diverse socially and culturally as Brazil, and in many ways is more representative of Spanish
America in general than is any other one of the eighteen
nations in the group. By concentrating upon Brazil and Co-

lombia I have sought to use as fully as possible the comparative method mentioned above. From the standpoint of the subject matter, the selections are organized into the following parts of sections: (1) those dealing with the development of the sociological study of Latin American societies; (2) those treating various aspects of the population of Latin America; (3) those containing analyses and descriptions of the social structure and selected social institutions; and (4) those having to do with a closely related set of subjects involving maladjustments, values, change, and development.

PART I

THE DEVELOPMENT
OF THE
SOCIOLOGICAL STUDY OF
LATIN AMERICAN SOCIETIES

Introductory Note

FEW TITLES have been published that trace in any detail the development of the scientific study of societies in Latin America. This writer himself has endeavored to gain as full an understanding as possible of the growth of knowledge in this field, but has limited his publications on the subject to the two short treatises that make up this section. Selection Number 1 was prepared in 1954, a year after a section on "Sociology," for which he served as editor, began appearing in the *Handbook of Latin American Studies* (which has been published annually since 1934 under the general editorship of members of the staff of the Hispanic Foundation of the Library of Congress). It was written to supply users of the *Handbook* with a short introductory sketch of the development of an interest in Latin America on the part of sociologists working in the United States. A few years later the text of Selection Number 2 was prepared. It was done in connection with a general report (T. Lynn Smith, *Rural Sociology: A Trend Report and Bibliography*, published as *Current Sociology*, Vol. VI, No. 1, 1957) made by assignment for the International Sociological Association and UNESCO. Because of the limitations of space, the section dealing with Latin America was deleted, but the text of the same and the bibliography were published in the *Revista Mexicana de Sociología* (Vol. XIX, No. 1, No. 2, and No. 3, 1957). The analysis of the reasons for the slowness of the development of rural sociology in Latin America apply fully as well to sociology in general and all of its branches.

1 The Development of
Sociological Studies of Latin America
in the United States

A SERIOUS interest in Latin America on the part of sociologists in the United States is a comparatively recent development. This is true both with respect to the Latin American area as a fruitful field in which to carry out sociological research projects and with relation to Latin American materials as the content for college and university courses in sociology. It is even true with regard to a knowledge of and concern about the publications of sociologists and other social scientists in the Latin American countries. Prior to 1935 anything dealing with Latin America on the part of a sociologist in the United States was conspicuous by its absence. Even at that, however, Latin America was one of the first great world areas in which sociologists in this country developed an abiding interest.

Some steps, it is true, had been taken before 1935, and it is well to commence by turning briefly our attention to them. The first item deserving mention is Frank W. Blackmar's study of *Spanish Institutions of the Southwest*. It was published in 1891 at the Johns Hopkins University Press as one volume in a highly important series on social and political history. Although done before Blackmar was fully identified as a sociologist and dealing with the Spanish cultural heritage in parts of the United States, the book is an important landmark for all those interested in sociological studies of Latin America. Publications by North American sociologists relat-

---

From T. Lynn Smith, "Sociology," in *Handbook of Latin American Studies,* Francisco Aguilera, ed., 1951, No. 17, prepared by The Hispanic Foundation in the Library of Congress, Gainesville: University of Florida Press, 1954, pp. 234–238. Reprinted by permission of the publisher.

ing to the Latin American countries themselves were still many years in the future.

To E. A. Ross, the pioneering father of sociology who was most noted for his interest in travel, ability as a lecturer, and skill as a writer, must be given the credit for two of the first items sufficiently important to demand recognition. Not long after Ross' tour of the Orient resulted in a book on *The Changing Chinese* (1911), the keen sociological observations and interpretations made in the course of his trip around South America were published under the title *South of Panama* (New York: The Century Company, 1915). A few years later his perceptive mind found in the Mexican Revolution the theme for another book, *The Social Revolution in Mexico* (New York: The Century Company, 1923), long before there appears any substantial evidence that his interest in the hemisphere-stirring upheaval was shared by any of his colleagues.

L. L. Bernard is another who early sensed the importance of Latin America's social problems, began concerted efforts to learn about them, and made substantial attempts to interest his fellow sociologists and other social scientists in the Latin American area. Bernard's major activities in the field, however, appear to have been limited to a voluminous correspondence with Latin American scholars and to contributions to the periodical literature. On frequent occasions by extensive reviews of batches of Latin American publications and by articles on sociology in Latin American countries, he sought to inform sociologists, political scientists, and those interested in jurisprudence in the United States about the work and publications of their fellows in the other American republics. Major articles include his "Sociology in Argentina (Topical Summaries of Current Literature)" in the *American Journal of Sociology,* XXXIII (July, 1927), 110–117, and "The Development and Present Tendencies of Sociology in Argentina," in *Social Forces,* VI (September, 1927), 13–27. Another, "The Negro in Relation to Other Races in Latin America," on which his wife, Jessie Bernard, collaborated, appeared in *The Annals of the American Academy of Political and Social Science,* CXL (1928), 306–318. Following the establishment of the *American Sociological Review* in

1936 much of his comment appeared in that journal; the first issue itself contained a review in which he sought to introduce 23 Latin American books to his fellows in the American Sociological Society.

Emory S. Bogardus is a third sociologist whose early interest in Latin American studies deserves recognition. As professor at the University of Southern California and editor of *The Journal of Applied Sociology*, now called *Sociology and Social Research*, Bogardus early was challenged by the problems of the Spanish American ethnic group in Los Angeles and other parts of the Southwest. As a result space was given in the Journal to articles about the local scene, and the interest soon was broadened. He opened his journal to articles by others on subjects of direct concern to those interested in Latin America and he, himself, travelled in Mexico and wrote on Latin American topics.

The work of the Commission on Cuban Affairs is the fourth and final step of significance, prior to 1935, in the development of studies of Latin American phenomena by the sociologists of the United States. This Commission was appointed by the Foreign Policy Association in response to an invitation extended by President Carlos Mendieta early in 1934. Among the members were sociologists Carle C. Zimmerman of Harvard University and Leland Hamilton Jenks of Wellesley College, and in addition Helen Hall of the Henry Street Settlement in New York and M. L. Wilson, agricultural economist, then director of the Division of Subsistence Homesteads of the U. S. Department of the Interior and afterwards director of the United States Agricultural Extension Service. The Report of this Commission published by the Foreign Policy Association in 1935 under the title *Problems of the New Cuba* reflects, for the first time, the application of North American empirical research techniques in the sociological study of a part of the Latin American area. Particularly important for sociologists are the chapters entitled "Population Elements," "Family Organization and Standards of Living," "Social Welfare," "Social Aspects of the Sugar Industry," and "Land Colonization and Diversification." Undoubtedly their form and content were due largely to Zimmerman's work as a member of the Commission.

About 1935 there was a definite awakening of interest in the Latin American societies on the part of sociologists in the United States. Robert E. Park of the University of Chicago had just returned from a world tour, in the course of which the social problems of Brazil and the West Indies seem to have impressed him greatly. As a result he did much to stimulate an interest at Chicago, at Fisk University, and at other centers of learning in the subject of race and culture in Latin America. One of his students, Donald Pierson, went to Bahia, Brazil, in 1935 to collect materials for his Ph.D. dissertation, eventually published under the title *Negroes in Brazil* (Chicago: University of Chicago Press, 1942). In 1935, too, Eyler N. Simpson was in Mexico finishing the work on his classical study of the Mexican agrarian revolution, *The Ejido: Mexico's Way Out* (Chapel Hill: University of North Carolina Press, 1937), a volume which did much to interest young sociologists in the United States in the great rural civilizations of Mexico, Central America, and South America. In 1935, too, Carle C. Zimmerman extended his Latin American interest to Mexico, and was accompanied by T. Lynn Smith in a brief reconnaissance survey of some of the principal rural areas of that country. The following year Samuel H. Lowry went as a professor to the University of São Paulo, probably the first sociologist from the United States to fill such a role in Latin America; and Charles David Kepner published his *Social Aspects of the Banana Industry* (New York: Columbia University Press, 1936). At about this time, also, James G. Leyburn was actively engaged in the studies of Haitian society, which led to his *The Haitian People* (Yale University Press, 1941), and Lowry Nelson taught for a few months in Chihuahua, Mexico.

These activities on the part of a handful of North American sociologists did much to lay the groundwork for future developments, but, of course, they did not revolutionize the organization and conduct of sociological teaching and research in the United States. A survey by the Pan American Union of course offerings in Latin American studies showed that, in 1935–36, only one university in the United States was offering a sociology course of Latin American content, and three years later, for 1938–39 another survey revealed that only two colleges and universities offered such courses. (*Courses on Latin America:* Pan American Union, Washington, 1949, p. xxxi.) Nevertheless, the groundwork was being laid for important developments. In 1939 T. Lynn Smith, aided financially by the Julius Rosenwald Fund, spent four months visiting the Latin American countries, observing patterns of race relationships, and studying the problems of exchanging professors and students between universities in the United States and those in the Latin American countries. In 1939, too, Donald Pierson returned to Brazil to begin his long service of teaching research at the Escola de Sociologia e Política in São Paulo. In 1940–41 E. Franklin Frazier of Howard University spent a year in Brazil and the West Indies as a fellow of the John Simon Guggenheim Memorial Foundation. The same academic year, assisted by the General Education Board, Smith brought the noted Brazilian authority on the Negro, Arthur Ramos, to the Louisiana State University as visiting professor, where he gave a course on race and culture and another on the peoples and cultures of Brazil. Henceforth a course on Latin American Institutions was to be offered regularly at that University.

The Second World War which did so much to expand the economic, political, and social horizons of the people of the United States, proved to be a great stimulus to the further development of sociological study of Latin American society on the part of sociologists in this country. Before mentioning a few of the more important happenings, however, it seems appropriate to quote briefly from a survey of personnel and activities in the Latin American aspects of the humanities and social sciences at twenty universities of the United States. The study was done in 1942 under the auspices of a committee of the American Council of Learned Societies and the Social Science Research Council. Pertinent conclusions relative to the status of sociological studies are as follows: "One of the most neglected disciplines, while one of the most essential for an understanding of Latin America in the United States, sociology would seem one of the most indispensable corollaries of studies of such subjects as Latin American education. Activities in sociology were confined, in the universities visited, to New Mexico, where it is studied in its practical aspects associated with the special problems of that locality, and to Louisiana State University. . . . The illimitable possibilities and pressing necessity of research in this important discipline seem unrealized in this country." (*Notes on Latin American Studies*, No. 1, April 1943, pp. 39–40.)

Late in 1941 the United States Department of State, advised and assisted by the Office of Foreign Agricultural Relations of the United States Department of Agriculture, decided to send three sociologists who had specialized in the study of rural life to the three largest Latin American countries. As a result, in 1942, Carl C. Taylor went to Argentina, T. Lynn Smith to Brazil, and Nathan L. Whetten to Mexico, where each undertook the studies needed for securing as accurate a knowledge as possible of the basic patterns of rural society in the country to which he had been assigned. In addition to the reports prepared for the State Department, eventually the basic materials gathered in the countries themselves, supplemented by several years of additional work, after they had returned to the United States, resulted in Smith's *Brazil: People and Institutions* (Louisiana State University Press, 1946), Taylor's *Rural Life in Argentina* (Louisiana State University Press, 1948), and Whetten's *Rural Mexico* (University of Chicago Press, 1948). A few years later a fourth sociologist, Lowry Nelson, was sent to Cuba under a similar arrangement, and his volume, *Rural Cuba* (University of Minnesota Press, 1950), took its place alongside the others.

The years of the Second World War were ones in which the Office of Foreign Agricultural Relations of the United States Department of Agriculture, in close cooperation with the State Department, was experimenting with a technical assistance program in other countries, a line of activity which eventually came to be known as the Point-4 Program. This contributed significantly to the development of Latin American sociological studies in the United States, for Latin America was the first area in which such collaboration was attempted and a few rural sociologists were among the first specialists assigned. Undoubtedly the chaotic condition of the man-land relationships in many of the countries was responsible for this. In any case very early in the program T. Lynn Smith was assigned to Colombia as advisor on colonization and settlement and he later went to Brazil to advise on agrarian reform, Charles P. Loomis went to the cooperative agricultural experiment station at Tingo Maria in Peru, and Olen E. Leonard, after briefer periods of work in Ecuador and Peru, spent about two years as director of the cooperative agricultural experiment station in Bolivia. The opportunities for observation and study which these assignments afforded resulted in numerous articles in the professional sociological journals and several substantial monographs published in both Spanish and English editions. The latter include, T. Lynn Smith, Justo Díaz Rodríguez, and Luis Roberto Garcia, *Tabio: A Study in Rural Social Organization* (Washington, Office of Foreign Agricultural Relations, 1945; Spanish edition, Bogotá, Ministerio de la Economia Nacional, 1944); Olen E. Leonard, *Pichilingue: A Study of Rural Life in Coastal Ecuador* (Washington, Office of Foreign Agricultural Relations, 1947); Olen E. Leonard, *Canton Chulpas: A Socioeconomic Study in the Cochabamba Valley of Bolivia* (Washington, Office of Foreign Agricultural Relations, 1947; Spanish edition, La Paz, Ministerio de Agricultura, Ganaderia y Colonización, 1947); and Olen E. Leonard, *Santa Cruz: A Socioeconomic Study of an Area in Bolivia* (Washington, Office of Foreign Agricultural Relations, 1948; Spanish edition, La Paz, Ministerio de Agricultura, Ganaderia y Colonización, 1948); and Charles P. Loomis, *Studies in Rural Social Organization* (East Lansing, Michigan State College Bookstore, 1945). Eventually Leonard's work resulted in his *Bolivia: Land, People and Society* (Washington, The Scarecrow Press, 1952), the fifth comprehensive treatment of a Latin American Society to be produced by specialists in the sociology of rural life in the United States.

In the meanwhile, in a variety of ways, other sociologists from the United States were getting into Latin American countries for professional work. These include John and Marvis Biesanz who produced *Costa Rican Life* (Columbia University Press, 1944), and numerous subsequent articles dealing with social problems in Panama; Kingsley Davis, who wrote on the process of urbanization in Latin America; Clarence Senior, who early had undertaken studies of agrarian reform in Mexico (*Democracy Comes to a Cotton Kingdom,*

Mexico, Centro de Estudios Pedagogicos e Hispano Americanos, 1940), who studied intensively Puerto Rico and the problems of Puerto Rican migrants in New York City; George W. Hill, who began with work on immigration and colonization in Venezuela, and who has remained to teach in that country; Norman S. Hayner who has analyzed the ecological patterns of Mexico City; Norman D. Humphrey who has written on social stratification in a Mexican town; A. Rex Crawford, who served as cultural attaché at the American Embassy in Rio de Janeiro, and whose *A Century of Latin American Thought* (Harvard University Press, 1944), is an invaluable reference work; Melvin M. Tumin who surveyed a community in Guatemala; Wilson Longmore who worked on the health problems of several countries; and Harry B. and Audrey R. Hawthorn who made ecological studies of Sucre, Bolivia.

Probably the most important recent development in the sociological study of Latin American phenomena by North American scholars is the growing number of Ph.D. candidates who are going to Latin American countries for the intensive period of observation and study involved in gathering data for their dissertations. A partial list of those who have undertaken such studies in recent years includes Chester W. Young (rural life in Haiti), from Louisiana State University; Reed M. Powell (social stratification in Costa Rica), from Michigan State College; Paul H. Price (assimilation of Poles in Brazil), Marion T. Loftin (assimilation of Japanese in Brazil), Thomas R. Ford (Agrarian Reform in Peru), and Clark S. Knowlton (Assimilation of Syrians in Brazil), from Vanderbilt University; Leo A. Suslow (social reform in Guatemala), from Colgate University; and Sam Schulman (the positivist movement in Chile), on a grant from Princeton University.

As we enter the second half of the twentieth century, sociological studies of Latin American civilizations in the United States are far from maturity. Definitely they are in a secondary position in comparison with historical, geographical, or anthropological studies; and probably they do not rival the work in economics and political science. Nevertheless, great progress has been made in the last fifteen years. Much of what has been done will compare favorably from the qualitative standpoint with that in the related disciplines, or that of sociological studies of other areas. The most encouraging feature is the fact that there already are a few dozen well-trained young sociologists personally experienced in the Latin American area and equipped with the language and other requirements for lifetimes of productive work on the sociological studies of Latin American problems. Each year that passes sees several more added to their number. Compared with the situation 25 or even 10 years ago the prospects are highly encouraging.

2 The Development of
Rural Sociology in Latin America

———◆———

RURAL SOCIOLOGY is in the vanguard as a newer and more pragmatic type of sociology is developed throughout the Latin American countries. Even so, in most countries the progress is not spectacular and the changes are striking only to one who is familiar with the situation in the past. The fact is that all forms of specialization within the field of sociology have been slow in getting underway throughout most parts of Latin America, and this state of affairs seems likely to prevail for at least another decade. Courses in rural sociology in the various institutions of higher learning, the specific features of colleges and universities in the United States and Canada which provide the livelihood or part of it for several hundred professional rural sociologists, are conspicuous by their absence. Even fewer professional positions in research organizations, comparable to the places on the staffs of the agricultural experiment stations in the United States, are available to the Latin American who would like to devote his life to rural sociological research. There is little chance of great expansion in the immediate future, either in teaching positions or in research activities, and without such, almost no likelihood of any general, rapid, and sustained development of rural sociology as a science in the countries lying between the Rio Grande and Cape Horn.

Factors Retarding the Development of Rural Sociology

The nature of the factors or forces obstructing the development of rural sociology in Latin America deserve brief analy-

This is the English text of "El Desarrollo de la Sociología Rural en Latinoamerica," *Revista Mexicana de Sociología,* Vol. XIX, No. 1 (Jan.–April, 1957), pp. 1–14.

sis and description, since they are the ones that also are retarding many other aspects of intellectual progress in the area
under consideration. The explanation lies, primarily, in the
nature of the class system. As is well known most Latin American societies are sharply divided into a small aristocratic
element at the apex of the social pyramid and a large mass
of people at the base, with few persons of middle-class status
between the two. This, in turn, has engendered and maintained definite patterns of expectation relating to facilities for
higher education, the qualifications of those who should hold
professorships in them, and the extent to which any except
those who are born to high social positions should have access to the universities. Briefly the number of institutions of
higher learning throughout Latin America is very small, and
the total enrollment in them is negligible in relation to the
population. As a result there simply are not enough university teaching positions to offer employment to any considerable number of sociologists, general or rural. The same is
true, of course, in the other fields with the exception of law
and medicine.

Even the existing professorships are not filled by persons
who devote full time to university work. Rather they are
part-time positions occupied by intellectually inclined members of the upper class who devote the great bulk of their
time and energy to various professional, business, political,
and other interests outside the university. The professor who
devotes his life largely to sociological activities, not to say
teaching and research in rural sociology, is almost unknown
throughout Latin America.

At present the situation is changing to a considerable degree. The numerous descendants of those who have occupied
the high positions in Latin American society, along with the
members of the rapidly increasing middle classes, are demanding more and better facilities for higher education. Some
expansion is taking place. Social differentiation and specialization are making considerable headway. Nevertheless in most
institutions the offerings in sociology consist of a single course
in general sociology, or at least two or three courses, almost

none of which is devoted to rural sociology. Likewise professional research positions are almost impossible to find. Institutionalized facilities for agricultural research themselves are few and those established to date concentrate almost exclusively on technical agriculture. In these agricultural research agencies the deficiency with respect to rural sociology and the other social sciences is particularly acute.

In spite of all the obstacles, however, a few notable treatises dealing with rural society or rural social problems early were produced in the Latin American countries, and today, at a few selected locations, significant progress is being made in the cultivation of rural sociological studies.

Notable Early Treatises

It is not strange that some of the most important early work should have been done in Brazil. That country's great size, the fact that it contains one third of the people of Latin America, and, until recently, the overwhelming extent to which it was rural, pastoral, and agricultural no doubt had much to do with turning the course of events. Any intellectual who grappled realistically with some of the nation's most challenging problems, or who studied the growth and development of Brazilian society, almost had to produce something closely related to the field of rural sociology. Such contributions there were, and in considerable number. Here only four, all of them of excellent quality, are mentioned.

Euclydes da Cunha's classical study,[1] which was first published in 1902, deserves a place with the best produced in any country. Indeed it is considered generally as the greatest book ever written by a Brazilian. It contains the facts of rural life as seen and described by a military engineer who during the closing quarter of the nineteenth century fought campaign after campaign in Brazil's great hinterland. The first one-third of the book describes the environment, the people,

[1] *Os Sertões* (*Campanha de Canudos*), 15th ed., Rio de Janeiro, Livraria Francisco Alves, 1940. (English edition, translation by Samuel Putnam, *Rebellion in the Backlands,* Chicago: University of Chicago Press, 1944).

and the society in Brazil's great drought-ridden northeastern region; and the remainder of the volume recounts the experiences of the various expeditions sent to put down a sect that under the leadership of Antonio Conselheiro was engaged in building a New Jerusalem and openly defying state and federal authorities.

Oliveira Vianna's noted volumes are true rural sociological studies. In analyzing how Brazil's society developed its characteristic features, Vianna, one of the country's best legal minds, produced volumes that were abreast of, if not ahead of, comparable work in other countries at the time. Two of his books are of special interest to those of us who are interested in the study of rural societies. The first of these[2] appeared in 1918. A strictly sociological study of the rural populations of the states of São Paulo, Rio de Janeiro, and Minas Gerais, it is one of the earliest systematic treatments of rural society produced in America, and it also is one of the most important books ever written in Brazil. For one who would include Brazil in any comparative study of rural society, it is an indispensable source. In its pages one will find expositions dealing with such subjects as the following: the formation and roles of the rural aristocracy, the ethnic composition of the social classes, social psychology of the masters, the latifundium and its function in Brazilian society, the genesis and spirit of the clan, the institutions of social solidarity, local governmental institutions, and the social psychology of revolutions.

Oliveira Vianna's second monumental study of Brazilian rural society appeared in 1922 and was published as the Introduction to Brazil's 1920 census.[3] In this book Vianna focused upon the evolution of Brazilian society, the evolution of the race, and the evolution of political institutions respectively, all in the matrix of the overwhelmingly rural so-

[2] F. J. Oliveira Vianna, *Populações Meridionaes do Brasil; Historia—Organização—Psycologia, Primero Volume, Populações Ruraes do Centre-Sul: Paulistas-Fluminenses—Mineiros,* 4th ed., São Paulo: Companhia Editora Nacional, 1938.

[3] "O Povo Brazileiro e sua Evolução," *Recenseamento do Brazil Realizado em 1 de Setembro de 1920, Volume I, Introdução,* Rio de Janeiro: Typ. da Estatistica, 1922.

ciety in which they occurred. It should be indicated that Vianna's racial theories are hardly in accord with contemporary sociological and anthropological theory, but that in other respects this volume is of utmost importance for one who would understand Brazilian society.

Gilberto Freyre's *Casa Grande e Senzala*[4] has received the widespread acclaim that it deserves. It is probably the greatest sociological study produced in Latin America. In it a trained social scientist through his study of the plantation districts along Brazil's northeastern coast found a key to the development of the country's civilization.

A noted Brazilian educator, Carneiro Leão, also working in the northeast, found in the nature of rural social problems, which he carefully observed and then described, the realities that had to be taken into account before Brazil's educational system could be reorganized along more realistic lines. His book[5] is the first general, systematic sociological study of rural society to be published in Latin America. It contains internal evidence that Carneiro Leão knew and was influenced by the writings of Kenyon L. Butterfield, P. A. Sorokin, Carle C. Zimmerman, Paul L. Vogt, James M. Williams, and others who contributed to the development of rural sociology in the United States. In turn what he has to say about Brazil's social problems, and especially those related to diet, health, rural housing, rural work patterns, migration from the rural districts, banditry, the milling around of population within the rural districts, and education is of fundamental importance.

Similar factors produced somewhat similar results in other countries. Unfortunately for the development of rural sociology, though, much of the writing on rural society and rural problems took the form of fiction. Nevertheless in Chile a noted humanist, Amanda Labarca H., by attending to the

---

[4] *Casa Grande e Senzala. Formação da Familia Brasileira Sob o Regime de Economia Patriarchial*, 3rd ed. Rio de Janeiro: Schmidt, 1938. (English translation by Samuel Putnam, *The Masters and the Slaves*, New York: Alfred A. Knopf, 1946.)

[5] *A Sociedade Rural; Seus Problemas e Sua Educação*, Rio de Janeiro: A Noite, 1939.

needs and possibilities of the humble rural inhabitants of her country, produced in *El Mejoramiento de la Vida Campesina*[6] a contribution that deserves special mention. Particularly important are her observations relative to the pitiful situation (*miseria*) of Chile's rural masses and the kind of an educational program needed to better their lot.

Recent Developments

During the last decade substantial headway has been made in the development of rural sociological research and teaching throughout the Latin American countries, gains that bid fair to continue and increase in the years immediately ahead. A number of the specific developments will be mentioned briefly.

Late in the 1940's Argentina's Ministry of Agriculture established a section on rural sociology. This was organized and headed for a time by the man who had served as assistant to Carl C. Taylor during the time the latter was gathering the material for his *Rural Life in Argentina.*[7] Perhaps because of this, perhaps for other reasons, there was a tendency for various other countries to recognize that part of the work already being carried on in the ministries, and especially the activities connected with colonization and settlement, properly should be labeled as rural sociology. In any case in Uruguay and Brazil, and possibly elsewhere as well, work designated as rural sociology began to figure in the programs of the ministries of agriculture. This supplemented, in a somewhat more professional manner, the more extensive observation, analysis, and writing about rural sociological topics on the part of numerous officials in the agricultural and other ministries of the several countries. The latter have added many significant items to the bibliography.

Likewise there have been substantial efforts to establish rural sociology courses and research in some of the institutions of higher learning throughout Latin America. Leading the way in this respect was the agricultural college at Viçosa, Minas Gerais, Brazil, followed by the Universidade Rural,

---

[6] Santiago: Ediciones de la Union Republica, 1936.
[7] Baton Rouge: Louisiana State University Press, 1948.

Brazil's national agricultural college located about 30 miles from the city of Rio de Janeiro, and the Central University in Caracas, Venezuela. At the present time there is a movement in Brazil for the introduction of a course in rural sociology in each of Brazil's universities, but it is still too early to foresee the results. A similar ferment is underway in Mexico. This arose largely as a result of the sociological and ethnological research carried on by the Instituto de Investigaciones Sociales in the Universidad Nacional Autónoma, and it gained headway during the course of the Sixth National Congress on Sociology, held at Morélia in the state of Michoacan in 1955, and devoted exclusively to rural sociology.[8]

One of the more significant expressions of a more widely developed interest in the general aspects of rural sociology throughout Latin America has been the publication in various places of comprehensive treatments of the subject as a whole, volumes suitable both for the general reader and for use as texts in the universities. Among the books of this type that have come to the attention of your speaker are: (1) Hernani de Carvalho, *Sociologia da Vida Rural* (*Subsidios para o seu Estudo*);[9] and Aldo E. Solari, *Sociología Rural Nacional*.[10]

In part the broader awareness of the importance and role of rural sociology in Latin America is due to the work of the international organizations and particularly to that of the Organization of American States. The Inter-American Institute of Agricultural Sciences at Turrialba, Costa Rica, especially, has done much to develop this interest. Indeed work in rural sociology and agricultural economics have figured

---

[8] See *Estudios Sociológicos* (*Sociología Rural*), 2 vols., Mexico: Instituto de Investigaciones Sociales, 1955, and especially "Que es la Sociología Rural?," pp. 77–88, by Lucio Mendieta y Núñez and "El Mundo Rural y sus Procesos Sociológicos," pp. 191–229, by Roberto Agramonte. See also Agramonte's report on this conference published as *Hacia una Sociología del Surco: Resultados de Sexto Congreso Nacional de Sociología de Morélia,* Havana: Universidad de Havana, 1956.

[9] Rio de Janeiro: Editora Civilização, Brasileira, 1951.

[10] Montevideo: Universidad de Montevideo, 1953; revised edition, 1958.

very prominently in the activities of the Institute.[11] The branches of the Institute, supported by special appropriations, and serving the northern portions of Latin America, the Andes, and the southern zone, respectively, have also had considerable influence in making rural sociology an integral part of agricultural education in Latin America. The conferences and short courses sponsored by them have had significant roles in this.

The Food and Agriculture Organization of the United Nations also has played an important part in helping turn and develop general interest in rural life and rural problems into more competent professional activities in the field of rural sociology. Especially significant was the training center organized in Concepción, Chile, in 1954, during which over a period of three months selected Latin Americans were given an intensive introduction of the field and methods of rural sociology.

The contacts of Latin American students and scholars with rural sociologists in the United States also have helped produce an increase in rural sociology in the various Latin American countries.[12] Those rural sociologists from the United States who have taken assignments in the various Latin American countries have left a nucleus of persons interested in rural sociological research in each of the countries visited; several of them have taught courses in rural sociology; and in various other ways they have helped promote an appreciation of the theoretical and practical value of the discipline. The articles they have published in Spanish or Portuguese in the Latin American journals are important examples of the latter.

[11] For substantial evidence of the accomplishments by the Inter-American Institute of Agricultural Sciences in the field of rural sociology, see Charles P. Loomis, Julio O. Morales, Roy A. Clifford and Olen E. Leonard, *Turrialba: Social Systems and the Introduction of Change,* Glencoe, Illinois: The Free Press, 1953.

[12] For a brief sketch of the development of a sociological interest in Latin American society by rural sociologists and others in the United States, see T. Lynn Smith, "Sociology," in Francisco Aguilera, editor, *Handbook of Latin American Studies: 1951,* no. 11, Gainesville: University of Florida Press, 1954, pp. 234–238.

Finally, the students from Latin America who have been in the United States for graduate training in rural sociology are among those who have done most to develop rural sociology in their homelands. The list of these is already a long one. Despite the lack of established positions in the government bureaus and in the universities, gradually they are finding or developing places in which their professional qualifications are needed.[13] As the countries grow and develop, as social differentiation proceeds, and especially as the facilities for higher education are multiplied and elaborated, this variety of the new Latin American intellectual should find it less and less difficult to find employment in the professional activities for which he has been trained.

[13] José Arthur Rios, *Educação dos Grupos,* Rio de Janeiro: Ministerio da Saúde, 1954; Orlando Fals Borda, *Peasant Society in the Colombian Andes: A Sociological Study of Saucio,* Gainesville: University of Florida Press, 1955; and Orlando Fals Borda, *El Hombre y la Tierra en Boyacá,* Bogotá: Editorial Antares, 1957, are outstanding examples of the publications by members of this group of young Latin American rural sociologists.

PART II

THE POPULATION OF
LATIN AMERICA

Introductory Note

COMPREHENSIVE, reliable, and up-to-date materials about the populations of the Latin American countries are essential for all who would understand social, economic, political, educational, industrial, and agricultural trends in the southern part of the Western Hemisphere. The demographic study of Latin America long has been one of my principal professional interests. Opportunities along this line were greatly enhanced when the award of a Guggenheim fellowship in 1951 enabled me to spend four months visiting census and other statistical offices in all of the Latin American countries. This was done to gather materials from the 1950 Census of the Americas and to establish the contacts that would help insure that I would receive the reports of the censuses as they became available. The studies from which we have taken the selections used in this section would have been impossible had it not been for these early efforts.

In order to give an over-all view of recent population trends in Latin America, Selection Number 3 is included. It was prepared originally as one in a series of talks on population matters that were recorded for broadcast throughout the various countries of the world over The Voice of America. Subsequently this series was published in slightly revised form in the small volume entitled *Population: The Vital Revolution*. Selection Number 4 is a study made at the request of The Select Commission on Western Hemisphere Immigration, a joint committee of the Senate and House of Representatives of the United States. Originally issued only in mimeographed form, subsequently it was published as one of the appendices in the *Survey of the Alliance for Progress* made by one of the subcommittees of the Senate Committee on Foreign Relations.

In many ways, including the racial or ethnic composition

of its population, Colombia stands near the middle of the range in an array of the Latin American countries. To help answer the many questions as to what is the absolute and relative importance of the principal components (red, black, and white) of the population of the Spanish American countries, Selection Number 4 was chosen. Those interested in comparable materials for Brazil will find a chapter on the same subject in any of the various editions of my *Brazil: People and Institutions*.

The extremely high birth rates are among the most distinctive and portentous features of the population of Latin America. Very little was known about this subject until recently, but for centuries throughout Latin America the high birth rates were offset by very high death rates so that the increase of population was not rapid. As the health work of the Rockefeller Foundation, the Pan American Sanitary Bureau, the governments of the respective countries, and lately the World Health Organization began to get results, however, the picture changed drastically. Birth rates of above 40 per 1000 were then no longer accompanied by death rates of 25 to 35, and the rate of natural increase rose from about 1.5 percent to about 3 percent or 30 per 1000 annually. As a result in about 1950 the various countries and the world as a whole were confronted with a situation in which the population was increasing at an astounding rate, and problems of every kind were rampant. The selections in Part IV of this volume give details about many of these; but for this section it was considered essential to present one item, Selection Number 6, dealing specifically with the rate of reproduction in various parts of Latin America.

Along with the burgeoning of population, the mass transfer of millions of people from rural to urban areas—the whole matter of rampant and "wildfire" urbanization—is at the heart of the momentous changes which are now taking place in Spanish America and Brazil. Several of the more significant aspects of urbanization are discussed in the selections that appear in Part IV, but to help round-out the picture a study of rural-urban migration is included here as Selection Number 7.

3   The Population of Latin America

————◆————

MANY STRIKING superlatives are being used nowadays to describe the phenomenal increase of population that is taking place throughout the world; but their use is more appropriate in connection with the changes now going on in the twenty American nations which collectively make up what is commonly known as Latin America than for any other large portion of the earth. At least since 1925 the populations of Mexico, Central America and Panama, the three island republics, and South America have been characterized by exceptionally high rates of natural increase and consequently by rapidly mounting numbers of persons. Furthermore since 1950 the rates of growth have risen to even higher levels than those attained before mid-century, and there is every reason to suppose that between 1960 and 1970, and possibly until 1980, the population of Latin America will maintain its record-breaking rates of increase.

A few statistics assist one to place the recent rates of population increase in Latin America in perspective. However, for periods before 1900 the results are clouded by a lack of census data and by the obvious inconsistencies in, and unreliability of, the various population estimates. By the turn of the century, though, it appears that the world's population had mounted to about 1,630 millions, of whom some 43 millions, or 2.7 per cent, were Latin Americans. Twenty years later, or just after the close of the First World War, the earth's inhabitants had increased to about 1,811 millions, whereas the population of the twenty Latin American countries had swol-

---

From *Population: The Vital Revolution*, Ronald Freedman, ed., Garden City: Doubleday & Company, 1964, Chapter 13. Copyright © 1964 by Doubleday & Company, Inc. Reprinted by permission of the publisher.

len to about 89 millions, or 4.9 per cent of the total. After 1920 there was a quickening of the pace at which the population of the earth was increasing, and by 1940 it reached 2,250 millions; but the speed with which the Latin American peoples were multiplying rose even more rapidly, so that by 1940 they alone numbered about 123 millions, or 5.5 per cent of the world's total population. Even the mass destruction and loss of life accompanying the Second World War did not halt the increase of world population, although it slowed its rate temporarily. In the Latin American countries, though, the war did not lessen the rapid rate of growth. As a result, by 1950, when the earth had come to have about 2,510 million inhabitants, 154 millions of them, or 6.1 per cent, were Latin Americans. Finally, between 1950 and 1960 the earth's total shot up to a mark of about 2,995 millions, with the rate of increase in Latin America still in the vanguard. As a result by 1960 the combined population of the twenty countries involved had mounted to 202 millions, or approximately 6.8 per cent of all the people on the earth.

In 1900 only 1 out of every 37 members of the human race was a Latin American, whereas in 1960 this ratio had risen to 1 in 15. In summary form this indicates that a phenomenal change is underway. With the passage of each decade the relative importance in world affairs of the population of Mexico, Central America, the three island republics, and South America is mounting rapidly. Moreover, as will be indicated later, the factors responsible for the rapid increase of population in Latin America will probably retain their force until at least 1980. Then, in all probability, a substantial fall in the birth rate may get underway. In the meanwhile, though, the proportion of Latin Americans among the earth's inhabitants probably will rise to about 1 in every 13 by 1970 and to 1 in 12 by 1980.

Rates of Growth

It is no easy task to determine with a fair degree of reliability the rate of growth of the total population of Latin America or of many of its parts. It is likely, however, that the growth rate for Latin America as a whole from 1950 to

1960 was at least 3 per cent per year, and that the rate for
the preceding decade was approximately 2.5 per cent. An
annual increase of 3 per cent is of record-breaking proportions. In all probability throughout the entire history of mankind no other large section of the earth, except the United
States during the years 1790 to 1860, has ever experienced
a rate of growth as high as 3 per cent per year. Such a growth
rate indicates, for example, that during the opening years of
the 1960–70 decade there were over six million more Latin
Americans alive at the end of a year than at its beginning,
and that there will be about eight million more Latin Americans on December 31, 1969, than on January 1 of the same
year.

The generality of these extremely high rates of increase
among the diverse portions of Latin America is another feature deserving of comment. Consider, first, that in the Brazilian half of South America the population growth indicated
by the censuses of 1950 and 1960 amounted to 37 per cent.
This was closely rivaled, however, by a gain during the same
period of more than 35 per cent in Mexico, second most
populous of the Latin American countries. Even the phenomenal rapidity of population growth in Brazil during this decade was exceeded, however, by increases of 46 per cent in
Costa Rica, 43 per cent in Venezuela, 41 per cent in the
Dominican Republic, and 40 per cent in Nicaragua; and the
rate in Mexico was less than those of Guatemala, Honduras,
and Ecuador, and equaled by that of Panama. Indeed, except
for the 13 per cent increase for the small country of Haiti,
the lowest relative increases for any of the countries are 19
per cent for Argentina and 24 per cent for Cuba.

The Primary Factors

For most parts of Latin America the data are woefully
inadequate concerning the three primary factors that influence the rate of population growth—i.e., fertility, mortality,
and migration. In spite of this, however, the role that each
of these three primary factors is playing in the phenomenal
increase of population is fairly certain. In brief, it is evident
that for centuries both the birth rates and the death rates

must have been very high in all twenty of the countries, with the former averaging somewhere between 40 and 50 and the latter between 30 and 40 per 1000 population. Except in Argentina and Brazil, and, for a brief period following the close of the Second World War, in Venezuela, immigration from overseas has been so slight as to be negligible in helping to account for population growth. Even in these countries it is unlikely that more than about 10 per cent of the increase during any decade may reasonably be attributed to immigration of Europeans or Asians. The movement from one country to another occasionally has assumed sizable proportions —as, for example, the migrations from El Salvador to Honduras, from Bolivia to Argentina, and from Paraguay to Argentina—but it has had little influence upon rates of population growth.

Since the role of immigration has been relatively unimportant, it is fairly certain that at least until 1900, and probably until 1920, the excess of births over deaths produced the fairly moderate recorded increases of population. Certainly, prior to 1920 there were few dramatic increases of the kind presently going on throughout the twenty Latin American countries.

By 1920 a great demographic revolution had begun. throughout Latin America. In large measure this was due to the comprehensive health programs of the Rockefeller Foundation and the world health agencies, working in close cooperation with governments. These programs were highly successful in controlling communicable diseases such as smallpox, malaria, and the dysenteries—all of the causes of death that are susceptible to arrest by such means as vaccinations, injections, and the safeguarding of milk and water supplies. As a result, the death rates in the Latin American countries began to fall sharply and substantially. As yet this dramatic achievement has not been accompanied by a comparable reduction in the birth rates. As a matter of fact, other than the tendency for the rate of reproduction to fall in some sections of the small, but rapidly increasing, urban population, the fertility rates throughout Latin America have maintained their previous very high levels. This means, of course, that for the areas as a whole the rate of natural increase, or the difference between the birth rate and the death rate, has increased within the last few decades from around 1 or 1.5 per cent to at least 3 per cent per annum. Thus we must attribute the recent large and sustained upsurge of population throughout the Latin American countries to the reduction of the death rate, and almost exclusively to the control of communicable diseases.

There is some evidence to indicate that many residents of the rapidly growing cities are beginning to practice birth control on a fairly large scale. This appears to be the case especially on the part of the numerous descendants of the upper classes who find it extremely difficult to maintain even an appearance of upper-class status; and it also seems evident on the part of those who are genuine members of the middle class. In view of this it is likely that by about 1980 a sharp reduction of the birth rate, comparable to that which took place in the United States between 1900 and 1935, will get underway throughout Latin America. As a matter of fact the fall in the birth rate in Latin America may be even more precipitous and dramatic than that which brought about such tremendous social and economic changes in the United States. Meanwhile, though, the tidal wave of population growth in Latin America is likely to continue rising until it crests, probably about 1970, at a rate of about 3.5 per cent per year. Thereafter the influence of further successes in the control of mortality probably will be more than offset by the quickening pace of a falling birth rate.

Redistribution

Rivaling in importance the spectacular rates at which the populations of the Latin American countries are growing are the drastic changes now underway in their spatial distribution. The South American continent contains, of course, a major portion of the unused and underutilized land on earth. This land is sufficiently favored by climate, soil, and other features to permit it, in our present stage of cultural development, to maintain large numbers of human beings. There are also extensive areas still awaiting the fructifying effects of man's efforts in Mexico and the Central American countries. Extensive portions of such countries as Brazil, Venezuela, Colombia, Peru, Bolivia, and Paraguay are almost devoid of inhabitants, and other large areas in the same countries are very sparsely populated. In many other parts of Latin America there are also other immense tracts of land fully capable of supporting large populations and still awaiting man's efforts to conquer the tropics. However, the push of settlement into virgin territory is involved only to a limited extent in the drastic changes in the distribution of population now underway in the Latin American countries. Rather, the tendency of overwhelming importance (and that which for better or worse is affecting economic and social development in all twenty of the countries under consideration) is the extreme concentration of population growth in the already densely populated areas of the various countries. Most of the population increase is accounted for by the mushrooming of existing cities and by the rapidly mounting numbers of people in extensive suburbs, or "bands of misery," which surround all of the principal urban centers. This huge expansion of the urban and suburban populations is most spectacular in the metropolitan districts of great cities such as Buenos Aires, São Paulo, Rio de Janeiro, Mexico City, Santiago, Lima, and Cali, in which industrialization is making vast strides. But it is also taking place in many other localities, such as the cities and towns of northeastern Brazil, the urban centers of Haiti, and the population centers of Bolivia, Ecuador, and Paraguay, in which jobs in industry for the heads of the families involved are conspicuous by their absence. It seems well to comment briefly in turn about the two important aspects of the redistribution of population presently taking place throughout Latin America.

THE EXTENSION OF SETTLEMENT. Perhaps the tendency for the population not to push out into the unsettled portions of North and South America is best illustrated by the case of Brazil. For that huge half continent, fully one half of which is almost totally unoccupied, the 1960 census data already are available to use along with those for 1950 in making the necessary comparisons. A study of detailed maps of the changes that took place between 1950 and 1960 indicates that the only portions of the great Brazilian land mass in which in recent years there have been any substantial efforts to bring new areas into agricultural production are the following: the northwestern part of the state of Paraná, the northcentral portion of the state of Maranhão, the sections of the state of Goiás which are fairly close to the new national capital (Brasília), the northern portions of the state of Minas Gerais, and the extreme northwestern part of the state of São Paulo.

In Argentina the days of the agricultural frontier largely have passed, and it is probable that when the detailed figures from the 1960 census are published, the general pattern will be seen to be one of rural depopulation rather than one of agricultural expansion.

In the Andean countries there is some tendency for settlement to push downward from the densely populated highlands and out onto the plains at the base of the mountains. To some extent this is taking place in Bolivia, Peru, Ecuador, Colombia, and Venezuela. In Ecuador this new settlement is moving into the previously largely vacant sections of the Pacific coastal plain, but in the other countries it is almost entirely down the eastern slopes of the Andes and out onto the plains and into the jungles at their base. Likewise in Central America and in Mexico there are a few areas in which new agricultural settlement is going on, but in Mexico and Central America, as in South America, all of this is dwarfed in importance by the immense flow of population from the rural districts to the cities and into the mushrooming suburban slums that surround almost all the important urban places.

THE PHENOMENAL GROWTH OF CITIES AND TOWNS. As mentioned earlier, the rapid growth of cities and towns and the mushrooming of the huge bands of suburban slums surrounding most of them are the most striking features of the great current redistribution of the population of Latin America. The statistical compilations needed in order to determine precisely how the present rate of urbanization in the twenty countries under consideration compares with the rates of urban population growth at various times and places throughout the world have never been made. Nevertheless the developments in this respect probably are among the most unusual in world population history. This is because until recently the level of urbanization in most of the countries was very low; the present rates of population growth in the urban portions of Latin America greatly exceed those in the rural areas; and the entire process is being fed by a rate of increase of the total population of at least 3 per cent per year.

Let us consider a few of the data. In 1950 only about 19 millions, or 36.5 per cent, of the Brazilian population were classified as urban. Nevertheless during the ensuing ten years Brazil's urban population increased by more than 13 millions, or 70 per cent, whereas the rural segment which totaled almost 33.5 millions in 1950 increased merely 5.8 millions, or by only 18 per cent. During this decade 69 per cent of the total increase in Brazil's population took place in her cities and towns. The most publicized aspects of this phenomenal growth of urban population in Brazil are, of course, the immense concentrations of people in the cities of Rio de Janeiro and São Paulo, each of which is now a conurbation containing at least 5 million inhabitants. But the rush of Brazilians to the cities is by no means confined to the migrations to these two huge giants. Between 1950 and 1960, for example, the urban population of the state of Minas Gerais increased by more than 1.6 million and that of Rio Grande do Sul by well over 1,023,000. Indeed, on the relative basis, the burgeoning of such cities as Belo Horizonte (with about 700,-000 inhabitants by 1960) and Fortaleza (with well over 500,-000 residents in 1960) was even more spectacular than the growth of São Paulo and Rio de Janeiro. Moreover, Recife and Salvador both developed so rapidly that each probably will pass the one million mark before 1970. In Brazil as a whole, places of 2000 or more inhabitants increased from 900 in 1940 to 1,174 in 1950, and to 1,799 in 1960.

Similar developments took place in Mexico, second most populous of the Latin American nations. In 1950 fewer than 43 per cent of its 26 million inhabitants were living in urban centers. Between 1950 and 1960, however, this urban segment increased by 61 per cent, whereas the rural population grew by only 16 per cent. As a result, in 1960 Mexico's urban population actually was slightly more numerous than her rural population, the reported numbers being 17,705,000 and 17,218,000 respectively. In 1960 the Federal District, which now is too small to contain all of the huge community of Mexico City (the nation's capital) alone had 4,871,000 residents. But its rate of growth of 60 per cent between 1950 and 1960 did not quite equal the rate of urban growth in Mexico as a whole. This indicates that the increase of urban population is by no means confined to the capital.

For Argentina, third most populous Latin American country, the recent census data are fragmentary and are still lacking the rural-urban classification that is so essential for present purposes. Nevertheless it is evident that the bulk of the growth of population between 1947 and 1960 took place in the urban districts and especially in the huge half-moon of dense settlement immediately adjacent to the federal capital of Buenos Aires. Thus during the latest intercensal period the seventeen civil divisions, or *partidos,* in this area more than doubled in population, with a numerical increase from 1,741,000 inhabitants in 1947 to a total of 3,647,000 in 1960. . . .

In Peru, between 1940 and 1961, the urban population increased by 122 per cent, whereas the rural population grew by only 37 per cent. This difference was produced, for the most part, by the migration of people from the rural districts to Lima. As a result, that capital had almost three times as many inhabitants in 1961 as it had at the time of the 1940 census. At present the city, along with its extensive suburban slums, makes up a metropolitan community of at least 2,500,000 inhabitants. During the same period (1940–61) comparable percentage increases of population were taking place in and about the other important cities in Peru.

Consider also the case of Panama. In 1950 that nation's population was only 805,000, with about 16 per cent of the total in Panama City, capital and largest city in the country. Ten years later, in 1960, the population of the Republic had increased to about 1,076,000; but so rapid had been the growth of the capital that more than 25 per cent of Panama's inhabitants were residents of Panama City. Finally, although recent census data for most of the other countries are lacking, the regular traveler to Central and South America surely must be convinced even by casual observation that the tendency of population to concentrate in the cities and towns of

Colombia, Venezuela, Ecuador, Uruguay, and the rest of Latin America is fully as great as it is in Brazil, Mexico, Argentina, Peru, and Panama, the places for which data have been presented.

Population Growth and Social and Economic Development

In some respects the implications of population growth for social and economic development in Latin America are more puzzling than they are for the development of other parts of the earth. Until very recently the lack of population was generally considered as a factor retarding development in most of the countries. Indeed, the theme song of Brazilian history, *falta de braços,* or lack of hands, had its philosophical counterpart in many of the other countries, as evidenced, for example, by their programs for promoting immigration. Even today in most parts of Latin America a survey probably would show that attitudes in general are favorable to a rapid increase of population.

As larger proportions of the lower classes of Latin American societies assemble in and about the larger cities, however, there is a growing tendency to question the belief that a rapidly increasing population is an evidence of social and economic development. In part this seems to be due to problems inherent in producing and distributing enough food and clothing to meet the most basic needs of the people. But the difficulties encountered in the attempt to build houses, expand public utilities, and establish schools fast enough to keep pace with the increasing population cause many to despair; and others are gravely concerned about the social, political, and ideological complications that arise among the transplanted populations. Today the problem of the suburbs is generally recognized in many of the countries as their most serious social problem, although the nature of the problem is very different in developing and already developed countries.

That population increase can be a problem in countries in which there still are millions of acres of virgin lands strikes many as paradoxical. A few recognize that fundamental reforms are necessary if the problems of rural unemployment and underemployment are to be solved and if any considerable part of the natural increase of population is to be directed to the frontier instead of going to the cities. They know that there must be changes in the systems of surveying and deeding public lands, in the prevailing systems of land tenure, in the existing concentration and control of property in land, in the antiquated systems of agriculture still in use in vast areas, and in the tax system. But there is little agreement about the ways and means of accomplishing such reforms, and there is little reason to suppose that such agreement will be reached in the very near future. Until such reforms are accomplished, however, the rapid growth of population and the maldistribution of the population are likely to serve as severe brakes upon social and economic development throughout much of Latin America.

Summary and Conclusion

1. The Latin American countries make up the great world subdivision in which the rate of population increase is the greatest. This has been true at least since 1920, was especially pronounced between 1950 and 1960, and remains true during the present decade.

2. Between 1900 and 1960 alone, the proportion of Latin Americans among the earth's inhabitants increased from 2.7 per cent to 6.8 per cent.

3. The rapidly falling death rate is chiefly responsible for the currently high rates of population increase in Latin America.

4. Although South America and other sections of Latin America contain a major portion of the earth's usable unsettled lands, very little of the phenomenal increase of population in Latin America is taking place in newly opened agricultural districts.

5. The recent large and significant increases of population are occurring almost exclusively in and about the already densely settled cities and towns of the twenty Latin American countries.

4 The Growth of Population in Central and South America, 1940 to 1970

———◆———

THIS STUDY represents an endeavor to update and supplement to some extent an earlier analysis, "The Growth of Population in Central and South America," which was prepared for Subcommittee No. 1 of the House of Representatives, Committee on the Judiciary in 1963.[1] Special attention is focused upon the changes in number of inhabitants and the rates of growth during the decades 1940 to 1950, 1950 to 1960, and 1960 to 1970, and also upon the three primary factors (fertility, mortality and immigration-emigration) which determine the absolute and relative changes in population.

Improvement in the Amount and Quality of the Data

One who works with demographic data for the various countries of Central and South America in 1967 enjoys a

Prepared for the Select Commission on Western Hemisphere Immigration, June, 1967, and published subsequently in the *Survey of the Alliance for Progress: Hearings before the Subcommittee on American Republics Affairs of the Committee on Foreign Relations, United States Senate,* Washington: U. S. Government Printing Office, 1968, pp. 265–274.

[1] *Study of Population and Immigration Problems,* Special Series No. 6, Washington: U. S. Government Printing Office, 1963, pp. 151–176. This report, in turn, was based to some extent upon materials collected and analyzed in extensive studies of the population of the Latin American countries which began in 1950 and were reported upon in T. Lynn Smith, *Latin American Population Studies,* University of Florida Monographs, Social Sciences, No. 8, Gainesville: University of Florida Press, 1960, and in numerous articles in professional journals published in the United States, Europe, and some of the Latin American countries.

vast advantage over his predecessor who attempted analyses of the populations of those areas in the 1940's, the 1950's, or even the opening years of the present decade. The principal improvements have been in the censuses.

Prior to 1940 only a few of the Central and South American countries had devoted any particular attention to taking periodic censuses of their populations. As a result, as late as 1945 anyone needing comprehensive data on the number, distribution, and characteristics of the populations of these important parts of the Western Hemisphere was beset by all sorts of difficulties and perplexities, many of which are insuperable. Only for El Salvador, Honduras, Panama, Chile, Colombia, and Venezuela were there available the essential materials assembled in fairly recent censuses. Older but useful data also were available for Costa Rica, Guatemala, Nicaragua, and Brazil.[2] Distinct advances were made in 1940 when Brazil, Nicaragua, and Peru were added to the list of the countries with fairly adequate censuses; and Guatemala also undertook a census that year, the results of which have been seriously challenged.

Venezuela made another enumeration of her population in 1941, Honduras in 1945, and Argentina, which had not made a count of her inhabitants since 1914, moved out of the ranks of "demographic darkness" with a census in 1947.

Prior to 1950 the comparability of the data gathered in the censuses taken by the various Central and South American countries left a great deal to be desired. Each nation went its own way relying upon the ingenuity of its own technicians for all decisions with respect to the questions to be asked, the ways in which they were to be phrased, and the manner in which the results were to be tabulated and published. In not a few cases the originality exhibited in these respects proved to be a nightmare for those attempting to analyze the results. For this reason the Census of the Americas, undertaken as a cooperative venture in which all of the American countries agreed to take a census in 1950 and in which

[2] In the preparation of the first edition of his *Brazil: People and Institutions,* published by the Louisiana State University Press in 1946, the present writer had to rely almost exclusively upon the 1920 census for materials pertaining to the population.

they further agreed to include certain basic questions and to tabulate the materials in comparable ways, represented a tremendous step forward. Unfortunately, not all of the Central and South American countries were able to keep the commitments they had made in the international gatherings wherein the agreements were reached. In the case of Argentina this was not serious, because the census of 1947 was recent and fairly well done. It was more serious in that of Peru, where political changes prevented the taking of the census, although even there its census of 1940 was still useful. The facts that Colombia could not carry through its plans for a census until 1951 and Chile until 1952 were of minor consequence. Extremely disappointing, however, was the failure of Uruguay to participate in the actual census taking, for its most recent enumeration was one made in 1908, and, as was proved when the results of its 1963 census finally became available, the official estimates of its population and those made by the United Nations and the Inter-American Statistical Institute were grossly inflated. All of the other countries, though, fulfilled their pledges, so that by the mid-1950's recent counts of their populations and tabulations showing many of the characteristics of their inhabitants were available for study.

A repetition of the Census of the Americas was planned for 1960, and all of the countries involved in this report except Bolivia took censuses either then or shortly thereafter. (See Table I for the dates.) Preliminary results from some of them were available by 1963, when the study referred to above was made, and in June, 1967, the preliminary results of all are available, although the final reports by some of them, including huge Brazil, are still being awaited.

In summary, the basic sources for the primary data on the growth of population between 1940 and 1950, between 1950 and 1960, and between 1960 and 1970, for the various countries are censuses taken in the following years: Costa Rica, 1927, 1950, and 1963; El Salvador, 1930, 1950, and 1961; Guatemala, 1921 (that taken in 1940 is too suspect for use), 1950, and 1964; Honduras, 1945, 1950, and 1961; Nicaragua, 1940, 1950, and 1963; Panama, 1940, 1950, and 1960; Argentina, 1914, 1947, and 1960; Bolivia, 1900 and 1950; Brazil, 1940, 1950, and 1960; Chile, 1940, 1952, and 1960;

Colombia, 1938, 1951, and 1964; Ecuador, 1950 and 1962; Paraguay, 1950 and 1962; Peru, 1940 and 1961; Uruguay, 1908 and 1963; and Venezuela, 1941, 1950, and 1961.

Rates of Growth

Presently three features of the growth of population in Central and South America deserve special attention. These are: (1) The knowledge about current rates of growth is now considerably more accurate than was the case in 1963 when the study referred to above was made; (2) The appearance of additional census materials and the improved data relative to births and deaths for many of the countries fully support the conclusion, arrived at earlier on the basis of fragmentary information, that the rate of growth was much higher between 1950 and 1960 than was the case between 1940 and 1950; (3) The very rapid increases of population which characterized the Central and South American countries during the decade ending in 1960 have continued since that time. Each of these will be considered briefly in its turn.

IMPROVEMENTS IN THE ACCURACY OF THE INDICATORS. A higher degree of reliability of the various indicators of the speed with which the population is growing and particularly in the annual rate of growth and the percentage increase between two established dates is one of the natural consequences of the appearance of the results of important censuses taken from 1960 to 1964. In order to present in summary form some of the most pertinent data from these censuses, along with the changes in population during the latest intercensal periods, on both the relative and the absolute bases, Table I was prepared. For each of the countries in Central and South America it gives the dates of the two latest censuses, the enumerated population shown by each of them, the increase in number of inhabitants during the intercensal period, the percentage increase of population during the same period, and the annual rate at which the population grew during the interval between the two demographic inventories. These, it should be emphasized, are the basic ingredients which those responsible for making any computations, estimates, and projections of the populations of Central and

South America must use. It is important to note that the demographer presently has available materials from censuses taken in 1960 or subsequently for Costa Rica, Guatemala, Nicaragua, Colombia, Ecuador, and Uruguay, whereas in 1963 the latest information available was from censuses taken in 1950 for all of them except Colombia; where the census was taken in 1951, and Uruguay, which had taken no census of population since that of 1908. At the present time only Bolivia out of all the nations of Central and South America lacks an up-to-date census of population. Among other things, the more adequate materials presently available means that the rates of growth of the population throughout these areas, and for each of them as a whole, now can be determined with a much higher degree of accuracy than was the case four or five years ago. Perhaps, however, it is well to specify exactly how the rates of growth included in Table I compare with the best that could be made in 1963. This may be done country by country as follows:

Country	Annual rate of growth given in Table I	Annual rate of growth given in the 1963 tabulation[1]
Costa Rica	4.0 per cent (1950-1963)	2.3 per cent (1927-1950)
El Salvador	2.8 per cent (1950-1961)	Same as given in Table I
Guatemala	3.1 per cent (1950-1964)	1.2 per cent (1921-1950)
Honduras	3.0 per cent (1950-1961)	Same as given in Table I
Nicaragua	2.9 per cent (1950-1963)	2.4 per cent (1940-1950)
Panama	2.9 per cent (1950-1960)	Same as given in Table I
Argentina	1.7 per cent (1947-1960)	Same as given in Table I
Bolivia	1.0 per cent (1900-1950)	Same as given in Table I
Brazil	3.1 per cent (1950-1960)	Same as given in Table I
Chile	2.8 per cent (1952-1960)	Same as given in Table I
Colombia	3.2 per cent (1951-1964)	2.2 per cent (1938-1951)
Ecuador	2.8 per cent (1950-1962)	Entirely unknown
Paraguay	2.6 per cent (1950-1962)	Entirely unknown
Peru	2.5 per cent (1940-1961)	Same as given in Table I
Uruguay	0.7 per cent (1908-1963)	Entirely unknown
Venezuela	3.9 per cent (1950-1961)	Same as given in Table I

[1] The expression "same as given in Table I" in this tabulation actually means "essentially the same," because in the 1963 study no attempt was made to adjust the rates of increase for the fractions of the years included in the intercensal periods, whereas the rates given in Table I do reflect such adjustments.

Table I. Populations Enumerated in the Two Most Recent Censuses and Growth of Population During the Intercensal Period for Each of the Countries in Central and South America*

Country	Population at beginning of period	Population at end of period	Increase Number	Increase Percent	Annual rate of growth
Central America					
Costa Rica	800,875	1,336,274	535,399	66.9	4.0
El Salvador	1,855,917	2,510,984	655,067	35.3	2.8
Guatemala	2,790,868	4,284,473	1,493,605	53.5	3.1
Honduras	1,368,605	1,884,765	516,160	37.7	3.0
Nicaragua	1,049,611	1,535,588	485,977	46.3	2.9
Panama	805,285	1,075,541	270,256	33.6	2.9
South America					
Argentina	15,897,127	20,008,945	4,111,818	25.9	1.7
Bolivia	1,555,818	2,704,165	1,148,347	73.8	1.0
Brazil	51,976,357	70,967,185	18,990,828	36.5	3.1
Chile	5,932,995	7,374,115	1,441,120	24.3	2.8
Colombia	11,548,172	17,482,420	5,934,248	51.4	3.2
Ecuador	3,202,757	4,476,007	1,273,250	39.8	2.8
Paraguay	1,328,452	1,816,890	488,438	36.8	2.6
Peru	6,207,967	10,364,620	4,156,053	67.0	2.5
Uruguay	1,042,686	2,592,563	1,549,877	148.6	0.7
Venezuela	5,034,838	7,523,999	2,489,161	49.4	3.9

*Compiled and computed from data given in the official census reports of the various nations, the United Nations, *Demographic Yearbook, 1965*, New York: The United Nations, 1966, and the Inter-American Statistical Institute, *America en Cifras*, 1965, Situación Demográfica: Estado y Movimento de la Población, Washington: Pan American Union, 1966.

Obviously the facts that recently it has become possible to determine rates of growth of population in three countries for which this was impossible in 1963, and to calculate rates for periods extending well into the 1960's for four other countries for which this could not be done at the time of the earlier study signify substantial improvements in the basic demographic materials for the areas under consideration.

HIGH RATES OF POPULATION GROWTH THAT RECENTLY BECAME EVEN HIGHER. It now can be established that the rapid rates of growth of population in Central and South America known to have prevailed during the decade 1940 to 1950 became substantially greater during the one ending in 1960. This could be discerned even on the basis of the fragmentary recent materials available in 1963, but presently, with the results from the most recent enumerations at hand, it can be established definitely and even the amounts by which the rates have risen can be ascertained with a considerable degree of accuracy. In order to present the most pertinent of the data that have been assembled, with the materials placed on bases that are as comparable as possible, Table II was prepared. In it the information has been adjusted so as to give the populations of each of the countries and the areas as wholes as of July 1 for the years 1940, 1950, and 1960, respectively, along with computations showing the increases in number of inhabitants, the percentage changes, and the annual rates of growth between 1940 and 1950 and between 1950 and 1960. These computations represent a considerable degree of refinement over those attempted in the 1963 study, but the fuller census coverages and the recency of the latest enumerations now make such adjustments feasible. Actually, the lack of any Bolivian census subsequent to that of 1950 presently is the only severe limitation upon the computations of the type given in this tabulation.

The magnitude of the rates and changes, and the consistency with which already exceptionally high rates became even higher are easily noted by an examination of the data presented in Table II. These materials make it evident that, even if we make allowances for possible inaccuracies in the data, the recent increases in the rates at which the populations of Central and South America are growing are truly

Table II. The Absolute and Relative Increases of Population in Central and South American Countries, 1940 to 1950 and 1950 to 1960

Country	Number of inhabitants on July 1 (000's)			Increase 1940 to 1950			Increase 1950 to 1960		
	1940	1950	1960	Number (000's)	Percent	Annual rate	Number (000's)	Percent	Annual rate
Central America	7,320	8,660	11,940	1,340	18.3	1.7	3,280	37.9	3.2
Costa Rica	620	800	1,250	180	29.0	2.6	450	56.3	4.2
El Salvador	1,630	1,850	2,450	220	13.5	1.2	600	32.4	2.9
Guatemala	2,500	2,790	3,900	290	11.6	1.1	1,110	39.8	3.4
Honduras	1,110	1,370	1,840	260	23.4	2.1	470	34.3	3.0
Nicaragua	840	1,050	1,430	210	25.0	2.3	380	36.2	3.2
Panama	620	800	1,070	180	29.0	2.6	270	33.8	3.0
South America	87,470	108,100	142,630	20,630	23.2	2.1	34,530	31.8	2.8
Argentina	14,160	16,760	19,960	2,600	18.4	1.7	3,200	19.1	1.8
Bolivia	2,600	3,000	3,700	400	15.4	1.5	700	23.3	2.1
Brazil	41,200	51,900	70,500	10,700	26.0	2.4	18,600	35.8	3.1
Chile	5,000	5,750	7,250	750	15.0	1.4	1,500	26.1	2.4
Colombia	9,090	11,300	15,660	2,210	24.3	2.2	4,360	38.6	3.3
Ecuador	2,600	3,190	4,200	590	22.7	2.1	1,010	31.7	2.8
Paraguay	1,110	1,340	1,740	230	20.7	1.9	400	29.9	2.7
Peru	6,200	7,800	10,120	1,600	25.8	2.3	2,320	29.7	2.6
Uruguay	1,800	2,060	2,460	260	14.4	1.4	400	19.4	1.8
Venezuela	3,710	5,000	7,040	1,290	34.8	3.0	2,040	40.1	3.5
Central and South America	94,790	116,760	154,570	21,970	22.9	2.1	37,810	32.2	2.9

phenomenal. Perhaps one may have some doubts that the rate for Guatemala actually trebled from the one decade to the next, but there are less reasons for being skeptical about the indicated more than doubling of the index for El Salvador and the near doubling of the one for Chile. Even more phenomenal in many ways is the rise from 2.6 to 4.2 per annum in Costa Rica. For the years 1940 to 1950 only Venezuela was characterized by a rate of growth as high as 3.0 per cent per annum, a fact that was very difficult to accept when the results of its 1950 census first became available; whereas for the decade 1950 to 1960 it was joined in that class by Costa Rica, Guatemala, Colombia, Nicaragua, Brazil, Honduras, and Panama. As a result for the second of the decades under consideration, one half of the countries of Central and South America and considerably more than one half of the populations of those nations were characterized by annual rates of increase of 3.0 per cent or more per year. Moreover, during the 1950's only Argentina and Uruguay showed annual rates of less than 2 per cent, and the next lowest indexes were those of 2.1, 2.4, and 2.6 for Bolivia, Chile, and Peru, respectively. Finally, one should emphasize that the substantial increase in already high rates of growth is dramatized by the upswing between the decade 1940 to 1950 and that from 1950 to 1960 from 1.7 per cent to 3.2 per cent per annum in Central America, from 2.1 per cent to 2.8 per cent per annum in South America, and from 2.1 per cent to 2.9 per cent for the two areas combined. That during a full decade the growth for the 16 countries in Central and South America actually attained a rate of 2.9 per cent per annum dramatizes the great velocity of current population change in these large sections of the earth's territory.

HIGH RATES HAVE CONTINUED AFTER 1960. Any precise determination of rates of population growth in Central and South America since 1960 must, of course, await the appearance of censuses that will be taken in 1970 or shortly thereafter. Therefore, any estimates or projections of populations for the sixteen nations under consideration in this study must remain conjectural until about 1973. In the years immediately ahead, however, we certainly will be presented the results of a considerable number of endeavors to portray the changes that have taken place since 1960 and those believed to be indicators of what the populations will be in 1970, 1975, 1980 or some other date in the future. Most of these will result from giving clerks or mechanical computers certain instructions, and then using the results of the computations as the estimates or projections that are presented. Also most of them will be based merely upon the assumption that recent rates of increase will prevail in the future, or that the recently noted increases in the rate of growth will continue quickening the pace of the changes on into the years to come. In most cases, not just one most likely estimate or projection will be given, but the reader will be confronted with three or more figures for a given year, each based on somewhat different basic assumptions.

The conclusion given in this study that the high rates of growth of population in Central and South America shown to have prevailed during the 1950's are continuing through the 1960's, and also the estimates of the growth of population between 1960 and 1970, are based upon several lines of reasoning. First, it is considered unlikely that the factors which have held the birth rate at an extremely high level, while the death rate was falling precipitously, have quickly lost their power, but rather than it probably will require another decade or two before a new and powerful set of factors comes fully into play. For example, a large and important campaign for "family planning" or the control of fertility presently is getting underway throughout the areas we are considering. Given a little time either this, or other forces, such as the rising standards and levels of living and the changing mores generated by the rapid transition from a rural to an urban way of life, or both, may produce a precipitous drop in the birth rate comparable to that which took place in the United States and northwestern Europe between 1850 and 1930. However, as is indicated below, there still are few if any indications that this has begun as yet, and it probably will not take place on any large scale until at least another decade has passed. Second, the birth rate about 1960 already was so high, and the death rate had fallen to such an extent, that it seems unsafe to count upon any additional large increment to the present high rate of natural increase. In other words we do not expect that the very high rate of increase will continue to become higher. Third, the fragmentary information that is available relative to the natural increase of the population since 1960, that is the data on births and deaths for some of the countries, support neither the idea that the rate of increase continues to quicken nor that the high rate already has begun to fall. Some of the data related to this are presented in the section dealing with the factors in population increase. Here, it should be stressed again, however, that the high rates of population increase which prevailed throughout Central and South America during the 1950's have continued during the decade that will end in 1970.

Primary Factors in Population Changes

Because the rates of increase of the population in Central and South America are so extremely high and because between 1950 and 1960 the already phenomenal speed of population growth was substantially quickened, demographers must scan with attention every indicator that might presage the slackening of the pace at which the number of inhabitants is mounting. This certainly must come sooner or later; but in the piecemeal information relative to the three primary factors responsible for population changes (namely, births, deaths, and migrations), there is as yet little hint that the rate of population growth in the countries we are considering is about to slacken. The velocity already attained seems certain to carry through 1970 and perhaps well into the decade ending in 1980 as well. Before our estimates or projections of the populations of the Central and South American countries for 1970 are presented, let us consider briefly each of the three primary factors involved in the changes.

IMMIGRATION AND EMIGRATION. Except for the considerable influx of immigrants of European origin in Venezuela during the decade after the close of the Second World War, overseas migrations have played inconsequential parts in the growth of population throughout Central and South America in the decades since 1940. It is true that Argentina and Brazil, which traditionally have been on the receiving end of large numbers of immigrants from Europe and (in the case of Brazil) from Japan, have continued to attract some immigrants from the countries of origin of the parents and grandparents of so many of their citizens; but from the standpoint of influencing the number of inhabitants of either Argentina or Brazil, the numbers involved are inconsequential.

The movements of people from one of the Latin American countries to another is of considerable significance in slowing the rate of increase of population in a few of the countries and in speeding up that in their neighbors. Unfortunately, however, this aspect of the subject has received practically no attention from those who have been studying population matters in various parts of Latin America. In a paper presented at the International Population Conference held in Vienna in 1959, though, the present writer attempted to identify and describe briefly a few of the principal exchanges of population between the various countries of Central and South America.[3] Several of these are sufficiently important to be of significance in recent and future rates of growth in the countries under consideration. They may be mentioned briefly as follows: (1) there has been for several decades and continues to be a heavy flow of population from El Salvador to neighboring Honduras; (2) much of the recent spread of settlement into the lowlands of Costa Rica, both into the Guanacaste Peninsula and other sections along the Pacific Coast and throughout the Caribbean Coastal Plain, has been due to an influx of persons from neighboring Nicaragua who are adjusted biologically and culturally to life in these tropical areas; (3) a huge movement of Bolivians into the northern provinces of Argentina, much of it seasonal but a large part of it of a more permanent nature, is an important factor in reducing the rate of growth of the population in Bolivia and contributing in some measure to the growth of population in much larger and more populous Argentina; (4) a heavy tide of migration from Paraguay to Argentina, some of it made up of political refugees but a much larger part probably repre-

[3] See T. Lynn Smith, "Migration from One Latin American Country to Another," in Louis Henry and Wilhelm Winkler, eds., *International Population Conference,* Vienna: Christophe Reisser's Söhne, 1959, pp. 695–702.

senting the long-continued tendency for Paraguayans to leave their own predominantly rural country for the attractions and opportunities offered in Buenos Aires, is another important feature of the interchange of populations between the various South American countries; and (5) there also is a considerable emigration of Paraguayans into Brazil, particularly to the State of Mato Grosso, where they constitute an important part of the labor force in the mate industry, and also are heavily represented in the various cities and towns. Finally, although it was not singled out for attention in the paper just mentioned, the huge "immigration" and subsequent "emigration" which are generated by Uruguay's divorce mills is a factor complicating all endeavors to understand the relative importance of the three primary factors in accounting for population changes in that country. As far as the present writer has been able to ascertain no one as yet has made any substantial analysis of this significant demographic and sociological matter.

THE BIRTH RATE. The birth rate is, of course, the primary factor in what will happen to the population of Central and South American countries in the next few decades. As is well known the basic reason for the present almost unprecedently high rates at which the populations of these countries are growing is because the traditionally high birth rate in Latin America has not changed appreciably, whereas during the last quarter of a century the equally traditional high death rate has fallen precipitously.

Thanks to the efforts of the Statistical Office of the United Nations and the work of the Pan American Union, such materials on vital statistics as have been gathered in the Central and South American countries are now available for study and analysis; and we have made use of those for the three years 1959–1961 in order to compute the rates that are presented in Table III. Specifically we have employed the data given in the Pan American Union's *America en Cifras* for the years 1960, 1961, and 1965, which correspond rather closely in most cases to those carried in the *Demographic Yearbook of the United Nations,* along with the 1960 populations as given in Table II, as the bases for computing the birth rates, death rates, and rates of natural increase for the countries

considered in this study. It is unlikely that any indexes that
are more reliable can be computed until after the passage of
another six or seven years when we may hope that the vital
statistics will have been improved and when the preliminary
results of the next censuses of population should be becoming available.

For the present we can merely warn that no one should
place much reliance upon the reliability of the rates that we,
or anyone else for that matter, may compute for many of the
countries involved. Even the birth rates for some of the countries, high as they may appear to be, probably are gross under-
statements of the actual indexes. In Colombia, for example,
the data on births in reality are reports of baptisms by the
Roman Catholic Church, and the actual birth rate, rather than
being 39 as shown in Table III, probably is at least 45 and
may be as high as 50. For Paraguay, the number of children
under 5 per 100 women aged 15 to 44, as shown by the 1962
census, is 83, which signifies that the birth rate cannot be
much below 50. Likewise the birth rate in Peru must be considerably above 45 and that in Bolivia probably is equally
high. However, the relatively low birth rates for Argentina
and Uruguay seem to be fairly reliable, as also is the case
with the high birth rates for the seven countries in which the
indexes given range from 44 to 48. It is unfortunate that
Brazil, with its huge population, has lagged so greatly in perfecting an organization for registering the births and deaths
in that tremendous nation. For that country, however, I personally have made estimates which place the birth rate at
about 48, the death rate around 17, and the rate of natural
increase at about 3.1 per cent per year.

THE DEATH RATES. Almost all of the death rates given in
Table III probably are substantially too low. It may be that a
few of the countries have rates that actually are as low as 10
per 1000 population, and it of course is possible that some
have indexes even lower than that. In general, however, these
facts must be verified by substantial analyses which are still
to be made.

It should be stressed, though, that even if the death rates
are highly questionable in most cases, they still undoubtedly
are only fractions of what they were as late as 1940. Still it

would appear that the precipitous drop in mortality that has taken place during the last quarter of a century has about exhausted the possibilities. Most of the results that can be achieved by fast, relatively inexpensive preventative measures (vaccinations, injections, the use of the "wonder drugs," the safeguarding of milk and water supplies, rudimentary sanitary installations, etc.) already have been attained. It will not be as easy and as inexpensive to achieve further reductions, nor is it likely that substantial results can be obtained quickly. To reduce the death rate by another two points in the years immediately ahead may prove to be far less feasible than was the task of bringing it down by 10 or 15 points only 25 years ago.

Table III. Birth Rates, Death Rates, and Rates of Natural Increase in Central and South American Countries, 1959-1961

Country	Birth rates	Death rates	Rates of natural increase
Central America			
Costa Rica	47.0	8.0	3.9
El Salvador	49.2	11.9	3.7
Guatemala	48.5	16.4	3.2
Honduras	44.7	9.8	3.6
Nicaragua	44.2	8.6	3.6
Panama	39.0	8.1	3.1
South America			
Argentina	23.8	8.8	1.5
Bolivia	26.8	7.8	1.9
Brazil	—	—	—
Chile	38.0	12.9	2.5
Colombia	39.0	11.4	2.8
Ecuador	48.1	14.2	3.4
Paraguay	26.0	5.3	2.1
Peru	36.3	11.2	2.5
Uruguay	24.7	9.6	1.5
Venezuela	47.7	8.0	4.0

The Changes Between 1960 and 1970

Finally, in this study we attempt the task of estimating or forecasting what the populations of each of the Central and South American countries will be as of July 1, 1970. Strictly speaking these are not projections, since we have applied no one standard formula, such as assuming that the population between 1960 and 1970 would grow at the same rate as that which prevailed between 1950 and 1960. Rather, we have made and studied a number of such projections, have checked these against variations and trends in the birth rates and death rates, have made allowances for certain happenings (such as recent, severe famine in southern Peru), and finally have arrived at our own best judgment or guess as to what the population will be three years hence. In this connection, however, it should be stressed that in making the estimates or forecasts, each nation was studied as a unit, and that greater reliance was placed upon some factors in the process of arriving at the figure for a given country than was true in the case of another. In the estimate of Argentina's 1970 population, for example, considerable significance was attached to the fact that the vital statistics (believed to be fairly accurate) for the years 1960 to 1963, inclusive, indicate a lower rate of

Table IV.   Growth of Population (Estimated) in Central and South America, 1960 to 1970

| Country | Population on July 1 | | Increase of population | | |
| | 1960 | 1970 | 1960-1970 | | |
	(000's)		Number	Per cent	Annual rate
Central America	11,940	16,040	4,100,000	34.3	3.0
Costa Rica	1,250	1,750	500,000	40.0	3.5
El Salvador	2,450	3,300	850,000	34.9	3.0
Guatemala	3,900	5,100	1,200,000	30.8	2.8
Honduras	1,840	2,490	650,000	35.3	3.1
Nicaragua	1,430	1,950	520,000	36.3	3.2
Panama	1,070	1,450	380,000	35.5	3.1
South America	142,630	185,760	43,130,000	29.0	2.6
Argentina	19,960	23,160	3,200,000	16.4	1.5
Bolivia	3,700	4,500	800,000	21.6	2.0
Brazil	70,500	95,000	24,500,000	34.7	3.0
Chile	7,250	9,150	1,900,000	26.2	2.4
Colombia	15,660	21,160	5,500,000	35.1	3.1
Ecuador	4,200	5,450	1,250,000	29.8	2.6
Paraguay	1,740	2,240	500,000	28.1	2.5
Peru	10,120	12,750	2,630,000	26.0	2.4
Uruguay	2,460	2,810	350,000	17.1	1.6
Venezuela	7,040	9,540	2,500,000	35.5	3.1
Central and South America	154,570	201,800	47,230,000	30.6	2.7

natural increase than that prevailing earlier; whereas no such importance was attached to the reported variations in numbers of births and deaths in Bolivia, Colombia, and Paraguay. The results of the estimates, along with the corresponding percentage increases and annual rates of growth are presented in Table IV. In interpreting these now, and also after the censuses that will be taken in 1970 and shortly thereafter have been made and their results published, it should be borne in mind that the completeness of the enumerations is an unknown that may seriously affect the calculations for past decades as well as estimates, projections, or forecasts of future populations. Prior to the 1960 census of population in Brazil, no one, in Brazil or out of it, was prepared to venture the proposition that Brazil's population in 1960 would be more than 66 million. The enumeration of 1960 accounted for almost 71 million. But it still is to be determined how much, if any, of the stupendous increase was due to a more complete coverage in 1960 than in 1950, and how much of it represented an actual increase in the number of inhabitants. Much the same can be said with respect to many of the other countries. In this connection it should be recalled also that presently it is believed that the United States Census of population taken in 1960 missed more than three per cent of the nation's inhabitants.

If the estimated rates for 1960–1970 are compared with the calculated rates for 1950–1960, it will be noted that the former tend to be slightly lower, although in a few instances they are the same or even slightly higher. The greatest differences are those for Costa Rica, Guatemala, and Venezuela, for which it would seem practically impossible for the exceedingly high indexes for the 1950 to 1960 period to be maintained. It is conjectured, by these estimates, that eight of the sixteen countries will have annual rates of 3.0 per cent or more during the decade through which we are passing. For Central America as a whole the indicated rate for the decade 1960 to 1970 is two points lower than the one for the 1950's, for South America the comparable difference is also two points. For both Central and South America taken together the two annual rates are 2.9 per cent for the period 1950 to 1960 and 2.7 per cent for the one 1960 to 1970, respectively.

Conclusion

The annual rates of increase of population in Central and South America were high during the decade 1940 to 1950. Between 1950 and 1960 they rose to almost unprecedented heights, many of them coming to exceed 3 per cent per year, with the average for the 16 nations involved being at the extremely high level of 2.9 per cent per annum. These high rates probably are being maintained during the period 1960 to 1970, although there seems to be a slight reduction overall. Finally, the present writer believes that between 1970 and 1980 the factors and forces now being brought into position to bring about a reduction in the birth rate will begin to become effective and that the annual rate of increase of population will probably start dropping sharply during that decade.

5 The Racial Composition of the Population of Colombia

———◆———

THE REDMAN, the Negro, and the white man were the three colors in the human palette of Nueva Granada. With these and their derivatives time has worked, during the course of four centuries, to create every possible mixture, blend, and shade of mankind, every human color possible without the addition of the yellow element from Asia. But the more important blendings were those of the white and Indian to form the great mestizo group of the highlands and of the white and Negro to produce the mulattoes who share the hot, sultry lowlands with the more pure-blooded descendants of the Africans. In the twentieth century the immigration of a few hundred Japanese, who settled in the Cauca Valley, has added the last of the major human types to the population of Colombia.

It is much easier, however, to identify the racial elements that have contributed to the formation of the present population of Colombia than it is to determine their relative importance in the nation as a whole or in its several parts. The latest three censuses of Colombia avoided the racial or color classification altogether, and those of 1918 and 1912 placed all those judged to be of mixed descent in a single category. Therefore, one who observes personally the fact that there is a large racially white population scattered about in the rural districts of the highlands to the north of Bogotá and another in the uplands of Antioquia and Caldas has no comprehensive statistical information with which he may test his observations. Likewise one who interviews hundreds of families along

From the *Journal of Inter-American Studies,* Vol. VIII, No. 2 (April, 1966), pp. 213–235. Reprinted by permission of the publisher.

the Cauca River in the southern part of the *departamento* of
Valle del Cauca and the northern portion of the *departamento*
of Cauca may note that Negroes and mulattoes form the bulk
of the population; if he visits the sticky overcast Chocó, drops
down into the Valley of the Patia in Nariño, ventures out on
the plains of Bolívar or makes his way up the Sinú River he is
certain to conclude that the Negroid elements predominate
in the population; and if he surveys the heavily populated
Banana Zone in Magdalena or finds his way into the numerous, small, remote, backwoods settlements on the opposite side
of the Santa Marta Mountains he will know that the majority
of the population in those parts are of Negroid descent. But
in all these cases, and in dozens of other localities he may
have occasion to visit during his travels through Colombia, he
will have no over-all quantitative data in which to anchor his
conclusions. Finally, an observant person cannot miss the fact
that the mestizos constitute a large share of all the people in
the hundreds of heavily populated *municipios* which are scattered along both sides of the eastern range, that in many of
them the Indian ancestry is only slightly diluted with the
white, and that the people in the heavily populated, mountain valleys of Nariño are mostly of the Indian race; but again
he will have to depend on general impressions and will have
no careful enumerations to aid him in arriving at accurate
generalizations.

Relative Importance of the Various Elements

In view of the unsatisfactory nature of the data, any attempt to determine the absolute and relative importance of
whites, Indians, Negroes, and the various crosses of the three
in Colombia can be little more than a considered guess. Representative compilations and estimates made by various authorities from the time of independence to the present have
been assembled in Table I. They are of interest, chiefly, as a
demonstration of the differences of opinion among the authorities, even those of recent date. There is general agreement, however, upon the fact that mixed bloods of one kind
or another constitute the bulk of the Colombian population.

Table I.   Population of Colombia by Race, According to
Various Authorities*

Authority	Date	Number of inhabitants
Vergara y Velasco	1778	828,775
Vergara y Velasco	1810	1,095,000
Mollien	1823	1,744,600
Mosquera	1851	2,299,256
Perez	1883	4,000,000
Vergara y Velasco	1901	5,000,000
Census	1912	2,611,147
Census	1918	5,855,077
Bureau of Information	1926?	7,000,000
James	1941	8,701,816
Rosenblatt	1945	9,206,283
Brand	1947	10,580,000
James	1959	13,227,000
Camacho-Leyva	1962	15,000,000
Banco de la República	1963	15,000,000

Sources: Banco de la República, *Atlas de Economía Colom-*
tion of Latin America," in *Some Educational and Anthropological*
1948), p. 51; Ernesto Camacho-Leyva, ed., *Quick Colombian*
1962), p. 174; Colombian Government Bureau of Information In
[?]), p. 31; Preston James, *Latin America* (New York: The Odys-
101–102; G. Mollien, *Travels in the Republic of Colombia in the*
Mosquera, *Memoir on the Physical and Political Geography of*
1853), p. 97; Felipe Pérez, *Geografía general, física y política de*
Ciudad Bogotá (Bogotá: Echeverría Hermanos, 1883), p. 171;
hasta la actualidad (Buenos Aires: Institución Cultural Espanola,
(Bogotá: Imprenta de Vapor, 1901), pp. 841–842.

Whites	Indians	Negroes	Percentages of Mestizos	Mulattoes	Zambos
24.7	19.7	7.3	[—	48.3	—]
20.5	15.9	6.6	[—	57.1	—]
14.3	25.8	5.4	22.9	31.5	—]
19.0	17.7	3.3	42.7	11.8	4.3
50.0	15.0	35.0	No mixed groups considered		
12.0	8.0	5.0	[—	75.0	—]
32.5	8.6	10.2	[—	48.7	—]
28.1	8.7	9.3	[—	53.9	—]
20.0	7.0	5.0	50.0	18.0	—]
10.0	10.0	30.0	50.0	with Negroes	
23.6	1.6	4.5	46.0	24.3	—]
20.0	12.0	9.0	59.0	with Negroes	
20.0	7.0	5.0	68.0	with Negroes	
20.0	1.0	4.0	58.0	14.0	3.0
20.0	2.2	6.0	47.8	24.0	—]

biana (Bogotá, 1963); Donald Brand, "The Present Indian Popula-
Aspects of Latin America (Austin: University of Texas Press,
Facts, 1962 (Bogotá: Instituto Colombiano de Opinion Publica,
New York, *Colombia Yearbook,* 1925–1926 (New York: 1926
sey Press, first edition, 1942), p. 81; and third edition, 1959, pp.
Years 1822 and 1823 (London: C. Knight, 1824), p. 352; T. C. de
New Granada, tr. by Theodore Dwight (New York: T. Dwight,
los Estados Unidos de Colombia y Geografía particular de la
Angel Rosenblatt, *La población indigena de America, desde 1492*
1945); and F. J. Vergara y Velasco, *Nueva geografía de Colombia*

Vergara y Velasco is considered by many Colombians as their leading authority on geography. His estimates are particularly interesting on account of the extreme emphasis he placed upon race mixture,[1] and the very small proportions of the population he was willing to consider as being either white, Negro, or Indian. One may be inclined to think that his dream of the time when all the racial elements in the Colombian population would have become fused into a new homogeneous type may have interfered with the objectivity of his analysis.[2] It is interesting to note that of the 75 per cent classified as mixed in his estimate for 1901, the most recent date, he distinguished 13 per cent of them as colored and 62 per cent as light (*pálidos*).

Mollien was a French traveler, apparently regarded as a spy by the revolutionary leaders, and his information was secured at a time when the data were rough approximations

---

[1] "At present a little less than five million inhabitants make up the Colombian nation, a product of the juxtaposition and mixing of the white, American, and Negro races, so that in the greater part it is composed of mixed bloods because now there does not exist one million representatives of what could be called the pure races. In a word: the ethnographic elements, which the Conquest accumulated in the national territory, tended to fuse more and more, with the positive advantage for the whole, which some day will have a perfect unity, having been suppressed forever the grave danger of race conflict, because they have come to consider each other as brothers in the Christian meaning of the term." F. J. Vergara y Velasco, *Nueva Geografía de Colombia* (Bogotá: Imprenta de Vapor, 1901), I, 840.

[2] The belief that the contact and mingling of races results in complete fusion, with all the original types losing their identity in a new one that is uniform and homogeneous is extremely widespread. Except for a few unique cases such as that of Pitcairn Island, in which the maintenance of a white strain was impossible because all the crew of the Bounty were males, it is difficult to see the basis upon which it has been founded and why it should have received such widespread acceptance. The evidence seems to show that when two or more races meet and mix a very complex situation results. There is preserved in relatively pure form at the several extremes groups of each of the original elements and in between them are produced various shades and colors to fit all the possible gradations.

at best. General Mosquera was one of the most enlightened men of his time, and his considered judgment as to the racial composition of the people whom he served as military leader and president should not be discarded lightly. His is one of the few efforts to differentiate the Indian-Negro cross (the Zambos) from the other mixtures. Of a total of 98,600 persons of this origin in the Republic, he credited the single *departamento* of Magdalena with 90,000.

The censuses of 1912 and 1918 contain the most comprehensive and basic data extant relative to the races and their distribution in Colombia. Unfortunately the *departamento* of Magdalena, in which Negroid elements are highly important, withheld the returns on the racial classification in both 1912 and 1918. At the later date it was joined in this regrettable behavior by Bolívar, another *departamento* in which the percentages of Negroes and mulattoes are high. These censuses also suffer from the serious defect that the mestizos and other gradations of the white-Indian crosses were not distinguished from the mixtures in which the white and the black races were the original stocks.

One of the most interesting sets of estimates is that which was compiled and published in English and Spanish by the Colombian Government Bureau of Information in New York City. The following comments on the general situation accompanied the figures:

On the coasts and on the river banks a great deal on intermixture of white and Negro blood is noticeable. In the high sections of the country the race is greatly improved. This is due to the fact that the Spaniards selected whenever possible climates similar to those prevailing in Spain for building cities. The aristocratic families resided in cities the climate of which is temperate and always kept aloof from other races, thus avoiding any intercourse with them. This custom had some exceptions in the beginning of the Conquest when it was not considered dishonorable for the conqueror to marry the daughter of an Indian chief. But, as a general rule, and excepting families boasting of noble descent, the Spaniards mixed with people of the Indian and Negro races, the result of this being the diversified elements which make up the population of the Republic of Colombia.[3]

Among the most defective of the estimates are those by Brand. They give far too little importance to the African strain in the population. Although he based the estimates upon "a perusal for more than a decade of nearly all available literature" and upon personal observations, and although his Negroid category includes all individuals with "perceptible Negro blood," he arrived at the extremely low figure of only 9 per cent for the country as a whole.[4] James' revised estimates are even more extreme in this respect, however, than those of Brand. His original figures are probably more representative of the actual situation.

On the basis of all he has been able to learn on the subject by analyzing the census reports, studying the works of those who have written on the subject, making extended trips of observation through all of the most important sections of the country, and this over a period of more than 20 years, the present writer believes the racial distribution of the population in 1950 to be approximately as follows:

Category	Number	Per cent
Total	16,500,000	100
Whites	4,170,000	25
Indians	720,000	5
Negroes	1,300,000	8
Mestizos	6,900,000	42
Mulattoes	3,300,000	20

Whites, Indians, and Negroes, respectively, are considered to be those of a given race in whom there is little or no trace of any admixture of either of the other principal stocks. Mestizos

[3] Abraham Martinez, *Colombian Yearbook, 1925–1926,* New York: Colombian Government Bureau of Information, 1926 [?], p. 31.

[4] Another who certainly has greatly underestimated the importance of the Negro element in Colombia is Sir Harry H. Johnston, (*The Negro in the New World,* New York: The Macmillan Co., 1910, p. 483) who calculated that the number of Negroids in Colombia and Venezuela combined was "say 60,000." The same author omits all reference to Cartagena as a center of the slave trade.

include the white-Indian crosses of various degrees, and mulattoes the corresponding mixtures of whites and Negroes. No effort is made to distinguish the Zambos, because in a large measure they have been thoroughly mixed with the mulattoes.

Distribution of the Races

The lack of a racial classification in the most recent censuses and the grouping of all those of mixed blood together in the 1912 and the 1918 enumerations, make it difficult to determine the present distribution of the principal racial stocks in Colombia. Affirmations as to the situation are not lacking, but not many of them are of any great value. An exception to this rule is the generalization by Professor López de Mesa who observed that a slightly waved line drawn from Río Hacha on the shores of the Caribbean to Ipiales on the Ecuadorian frontier divides Colombia into two great racial zones. To the east of this line the mestizo type prevails, to the west of it the mulatto.[5] This is essentially the same conclusion as that which has been presented by many writers, Colombians and visitors, for a good many years. Thus a French traveler who visited Colombia just at the time the wars for independence were coming to an end wrote as follows:

The greatest number of Negroes is found in the maritime provinces. Those of Antioquia, the Magdalena, of Cauca, of Guayaquil, and of Chocó, contain a great number; they have increased there in such a manner that the whites are noticed as in our [the French] colonies. In the eastern branch of the Cordilleras there are none but whites and Indians.[6]

It is also possible to find many excellent descriptions of the specific situation in certain parts of the country. These thoughtful, unemotional attempts to appraise various aspects of the racial composition and distribution of the population by persons long familiar with given sections of the country

[5] Luis López de Mesa, *Como se ha formado la nación colombiano* (Bogotá, 1934), pp. 48–49: cf. Justo Ramón, *Geografía de Colombia* (Bogotá: Librería Stella, 1943), p. 106.

[6] G. Mollien, *Travels in the Republic of Colombia in the Years 1822 and 1823* (London: C. Knight, 1824), p. 351.

deserve serious attention. But few of them will equal the description provided by Ramón Franco R. for the "Caucano" nucleus. Therefore it has been deemed advisable to give in translation his rather detailed characterizations of the population in five different sections of this important part of Colombia. These are as follows:

1. A coastal belt of the African race, which extends inland along the banks of the rivers as far as Dagua, Buenaventura, and Puerto Tejada. In the Patia Valley is found the pure Negro, formerly a miner, who today devotes himself to cattle-raising, loafing, and vandalism. Displaced from the mines by the foreign companies and their machinery, and incapable of agricultural work, he has dedicated himself to the calling which gives most leeway to his idleness: raising and stealing cattle. On the shores of the Pacific the Negro continues his boating, his hunting, and his fishing. He is happy, unmoral, without esthetic notions, fetishistic, affectionate, and lying.

2. The mulatto group, wheat colored, whose members today exercise hegemony in political affairs (the Indostanes), the economic field, administrative activities, and even in social matters, overspreads almost all the Valley and parts of the mountains.

3. The mestizo region which commences on the slopes of the Cordillera of the Quindio and mixes with the Tolimense population at the limits.

4. The Indian of the Tierradentro region, a remnant of the ancient nation of the Paeces, of which there still exist 22 fragments in those Andean masses, in addition to two per cent of the population of the Valley.

5. The white nucleus of Popayán, "with shoots of good family in Cali, Palmira, Tulua, Buga, and Cartago." It is traditionalist and as such lives from its high traditions; it practices a Dionysian philosophy of life and from the economic standpoint is improvident and negligent. It represents the remnant of the old feudal masters of the land, of noble intelligence, of exclusive culture, latinist, and poetic. This group has its major branch in Popayán, and about the Master Valencia consecrates itself to art and thought. . . .[7]

[7] Ramón Franco R., *Antropogeografía colombiana* (Manizales: Imprenta del Departamento, 1941), p. 194.

Similar generalizations for other sections of the country are not lacking. One of the most important probably is that for Antioquia. This is because the high rate of reproduction and the tremendous migration to other areas have brought about the situation in which approximately one person out of two in Colombia either lives in Antioquia and Caldas, or is a migrant or the child of a migrant from one of those *departamentos*. It is interesting to note that although the anonymous author or authors of the statement we quote in translation are skeptical about the possibility of arriving at an accurate inventory of the racial composition of the population by census procedures, it was not thought necessary to express any doubts or give any qualifications of the generalizations presented. Thus we are informed that:

In the Departamento of Antioquia there is a wide field of study, but, unfortunately, there are no censuses with the registration of the races nor will it be possible to obtain them, since the declarations on this subject are generally false. That which today is observed in the Departamento is that the indigenous influence upon the racial make-up has been very slight or totally absorbed by the other races; that in the cold areas is encountered a population belonging to the white race; and that along the Atrato, Cauca, Nechí, and Magdalena rivers is found a population mass almost pure Negro. Between these two extremes there is the great body of population, the product of a cross between the white and Negro races, or the *morenos* of whom Dr. Manuel Uribe Angel writes in his *Geografía general del Estado de Antioquia*.[8] . . .

[8] *Geografía económica de Colombia: I, Antioquia* (Bogotá: Imprenta Nacional, 1935), pp. 120–121. Manuel Uribe Angel *Geografía general y compendio histórico del Estado de Antioquia en Colombia* (Paris: Victor Goupy y Jourdan, 1885), p. 113, gives the following interesting statement concerning the ethnic origins of the people of the Medellín Valley, one of the most important centers of dispersion in Antioquia: "Before the foundation of Envigado (1775), its *campos* were occupied by families of Spanish origin for the most part, by some Negro slaves, and by a few mestizos. The indigenous race had disappeared from almost all the valley, leaving only a few families in the pueblo de Estrella and on the headwaters of the Rio Aburrá. These Spanish *campesinos* of Envigado and the rest of the Medellín Valley were people of pure

The Racial Elements

THE INDIANS

Much remains to be done by the anthropologists before it will be possible to sketch a brief and accurate account of the numbers, types, distribution, and tribal groups of the Indians who were living at the time of the Conquest in what is now Colombia. There can be no doubt that the population was large, the diversity of human types great, and the tribal differentiations considerable, but there is no single place to which one may go for a brief and accurate exposition of essential facts. In the literature the pertinent materials occur in such a maze of place names and group designations that it is difficult for one to grasp even the broadest outlines of the general picture.

One authority, Padre José Agustín de Barranquilla,[9] whom we follow, does attempt a systematic listing of the major groups, along with indications of the habitat of each. According to this Capuchin father the Indians occupying the coast between Río Hacha and the mouth of the Magdalena were called Taironas, those more to the interior, Bondas and Chimilas. In what are now the *departamentos* of Atlántico and Bolívar were the Calamaris, Yurbacos and Fizenus. Along the Gulf of Urabá were the Caribs, related to the groups in the Antilles. From Panama some of the Guaímies extended along the Pacific Coast into Colombia, neighbors of the Cunas who lived on the Isthmus of Darién and to the

blood, mountaineers most of them, and all of them of patriarchial customs, honorable, industrious and old Christians in the best sense of the term."

[9] *Asi es la Guajira* (Barranquilla: Emp. Litográfica, 1946) pp. 47–49. Cf. Julian H. Steward, Editor, *Handbook of South American Indians,* Bureau of American Ethnology, Bulletin 143 (Washington: Government Printing Office, 1946), II, 50–57; 865–974; III, 763–798; and IV, 1–40; 297–385. James G. Leyburn, *Handbook of Ethnography* (New Haven: Yale University Press, 1931), lists 119 tribal names for the Indians of Colombia. Vergara y Velasco, *Nueva geografía,* pp. 877–906, discusses at some length the Colombian tribes.

south. Between the Cauca and the Pore rivers were the Tahamíes. The Catíos lived along the Atrato, the Sierra de Abibe, and extended to the Gulf of Urabá. South of them, and extending to the Quindío divide in the central range, were the Quimbayas. Along the Pacific Coast to the west were found the Barbacoas; the Indians of the Cauca Valley were the Lili or Cali; and those to the south of them in the Popayán area were the Patianos and Pastusos. Along the Magdalena in Tolima and Huila were distributed the Pantágoras, and above them on the slopes of the eastern cordillera, the Pijaos and Timanes. On the high plains of Bogotá were the Chibchas or Muiscas, while to the west about Facatativá were the Panches and Agatáes. To the north in the mountains around Pamplona lived the Chitagáes, while the section between the Sogomoso River and the Minero was inhabited by the Laches and the Muzos. The eastern slope of the eastern range was the home of the Andaquíes. At the base of the Andes and extending to the Meta, the Apure and the Orinoco were the Chicaráes and the Guahibos. And finally in the territory of Guajira were the Indians which our author studied in detail, the Arhuacos and Guajiros.

Even though such a sketch does not do justice to the complexity of peoples in the southern part of the country, or those living along the headwaters of the Amazon in Colombia, It does take into account the major groups of indigenes through the parts of Colombia that have been incorporated into the economy and society of the nation or extinguished entirely.

Probably we shall never know with any degree of certainty the numbers in the aboriginal population of Colombia at the time of the Conquest. Many sections were densely populated and it seems likely that the total could not have been less than 500,000, and it may very well have been considerably more. Even more important is the fact that only certain parts have contributed very much to the present population, others having been exterminated before they had any significant effect upon the ethnic composition of the modern nation. Thus the contributions of the Chibchas and other groups inhabiting the upper portions of the eastern cordillera were great, as were those of the tribes who possessed the inter-mountain basins of

Nariño. In both cases peoples who had already developed their social organization to a considerable degree rather docilely accepted the yoke of the new white oligarchy. On the other hand the coastal Indians, those in the mountain fastnesses of the central range, and the inhabitants of the Cauca Valley put up such a fierce resistance to the Spaniards that most of them were exterminated.

THE WHITE MEN

To a relatively few conquerors and late-comers Colombia owes the genes which determine the zoological nature of the 25 per cent of her population that is white, and contribute along with those from Indian and Negro sources in the third of her people who are mestizos and the quarter who are mulattoes. The conquistadores were not numerous, other settlers from Spain did not come in any great numbers, and the number of immigrants from European countries other than Spain has been negligible. Says Vergara y Velasco:

> Few were the Spaniards who came to the Colony before 1550: they would not total 10,000, half of whom died in the conquest, and at least as numerous were the first mestizos, considered naturally as Creoles; such was the origin of the 220,000 white Creoles who existed in Colombia in the epoch of Independence.[10]

There is much reason in the insistence of this authority upon the point that an Indian strain runs through a good share of the population considered as white. It is true that some of the upper class families have carefully guarded the purity of their white heritage. It is not at all unusual to find one of their members who will stoutly insist that race prejudice is lacking in Colombia, and that the three races are blending harmoniously into new combinations. This same person, however, will be rudely shocked by any questions designed to discover if any of his ancestors, however remote, might have had a strain of Indian blood. But the fact remains that a great many persons of mixed blood have in the past been accepted as part of the white community. In the first

[10] *Nueva geografía*, p. 871.

place, the conquistadores did not hesitate to take daughters of the principal caciques as their wives, and to consider their children as equal in every respect to those whose mothers were whites. In the second place, the King gave out strict orders just at the time of the conquest of New Granada to the effect that the children of Spaniards were to be recognized as such, were to be cared for and were not to be "lost among the Indians." Even though the mixed bloods were not the issue of any legal marriages it was provided that the mestizos and their mothers were to be collected into one place in order that they might be cared for. Those proved to be the children of men able to do so were to be taken care of by their fathers. The others were to be placed in the families of the *en-comenderos*.[11]

By the time Padre Vicente de Oviedo made his classification of the parishes in the Archbishopric of Santa Fé de Bogotá in 1763, race mixture had proceeded to the point that it was very difficult for the good priest to distinguish between those who should be characterized as Indians and those who should be admitted to the category of whites. The "Thoughts and Facts Selected for Utility to the Priests" by this authority included (along with data about the climate, the remoteness from the capital and the state of the roads, and the income to the church) estimates on the numbers of Indians and whites in the respective community. Time after time Oviedo repeated that the "cities and places" of the Spaniards were called *parroquias* while the villages and towns of the Indians were designated as *pueblos,* but in the long enumeration of specific localities about which he informed his fellow priests, few exclusively Indian settlements are to be found. As a matter of fact the padre himself generalized to this effect in connection with his comments upon bullfighting:

> . . . but in all parts and most abundant within the jurisdiction of Tunja, there are very wild bulls, and each year in fiestas for three or four days they fight ten or twelve bulls, not only in the cities and places of the Spaniards,

---

[11] Ministerio de Trabajo y Prevision (of Spain), *Disposiciones complementarias de las leyes de Indias* (Madrid: Saez Hermanos, 1930), I, 236.

which here are called parroquias, but also in the other
pueblos of the Indians, because in all of them there is a
large group of Spaniards. . . .[12]

In another paragraph he stated specifically the meanings he
attached to the Indian and white categories in the following
words:

> . . . Ubaté . . . should have more than 700 Indians,
> and I warn that when I put the number of Indians it
> generally is all of them and not precisely those who pay
> tribute. It has more than 1,000 white citizens, in which
> are included all the mestizos and other breeds that are
> called whites . . . and this rule is general in all that we
> have to say.[13]

Don Jorge Juan and Antonio de Ulloa also took the trouble
to inform their readers as to the actual origins of some of the
population who prided themselves on being white.[14]

There have been some attempts to establish the origins of
the Spaniards who settled in various parts of what is now the
Republic of Colombia. Indeed much controversy has arisen
about the extent, if any, to which persons of Jewish origin
took part in the development of Antioquia. On the other aspects not so much has been written, but Justo Ramón[15] has
summarized the accepted ideas on this subject as follows:
along the Caribbean coast in Bolívar, Atlántico, and Magdalena, the Andalusians predominated; in Antioquia and Caldas
most of the Spanish settlers were Basques, Andalusians, and
Castilians; those of the Santanders were Navarrians, Galicians,
and Asturians; in the highlands of Cundinamarca and
Boyacá most of the Spaniards were Andalusians and Castilians; those establishing themselves in Huila and Tolima were
Estremadurians; in Nariño the Spanish contingent were
Basques, Castilians and Andalusians; and in El Valle del
Cauca and Cauca they were Castilians.

---

[12] Basilio Vicente de Oviedo, *Cualidades y riquezas del Nuevo
Reino de Granada,* edited by Luis Augusto Cuervo, Biblioteca de
Historia Nacional (Bogotá: Imprenta Nacional, 1930), XLV, 52.
[13] *Ibid.,* p. 96.
[14] See the extract from their writings which is given below.
[15] *Geografía de Colombia* (Bogotá: Librería Stella, 1943), p.
103.

Little definite has come to my attention concerning the widely diffused belief that persons of Jewish descent formed an important element in the settlement of Antioquia. (Numerous, however, are the writers who assert that there is no basis for such a belief.) But José M. Samper, after characterizing the Antioqueño as "very interesting, the most beautiful physically in the country, and strong for his characteristics and his influence in the Confederation," wrote as follows:

The old province of Antioquia (today a federal State of the same name) conquered by Robledo and Heredia, naturally attracted an immigration of the first Spaniards, on account of its prodigious deposits of gold and the excellent climate of its mountains. Later, the Jews persecuted in Spain, even those converted by force, organized an emigration of 200 families of this race, converted to Catholicism, who obtained permission to go establish themselves in the province of Antioquia. There disappeared all the obstacles which had made fusion impossible in the Peninsula. Spaniards, Israelites, and Creoles crossed freely and produced the most beautiful and energetic mestizo-European race that is known in Hispano-Colombia. Today the State of Antioquia has more than 300,000 inhabitants of whom at least 250,000 are of the mixture in which the Jewish element has figured.[16]

Finally, one should not close the discussion of the white stocks which have entered into the ethnic composition of Colombia without mentioning that a considerable number of persons of low estate made their way into this and other Spanish colonies. There they contributed not a little to the genes of white origin which are now part of the hereditary makeup of large numbers of the mulattoes and mestizos. In this connection one can do little better than to present in some detail the facts as given by Jorge Juan and Antonio de Ulloa in their account of Cartagena.

[16] *Ensayo sobre las revoluciones políticas y la condicion social de las repúblicas colombianas* (Paris: E. Thunot y Co., 1861), p. 85. Cf. Ricardo Uribe Escobar, *El Pueblo Antioqueño* (Medellín: Universidad de Antioquia, 1942), pp. 9–10; A. C. Veatch, *Quito to Bogotá* (London: Hodder & Stoughton, 1917), pp. 206–207; and Edward Alsworth Ross, *South of Panama* (New York: The Century Co., 1915), pp. 14–15.

Those who on board of the gallions are called Pulizones, as being men without employment, stock or recommendation; who leaving their country as fugitives, and, without license from the officers, come to seek their fortune in a country, where they are utterly unknown; and therefore, after traversing the streets till they have nothing left to procure them lodging or food, are reduced to have recourse to the last extremity, the Franciscan hospital, where they receive not in a quantity sufficient to satisfy hunger, but barely to keep them alive, a kind of pap made of casava, which, as the natives themselves will not eat it, the taste, to wretched mortals never used to such food, may be easily conceived. As this is their food, so their lodging is the entrance of the squares and the porticos of churches, till their good fortune throws them in the way of hiring themselves to some trader going up the country, and who wants a servant. For the city merchants, standing in no need of them, shew no great countenance to these adventurers, as they may very justly be called. Affected by the difference of the climate, aggravated by bad food, dejected and tortured by the entire disappointment of their romantic hopes, they fall into a thousand evils, which cannot well be represented, and among others, that distemper called at Carthagena, Chapetonada, or the distemper of the Chapetones, without any other succour to fly to than divine providence; for none find admittance into the hospital of St. Juan de Dios, but those who are able to pay, and, consequently, poverty becomes an absolute exclusion. Now it is that the charity of these people becomes conspicuous. The Negro and Mulatto free women, moved at their deplorable condition, carry them to their houses, and nurse them with the greatest care and affection. If anyone die, they bury him by the charity they procure, and even cause masses to be said for him. The general issue of this endearing benevolence is, that the Chapetone, on his recovery, during the fervour of his gratitude, marries either his Negro or Mulatto benefactress, or one of her daughters; and thus he is settled, but much more wretchedly than he could have been in his own country, tho' he had only his own labour to subsist on.

The disinterestness of these people is such, that their compassion towards the Chapetones must not be imputed to the hopes of producing a marriage, it being very common for them to refuse their offers either with regard to themselves or their daughters, that their misery may not be perpetual, but endeavour to find them a master whom they may attend up the country, to Santa Fé, Popayán, Quito and Peru, whither their inclination on the fairest prospects lead them.

Those who remain in the city, whether bound by one of the above marriages, or, which is but too common, are in another condition very dangerous to their future happiness, turn Pulperos, Canoeros, or such like mean occupations: In all which, they are so harrassed with labour, and their wages so small, that their condition in their own country must have been miserable indeed, if they have not reason to regret their quitting it. And the height of their enjoyment after toiling all day and part of the night, is to regale themselves with some bananas, a cake of maize or casava, which serves for bread, and a slice of tasajo, or hung beef; without ever tasting any wheat bread during the whole year.

Others, and not a few, equally unfortunate with the former, retire to some small Estancia, where in a Buhio, or straw-hut, they live little different from beasts, cultivating, in a very small spot, such vegetables as are at hand, and subsisting on the sale of them.[17]

Nor should one who seeks to understand the racial backgrounds of Colombia's population neglect the fact that a few upper-class men left huge progenies, many of them of white mothers and born in wedlock, but not a few of them of mixed blood. In this way the genes of a handful of men contributed out of all proportion to the present-day make-up of the population, and introduced not a little white blood into the lower social strata.[18]

[17] *A Voyage to South-America, etc.* (London: L. Davis and C. Reymers, 1758), I, 37–39.

[18] For one author's comment upon the facsimiles of renowned men to be observed in small towns, see J. Steuart, *Bogotá in 1836-7* (New York: Harper & Brothers, 1838), pp. 92–93. Of course the story of the small community, all of whose members are descendants of the old village patriarch, crops up in all of the Latin American countries, in many cases with more than a shred of evidence in its favor. Cf. Eric Pixton, *De Buenos Aires a Misiones en canoa* (Buenos Aires: Editorial Claridad, 1937), pp. 91–92. As a matter of fact, if everything necessary in order to attain a high degree of civilization and culture were to develop a population of almost pure blood descent, certain parts of Latin America would have attained the pinnacle of perfection.

THE NEGROES

In spite of all that has been written about the Negro in the New World and the slave trade there is a lamentable lack of organized material dealing with the importation of slaves into the territories that now constitute the Republic of Colombia. Such authorities as Sir Harry H. Johnston, one of the few who has tried to give a comprehensive picture for both North America and South America, almost completely ignore this part of the Spanish possessions. This is all the more to be regretted because the documents establish definitely that Cartagena was one of the chief slave marts of the New World. As early as the beginning of the seventeenth century this famous port, probably the most heavily fortified stronghold in the world at that time, was not merely the point at which the Spanish galleons were assembled into convoys for the voyage to Spain. It was also an important market for the "black ivory" or the *piezas de Indias* from Africa. The *Catholic Encyclopedia* states that as many as 12,000 slaves were landed each year at that port, most of them in a wretched condition. It was here that the Jesuit, Pedro Claver, the Apostle of the Negroes, lived and performed the great humanitarian work which eventually resulted in his being numbered with the Saints of the Church.

But although the work of collation, analysis, and synthesis pertaining to the slave trade in this part of the world is still to be done, a little research indicates that there are many materials on which such a study could be based. Aside from the voluminous legislation on Negroes and slaves in the Laws of the Indies, most of which is general and applies to all the colonies, there are many other documents which have a bearing on the subject.[19] To illustrate this we call attention to a

[19] A good beginning on the type of synthesis needed has been made by José Rafael Arboleda, S.J., "Nuevas investigaciones afrocolombianas," *Revista Javeriana,* (May 1952); and Aquiles Escalante, *El negro en Colombia,* Monografias Sociológicas No. 18 (Bogotá: Facultad de Sociología, Universidad Nacional de Colombia, 1964).

few pertinent facts and events, most of them drawn from a single study which was made during the latter half of the nineteenth century.[20]

One of the first events of interest is the slave rising which took place at Santa Marta in 1529,[21] not long after the Spaniards from the West Indies established themselves on the mainland and before Jiménez de Quesada began his long climb to the Savannah of Bogotá. In 1537 Vadillo, who had gone to Cartagena to *residenciar* or examine the conduct of the Governor, Pedro de Heredia, noted that there were many Negroes in the city, females as well as males; and two years later there is a document which indicates that Negroes had already been introduced into the settlement of Anserma in the Province of Popayán.[22] Then as later there undoubtedly was so much smuggling that official records would have been quite inadequate, even if they were available. But materials such as the letter dated July 24, 1545, which the Licenciado Miguel Diez Armendariz sent to the King indicate that not only were there already many Negroes in the colony but that not a few of them had got completely out of hand. This official raised grave accusations against the government of Cartagena, alleging that for more than nine years escaped Negroes had been out of control, forcing the Indians to work for them, sacking haciendas, and stealing women. When he wrote the escaped Negroes had just completed an assault upon the Pueblo of Tafeme where they killed over 20 persons, stole the gold and other valuables, destroyed the fields of corn, and carried away more than 250 Indians. The letter continues as follows:

> They have . . . their seat about 40 leagues from the Villa of Santiago de Tolú. For this reason that province is in a state of great alarm and some of the Indian pueblos have been deserted. It is a shame to see such vile people go so long unpunished. . . . I have promised rewards to those

[20] José Antonio Saco, *Historia de la esclavitud de la raza africana en el nuevo mundo y en especial en los paises americo-hispanos* (Habana: Cultural, S.A., 1938).

[21] *Ibid.*, I, 242.

[22] *Ibid.*, p. 289.

that kill them, and greater ones to those who bring them in alive.[23]

Another uprising of slaves at Santa Marta is reported for 1550, and that the traffic was becoming great enough to demand attention from the busy body of men who made up the Council of the Indies is indicated by the fact that a Royal Cedula of June 6, 1556, fixed ceiling prices on slaves at various places. In the list one finds Cartagena, Tierra Firme, and Santa Marta in which the limit was placed at 110 *ducados* per head; and Nuevo Granada and Popayán, both far inland, where it was set at 140 ducados.[24]

The seventeenth century was one in which the trade in slaves in the Spanish colonies was regulated by a series of contracts (*asientos*) giving exclusive privileges to some entrepreneur. One of these signed on May 13, 1601, with Juan Rodríguez Cutiño (João Rodrigues Coutinho?), a Portuguese, called for the introduction of 500 slaves each year at the ports of Santa Marta, Río de la Hacha, Margarita, Cumaná and Venezuela;[25] and another with the Portuguese Antonio Rodríguez Delvas signed on September 27, 1615, and to last for eight years provided for the delivery of up to 5,000 Negroes, but not fewer than 3,000 live ones, at Cartagena and Vera Cruz.[26] Cartagena had come into its own as a slave emporium.

Not long after this, on August 8, 1621, the Negroes of the fortress city were the object of a special decree handed down by Philip IV. After noting that "in the City of Cartagena there are many Negroes and Mulattoes, from whose unrest has come many killings, robberies, crimes, and destructions, be-

[23] *Ibid.*, II, 11. In this connection it is interesting to note that this part of what is now the Departamento de Bolívar is one of the few places in Colombia from which come reports of Negro communities in which the African language, dances, and customs, are still preserved. These small groups of Negroes are said to insist absolutely on endogamous marriage. See, *Geografía económica de Colombia, Tomo V, Bolivar* (Bogotá: Editorial El Grafico, 1942), pp. 152–154.

[24] Saco, *Historia de la esclavitud*, II, 27, 42.

[25] *Ibid.*, pp. 100–101.

[26] *Ibid.*, pp. 115–116.

cause the officials have consented for them to carry arms and knives . . ." it was ordered that this practice should cease and that no slave be permitted to carry arms or a knife, even though he was accompanied by his master, except through license from the King himself.[27] Cartagena, as a slave market was also the object of another law three years later, one that levied a tax of from 6 to 8 *reales* upon each Negro debarked at the port. The proceeds were to be used to pay the expenses of an armed guard to be formed for the purpose of pursuing runaway slaves.[28] By this time ships of considerable size were engaged in carrying slaves to this part of the New World. One of them which sank within sight of Cartagena had aboard some 900 Negroes, of whom only 30 were saved.[29]

During the second half of the seventeenth century the trade seems to have been handled in much the same manner as it was in the first, except that the volume perhaps was larger. In any case there was a contract signed with Domingo Grillo and Ambrosio Lomelín on July 5, 1662, which provided for the delivery within seven years of 24,500 *piezas de Indias, i. e.,* Negroes measuring 7 *cuartas* (about 57.6 inches) or more in height.[30] About 12 years later another one with Antonio García and Sebastián Siliceo provided for the bringing of 4,000 slaves each year for five years of whom 700 *piezas de Indias* were to be for Cartagena, and 50 for Santa Marta and Río de la Hacha.[31] Shortly after this, on January 27, 1682, another contract containing almost exactly the same provisions was signed with Nicolás Porcio acting for Juan Barroso de Pozo.[32]

The asientos entered into during the eighteenth century did not specify the ports at which the slaves were to be landed, but one may be sure that Cartagena received her share. We con-

[27] *Recopilación de las Leyes de las Indias,* Libro 8, Titulo 5, Ley 17.

[28] *Ibid.,* Libro 8, Titulo 18, Ley 7.

[29] Saco, *Historia de la esclavitud,* II, 145.

[30] *Ibid.,* pp. 157–158; cf. Ministerio de Trabajo y Prevision, *Disposiciones complementarias de las Leyes de Indias* (Madrid: Saez Hermanos, 1930), I, 250–261.

[31] Saco, *Historia de la esclavitud,* II, 163.

[32] *Ibid.,* p. 167.

clude this brief résumé with a translation from an account of another experience with runaway Negroes, this one dealing with the Santa Marta area:

> More successful were the works of the priest of the Indians at Santa Cruz de Masinga, Friar Andrés de Picó, with the savage Negroes who, fleeing from the maltreatment they received from their masters on the haciendas, had taken refuge in the Sierra Nevada of Santa Marta, where they not only lived independently but insolently confronted the forces which went out in search of them.
>
> Authorized by the provincial of the Franciscans, Friar Sebastián Barroso, and by the Provisor Vicar governor of the Bishopric, the Licenciate D. Antonio Barranco, and counting on the aid of the Governor of Santa Marta, D. Alonso Valero Caballero of the Order of Santiago, Padre Picó succeeding in arriving, after suffering a thousand hardships, at the stockade which the Negroes had constructed. His preaching brought forth good fruits and on March 12, 1704, he entered Santa Marta with some converted Negroes among them the Captain or chief of the stockade; these swore obedience to the Governor in their own names and those of all their companions, and two days later were solemnly baptized in the Cathedral. The remainder of the Negroes in the stockade were also converted to Catholicism, and all were declared free and authorized to leave the Sierra and to trade. In order that this should not serve as a stimulus for desertions, these privileges were not extended to those who later should attach themselves to the stockade.[33]

Racial Succession

When the first Spaniards set foot upon the Caribbean shores of what is now Colombia, racial succession, the process by which the members of one race are pushed out of the territory they have been occupying and supplanted by those of another, began. It continues unabated today. At first all of the receding was done by the members of the red race, all the encroaching by the whites and the Negroes who served

[33] D. Jerónimo Bécker and D. José M. Rivas Groot, *El Nuevo Reino de Granada en el Siglo XVIII* (Madrid: Biblioteca de Historia Hispano-Americana, 1921), pp. 10–11.

them as slaves on the plantations and in the mines they established at the "cutting edge of civilization." Some of the black men, however, were not long in fleeing the settlements and doing a little encroaching strictly on their own. As the centuries have passed, the pressures upon the Indians have not lessened, until at present there are very few places in which they have succeeded in retaining any of the better lands. Rather they are crowded into the out-of-way places, high on the slopes of the mountains, and back deeper into the jungles. But in recent years the pressures also have been upon the Negroes and they, too, have been forced to relinquish many of the areas they once enjoyed to their fellows of the white or the mestizo racial groups.

It would be possible to write a fairly adequate history of the people of Colombia strictly in terms of racial succession. Here no such comprehensive task is attempted, but an effort is made to illustrate the general process by brief reference to a few of the more important developments. The manner in which the Indians receded before the whites varied greatly from one part of what is now Colombia to another. Along the coastal plains in the north, in Antioquia, and in the Cauca Valley, the changes came about swiftly and violently, while along the heavily populated slopes of the eastern cordillera and far to the south in the upland portions of Nariño, the changes were slow and gradual. In the former the aborigines were less developed in many ways than the sedentary, agricultural Chibchas and their neighbors who inhabited such temperate climes as the Savanna of Bogotá and the high plateaus of Boyacá; or those who made their homes in the Pasto Basin, and many other parts of the *tierra fria*. In particular their political organization seems to have been of a more primitive form. But in any case while the inhabitants of the cool savannas and the high plateaus rather docilely accepted the white man's yoke, those in the coastal plains, the mountains of Antioquia and Caldas, and the Cauca Valley resisted bitterly. As a result the latter were exterminated by the tens of thousands, their lands seized immediately and converted into pastures and plantations, and their places taken by a few hundreds of white people from Spain and thousands of Negroes from Africa. In these sections of the country, the process was swift and violent as will be documented below.

In the high temperate zones to which Jiménez de Quesada and his followers fought their way, and in which they established their capital called Santa Fe de Bogotá and other garrison towns, the overlordship of hundreds of Indian villages passed from the native *caciques* to the conquistadores without such a widespread extermination of the Indians. The handful of Spaniards merely settled themselves in a few new towns and set about to enjoy the better things of life to which they were entitled through participation in the Conquest. In particular they devoted themselves to three things: (1) the breeding of cattle and horses on the private allotments of the richest and most desirable lands which were at once handed over to them by the representative of the king, on his own behalf or through the local cabildo, and on the extensive tracts of common pasture called *ejidos;* (2) the levying and collection of tribute from the Indians assigned to them in *encomienda,* a tribute that the Indians had to wrest from the less desirable lands, generally those on the steep slopes above those in the valley bottom that had been seized for the private uses of the stockraising conquerors; and (3) mining activities conducted with the labor force which the institution of the *mita* gave them a right to conscript in the villages of the *encomiendas.* But for none of these activities was it necessary to import large bodies of Negro slaves. As a result as the centuries have passed and as the Indians and the mixed breeds who lacked status in the Spanish community have been crowded higher and higher onto the slopes, back into the small tortuous valleys, and out onto the poorest lands generally, the Negro has not been among the racial groups replacing them. The pressures have come from those who are racially white, and that portion of the mestizos who have been incorporated to some extent in the white community. Even today, after communications have developed to the point where the automobile, the airplane, and the railway can all play a role in scrambling the racial groups in Colombia, one rarely sees a person of Negroid descent in Bogotá or the other highland cities. A few students at the national university and some of those who represent the coastal districts in the National Congress are about the only ones seen in the capital, and in the smaller cities members of the black race are hardly to be encountered.

The evidences that the Coastal Indians, those of Antioquia and Caldas, and those once inhabiting the Cauca Valley were killed off by the tens of thousands, the survivors driven back into the forests and up into the mountains, and the lands immediately utilized by the Spaniards and their slaves are so abundant that they alone would fill volumes. Among the whole lot, however, no description more adequate and illuminating than that given by Pedro Cieza de León, himself one of the conquistadores who was rewarded with an *encomienda* of Indians at Arma, in what is now Caldas, has come to the writer's attention:

All this valley, from the city of Cali to these rapids, was formerly very populous, and covered with very large and beautiful villages, the houses being close together and of great size. These villages of the Indians have wasted away and been destroyed by time and war; for, when the Captain Don Sebastián de Belalcazar, who was the first captain to discover and conquer this valley, made his entry, the Indians were bent on war, and fought with the Spaniards many times to defend their land, and escape from slavery. Owing to these wars, and to the famine which arose on account of the seeds not having been sown, nearly all the Indians died. There was another reason which led to their rapid extermination. The Captain Belalcazar founded, in the midst of the Indian villages in this plain, the city of Cali, which he afterwards rebuilt on its present site. The natives were so determined not to hold any friendship with the Spaniards (believing their yoke to be too heavy) that they would neither sow nor cultivate the land; and from this cause there was such scarcity that the greater part of the inhabitants died. When the Spaniards abandoned the first site, the hill tribes came down in great numbers, and, falling upon the unfortunates who were sick and dying of hunger, soon killed and ate all those who survived. These are the reasons why the people of this valley are so reduced that scarcely any are left.[34]

[34] *The Travels of Pedro de Cieza de León,* translated and edited by Clements R. Markham (London: The Hakluyt Society, 1864), pp. 93–94.

Nor is it either practicable or necessary to multiply descriptions designed to show how the Indians were crowded out of the rich fertile valleys and forced to go high up the mountain slopes in order to make their modest little plantings of corn, potatoes, and barley.[35]

But the process eventually reached a critical point in such *departamentos* as Cundinamarca, Boyacá, Santander, and Norte de Santander. Much of the soil erosion which has made huge sections of these states into absolutely unreclaimable badlands had its origins in the type of racial succession under discussion. Since the agricultural Indians and mestizos were crowded out of the valleys and off from the light slopes at the base of the mountains, in order that these could be converted into pastures for the livestock of the conquerors and their heirs, a situation developed in which the lands most suited for agriculture were practically all in grass while those most fitted for pastures were under cultivation. This may be observed today by anyone who travels overland from Bogotá to Tunja, or Leiva, and in almost any other section of the uplands. But the prevailing situation probably has never been described more concisely nor accurately than by Manuel de Ancízar, secretary to the Codazzi Commission, who 100 years ago wrote as follows:

From Sogamoso to Iza it is something over four leagues of level road, happy and clear through a pretty, green valley occupied by a *hacienda* called la Compañía, in commemoration of the Jesuits, first owners of that valuable *finca*, the only one in the canton in which the large extension of land included in this valley is concentrated in the hands of a single family, because happily the remainder of its soil is divided into small holdings, the property of many proprietors. *La Compañía* is simply a pasture for fattening cattle, so that the plantings of the *colonos* which surround it appear like refugees upon the slopes and sides of the surrounding mountains; and the rich plains possessed by herds

[35] This process has been described in more detail in T. Lynn Smith, "Land Tenure and Soil Erosion in Colombia," in the *Proceedings of the Inter-American Conference on the Conservation of Renewable Natural Resources* (Washington: U. S. Department of State, 1949), pp. 155–160.

of sheep and larger animals, and by numerous troops of mules, incontestible sign of the infancy of our country, it is with agriculture dislodged from its legitimate lands by livestock.[36]

[36] *Peregrinación de Alpha,* (Bogotá: Arboléda y Valencia, 1914), p. 276.

6 Rate of Reproduction

SERIOUS STUDY of the birth rates of Latin American populations is still in the beginning stages. Only in a few of the countries have well-planned efforts been made to determine the level of the rate of reproduction, the way it varies from group to group, place to place, and time to time, and the factors responsible for such variations; and for the area as a whole, the bibliography is practically lacking in titles. It should be indicated, however, as will be stressed below, that prior to 1950 the data available for comprehensive investigations of the fertility of the population in most parts of Latin America were so incomplete and unreliable that substantial amounts of work, even by the most experienced students of population, probably would have produced relatively modest results.

This is not to say that much has not been written about the birth rate in various Latin American countries. Many economists, geographers, sociologists, and historians who have studied social and economic matters in Latin America have included in their books and articles some mention of the birth rate. On occasion some of them have given the statistical data as compiled by the official agencies of the various countries. But it is meant to indicate that as a general rule sufficient care has not been taken to determine the degree to which such data could be relied upon, and in the analysis of the information that was presented.

Alejandro Bunge, noted Argentine economist, appears to have been the first to undertake substantial study of the birth rate in various Latin American countries. In connection with

From T. Lynn Smith, *Latin American Population Studies*, University of Florida Social Sciences Monographs No. 8, Gainesville: University of Florida Press, 1960, Chapter 3. Reprinted by permission of the publisher.

his thesis of the splendor and decline of the white race, he assembled data designed to show that the birth rate was declining in Argentina, Chile, and Uruguay, and not merely in various countries of Europe, the United States, Canada, Australia, and New Zealand.[1] The efforts of Forrest E. Linder (1941) to assemble birth statistics for various countries in the Caribbean area,[2] and the projects undertaken by the United States Bureau of the Census in cooperation with the Office of the Coordinator of Inter-American Affairs for the purpose of assembling and publishing a series of birth statistics for each of the Latin American countries,[3] are other landmarks in the development of the scientific approach to the study of the rate of reproduction throughout Latin America. Linder knew, as did the demographers responsible for the compilations for the various countries, that the reported birth rates were not indicative of the true rates of reproduction, but none of them attempted to determine the degree of accuracy of the indexes. It seems that T. Lynn Smith[4] and Giorgio Mortara,[5] working separately with Brazilian data, were the first to publish results of any efforts to determine the extent to which the official statistics failed to indicate the magnitude of the birth rates actually prevailing. By 1944 the former had concluded that the birth rate in Brazil was at least 38, and not 12 as reported in that nation's official publications;[6] and two years afterwards the latter concluded that the true birth rate was somewhere between 39.5 and 47.8.[7] Smith eventually extended his efforts to include

[1] *Una Nueva Argentina* (Buenos Aires: Guillermo Kraft Ltda., 1940), Chapters I and II.

[2] "Population and Population Statistics of the Caribbean Area," *Vital Statistics—Special Reports*, XII (1941), 559–571.

[3] See *Argentina: Summary of Biostatistics* (Washington, 1945); and comparable volumes for nineteen other countries issued at about the same time.

[4] *Brazil: People and Institutions* (Baton Rouge: Louisiana State University Press, 1946), Chapter VIII.

[5] *Estimativas da Taxa de Natalidade para o Brasil, as Unidades da Federação e as Principais Capitais*, "Estudos de Estatística Teórica e Aplicada, Estatística Demográfica," No. 4 (Rio de Janeiro: Instituto Brasileiro de Geografia e Estatística, 1948).

[6] *Op. cit.*, pp. 231–234.

[7] *Op. cit.*, pp. 11–12.

all the other Latin American countries, beginning with El Salvador,[8] where he found the birth rate to be about 45. In 1953 he presented preliminary results of his attempts to determine the levels of the rate of reproduction throughout Latin America, and in 1958 he published more definitive materials on the subject.[9]

Among the efforts to measure the fertility of the population in specific Latin American countries, the following deserve special mention: Giorgio Mortara, "The Brazilian Birth Rate: Its Economic and Social Factors";[10] John V. D. Saunders, *Differential Fertility in Brazil;*[11] and Julio Durán Ochoa, *Población.*[12]

Indexes and Data

Those interested in the fertility of the population in Latin America must give more attention to some elementary aspects of demography than is required if they are concerned with Europe, Japan, the United States, Canada, Australia, or New Zealand. Specifically they must be exceptionally careful in the selection of the indexes to be used and they need to be very judicious in the evaluation of the data with which they are working.

INDEXES—Demographers rely for the most part upon two basic indexes for measuring the rate at which populations are reproducing. These are the birth rate and the fertility ratio.[13] There is still little to be gained by applying in Latin America any other gauges of the fertility of the population. In its sim-

[8] "Notes on Population and Rural Social Organization in El Salvador," *Rural Sociology,* X (December, 1945), 366–367.
[9] "The Reproduction Rate in Latin America," *Eugenical News Quarterly,* XXXVIII (September, 1953), 64–70; and "The Reproduction Rate in Latin America: Levels, Differentials and Trends," *Population Studies,* XII (July, 1958), 4–17.
[10] In Frank Lorimer, *Culture and Human Fertility* (Paris: UNESCO, 1954), pp. 405–503.
[11] Gainesville: University of Florida Press, 1958.
[12] Mexico: Fondo de Cultura Económica, 1955. Pages 55–91 of this volume contain a substantial study of the level of reproduction in Latin America's second most populous country.
[13] Cf. T. Lynn Smith, *Fundamentals of Population Study* (Chicago: J. B. Lippincott Company, 1960), Chapter 11.

plest and crudest form the birth rate is merely the ratio between the number of live births during a stated period (one
year if possible) and the number of persons in the population,
with the resulting figure multiplied by a constant in order to
convert the index into a simple number of two digits. Naturally several requirements must be met before the birth rate
can be used with any degree of confidence, and before there
is any reason for attempting any substantial refinement of the
crude birth rate. Obviously it is essential that birth registration
be fairly complete and accurate. However, in many parts of
Latin America, not to mention other parts of the world, this
requirement is not met. In other parts of Latin America only
recently have enough of the births been registered to make
the birth rate a fairly reliable index of the rate of reproduction
of the population. Even in the second half of the twentieth
century throughout Latin America the struggle for registration of all the births and significant classifications of them
is far from being won.

The population of the country or area must also be known
with a high degree of accuracy before the birth rate can be
determined even in an approximate manner. Before the results of the Census of the Americas of 1950 were published,
the reported birth rates for a number of the countries were
mere guesses simply because the estimates of the populations
of the countries were so unreliable.

Even if all the births are registered and if the population
counts or estimates are current and accurate, many other
requirements must be met before the birth rate may be used
as the basis for many of the more important comparisons in
the study of the fertility of the population. As is easily demonstrated, the populations of the various countries, and the rural
and urban portions, racial categories, and other groupings
within a given country, differ sharply from one another with
respect to age and sex composition. These two factors, in turn,
are closely linked to the rate of reproduction. For example,
. . . the age and sex make-up of Argentina's population is so
different from that of Brazil's or Mexico's that a comparison
of the crude birth rates of the three is almost certain to
prove misleading to all except the most experienced demog-

raphers. Likewise, because the age and sex distributions of their populations are so different, little is to be learned by a comparison of crude birth rates in the United States and most of the European nations with those for various Latin American countries. Moreover, in most parts of Latin America the data essential for the standardization of birth rates are lacking. This makes it difficult to explore even the most elementary aspects of the rate of reproduction in Latin America unless some substitute for the birth rate is employed.

The 1950 Census of the Americas has now made available fairly abundant and substantially improved demographic materials which may be used in the calculations of another valuable index of the fertility of the population in Latin America. This is the fertility ratio, which is based on the ratio between the number of young children and the number of women in the childbearing ages. Obviously, the specific age groupings used in tabulating census materials may cause variations in the actual age limits employed by different persons for different countries, but insofar as it is feasible the present writer prefers to use the number of children under 5 and the number of women aged 15–44. Instead of the conventional constant of 1000, he uses 100 in computing the fertility ratio. This index may be employed to gauge the level at which the population is reproducing even in a country such as Brazil where a large proportion of the births are not registered. Unlike the crude birth rate, it also is substantially standardized for differences in the age and sex composition of the populations which may be compared. In addition, it is important to note, often one can compute the fertility ratios for various residential and racial or ethnic groupings which figure in the tabulations of census data. This is of special importance in most of Latin America, because such categories are lacking in most of the classifications pertaining to births.

THE DATA.—The casual observer of standard sources is likely to gain the impression that a plethora of data relating to the rate of reproduction in the Latin American countries is readily available. Extensive materials from the registers of births help fill the *Anuario Estadístico* published annually in most of the countries. Tabulations of the number of births and computations of the birth rates for the various Latin American countries figure prominently in the numerous issues of the *Statistical Yearbook* of the League of Nations; they have been reproduced for the years 1905 to date in the several editions of the *Demographic Yearbook* of the United Nations; and the current issues of the *Statistical Bulletin* of the United Nations give the latest official data shortly after they are received from the member governments. In a *Summary of Biostatistics* for each of the countries in Latin America, prepared and published during the early 1940's by the United States Bureau of the Census in cooperation with the Coordinator of Inter-American Affairs, also are to be found tabular and graphic materials on births and birth rates going back to 1900 in the majority of the cases. These are only a few of the places in which one encounters extensive materials, so that offhand it is easy to conclude that the materials needed for intensive study of the birth rate in Latin America are readily available. . . .

The technicians employed by the United Nations have made a beginning in the evaluation of birth statistics in Latin America and throughout other parts of the world. As a result the various editions of the *Demographic Yearbook* contain some details relative to the extent to which the data are presented on the date-of-occurrence rather than the date-of-registration basis, the manner in which stillbirths are handled, the way in which multiple births are counted, and the coverage and completeness of the data. All of these are pertinent for one who contemplates making any use of Latin American birth statistics, particularly those for the past. For example, the exceedingly high birth rates reported by Cuba for 1926, Panama for 1924, and Paraguay for 1942 are indicative merely that births occurring in previous years helped inflate the rates for the years mentioned. As indicated by the 1958 issue of the *Demographic Yearbook* of the United Nations, the data for Cuba, the Dominican Republic, Honduras, Mexico, Nicaragua, Colombia, Paraguay, Peru, and Venezuela are known to be by year of registration rather than by year of occurrence; and the 1953 edition of the same fundamental compilation indicated that Costa Rica, El Salvador, Guatemala, Argentina, Ecuador, and Uruguay were then in the same category. The 1953 volume also indicates that the Peruvian data for 1925–1939 includes stillbirths; that certain countries, such as Cuba, Honduras, Bolivia (prior to 1948), and Ecuador, exclude from the reports liveborn infants dying within twenty-four hours of birth; that Argentina does not include liveborn infants dying before registration of birth; and that the materials for Colombia are those on baptisms taken from the church registers.

The staff of the United Nations evaluated the materials supplied by the various countries, and they also queried the officials of the agencies responsible for gathering and submitting the materials in each country relative to the coverage and reliability of the information. As a result of their work, the data on births in the various nations were classified into three large categories: (1) those in which there is "a complete, or virtually complete, coverage of the events occurring each year"; (2) those in which there is an incomplete coverage or one "subject to considerable irregularity"; and (3) those for which no comprehensive data were available.[14] Haiti and Brazil are the two Latin American countries still not reporting birth statistics to the United Nations, and they do not figure in the compilations given in the *Demographic Yearbook*. In the 1953 issue of the volume Mexico alone qualified for the first category, that in which the coverage each year is complete or virtually complete; Guatemala, Honduras, and Argentina fell in the third category; and all of the others were placed in the second group. By 1958, however, El Salvador, Guatemala, Panama, Argentina, Chile, Uruguay, and Venezuela had joined Mexico in the category of those having complete or virtually complete coverage.

As indicated above, there are many large and puzzling discrepancies between the data for the same area and period published in two or more of the official sources; it is necessary to emphasize also that the materials published for specific years in the various editions of the *Demographic Yearbook*

[14] *Demographic Yearbook, 1953,* p. 15.

of the United Nations are not always the same and that one making use of such sources must endeavor to use the most recent editions of that invaluable source. For example, the overestimation of the population of Guatemala prior to the 1950 census was so great that the birth rates for that country as published in the 1948 edition of the *Yearbook* were 33.8, 33.7, and 36.8 for the years 1945, 1946, and 1947, respectively. After more reliable population data became available, however, the recent issues of the *Yearbook* carry the rates of 48.7, 48.2, and 52.2, respectively, for the three years specified.

Generally speaking, the most important thing to be noted about any of the comprehensive series for the various Latin American countries is the utter lack of dependability of the reported birth rates. With few exceptions they are not indicative of the levels of the rate of reproduction in the various countries, nor of the changes or lack of changes that have taken place in the rate of reproduction in the course of the last fifty years. Possibly the data for Argentina, Costa Rica, El Salvador, and Mexico are fairly indicative of the real situation and trends, but even they should be used with a large degree of caution. At least until most recently the materials for all of the others are absolutely inadequate either as a basis for comparisons or for a study of trends. Therefore, for reliable information about the fertility of the population in Latin America, how it varies from country to country, how it compares in urban and rural districts or among the white and colored segments of the population, or how it is changing in the course of time, one cannot depend upon the birth rate as the measure to be employed.

The situation in this respect is reminiscent in many ways of that prevailing in the United States between 1900 and 1930. About 1930, however, the use of the fertility ratio as an indicator of the rate of reproduction came to be used by many of the more serious and experienced students of population, and, largely as a result, our knowledge of population matters developed rapidly. At present, it seems that the use of the fertility ratio in the study of the fertility of the populations of the Latin American countries is likely to yield substantial results. Unfortunately, however, the failure by many of the censuses to present the necessary age and sex distributions for such categories as the rural and urban parts of the population, the various racial or color groupings, and other significant segments of the population, properly cross-tabulated, greatly limits and complicates the use of this measure of the fertility of the population.

Table I. Indexes of the Fertility of the Population in the Various Latin American Countries.

Country	Average birth rate, 1949-1951	Fertility ratio, 1950	Reported birth rate as a percentage of the fertility ratio
Costa Rica	37.2	73.9	50.3
Cuba (1)	25.1	55.3	45.4
Dominican Republic	37.3	79.8	46.4
El Salvador	47.8	67.4	70.9
Guatemala	51.6	75.2	68.6
Haiti	----	49.7	----
Honduras	40.6	72.7	55.8
Mexico	44.9	68.4	65.6
Nicaragua	41.0	70.2	58.4
Panama	32.8	75.4	43.5
Argentina (2)	25.1	46.8	53.6
Bolivia	39.6	68.5	57.8
Brazil	----	70.5	----
Chile (3)	34.0	56.7	60.0
Colombia (4)	36.5	74.5	49.0
Ecuador	46.3	76.5	60.5
Paraguay	20.0	75.2	26.6
Peru (5)	26.0	71.5	36.4
Uruguay	18.6	----	----
Venezuela	42.8	76.7	55.8
Puerto Rico (6)	38.5	78.4	49.1
United States	24.0	47.9	50.1

Sources: Compiled and computed from data in the various issues of *Demographic Yearbook* and the census reports of the respective countries.

(1) Birth rate is for 1952; fertility ratio for 1953.
(2) Data are for 1946-1948 and 1947, respectively.
(3) Birth rate is for 1951-1953; fertility ratio for 1952.
(4) Data are for 1950-1952 and 1951, respectively.
(5) Birth rate is for 1940-1941; fertility ratio for 1940.
(6) Test in 1950 indicated the data on births to be 95.9 per cent complete.

Fertility Levels

The most important fact to be established about the rate of reproduction in Latin America, and for each of the countries, is the level at which it stands. From what has been said above, it should be evident that this is no simple task. For purposes of analysis, though, attention is directed to the materials on the birth rates as reported officially and fertility ratios as calculated by the writer given in Table I. Since 1950 is the year of the latest census in most of the countries, it is the one generally used. Wherever possible the birth rate presented is the average of those for the year preceding the census, the census year itself, and the year following the census. In order to facilitate comparisons between the birth rates and the fertility ratios for the various countries, the percentage that the figure representing the birth rate is of the one for the fertility ratio is presented for each of them. Recent materials for the United States and Puerto Rico are included for comparative purposes.

A study of these data leads to few definite conclusions except that almost uniformly throughout Latin America the rate of reproduction is exceedingly high. Only Argentina and Haiti have fertility ratios approximately as low as that of the United States in 1950, and it is unlikely that the one for Haiti is very accurate. In most of the countries the fertility ratios are above 70, which means that the fertility of their populations is comparable to the very high level that prevailed in the United States one hundred years ago. Two of the countries with fertility ratios only slightly below 70, El Salvador and Mexico, are those in which the birth statistics certainly are among the best. In the former the fertility ratio is 67.4 and the birth rate 47.8, and in the latter the ratio is 68.4 and the birth rate 44.9. It is doubtful, therefore, that the true birth rate is less than 45 in any of the countries in which the fertility ratio is 70 or above, namely, Costa Rica, the Dominican Republic, Guatemala, Honduras, Nicaragua, Panama, Brazil, Colombia, Ecuador, Paraguay, Peru, and Venezuela. The reported birth rates for Cuba, Argentina, and Chile may be fairly accurate, but those for the remainder of the countries are almost certainly above 40, except for Uruguay, where the lack of any modern census makes even intelligent guessing almost impossible.

In the second half of the twentieth century birth rates of 40 or above are exceedingly high. Other than those for Latin America, the only countries with indexes of these magnitudes throughout the entire world in 1950 as reported by the *Demographic Yearbook, 1955*, are as follows: Egypt, 44.4; Belgian Congo, 40.6; Mauritius, 49.7; São Tomé and Principe, 42.9; British Guiana, 40.4; Ceylon, 40.4; Formosa, 42.5; Brunei, 50.7; Federation of Malaya, 42.0; Ryukyu Islands, 41.1; Singapore, 45.7; the Maoris of New Zealand, 45.1; American Samoa, 43.3; Cook Islands, 41.8; and Western Samoa, 45.5. Among the independent nations of the modern world, those of Latin America have birth rates which stand in a class by themselves.

Similar is the conclusion if the comparison of the rate of reproduction in Latin America with that prevailing elsewhere is based upon the fertility ratio. As indicated by the data in Table I, the fertility ratio is above 60 in every Latin American country except Cuba, Haiti, Argentina, and Chile. In twelve of the countries, embracing far more than the majority of the Latin American population, it is above 70. Other than in Latin America, on the basis of the age and sex data from the 1953 issue of the *Demographic Yearbook*, among all of the countries and possessions for which the necessary materials are available fertility ratios above 60 are found only in the following: the Moslem population of Algeria, 76.7; Gold Coast of Africa, 61.2; Yukon and Northwest Territories, Canada, 76.4; Alaska, 61.5; Formosa, 86.6; India, 61.4; and Turkey, 66.3.

Costa Rica, Cuba, El Salvador, Mexico, and Chile are the Latin American countries in which the birth statistics probably are the best. The practice in El Salvador of making a birth certificate a prerequisite for baptism appears to be effective in securing the registration of nearly all births, and there may be comparable devices in use in some of the other countries. However, much remains to be done to improve the coverage. As was the case in the United States until very recently, the fertility ratios appear to be much more reliable indicators of the levels of reproduction throughout Latin America than are the reported birth rates. The birth rate in the United States is approximately 50 per cent as large as the fertility ratio, and in some other countries in which the registration of births is believed to be fairly complete, the corresponding percentages are as follows: Australia, 54.5; New Zealand, 43.7; Canada, 49.1; India, 40.4; and Japan, 48.5. In Europe, based on recent data, the corresponding percentages range from a low of 36.0 in Ireland (1950) to a high of 54.3 in Portugal (1950). In Latin America, however, because of the high infant and child mortality rates, the corresponding percentage is much higher. Even so, however, in any Latin American country in which the birth rate is less than 60 per cent as high as the fertility ratio, it is probable that a considerable proportion of the births are not registered.

Differential Fertility

Much interest and importance are attached to the facts with respect to the comparative rates of reproduction among the rural and urban, white and colored elements in the population of Latin America. Even greater significance may be attributed by some to any differences, much more difficult to establish, that may exist between the birth rates of those who belong to the lower social and economic classes and those who belong in the middle and upper classes of the respective societies. On these subjects a great deal of speculation has taken place, but it is difficult to find reliable, comprehensive, convincing data pertaining to them. However, now that the recent censuses supply more adequate information on the age and sex composition of the population, the elements needed for the computation of fertility ratios, it is possible to begin the study of such differentials in fertility.

RURAL-URBAN DIFFERENTIALS.—In Europe and the United States differences between the rates of reproduction in rural and urban areas have been widely studied. Almost without exception, whenever a fair comparison has been made, the rural population is shown to be multiplying more rapidly than the urban. Moreover, as demographic techniques were improved, it became fairly easy to establish that the pronounced tendency for the peoples of western societies to congregate in towns and cities, throughout the nineteenth century and the first one-third of the twentieth, was accompanied by a long, steady decline in the birth rate in those same societies. However, in the United States at least, this association ceased about 1935. Thereafter the curve representing the urbanization and industrialization of the population moved up at an almost unprecedented rate, but that depicting the birth rate not only ceased to fall, but moved up sharply. This has necessitated a thorough reappraisal of much population theory. The fact that the rise in the birth rate in the towns and cities was much more pronounced than that in the country has added to the perplexity. Nevertheless, even in the United States the rate of reproduction of the urban population still remains considerably below that of the rural population.

Although we are still uncertain about the specific factors associated with urban and industrial living which ultimately are responsible for the low birth rates in towns and cities, apparently those factors now are operating in about the same manner in Latin America as has been true elsewhere throughout the world. (See Table II.) If we compare the fertility ratios for the rural and urban populations of many of the countries, the results are strictly in line with those established previously by much more intricate and time-consuming improvisations. The rural-urban differential in fertility is pronounced. In fact, in country after country the fertility ratio of the rural population is greatly in excess of, and frequently almost double, that of the urban population. Moreover, in those countries whose censuses have failed to include the highly important age and sex distributions for rural and urban populations separately, the fertility ratio in the national capital is far below that for the remainder of the nation's territory. In one capital, Buenos Aires, a ratio of only 25 children under 5 per 100 women 15–44 was registered in 1947. For comparative purposes it is interesting to consider the data for the largest city in the United States, New York City, in which the corresponding index was 26.3 in 1940 and 34.2 in 1950. But in Latin America the low ratio for Buenos Aires is by no means matched in the other great metropolitan centers of the area. Note that in 1950 the fertility ratio for Mexico City

was 53.9 and the one for Caracas, Venezuela, was 60.3. The
one for Lima ten years earlier was 53.5. Even the lowest of
these is considerably above that (47.9) for the United States
in 1950.

Study of the data in Table II leads one to the following
generalization: the lower the general rate of reproduction in
a country, the greater the rural-urban differential in fertility.

Table II.   Rural-Urban Differences in the Fertility Ratios of the
Latin American Countries, 1950

Country	Number of children under 5 per 100 women aged 15-44		
	Nation	Urban areas	Rural districts
Costa Rica	73.9	54.3	86.8
Cuba (1)	55.3	41.5	79.2
Dominican Republic	79.8	54.2	90.9
El Salvador	67.4	53.7	76.7
Guatemala	75.2	———	———
Haiti	49.7	36.7	52.0
Honduras	72.7	———	———
Mexico (2)	68.4	53.9	70.7
Nicaragua	70.2	58.5	78.1
Panama	75.4	54.8	92.3
Argentina (3)	46.8	24.8	52.9
Bolivia	68.5	———	———
Brazil (4)	70.5	49.4	77.8
Chile	56.7	———	———
Colombia (5)	74.5	59.5	87.0
Ecuador	75.6	66.8	77.6
Paraguay (6)	75.2	42.5	82.8
Peru (7)	71.5	53.5	74.6
Uruguay	———	———	———
Venezuela (2)	76.7	60.3	79.7

(1)   Data are for 1953.
(2)   Federal District is considered as urban, remainder of the
country as rural for the purposes of this comparison.
(3)   Federal Capital considered as urban, remainder as rural.
Data are for 1947.
(4)   The urban category includes the suburban one as well.
(5)   The *cabeceras of municipios* considered as urban, remainder
as rural. Data are for 1951.
(6)   Asunción considered as urban, remainder as rural.
(7)   Province of Lima considered as urban, remainder as rural.
Data are for 1940.

Therefore, since the evidence leads one to expect the continued industrialization and urbanization of Latin America, the prevailing rural-urban differential in the birth rate is likely to be maintained for many decades to come. Eventually, the point may be reached at which this tendency will bring about a falling birth rate throughout the length and breadth of the area. Certainly as the urban population becomes a more significant proportion of the total population, national birth rates are likely to fall, and perhaps many of them will decline sharply.

RACIAL DIFFERENTIALS.—The differences, if any, between the rates of reproduction of the white, Negro, and Indian populations of the various Latin American countries is another feature of considerable interest to many people. The belief that the colored elements in these countries are reproducing more rapidly than the white has gained widespread acceptance, even among scholars of national and international repute. In this connection consider the generalization offered by Frank Tannenbaum, noted historian and long-time student of the Negro in the Americas. After pointing out that the Negro has physical occupancy or possession of a large part of the Western Hemisphere, graphically described as a huge half-circle stretching from Washington, D.C., to Rio de Janeiro, Brazil, this authority flatly states: "And the density as well as the extent of this empire is increasing because Negro fertility is relatively high in comparison to the white. The only place where this biological expansion is being challenged is in Trinidad by the East Indians."[15] Quite apart from the matter of the accuracy of this statement with respect to the southern portion of the United States, and the degree to which migration offsets any differential that may exist, this quotation serves to bring out the importance attached to the topic under discussion by persons of many shades of opinion.

Racial differentials in the fertility of the population of Latin American countries are much more difficult to determine than are the rural-urban differences discussed above. In some of the countries, it is true, births are classified according to color

[15] "Discussion," in Vera Rubin (ed.), *Caribbean Studies: A Symposium* (Jamaica, B.W.I.: Institute of Social and Economic Research, 1957), p. 62.

or race, and in many of them some kind of racial or ethnic classification of the population is made in the census tabulations. Almost never, however, is it possible to match the births so classified with the necessary population data in order to compute birth rates for the various racial or color groups; and if one could, there would still remain fundamental questions about the degree of completeness or incompleteness in the reporting of births. Even more disheartening to the analyst, however, is the fact that the age and sex distributions for the white and colored segments of the population, the data needed for computations of the fertility ratios, generally are lacking. Some analyses, though, are possible. For example, a considerable number of students, including the present writer, have for some time been convinced that differential fertility was helping to produce a rapid "bleaching" of the population in Brazil; and some of them have judged it likely that comparable changes were underway in some of the other countries. The improved classifications used in the 1950 Brazilian census reports make it possible to calculate with ease the indexes needed for putting such an hypothesis to a rigid test. . . . A study of these materials makes it readily apparent that whites are outbreeding the Negroes by a considerable margin. The fertility ratios for the Negroes throughout Brazil are consistently lower than those for the whites. The ratios for the mixed category are inflated, of course, by any racial mixing in which either the whites or the Negroes are involved, but despite this fact, the ratios for the whites compare very favorably with those for the mixed group. The difficulties the Negro woman has in securing a mate, and the relative freedom of access which the upper class (white or whitish) man has to the (colored) women in the lower social classes probably are the two most important factors in accounting for the differentials that prevail.[16]

Other than in Brazil the lack of the necessary age and sex data for the various racial groups makes it exceedingly difficult or impossible to determine whether or not there are any significant racial differentials in the fertility of the population.

[16] Cf. T. Lynn Smith, *Brazil: People and Institutions* (Revised Edition; Baton Rouge: Louisiana State University Press, 1954), pp. 160–161; and Saunders, *op. cit.*, pp. 119–120.

However, in a few of the countries certain comparisons may be made. Thus for Cuba in 1953 it is possible to compute the fertility ratios for the four race or color categories, and these are as follows: white, 52.4; Negro, 57.2; yellow, 57.8; and mixed, 68.8. Obviously the extent of miscegenation is the most striking fact reflected in these data, but one cannot determine from them the degree to which genes from white and Negro progenitors, respectively, are contributing to the racial make-up of the new generations of Cubans. In Costa Rica, where the Negro population is very small, the fertility ratios in 1950 were 74.3 for whites and mestizos combined and only 54.6 for Negroes; and in Panama, a veritable "melting pot," the fertility ratios for the various race or color groupings used in the 1940 census are as follows: white, 40.5; Negro,

Table III.   Number of Children Under 5 per 100 Women Aged 15-44 in the Latin American Countries at Recent Census Dates

Country	Date of census	Fertility ratio	Country	Date of census	Fertility ratio
Costa Rica	1892	68.3	Panama	1940	64.4
	1927	68.8		1950	75.4
	1950	73.9	Argentina	1914	67.2
Cuba	1931	62.2		1947	46.8
	1943	57.4	Bolivia	1950	68.5
	1953	55.3	Brazil	1920(1)	66.8
Dominican	1935	78.2		1940	68.9
Republic	1950	79.8		1950	70.5
El Salvador	1930	66.8	Chile	1940	52.3
	1950	67.4		1952	56.7
Guatemala	1940	72.2	Colombia	1938	67.6
	1950	75.2		1951	74.5
Haiti	1950	49.7	Ecuador	1950	76.5
Honduras	1935	56.6	Paraguay	1950	75.2
	1945	71.2	Peru	1940	71.5
	1950	72.7	Uruguay	—	—
Mexico	1930	62.1	Venezuela	1936	58.3
	1940	63.0		1941	64.1
	1950	68.4		1950	76.7
Nicaragua	1940	71.9			
	1950	70.2			

Sources: Computed from data given in the censuses of the respective countries.
    (1) 54.5 per cent of women aged 40-49 considered as being 40-44.

34.3; mestizo (largely mulatto), 68.9; and others, 55.2. All told these bits of data for other countries do not fully support the hypothesis, based on Brazilian materials, that the white elements in the population are reproducing more rapidly than the colored, but neither do they fortify the belief held by many that the opposite is true. New and greatly improved data are needed for adequate study of the subject.

Trends

Except for a recent and spectacular decline in the birth rate in a few of the more industrialized and urbanized sections of Latin America, the rate of reproduction remains high throughout the entire area. In 1950 the fertility of the population in most of the countries was still at levels comparable to those in the United States and Canada at the beginning of the nineteenth century. Only in Argentina and Cuba is there definite indication that the fertility ratio has been falling. (See Table III.) Indeed the indexes for most of the countries are so high that it is apparent little or no decrease in fertility could have taken place during recent decades. Furthermore, for eleven of the fourteen countries for which successive censuses make possible a determination of trends, the index for the most recent year is higher than the one at the time of the preceding census. One should hardly assert on the basis of these data that the birth rate is rising (improvement in census procedures is probably the best explanation of the observed changes), but the materials do lend strong support to the proposition that it is not falling significantly. Finally, there is little reason to suppose that the present high rates of reproduction in most of the countries will not continue to prevail for several decades in the future.[17]

[17] See T. Lynn Smith, "Current Population Trends in Latin America," *American Journal of Sociology*, LXII (January, 1957), 401.

7   Rural-Urban Migration

———◆———

THE RUSH of people from rural districts to urban centers which took place during the second quarter of the twentieth century and which continues at a more accelerated pace during the third quarter may well be considered as the most important current demographic fact in Latin America. To indicate something with respect to the magnitude of the movement, to identify some of the factors and forces responsible for it, and to suggest a few of its results are the objectives of this chapter.

The Extent of Rural-Urban Migration

The schedule of questions used in the modern census is a long one, the number of topics included formidable, and the tabulated results the most comprehensive set of data available to the social scientist. But despite the length of the schedules and the variety of the questions, the collection of essential data on rural-urban migration still is not one of the major objectives of those conducting the enumerations. As a result, one who would like to know the extent of the movement from rural to urban areas, that in the opposite direction, the characteristics of the migrants, and so forth, must resort to various improvisations and approximations. Most of our knowledge about the flow of population between country and city is derived from the study of the actual rates of increase of population in rural and urban areas in comparison with the rates of natural increase, analysis of the data in which the state of birth is cross-tabulated by state of residence, and

From T. Lynn Smith, *Latin American Population Studies,* University of Florida Social Sciences Monographs No. 8, Gainesville: University of Florida Press, 1960, Chapter 4. Reprinted by permission of the publisher.

meticulous comparisons of rural and urban age and sex distributions. The nature of the data that have been assembled for the Latin American countries imposes the necessity of such indirect approaches to the subject fully as much as, if not more than, is true in the United States, Canada, and the various European countries.

One who has traveled extensively throughout Latin America during the last quarter of a century knows, of course, from his own direct experiences and observations that a mass transfer of population from rural to urban areas has been taking place. The Latin Americans with whom he mingles, including intellectual, agricultural, governmental, and business leaders, are also thoroughly convinced that a mass exodus of population from the rural districts is under way, and not a few of them, in the city as well as in the country, are advocating radical measures to halt the movement or even to return to their former homes in the country part of those who have already migrated.[1] Statistically, too, it is possible to demonstrate that neither the visitor nor his Latin American friends have been misled by mere appearances. Such a demonstration is attempted in the paragraphs that follow.

Consider first the facts that the rate of population growth is much higher in the urban areas than it is in the rural, whereas the rate of reproduction of the urban population is much below that of the rural. The most striking difference in this respect is that in Venezuela. In that country during the latest intercensal period, 1941–1950, the urban population increased by 79 per cent and the rural population actually decreased slightly, although the 1950 fertility ratio for the urban population (60 children under 5 per 100 women aged 15–44) was substantially lower than that for the rural (80 children under 5 per 100 women aged 15–44). The slightest differential, on the other extreme, is that for Panama during the period 1940–1950, in which the percentage increase of

[1] By 1952 enough Latin American leaders had become convinced of the importance of the "rural exodus" that this topic was designated by the Social and Economic Council of the Organization of the American States as "one of the serious problems," and study of the matter was placed on the 1952–1953 work program of the Council.

the urban population was 38 per cent and that of the rural population only 25 per cent, despite an urban fertility ratio of only 55 in 1950 in comparison with one of 92 in the rural districts. In all of the other countries for which successive censuses and usable rural-urban classifications of the population are available, the rate of population increase in urban areas is at least double that in the rural, even though the rate of reproduction in the former is much lower than that in the latter. In Latin America, in contrast with the United States and Europe, there may be a slightly lower death rate in the city than in the country, but at most this is a minor factor in explaining the more rapid rate of increase of the urban population. Nor can immigration and the tendency for most of the immigrants to concentrate in a few of the larger cities account for very much of the differential. Therefore, the differences indicated above constitute a sound basis for inferring that, in recent decades and throughout Latin America, there has been a heavy net migration of people from the country to the city.

This conclusion is strongly supported by a detailed analysis of the comparative rates of population growth in the state or provincial capitals and in the remainder of the territory in each unit, and of the rates of growth in the seats of municípios, or counties, and the other parts of the municípios. The lack of space precludes the presentation of these data in this chapter, but it should be stated that throughout all of the countries for which such comparisons are possible the evidence is conclusive that the urban centers of all sizes are growing much more rapidly than the rural districts surrounding them. Inasmuch as the urban rates of reproduction are much below those of the rural, this can only mean that a substantial movement of population is under way from the rural districts to urban centers of all sizes.

The state-of-birth data when cross-tabulated with the materials on state of residence supply other facts that have a definite bearing upon rural-urban migration. This is particularly true for those countries, such as Brazil, Mexico, and Venezuela, in which a federal district containing the national capital and some of its suburbs figures as one of the principal subdivisions of the nation. According to the 1950 censuses, the proportions of the inhabitants of these federal districts who were born in other divisions of their respective national territories were 43.5, 46.4, and 48.6 per cent, respectively. Of course a part of these persons were born in other towns and cities, and, too, some of them may have transferred residence to their national capitals many years ago.

In the case of Brazil's federal district (or the city of Rio de Janeiro), however, the facts that similar materials were collected in both 1940 and 1950 and that an age distribution of those born elsewhere in the republic is given in each census enable us to estimate with some degree of reliability the numbers and proportions of those born outside the Distrito Federal and living there in 1950 who had moved to it since 1940. This is done as follows: (1) for each age group and separately for each of the sexes the number of native-born Brazilians born elsewhere and living in the Distrito Federal in 1940 is decreased by the same percentage that all Brazilians of corresponding ages fell off by the time they figured as the bracket ten years older at the time of the 1950 census; for example, the decrease that took place as the group aged 20–29 in 1940 became that aged 30–39 in 1950; (2) this number is then compared with that in the corresponding age group as reported in the 1950 census; and (3) the difference is attributed to migration from other parts of Brazil during the ten-year period between the censuses. Summing the data for the various age groups and the native-born children under ten years of age born outside the Distrito Federal for both of the sexes provides an estimate of the number of the migrants.

This method indicates that there were living in the Distrito Federal at the time of the 1950 census a total of 392,829 native-born Brazilians, 182,244 males and 210,585 females, who had moved there from elsewhere in Brazil since 1940. This figure is the equivalent of 16.5 per cent of the total population of the Distrito at the time of the 1950 enumeration. It seems fairly indicative of the tremendous influx of population from elsewhere throughout the nation that was getting under way in the years immediately following the close of World War II. Along with other data these estimates enable us to account for the increase of 573,310 in the population of the Distrito Federal between 1940 and 1950 as follows: immigration, −3.1 (there were 18,178 fewer persons of foreign birth in the Distrito Federal in 1950 than there were in 1940); natural increase, 198,659, or 34.6 per cent; and net migration from elsewhere in the Republic, 392,829, or 68.5 per cent.

The same method was employed to estimate the numbers of migrants from each of the various states who moved to the Distrito Federal in the decade under consideration. (See Table I.) Note the heavy influxes, preponderantly of the female sex, from the nearby states of Rio de Janeiro, Minas Gerais, and Espírito Santo. Note, too, the large numbers of migrants from the northeastern section, and especially from the states of Pernambuco, Paraíba, Alagoas, Ceará, and Rio Grande do Norte. From three of these states the migrants included much larger proportions of males than of females, and in the case of Paraíba, whose migrants and their music set the capital agog, the newcomers included almost three males for every female.

Migration to the município of São Paulo during the decade 1940 to 1950 was estimated by the same method. For this important metropolis the arithmetical computations indicate that 524,043 native-born Brazilians enumerated by the 1950 census as residing in the city of São Paulo and its immediate environs had migrated from elsewhere in Brazil subsequent to the 1940 census. This figure is equal to 23.8 per cent of the município's 1950 population. Of the migrants 253,633 were males and 270,410 females, or the sex ratio was 93.8. These figures and other data enable one to account for the increase of 871,835 in the population of São Paulo's great metropolis during the decade 1940 to 1950 as follows: immigration, 19,944 or 2.3 per cent; natural increase 327,848 or 37.6 per cent; and migration from other parts of Brazil, 524,043 or 60.1 per cent. Even though the persons actually migrating to the city of São Paulo during the period under consideration may have come in part from other urban centers, with their places being filled immediately by an influx to those places of persons from the surrounding rural areas, this figure attests to the tremendous role of rural-urban migration in the growth of São Paulo. There is little reason to

Table I. Estimates of the Numbers of Migrants to the Distrito Federal from the Various Brazilian States, 1940 to 1950, by Sex

States	Number of migrants			Percent of the total	Sex ratio
	Male	Female	Total		
Total	182,244	210,585	392,829	100.0	86.5
North					
Acre(1)	217	338	555	0.2	64.2
Amazonas(2)	1,025	1,857	2,882	0.7	55.2
Pará(3)	2,529	3,949	6,478	1.7	64.0
Northeast					
Maranhão	1,658	2,221	3,879	1.0	74.7
Piauí	748	845	1,593	0.4	88.5
Ceará	4,759	3,461	8,220	2.1	137.5
Rio Grande do Norte	3,667	3,226	6,893	1.8	113.7
Paraíba	11,139	4,603	15,742	4.0	242.0
Pernambuco	10,380	10,501	20,881	5.3	98.8
Alagoas	5,426	5,783	11,209	2.9	93.8
East					
Sergipe	3,441	3,958	7,399	1.9	86.9
Bahia	10,504	11,558	22,062	5.6	90.9
Minas Gerais	40,892	53,785	94,677	24.1	76.0
Espírito Santo	18,325	20,794	39,119	9.7	88.1
Rio de Janeiro	51,126	65,618	116,744	29.8	77.9
South					
São Paulo	7,557	8,439	15,996	4.1	89.5
Paraná	1,146	1,237	2,383	0.6	92.6
Santa Catarina	2,024	2,188	4,212	1.1	92.5
Rio Grande do Sul	3,933	3,933	7,866	2.0	100.0
West Central					
Mato Grosso	1,284	1,840	3,124	0.8	69.8
Goiás	464	451	915	0.2	102.9

(1) Territory.
(2) Includes Rio Branco.
(3) Includes Amapá.

suppose that its influence has been less in the increase of population in other cities throughout Latin America.

To complete this discussion of the extent of migration from the country to the city in Latin America, it is well to offer a few of the results from the Colombian census of 1951. Specifically, the information secured enables one to determine the proportions of the population enumerated in 1951 who were born in the município containing the city, in other municípios of the departamento in which the city is located, and in other sections of the republic. For present purposes the percentages born in other municípios of the departamento and in other departamentos are the most significant. Thus in Bogotá 43.3 per cent of the population was classified as being born in the município, 23.5 per cent in other municípios of Cundinamarca, the departamento of which it is the capital, 31.5 per cent in other departamentos, and 1.7 per cent in other countries. For Barranquilla the comparable percentages are as follows: in the município, 53.2; in other parts of the departamento of Atlántico, 10.9; in other departamentos, 34.1; and abroad, 1.8. And Medellín registered 44.5 per cent born in the município, 47.1 in other parts of Antioquia, 7.7 in other departamentos, and 0.7 abroad. The data for Cali were not made available. As in the case of Brazil, these materials reflect the very heavy rural-urban migration that is under way. Of course, again as in Brazil, some of these migrants may have come from other towns and cities throughout Colombia, but it is all a part of the same process. Any gaps in such places left by their departures were more than filled by the influx of others from the surrounding rural districts.

Factors, Forces, and Media

The factors, forces, and media involved in contemporary mass transfers of population from rural to urban districts throughout Latin America may be divided logically into two large categories. The first of these includes the great social and economic changes that have set the stage for the rural exodus and the mushrooming of towns and cities, and the second embraces the immediate influences or media acting upon specific individuals to induce them to transfer residence from the countryside to the urban district. Each of these will be discussed in turn.

Reams of paper could, of course, be filled with an enumeration and discussion of the *broad social changes* which have got under way in the various Latin American countries since 1900, and which, in the last analysis, are the factors or forces responsible for the tremendous currents of migration presently flowing from the rural to the urban districts throughout the area. Such an analysis might easily carry us far beyond the scope of the present work; but even in the most cursory treatment some of these forces or factors should be mentioned. Certainly these include: (1) the development and extension of modern means of communication and transportation, both those that link one country with another, and those that unite the various parts of a given country; (2) the first steps in developing what may eventually become a system of universal education in each of the countries; (3) greatly increased contacts between Latin American societies and those in other parts of the western world, and especially with those in which relatively strong middle-class standards and values and a high degree of industrialization have combined to produce exceptionally high levels and standards of living; (4) widespread social ferment among the masses, among the descendants of those who for centuries were so docile and tractable in the hands of the aristocratic elements of Latin American society; (5) the enactment in all of the Latin American countries of substantial bodies of social legislation relating to hours of work, minimum wages, security of tenure, paid vacations, severance pay, and so forth, all of which have been much more effective in the urban districts than in the rural, thus helping to broaden the differentials between working conditions in the two; (6) the growing conviction on the part of political and other leaders that industrialization offers the most promising solutions for a host of the acute and chronic problems with which their countries must deal; (7) the onslaught in some of the countries, and particularly in Colombia since 1947, of extended periods of great internal strife which have caused hundreds of thousands of rural people to seek safety for their lives in the towns and cities; and (8) some fundamental changes in the nature and functions of Latin American cities. Each of these will be commented upon briefly in turn.

Neither the application of steam in the propulsion of ships nor its use to move trains of cars over prepared roadbeds revolutionized the transportation systems in most parts of Latin America to the extent that, during the last half of the nineteenth century, they made for the rapid and inexpensive movement of persons and things from one place to another in Europe, the United States, and Canada. Even today few sections of Latin America have adequate rail facilities. Similarly the telephone and telegraph did relatively little to modernize communication facilities throughout most of Latin America prior to World War I. But since 1930, and especially since the close of World War II, the automobile and motor truck, the airplane, and radio and television have, almost overnight, made rapid means of communication and transportation integral portions of community life and intercommunity relationships in all sections of the Latin American area. Roads and trails in the interior of Brazil, Mexico, and Colombia, for example, on which scarcely a decade ago the writer personally spent days and weeks without sighting more than a score of vehicles, today are jammed with trucks, busses, and automobiles moving thousands of persons and tons of merchandise from one place to another. These expanded and improved facilities for communication and transportation are a major factor in setting the stage for the exodus of population from the rural areas.

In most parts of Latin America the condition in which two-thirds or three-fourths of the total population, and even higher proportions of the rural population, remained in a state of illiteracy throughout their lives no longer is regarded as natural, inevitable, or even tolerable. Many of the Latin American countries recently have made notable strides in the development of a system of schools open to all children, and already the country in which the percentage of illiteracy remains above 50 is the exception and not the rule. But the school—and the books and magazines it teaches people to read—are among the most powerful forces making for urbanization that have ever been unleashed in the world. For hundreds of thousands of those who have had the privilege of attending school for more than a year or two, the city has become a magnet of irresistible force. As in the United States and Canada, throughout Latin America the development of a system of general education is greatly stimulating the flight of the rural population from the land.

The increased contacts of persons in a given society with those from other parts of the world is one of the features which most distinguish the years since 1940 from all preceding epochs. In few parts of the world has this revolution been more pronounced than in Latin America, a change involving travel by increased numbers of Latin Americans to other parts of the world as well as the influx of persons from other countries to all sections of Latin America. Particularly numerous are the contacts between Latin America and the North American and European countries in which middle-class mentalities and industrialization have combined to produce exceptionally high average levels and standards of living. Almost inevitably the Latin American who has visited such countries helps speed up the process of urbanization in his country upon his return; whereas the foreign companies which train country boys to operate trucks, bulldozers, and other machinery play an important role in the mass movement of population from rural to urban areas in the countries in which it secures contracts.

The second half of the twentieth century is one of great social ferment among the rural masses who for so long have constituted the bulk of the population throughout most of Latin America. Once so docile and tractable, and so completely under the control of the large landowners and their representatives, these humble folk are growing increasingly discontented with their own lot and with the prospects for their children. This social ferment is a powerful influence in causing the rural masses to abandon the country for the city.

Ever since the close of World War I and the organization of the League of Nations, the various Latin American countries have been among the first to enact into law the various models of social legislation developed by the international agencies. In many of the urban districts this legislation has had substantial effect in bettering the lot of the workers, and word of this has quickly spread throughout the rural areas. This, too, is an important factor in leading many rural folk to flock into the towns and cities.

For many decades now Latin America has constituted a highly rural enclave in a world that has been governed largely by urban and industrial values. Apparently this has led to a conviction on the part of large numbers of Latin American leaders that only by urbanizing and industrializing can their societies hope to overcome the host of chronic social and economic problems with which they are afflicted. The efforts in which they have engaged to industrialize their respective countries have done much to speed up the migration of people from the farms to the cities.

In some of the countries extensive and prolonged civil war has produced so many massacres and so much rapine and pillage in the rural districts that hundreds of thousands of persons have fled to the city in search of safety.[2] This has been particularly true in Colombia since 1947, and it has been a powerful influence in the growth of Bogotá, Cali, Medellín, and other large cities throughout the republic.

Finally, the rapidly changing functions of Latin American cities must be regarded as a cause, as well as an effect, of the mass movement of population from rural to urban districts. In the colonial period the Spaniards and the Portuguese, who conquered the natives and took possession of the land in the names of their sovereigns, founded hundreds of towns and cities. Most of them were built according to a designated plan and all were approximately equal in the social and economic functions they performed. They were merely military, administrative, and residential centers from which the conquerors exercised their control over the native Indians, the mestizos whom they quickly helped to appear upon the scene, and the Negro slaves who were imported from Africa to work on the plantations and in the mines. Few of these new cities were commercial centers of any importance. Some, such as Cartagena, Rio de Janeiro, and Havana, were important as ports and centers of transportation; but they were the exception and not the rule. Most of the colonial towns and cities throughout Latin America were transportation centers only in the sense that from them radiated the mule trails or canoe routes which led to the interior. Indeed, those sociologists and economists who insist that a break in a transportation route has been the basic factor in determining the exact location of a town or city do well to overlook such cases as Mexico City, Guatemala City (and Antigua as well), San

---

[2] Cf. Orlando Fals Borda, *Peasant Society in the Colombian Andes: A Sociological Study of Saucio* (Gainesville: University of Florida Press, 1955), p. 58.

Salvador, Tegucigalpa, Managua, San José, Bogotá, Quito, Lima, La Paz (and Sucre as well), Santiago, Asunción, and Caracas, to mention only national capitals.

Even after most of the countries obtained their independence during the opening decades of the nineteenth century, there were no great changes in the functions performed by the various Latin American cities. They continued for another century as mere residential, administrative, and military centers. However, a dozen or so of them became important as ports, and the construction of railroads helped to increase the commercial and transportation functions of others. By 1900 Buenos Aires, Rio de Janeiro, Havana, and Montevideo were capitals in which transportation and commerce had come to be among the major bases of support for their populations; and throughout Latin America a considerable number of important centers had arisen in which the administrative function played little or no role. Rosario, Valparaíso, Barranquilla, Buenaventura, Callao, Salvador da Bahia, Pôrto Alegre, Belém, Manaus, and Recife deserve mention in this connection.

In the decades since the close of World War I the growth and development of true industrial centers throughout Latin America has been phenomenal. São Paulo, Medellín, Monterrey are names that flash into mind when industrial progress is mentioned, but by 1950 Buenos Aires, Havana, Santiago, Lima, Mexico City, Pôrto Alegre, and Bogotá were cities in which manufacturing and transforming activities led all others in supplying jobs for their breadwinners.

Along with industrialization, the development of transportation facilities, especially those connected with aviation, and the development of commerce and construction activities have done much to change the basic nature of Latin American cities. As a result, today most Latin American cities resemble much more closely the cities in other parts of the western world than they do the centers they themselves were only a quarter of a century ago. As indicated above, these changing functions of Latin American cities figure among the important general factors that have brought millions of rural people to urban districts.

The *immediate influences or media* which act upon specific individuals to cause them to transfer their residences from rural to urban districts are legion. Prominent in this category, though, are such factors as the following: (1) word-of-mouth reports and letters describing the advantages of life in the city which some of the migrants send back to their friends and relatives in the rural districts;[3] (2) the location of almost all secondary schools in towns and cities, which induces many a large landowner to move his family to one of them so that the children may continue their education; (3) the "scouring" of the countryside by high-born city women in search of servants for their mansions; (4) temporary transfer by the absentee landlord of a few of his retainers, male and female, from one of his estates to his palatial home and grounds in a state or national capital; (5) recruitment of workers in the rural districts for construction and other projects on which foreign and national companies are engaged; (6) the glib promises made to the girls they meet in the farming districts by the young Lotharios who pilot the trucks, busses, and automobiles from the cities over the newly opened trails and roads throughout the back country; (7) the advice and counsel of the urban-reared or urban-trained schoolteacher to the youths of the neighborhood in which she is employed; (8) visits by country people to relatives who previously have established themselves in the city; and (9) at least in Paraíba, Ceará, and other parts of northeastern Brazil, the glowing pictures of city life by the truck drivers who are engaged in transporting families and their possessions, often as many as fifty persons per load, over the long, rough, and hot road to Rio de Janeiro and São Paulo.

Recently the present writer lived in a home in Mexico City to which the servant had come seven years earlier from a small agricultural village in the state of Oaxaca. She got her job upon the recommendation of her predecessor in the position, a girl who had migrated earlier from the same village. My landlady told me that in this part of the city, the Colonia Napoles, in recent years nearly all of the servants had come from the state of Oaxaca. But the potency of this factor is

[3] *Ibid.*, p. 59.

not limited to contemporary Mexico. Just as letters and other personal reports to friends in the "old country" were the great factors in inducing the phenomenal movement of persons from European countries to the United States,[4] so from Mexico to Argentina at the present time letters and word-of-mouth reports from those already established in the city to friends and relatives back home are the basic things which cause Juanita García or João Castro to migrate to an urban center. Information gained in this manner, the rural youth feels he may trust. Such personal reports, advice, and assistance in obtaining positions is probably the most important single device in the current, heavy rural-urban migration throughout Latin America.

In most of the great rural portions of Latin America secondary schools are entirely lacking, and in immense sections of the area between the Rio Grande and Cape Horn such facilities are found only in state and national capitals or other major cities. In most of Brazil, for example, the well-to-do landowner in the interior early must choose among the following alternatives: (1) allow his children to grow up with no more schooling than the three or four years provided by the elementary schools in the município in which he resides; (2) send his children to board with friends or relatives in the capital or other city, usually on the coast, while they continue their schooling; or (3) move the entire family to one of the cities in which the desired facilities are located. Frequently the third alternative is the one selected, a factor of no slight importance in Brazilian rural-urban migration. In Spanish America, in which most members of the upper class habitually reside in the national or state capitals, this medium is of less importance; but even there it is not entirely lacking in significance, especially now that many members of the middle class and even some persons originating in the lower social strata are aspiring to educational attainments that will enable them to rise in the social scale.

The standards of living of upper-class Latin Americans demand an abundance of personal servants (maids, cooks, gar-

---

[4] W. I. Thomas and Florian Znaniecki, *The Polish Peasant in Europe and America* (5 vols.; Boston: Richard G. Badger, 1918–1922), *passim*.

deners, chauffeurs, laundresses, and so forth) in the elaborate
city mansions in which they live. Even members of the middle
class must have a servant or two if they are to keep up the
appearances demanded by their social position. When it becomes difficult to find such help in the city, at the prevailing
wages, and if the servants already on the job are unable to
locate others in the communities from which they have come,
many of the families comb the surrounding rural communities for the help they need. The area surrounding Bogotá,
for example, has literally been scoured by high-born city
women in search of servants for their homes in Chapinero
and other exclusive residential districts of the capital.

Closely related to the preceding is the transfer, intended to
be merely temporary, by large landowners of some of the
retainers from one of their great rural estates to their permanent residences in the city. Referring again to Colombia, in
which it has not been unusual for a large landowner to have
estates in the lowlands, in the intermediate ranges in which
coffee plants flourish, and in the high, cool intermountain
valleys, there long has been the practice of shifting families of
laborers seasonally from one of the places to another. When
help for their homes and gardens in the city become scarce,
at the prevailing urban wages, as frequently has been the case
in the last two decades, it is not unusual for some of the rural workers to be brought in to help staff the city residences
and grounds. Not infrequently such transfers become permanent, or if not, the return of these workers adds still more
to the social ferment in the rural areas and causes more and
more of the rural masses to "get completely out of hand" and
to join the rush to the urban centers.

Merely the construction that has taken place in building
Latin American cities during the last twenty-five years, along
with building the water systems, dams and power plants, and
so on needed to supply them, has required great armies of
workers, armies that for the most part could not be recruited
in the cities themselves. Accordingly the representatives of the
firms, foreign and national, holding the contracts for the projects have carried on extensive recruiting activities in the surrounding rural areas. This has been a major factor in causing Juan and José to leave the country and to take jobs

which meant that they would spend the remainder of their lives in the city and probably influence numerous of their friends and relatives to do likewise.

The drivers of fleets of urban-based busses, trucks, taxis, and other automobiles that now crawl like ants over the Latin American countrysides play a role not to be overlooked in determining that María, Louisa, or Dolores will decide to leave her home in the country for the bright lights of the city. These young Lotharios not only persuade the girls they meet—in the little country stores, in the inns at which frequently they spend the night, in the village parks, and so forth—that the city is the place for them, but the vehicles which they drive furnish the necessary transportation.

In Latin America as throughout the rest of the world, the school generally is the most urbanizing influence in the rural community. It would be practically impossible to get or prepare teachers who are not dominated by urban values, even if they are not urban-reared, and even if that were the objective of those in charge of administering the schools. As it is, the extent to which the teacher has an influence upon her pupils is almost the extent to which they are inspired to seek a life in the urban districts.

Kinship and friendship ties are very close and intimate throughout Latin American society, and this is changed little by the fact that one or more members of the group has left the rural districts for a life in the city. The migrant seeks every opportunity for a visit back home, and many of the friends and kinfolk go to see him in the urban center. This is a potent force in causing some of the rural relatives likewise to change their residences from the country to the town.

In some parts of Latin America, and particularly in northeastern Brazil, the transportation of those following long-established migration routes, such as those that lead from Ceará, through the entire Northeast, and on to Rio de Janeiro and São Paulo, is an endeavor in which hundreds of truck owners are engaged. Naturally these entrepreneurs do not overlook chances to indicate to their friends and acquaintances in the northeastern states the possibilities of work and life in the great cities of the south and to collect the established fee for providing the transportation. As early as 1951, almost immediately after the last link in the road had been completed, the state of Ceará attempted to combat the exodus this was producing, by enacting a law making it illegal to carry passengers across the state line by truck. This resulted in some inconvenience to the migrants, since they then had to get out of the truck at the state line, themselves take the few steps into the next state, and then reboard the truck in order to continue on several thousand miles to the south.

Effects

So far in this analysis the movement from the country to the city throughout Latin America has been considered as the dependent variable, as a result of other factors. But, as is the case in most social and economic equations, such an analysis is incomplete. It is fully as valid and important to reverse the equation, to consider the movement from rural to urban areas as the moving force or independent variable, and to seek to determine its effects upon other aspects of social and economic structures and processes. To the effects of rural-urban migration this section is devoted.

First to be listed, as it probably also is first in importance, is the fact that the migration from rural to urban areas is the principal factor in the remarkable growth of towns and cities that is going on throughout Latin America. Inadequate as are the data, still, as is evident in the cases of São Paulo and Rio de Janeiro, there can be little doubt that the natural increase of population in urban areas definitely is secondary in importance in the growth of towns and cities, and that the major factor in urban growth is the movement of population from the rural districts. The third factor that needs to be considered in the analysis, namely immigration, runs a very poor third in most cases, although in a few places, such as in the growth of Buenos Aires, Rio de Janeiro, São Paulo, and Caracas, it once played a significant role. But by all odds the important cause of the growth of towns and cities, large and small, throughout Latin America is the urbanward flow of population from the rural areas. Since the rapid urbanization of the area, in turn, must be considered as the major cause of the tremendous social, economic, and political changes now under way between the Rio Grande and Cape Horn, this fact alone brings out the importance of rural-urban migration.

Second, rural-urban migration is giving rise to a constellation of perplexing social, economic, and political problems in all of the countries from Mexico to Argentina. Throughout the rural districts the landowners are bemoaning the lack of hands that results from the exodus, whereas in the cities problems of housing, health and sanitation, and intraurban transportation, along with disorders, occasional food riots, and pressures upon the legislative bodies, are very much in the minds of the responsible officials and in the news. Many urban leaders, and especially the governmental officials, think that their problems would be greatly eased if the migrations from the country could be slowed down or even stopped altogether; and frequently, very frequently indeed, one hears expression of the belief that many of the migrants should be returned to the communities from which they came. Thus in large measure the tremendous problems of adjustment presently confronting all of the Latin American countries is due to the movement from the rural districts to the cities that is going on throughout the area.

Third, rural-urban migration and the backwash to the rural areas it engenders of ideas, values, techniques, and various other social and cultural items are beginning the work of eradicating the tremendous rural-urban and regional differences that long have prevailed throughout Latin America. This rural-urban movement of population must be thought of as a stirring process that is thoroughly mixing ethnic, social, and cultural elements in various sections of each country which not many years ago were almost hermetically sealed off from one another. In Brazil, for example, the trucking to Rio de Janeiro of hundreds of thousands of migrants from the rural sections of Paraíba, Ceará, Bahia, and other northeastern and eastern states during the years 1948–1955 had as one almost immediate effect the replacement of the *samba* by the *baião* as the most popular music and dance forms in Brazil. (With a lag of a few more years, this rhythm, not long since confined to a small region in northeastern Brazil, may even supplant "rock and roll," or some other of the latest crazes, in the United States.) But the migrants who return to their home districts, the relatives who visit them in the city, and the exchange of messages and letters are potent forces in the diffusion of food habits, technical skills, ideas, vices, and so forth from the advanced sections of southern Brazil to the more tradition-bound areas of the northeast. And so goes the homogenization of society throughout the length and breadth of Latin America. Local and regional ethnic, social, and cultural differences are being greatly reduced by the movement of persons from all parts of the republics into the national and state capitals and other towns and cities, and the subsequent diffusion of social and cultural traits to the rural areas. In addition, the process of stirring is itself favorable to the discovery of new combinations of previously existing traits and complexes, so that the whole process of social and cultural change is greatly facilitated by the rural-urban exchange.

A rise in standards and levels of living is another change throughout Latin America for which the rural-urban migrations must be considered as among the most important moving forces. The wants of the migrants, the things for which they are willing to put forth sustained effort, are tremendously expanded by a few years of residence in urban areas, and at the same time new skills, the protection afforded by social legislation, and the constant battle of wits forced upon them by city life, contribute greatly to their ability to earn the money needed to enable their level of living to keep pace with their rising standards. In turn, part of this seeps back into the communities from which they came. In no aspect of life is this more apparent than in the rising standards and levels in the educational fields. A waiter (he served the lunch the present writer enjoyed a few hours before he penned these lines) himself moved to Mexico's capital from a rural area some twenty years ago. Today one of his children is nearly through medical school, a second has just received a teacher's certificate, and the third is beginning high school. This is only one case, and the changes in Mexico may be more rapid than those in many of the countries, but such aspirations and accomplishments hardly were possible in the Latin America which existed in 1900.

PART III

SOCIAL STRUCTURE AND
SOCIAL INSTITUTIONS

Introductory Note

IN MANY ways the study of social structure and social institutions, or social organization in general, constitutes the very core of sociology. Hence those seeking to attain or to impart knowledge about Latin American societies must give high priority to these subjects. This section is made up of six items relating to them.

The first of these, Selection Number 8, deals in a general way with the rural community in Latin America. It was prepared for use as a paper for an annual meeting of the Rural Sociological Society and was published originally in *Rural Sociology*, the official journal of the Society. The following title, Selection Number 9, gives a somewhat more intensive study of the neighborhoods and communities in Brazil. It was prepared for one of the annual meetings of the American Sociological Association and was published in the official journal of that organization. To accompany these materials on the locality group structure of Latin American societies, two items were included to furnish information on the class structure. One of these, Selection Number 10, is an extract from a book-length study of social structure and the process of development in Colombia; and the other, Selection Number 11, gives details of the class structure of one small rural community in the same country. The survey from which the latter is taken was made under the auspices of Colombia's Ministry of Economy and appears to have been the first sociological survey of a rural community to be made in any part of Latin America. Tabio, the community studied, was selected as being fairly representative of hundreds of similar places spread throughout the densely populated Andean highlands of Colombia; and subsequent observation has indicated that it is not vastly different from other hundreds of small social entities in the high cool uplands of Venezuela and Ecuador.

Materials that deal with the domestic institutions are difficult to find in any convenient form by those who seek for sociological data pertaining to these fundamental features of Latin American societies. Selection Number 12, taken from our book on Brazil, presents information concerning the size and composition of the Brazilian household and pertaining to the functions performed by the Brazilian family.

8 The Rural Community with Special Reference to Latin America

———◆———

THE INVITATION to prepare this paper was warmly welcomed for two reasons: First, because of my belief that rural community studies are being sadly neglected by rural sociologists in the United States and, second, because I believe that thoroughgoing studies of the rural community are among the most fruitful endeavors in which rural sociologists interested in Latin America can hope to engage. I realize, of course, that one rarely if ever encounters nowadays little "community units" corresponding exactly to those identified and described by Galpin, Sanderson, and others in the days before the automobile and good roads had made their influence felt to a considerable extent in the rural portions of the United States. Nor do the units that still persist come "neatly wrapped and labeled" in the manner that the reports of some investigators lead one to think they may have expected. But today, fully as much as in 1915, the mind that is as discerning as were those of Galpin and Sanderson should be able to identify and describe throughout rural America, in both northern and southern hemispheres, intricate webs of association, mutual awareness, and interdependence which deserve to be designated as communities. We should not forget that in pre-Galpin days the farmer in the United States commonly was designated as "the man without a community."

In Latin America two types of rural community studies are urgently needed: (1) those that will delineate the boundaries of the various communities and neighborhoods of which a given governmental unit (municipio, department or state,

From *Rural Sociology*, Vol. 23, No. 1 (March, 1958), pp. 52–67. Reprinted by permission of the publisher.

or nation) is composed; and (2) those that will analyze and describe in detail the social forms and processes in representative community units. Such studies are important for the North American or European sociologist who seeks to expand the boundaries of knowledge by research in one or more of the Latin-American countries; and they are doubly so for the Argentine, Brazilian, Colombian, Cuban, Mexican, or Venezuelan sociologist, or for our colleagues in any of the fourteen other Latin-American countries. This is true, also, irrespective of whether the worker is attempting to make a contribution in the realm of pure science or whether his major concern is with the applied aspects of our ample and challenging discipline. As we all know, at the community level and in the community pattern one encounters social facts and social relationships in their most concrete and meaningful expressions. Therefore, it is far more unlikely that a logical mind will go seriously astray if the ideas it would generalize are subject to repeated, empirical tests at the community level. At this local level, too, are the most fruitful of all efforts to organize welfare services, effect agrarian reforms, raise levels and standards of living, establish and strengthen school systems, go forward with programs of colonization and settlement, or otherwise change the social system in ways to benefit the rural masses.

The origin, growth, and development of rural sociology in the United States came about very largely through studies of community delineation and studies of specific rural communities by men such as James M. Williams, Warren H. Wilson, Newell L. Sims, Charles J. Galpin, Dwight Sanderson, Carl C. Taylor, Carle C. Zimmerman, and a considerable number of others.[1] In Latin America, too, many of those who have

[1] For a general summary of these developments, see T. Lynn Smith, "Rural Sociology in the United States and Canada: A Trend Report," *Current Sociology*, VI (March, 1957), 10. The following are among the classic studies on the subject: James M. Williams, *An American Town* (New York: J. Kempster Printing Co., 1906); Warren H. Wilson, *Quaker Hill* (New York: Columbia University Press, 1908); Newell L. Sims, *A Hoosier Village* (New York: Columbia University Press, 1912); Charles J. Galpin, *The Social Anatomy of an Agricultural Community* (Wisconsin Agr. Exp. Sta., Bull. 34; Madison, 1915); Dwight Sanderson, *Locating*

led the way in the sociological study of rural society have attempted to secure their bearings by intensive study, using a well-ordered frame of reference and tested research procedures, of specific rural communities. But only the first steps have been taken. The first comprehensive work on community delineation is still to be done,[2] and many intensive studies of specific rural communities must be made, to supply the qualitative analysis, before much headway can be gained in the quantitative analysis of Latin American rural society.

Nature of the Rural Community

Most of what we know about the rural community grew out of the interest generated in the subject by North American sociologists from about 1910 to the present. At the beginning of the twentieth century, in Asia and much of Europe, in which the widespread use of the village pattern of settlement made the physical expression of the rural community evident to all, the nature and limits of the rural community could be taken for granted. One who left the towns and cities for the agricultural districts went "into the villages." "Village society" and "rural society" were largely synonymous terms. Under such circumstances there would have been very little point to the fine distinctions drawn by sociologists, even had the members of our fraternity been numbered among the intellectuals of those days.

In the United States, Canada, and several of the Latin American countries, however, during the nineteenth century a type of rural society had arisen in which the prevailing

---

the Rural Community (Country Life Series; Ithaca, N.Y.; N.Y. State College of Agriculture, 1920); and Carle C. Zimmerman and Carl C. Taylor, Rural Organization: A Study of Primary Groups in Wake County, N.C., (North Carolina Agr. Exp. Sta., Bull. 245; Raleigh, 1922).

[2] Intensive work of delineation has been done, though, in the Turrialba area of Costa Rica. See Norman W. Painter, "The Ecological Basis of Social Systems in Turrialba," in Charles P. Loomis, Julio O. Morales, Roy A. Clifford, and Olen E. Leonard, eds., Turrialba: Social Systems and the Introduction of Change (Glencoe, Ill.: Free Press, 1953), ch. vi.

locality groups were not cut to the familiar village patterns. The families of those who gained a livelihood by cultivating the soil lived widely separated from one another. Their homes were amid the fields and pastures and not in a cluster of any sort. The towns and villages which dotted the landscape were trade and service centers to which the farm people resorted occasionally. They were inhabited by tradesmen, artisans, professional people, retired farmers and their wives, the widows of deceased agriculturists, and others not engaged directly in the cultivation of the soil. Given these ecological arrangements, in such sharp contrast with the locality groups found in most parts of the old world, the existence and nature of the rural community were not readily apparent.

Charles J. Galpin[3] was the first to demonstrate the existence of a genuine rural community in the United States and to develop a practical method for delineating its boundaries. The stimulus he gave did much to place rural community studies in the forefront as sociology and rural sociology developed in the United States. His classical study of Walworth County, Wisconsin, revealed the basic locality-group structure of the county and demonstrated a feasible method of determining the limits of each rural community. On the basis of this study came the proposition that the rural community in the United States consists of two basic parts: (1) a village nucleus; and (2) a surrounding zone of open country in which the inhabitants are dependent upon the village center for commercial, financial, ceremonial, social, recreational, and other services. In recent years, however, the members of our group have given relatively little attention to the nature of rural locality groups or to the ways in which the rural community is changing as the full impact of modern and rapid means of transportation and communication is felt throughout the rural districts of the United States.

On the basis of his own studies in the United States, Europe, and Latin America, his contacts with other rural sociologists, and his study of the existing literature on the subject, the author believes it useful to sketch several general

[3] *Op. cit.*

propositions relative to the nature of the rural community.[4]

First, the rural community is one of the "natural areas" with which the sociologist deals. Each rural community has a specific physical expression; it is a small but definite part of the earth's surface. Even though its limits ordinarily do not figure on the geographer's maps along with streams, divides, and other so-called "natural" phenomena, its boundaries are indelibly stamped upon the minds of its inhabitants. Indeed, they are the limits that determine effectively the areas of social participation, mutual awareness and concern, and collective action of many types. Hence it is important to think of the community as a specific part of world, national, state, or county territory in which the residents realize that they all are "in the same boat" and thereby are impelled to effort for the welfare of the group over and above that brought forth in response to family and neighborhood interests, responsibilities, and obligations.

Second, the rural community also is an area of social interaction, one of the varieties in the general category of "locality groups." It differs fundamentally, however, from the other members of the group, such as the family and the neighborhood. To begin with, it is larger than either of these, and indeed a single community may encompass hundreds of families and dozens of neighborhoods. Whereas the family and the neighborhood are the classic examples of primary groups, i.e., those characterized by intimate, face-to-face association and of primary importance in the determination of human personality,[5] the community may include many persons and families who are unknown to one another. In fact there may be open hostility between families or between neighborhoods belonging to the same community. Just as the family is composed of intimately linked individuals, and the

[4] Among the author's previous efforts along these lines are T. Lynn Smith, *The Sociology of Rural Life* (3d ed.; New York: Harper, 1953), pp. 377–384; "The Role of the Community in American Rural Life," *Journal of Educational Sociology,* XIV (March, 1941), 387–400; and "Trends in Community Organization and Life," *American Sociological Review,* V (June, 1940), 325–334.

[5] Charles H. Cooley, *Social Organization* (New York: Scribner, 1925), p. 23.

neighborhood is a cluster of families, the community frequently consists of a fairly well-integrated group of neighborhoods. This means, of course, that the persons comprising a
specific rural community may be highly diverse in their social
characteristics and extremely individualistic in many of their
activities. Indeed, they may have very little in common with
one another except that they all reside in one specific frag-
ment of territory, depend upon its institutions and agencies for
the satisfaction of their basic needs, and participate for better
or worse in the vicissitudes of its existence.[6]

Third, as indicated above, where the village type of settlement prevails, the limits of the rural community are obvious
to almost anyone. It is easy to see their relationship to local
political subdivisions of the province or the state. But in such
countries as the United States, Canada, Brazil, Colombia, and
Argentina, in which the farm homesteads are dispersed over
the landscape, the boundaries of the rural communities are
not easily identified. In such cases there is considerable likelihood that the limits of political subdivisions, tax districts,
school attendance areas, and other significant boundaries will
cut directly across the middle of such "natural areas." Near
my own home in Florida, for example, is one rural community in which the village nucleus itself is split into halves by
the line separating two counties, and in which the surrounding open-country portion of the community is divided among
three counties. In Colombia, too, a good example of the lack
of correspondence between community boundaries and political boundaries appeared in our study of the municipio of
Tabio on the Savannah of Bogotá.[7] Families living in the
northern portion of this municipio were found to be dependent upon its small seat for religious, educational, and political
purposes; but they directed their footsteps for trading purposes to Zipaquirá, the much larger seat of an adjacent
municipio. However, in some parts of the United States, nota-

[6] Cf. Charles P. Loomis and J. Allan Beegle, *Rural Sociology:
The Strategy of Change* (New York: Prentice-Hall, 1957), pp.
31–33.

[7] T. Lynn Smith, Justo Díaz Rodríguez, and Luis Roberto Garcia,
Tabio: A Study in Rural Social Organization, (Washington: United
States Department of Agriculture, 1945), pp. 24–25.

bly in parts of Texas and Georgia, and in some portions of Latin America, such as the Brazilian state of São Paulo, the boundaries of the small counties or municipios seem to define fairly well the limits of the contemporary rural community.

Fourth, R. M. MacIver's statement that "any circle of people who live together, who belong together, so that they share, not this or that particular interest, but a whole set of interests wide enough and complete enough to include their lives is a community,"[8] adequately describes other essential features of the community. To meet such criteria any rural community must provide the basic institutions needed to minister to the domestic, economic, educational, political, governmental, religious, recreational, health, and welfare necessities of its members.

Finally, and by way of summary, the rural community is for the individual farm family the specific area covered by the web of life in which it is intricately involved—the territory included in the attendance area of its church and its school, the patronage areas of the stores at which it trades and the bank with which it deals, the service areas of the recreational facilities in which its members participate, and so forth. Naturally, within a given locality group the community attachments, contacts, and loyalties may be very strong or they may be very weak. A given family, or the various families in a community, may be largely engrossed in kinship matters and devote relatively little time, thought, or activity to the affairs of any larger unit; or neighborhood loyalties and activities may be the dominating elements, with the lives of the various persons almost completely submerged in the interests of that particular type of primary group. But, on the other hand, the web may be one in which the threads of interest and responsibility uniting the individual with society are woven into the warp and woof of a larger unit, one definitely beyond the realm of the primary group, to which we give the name of community. In addition, in a period of rapid change, such as has characterized the rural portions of the United States since 1915, and such as presently is getting under way

[8] *Society: A Textbook of Sociology* (New York: Long & Smith, 1937), pp. 9–10.

throughout the immense area known as Latin America, locality group relationships may be scrambled by the weakening of community loyalties once prevailing and the growing pains which accompany the emergence of new and larger areas of interdependence. Under such circumstances the individual farm family may share its patronage and loyalties with a number of trade and service centers of varying sizes, ranging from the nearby hamlet to the distant metropolis.[9] As will be indicated below, at the present time in many parts of the United States the town of from 3,000 to 10,000 inhabitants increasingly seems to be becoming the center of a web of life which embraces dozens of once fairly complete rural communities, hundreds of neighborhoods, and thousands of farm families. To identify, analyze, and describe the interlocking locality groups comprising these specific webs, and also to relate them to the nation's larger cities, is, the speaker believes, one of the largest challenges facing the present generation of rural sociologists.

Structural Types

On the basis of their structure the infinite variety of rural community forms to be observed throughout the world may all be classified into two basic categories or types. The first of these is the one which long ago British scholars designated as the "village community." The second is that which Galpin identified and defined as the rural community consisting of a village or town nucleus plus the farmsteads in a zone tributary to it.

Each of these two basic types consists, in turn, of two principal parts. In the village community these are: (1) the village nucleus; and (2) the surrounding gardens, fields, pastures, meadows, and woods which are used for agricultural, stock-raising, and collecting activities by the villagers and to which they commute daily for the performance of the necessary

[9] For an early description of this tendency, see T. Lynn Smith, *Farm Trade Centers in Louisiana* (Louisiana Agr. Exp. Sta., Bull. 234; Baton Rouge, 1933), pp. 54–56. Other literature on the subject is reviewed in Smith, *The Sociology of Rural Life*, chs. xv, xxiii.

tasks. In this type of community the village nucleus consists of the homes of agriculturists; the barns, sheds, and corrals for their livestock; the homes, stores, workshops, and offices of the few tradesmen, artisans, and professional persons who are found in the rural community; and all the community's ceremonial, recreational, administrative, and educational buildings. The surrounding zone, almost entirely devoid of buildings (other than temporary structures used for crop watching and herding), is easily identified and delimited, since the inhabitants of the village themselves cultivate or otherwise make use of the parcels of which it is composed. The extreme fragmentation of holdings usually found in this type of community also serves to diffuse family interests broadly throughout all parts of the community's area. Under such circumstances the nature and limits of the rural community are readily apparent to all, and the task of delineating community boundaries is reduced to the minimum.

Where either scattered farmsteads or the line-village pattern of settlement prevail, the second structural type of community also is to be found. In this case the village or town which constitutes the community's nucleus is not primarily a residential center for farmers and their families. Indeed there may be very few or no agriculturists living there. Instead it is a trade, service, and ceremonial center inhabited by families whose income is derived from the commercial enterprises in which they are engaged, the professional or other services which they render, or, perhaps, from the work of their breadwinners as artisans, casual laborers, and so on. Frequently villages and towns of this type are the seats of small manufacturing enterprises, and some of their inhabitants are engaged directly in manufacturing and processing. In such centers the cluster of buildings devoted to religious, educational, administrative, and recreational purposes may be substantial, but rarely does it contain all such facilities of the community.

Likewise, in this structural type the portion of the rural community lying outside the perimeter of the village or town nucleus differs substantially from that of the village community. As in the case of the latter, it also consists of fields, pastures, meadows, and woodlands; but in this type of community the gardens, arable lands, pastures, meadows, and

woodlands used by a specific farm family constitute a single
territorial unit, or at most of two or three segments. Each
farm family has its home, its barns and sheds, and its other
outbuildings located in a group amid the fields it works. This
serves greatly to restrict family knowledge and interests to a
small segment of the community's territory. The members of
the farm family commute to the village or town nucleus for
purposes of trade, for professional services, and, frequently,
for religious, educational, and recreational activities. But the
open country is not necessarily devoid of churches, school
buildings, commercial establishments, and processing plants
such as creameries, cheese factories, cotton gins, and grain
elevators. Under such circumstances the boundaries of the
rural community are not readily apparent, and indeed it required unusual genius to identify and describe the web of relationships of which such a community is composed.

Some Differences Between North American and Latin American Communities

Rural communities in the United States and Canada are far
from being a homogeneous lot. Those in the Midwest are not
exact duplicates of those in New England, the South, or the
West, or in any of Canada's various regions. Even within a
given social and cultural region there is considerable variation
from community to community. Nevertheless, the differences
one encounters in this respect as he moves about north of the
Rio Grande are very much less than those he observes when
he travels from Mexico to Argentina and Chile. Of course the
rural communities of Latin America have not been studied
as thoroughly as those of the United States and Canada, but
in the paragraphs that follow the author attempts to set forth
some of the more significant differences between the communities of the two great world areas as they appear to him
after the quarter of a century he has devoted to comparative
studies of Anglo-Saxon America, Spanish America, and Portuguese America.

1. Much larger proportions of the rural communities of
Latin America, in comparison with those of the United States

and Canada, fall into the village community category. As is well known, there are relatively few agricultural village communities north of the Rio Grande. Even though communities of this type were the first to be established in New England, at the present time they persist only in the Mormon settlements in the Great Basin and among some of the Spanish American sections of the Southwest. From the Atlantic to the Pacific and from the Gulf of Mexico to the northern limits of settlement in Canada, the prevailing type of rural community is that composed of the village or town nucleus plus the farm families living in the surrounding area. On the other hand, in such countries as Mexico, Guatemala, Ecuador, Peru, and Bolivia, the village community type prevails, and it is of considerable importance in some of the others, such as Honduras and Colombia. Frequently in countries like Mexico, Guatemala, Ecuador, Peru, and Bolivia, where aboriginal elements are strong, even the land is owned by the village, i.e., the community. Furthermore, over much Latin American territory the large sugar and coffee plantations, which generally employ the village pattern of settlement for their workers, actually are genuine village community units in and of themselves.

2. In the United States and Canada, exception being made of a few of the New England states, almost never does the territorial unit embraced within a given rural community have any legal basis, recognition, or standing. But in Latin America as a general rule the separation of state and church was slow in coming about, and even today the local government unit, designated as a municipio in most of the countries, corresponds exactly to the church parish. Furthermore, the boundaries of the municipios are almost always drawn with social and economic factors taken into consideration, so that they correspond much more closely to natural social areas than do those in the United States. Frequently this has the result of giving *de facto* legal status to the rural community unit. Of course in such states as Texas and Georgia, the improvement of facilities for communication and transportation, the comparative stability of county boundaries, and the various advantages enjoyed by county seats over their competitors, seem gradually to be transforming the county into a

genuine community. But this is not general throughout the United States.

3. In most parts of Latin America rural social organization remains in the neighborhood stage to a much greater extent than is true in the United States.[10] This is to say that most of the areas of association are restricted, that the web of life of the ordinary rural inhabitant is small with very few threads extending beyond the small area of daily, face-to-face contacts, that many of the things that cannot be provided within the small group must be done without, and that the person and family are closely identified with and bound up in the life of the immediate vicinity and only remotely conscious of and infrequently in contact with the activities of the larger and more complete areas of human interaction. Indeed, in immense portions of Latin America family, kinship, and neighborhood ties are so strong that the next level of association, the community, receives relatively little attention and loyalty. Of course where the village community prevails, it is difficult, if not impossible, to distinguish between community and neighborhood.

4. Trade and commerce are of much less relative importance in Latin American than in North American community relationships and processes. As is well known, the integrating force of trade has been so great in the rural portions of the United States that rural sociologists in general have referred to the village or town nucleus as the "trade center." In Latin America, however, the equivalents frequently are "ceremonial center" or "church center." Trade and commerce play relatively insignificant roles, with the weekly market or fair at the administrative and church seat being the occasion and the scene of the bulk of the exchange. In most of the countries, barter still figures prominently in the economic life of the community. As agriculture becomes more commercialized, though, as transportation and communication facilities are improved, and as the self-sufficiency of the farm family decreases, this may be expected to change rapidly and along the

[10] For Brazil, this point is developed in considerable detail in T. Lynn Smith, *Brazil: People and Institutions* (rev. ed.; Baton Rouge: Louisiana State University Press, 1954), pp. 509–523.

same general lines as such social differentiation followed in the United States and Canada.

5. In Latin America there are comparatively few forces that are dismembering the rural community, whereas in the United States various strong factors are cutting it into segments, pulling it apart, or at least preventing it from becoming a strong, solid, and well-integrated unit. In our country, unlike most Latin American countries, legal, administrative, juridical, and fiscal boundaries generally are drawn with complete disregard for the limits of the natural areas we designate as communities. As a result we should not wonder that the rural community is so weak; rather the wonder is that the spirit of association has been able to withstand, to the extent that it has, the mutilation that seems to be our regular procedure. Let us consider a few of the ways in which this cutting up, tearing apart, and other mutilation of the community unit goes on in the United States.

First, county lines are drawn without respect to community and neighborhood attachments of the farm families involved. Sometimes this procedure merely shears off a part of the open-country zone that is tributary to some town or village nucleus, thus making it necessary for some farm families to be involved for tax purposes, political activity, law enforcement, and so on, with a county seat quite different from the village or town with which they maintain the majority of their interests, business transactions, recreational activities, church relationships, and so forth. In some cases, though, even the community nucleus itself is divided by a county line, and the rural community itself may have segments that fall within three or even four counties. Perhaps for the reason that Latin American societies lack functional systems of parallel lines, such as those which define sections, townships, and ranges in the United States and Canada, the dividing lines they do employ are more likely to correspond to significant social and economic boundaries. In any case they appear to be far less artificial than those we customarily utilize.

Second, school districts and school attendance areas are drawn, and even school buildings themselves are located, with almost every consideration in mind except the limits of the complex web of social relationships which constitute the community. Likewise drainage districts, irrigation districts, and all sorts of other special entities, all with substantial powers to levy taxes, are established with little or no thought about the limits of the natural social groupings in the areas affected. All of this tears away at the unity and strength of the local community unit. So far there are no comparable developments in Latin America.

Third, the practice of allowing small population centers to incorporate, i.e., to set themselves apart and enjoy a corporate existence separate and distinct from the open-country portions of the same communities, is particularly effective in weakening the rural community in the United States. It also is a frequent cause of the town-country conflict which arises between the inhabitants of the two parts of the rural community. Nowhere in Latin America is such an unnatural division of fundamental community interests permitted. The same local governmental institutions, weak though they are, serve both parts of the rural community.

Fourth, our rapidly improving means of transportation and communication have greatly speeded up the process of social differentiation, thus tearing away at parts of existing community patterns of association and organization. The highly specialized retail units in distant towns and cities are enabled to attract the patronage of the farmers in the open country parts of the community, and even of the villagers themselves. This siphons off to the center of a larger unit a considerable part of the trade formerly enjoyed by village merchants. Perhaps in many parts of the United States it is adding a newer and higher level of integration to the three (family, neighborhood, and rural community), heretofore of greatest significance in the rural sections of the nation. Similar is the situation with respect to recreational activities, especially in Texas and other portions of the great plains, where many rural families think little of driving seventy-five or one hundred miles to attend a movie or participate in some other form of recreation.

Commuting by farm youths, who have finished high school, to junior colleges, colleges, and universities located in towns and cities far beyond the limits of the rural communities in which they live is another expression of the same process

of social differentiation; and the loyalties and attachments
formed in the college town by the students and their relatives,
especially in all that has to do with football and other sports,
constitutes another serious inroad upon the spirit of association and consciousness of mutual interest at the rural community level.

In brief, all of these expanding social and economic horizons made possible by our modern means of communication
and transportation are tearing away at the bodily structure of
the rural community. Even the television program, which
brings the representatives of distant business firms, recreational organizations, cultural groups, and so on into the living rooms of the farm and village families, helps to divide the
loyalty and attachments that once were concentrated largely
within the rural community. As yet in most parts of Latin
America, the effects of such forces are comparatively slight.

9 The Locality Group Structure of Brazil

———◆———

MAN IN his relationships with his fellows always divides the earth's surface up into areas of mutual aid, common living, and human association. In addition to the family, which is the smallest social grouping whose interests and activities converge in a definite locale, human societies are always segmented into neighborhood and community groups. Like the family, each of these occupies a definite part of the earth's surface, is an area of human association. The three together comprise the fundamental cells and tissues out of which the State and the Great Society are constituted. Even though the latter may disintegrate or fall into a state of anarchy, the smaller locality groups remain. This paper contains a brief analysis and description of Brazil's locality group structure.

The Similarity of Locality Groups in Brazil and the United States

Because in the colonization of Brazil, as in the settlement of the United States, extensive use was made of single farmsteads for arranging the population on the land, there have arisen many similarities between the locality group structures of the two countries. For the same reason Brazilian locality groups do not resemble closely those of Europe, or those that are found in most of the Spanish-speaking countries of America. Upon close inspection Brazilian neighborhoods and communities will be seen to possess characteristics which are very similar to those of the corresponding locality groupings in

Presented to the Thirty-eighth Annual Meeting of the American Sociological Society, New York, December 4, 1943, and published in the *American Sociological Review*, Vol. IX, No. 1 (February, 1944), pp. 41–49. Reprinted by permission of the publisher.

the United States and Canada, and to exhibit few affinities with those of the Old World. Along with our own locality groups and those of Canada, Brazil's farms, neighborhoods, and communities bear the stamp "Made in America."

When colonization was begun in the Western Hemisphere the farm in both Portugal and England consisted of a home and garden plot located in a hamlet or small village, plus several pieces of arable land scattered about in the fields that surrounded the residential center. Communal rights to the use of pastures and woodlands were customary. In other words, the farm, the smallest locality group, was not a clear-cut, well-differentiated territorial unit, but was fused with the neighborhood or the community. It did not stand out as an entity as does the *fazenda* in Minas Gerais or the farm in Iowa. The European neighborhood, on the other hand, was more clear-cut than those of Brazil or the United States. It consisted of a number of families whose homes were huddled together in a hamlet or small village, and the tributary farm land, pastures and woods. A sociologist might have had some difficulty in determining whether a given locality should be classed as a neighborhood, or as a larger community, but he would have had none in deciding which houses belonged in the unit.

Observation of locality groups in Brazil and in the United States shows how greatly they have diverged from the Old World patterns. Brazil never knew the village composed of small freeholders. In the Portuguese-speaking giant of the Southern Hemisphere, nucleated settlement patterns are present only on the large estates. Otherwise the cultivators and stock growers live scattered about on the land. The farm or *fazenda* stands by itself, clearly distinguishable, as a fundamental unit. The families who till the soil or manage the herds live amidst the fields and pastures and not in a nucleated center. The Brazilian village or town, like that of the United States, seems to have been an "afterthought"—it arose spontaneously to care for the multiplying social and economic needs of the population. As a result of this scattered farmsteads pattern of settlement, the Brazilian rural community is not readily visualized and defined; the village is by no means identical with the rural community. In the days before Dr.

C. J. Galpin contributed his illuminating analysis of social anatomy in North America, the Brazilian farmer, like his fellow in the United States, might have been classified as "the man without a community."

The Brazilian neighborhood also differs sharply from the European variety. Like the small locality group in the United States, generally it is not composed of the families who live together in a nucleated farming hamlet. Even when this is the case, the tiny village or hamlet is made up of the homes of workers on a plantation or ranch and is not a collection of the dwellings of freeholders who till the surrounding lands. But usually in Brazil, as in the United States, the neighborhood is made up of a small number of families who live on adjacent farms, whose members frequently come into face to face contact with one another, and who have established a system of mutual aid amongst themselves. Like those of the United States, Brazilian neighborhoods owe their integration to a wide variety of causes: to visiting and mutual aid among families who live in close proximity to one another; to the pooling of efforts in order to secure and maintain a chapel or a school; to a mutual dependence upon a landed proprietor, a sugar mill, a cotton gin, a grist mill, a co-operative marketing association, a creamery or a cheese factory, a railway station, a *venda* or store; to the grouping in close proximity of farm families who are intimately knit together by ties of kinship, national origins, language and religion; or to the fact that a few families have been thrown into close and constant contact with one another, and isolated from the larger world, through establishing their residence in a small cove, in a fertile oasis, on a small island, on a high river bank, or even on a *fazenda*.

THE NATURE OF THE BRAZILIAN COMMUNITY. Unlike the old village communities of Europe, Asia, and most of Spanish America, the Brazilian village is not identical with the community. In Brazil the rural community consists of two distinct parts. The first of these is a village or town nucleus whose principal function is not that of providing a location for the dwellings of agriculturists. Rather it serves as a residence and place of business for tradesmen, men skilled in the professions, money lenders, and workmen of all types; and as a center for schools, churches, and recreational institutions. The church is especially important but in this village or town center all the social and economic institutions converge. The second indispensable part of the Brazilian rural community consists of the farm families who live in the surrounding neighborhoods, who make the village their trading and social center, and who in many cases maintain a "town house" there for use on weekends, holidays, and on occasions of marriages or funerals. As deep rooted as the North American "go to town" is the Brazilian's *"ir ao commercio"* (go to do business). The two expressions have the same meaning. The fact that the Brazilian village or town has as its chief functions those of trade, manufacture, education, religion, and recreation, and that these are carried on chiefly to service the people who live on the surrounding farms or *fazendas,* definitely aligns her rural communities with those of the United States, and sets them apart from those of Europe and most Spanish American countries. Thus it may be said that in Brazil, as in the United States, the rural community is: (1) a geographic area consisting of a trade center and those surrounding farms and neighborhoods whose social institutions converge in the trade center; (2) an area within which there is a general consciousness on the part of the people of belonging together, or at least of identifying themselves with the neighborhoods in which they live, and the larger community area within which their farms and their neighborhood lie and of which they constitute integral parts; and (3) a consensus of opinion among the group of people living in this contiguous area which forms the community's locale that the fortunes of each individual in the locality are closely tied up with and affected by the welfare of the community as a whole.

Differences Between Brazilian and North American Communities

Although the basic similarities are great, there are also some significant differences between the structures of Brazilian and North American communities. These need to be pointed out. In Brazil, as in the Southern portions of the United States, the village-centered community embraces large estates, *fazendas* or plantations, which of themselves may be almost large enough and self-sufficient enough to qualify as communities. Frequently the proprietors of these possess "town houses" in the community center, in addition to their manor houses on the land. The social horizons of these elite members of society are far different from those of the laboring classes. Their attachments and contacts transcend local community and neighborhood boundaries. Sometimes they abandon residence on the land altogether. At best such class differences complicate arrangement of the locality group pattern; in their worse expressions they deprive the land of the watchful eye of its owner, and the local community of its leading citizens.

A second point requiring comment is the progressive tendency for the *município,* the Brazilian administrative unit that corresponds to our county, to function as a larger or *rurban* community. Rather rapidly in southern Minas Gerais and in São Paulo, the seat of the *município* is becoming the economic and social center for all the various communities and neighborhoods within its limits. The fact that Brazil does not allow the *cidade*, which is the seat of the *município,* to separate itself by incorporation from the open country parts of the area contributes to this trend. If the small Brazilian city or town becomes an urban "cyst" in the midst of a large rural population it does so contrary to the spirit of the law, and not with its aid and abetment, as frequently is the case in the United States. As roads and automobiles increase, in south Brazil the *município* will tend more and more to become one large community centered in the *cidade* which is its seat. Such a pattern of rural organization for the United States has been the dream of Dr. C. J. Galpin, the father of rural sociology.

In addition to the significant differences just mentioned, there are several other fundamental ways in which the Brazilian community differs from our own. First it may be indicated that in Brazil, as contrasted with the United States, the role of the village as a church center seems to be relatively more important. In the old days, before administrative and judicial lines were finely drawn, it was customary in counting the populations of Brazilian centers to include all within *toque de sino* (sound of the church bell).[1] This seems to indicate that the community area was then delineated mostly in terms of the service area of the church. In early days the boundaries of our own communities were thought of in terms of the "team haul." Today, although the Brazilian village may contain a number of churches, except in the South, they are generally all of the same denomination—the Roman Catholic. Furthermore, one of them is the mother church, and the others are its affiliated branches. If there are chapels on the surrounding *fazendas*, they, too, are affiliated with and serviced by the mother church or *matriz*. Because of this homogeneity in religious affairs, the boundaries of the religious community coincide closely with those of the general community.

Another difference that must be indicated is that ethnic and racial heterogeneity do less to confuse community and neighborhood patterns in Brazil than in the United States. Within the limits of the same community there are not many places where overlapping neighborhoods of whites and Negroes may be distinguished, as is so generally the case in the southern parts of the United States, that is, in those parts of our country in which Negroes live in open country areas. Today, as when Koster wrote at the beginning of the nineteenth century, "it is surprising, though extremely pleasing, to see how little difference is made between a white man, a mulatto, and a creole negro, if all are equally poor and if all have been born free."[2] Where persons of different colors live within the limits of the same community there is no great tendency, in most of Brazil, for the complexity of locality group structure brought about by class and other differences, to be further complicated by lines of cleavage that follow color lines. True it is that class differences are closely correlated with color shades; and any generalization about lack of race discrimination is less valid for São Paulo and the three states to the south of it than for the other parts of Brazil. Nevertheless, the comparative lack of population constellations based

[1] Cf. Sir Richard F. Burton, *Explorations in the Highlands of Brazil*, London: Tinsley Brothers, 1861, Vol. I, p. 81.

[2] Henry Koster, *Travels in Brazil*, London, 1816, p. 317.

on color, and the religious homogeneity make the internal structure of the Brazilian community much less intricate than that of the typical one in the United States.

Finally, there is a great difference between the communities of Brazil and the United States in the relative importance of trade and commerce and in the manner in which they are organized. In the United States trade is the principal function of the village which forms the community's center, while in Brazil the religious function usually occupies first place. There may be exceptions to this rule, but in general it will probably hold true, and it constitutes a fundamental difference.

The organization of business in the trading centers of the two countries also is considerably different. In the United States there is little remaining of the old-fashioned "market" or "fair," an economic institution which provides that on a designated day of the week a certain village or town is the place to which buyers and sellers from a considerable area will resort for the purchase, sale, and exchange of produce and merchandise. Brazil has retained this ancient institution as a keystone in the business structure of its rural areas. Nearly every village and town has its market place, and many of them, especially those in the East and North, have their weekly fairs or *feiras*. To hundreds of small centers would also apply the following description of the trading function of one of Pernambuco's small towns:

> Commerce consists of the local operation of weekly fairs, where the products of the region are sold, others from the outside, such as dry goods, notions, liquids, utensils, etc., which come from the outside, resold, the goods being displayed in mercantile establishments or in temporary sheds.[3]

According to Vasconcellos Torres "the fair is a complement of rural life in the North."[4] It comes once a week and its occurrence is the equivalent to a holiday. From all sides of the village arrive persons who come to sell or exchange

---

[3]Sebastião de Vasconcellos Galvão, *Diccionario Chorographico, Historico e Estatistico de Pernambuco*, Rio de Janeiro: Imprensa Nacional, 1921, Vol. III, p. 4.

[4] In the *Correio do Manha*, of Rio de Janeiro, for May 26, 1942.

their produce and to secure provisions for the period of a week. They carry baskets and sacks, and oftentimes travel several leagues in order to reach the market place. In the market place and on the *vendas* trade goes on at a busy pace. But the day is also one of recreation. One of the most popular amusements is that of listening to folk tales which are narrated in song by blind singers who accompany themselves on the *viola* or Brazilian guitar. These songs, dealing with the exploits of such noted characters as Lampeão, or summarizing recent world events such as those growing out of the perfidy of Japan, also are printed in small booklets and sold in the markets. Naturally, such weekly gatherings can serve as fertile spots for the planting of rumors by fifth columnists and these noxious elements have been exploiting them to the fullest extent. From these centers stories have spread that the rural people are to be dragged from their homes and sent overseas, and that those who leave to work in the Amazon Valley are really to be shipped to Africa.

VILLAGE AND OPEN-COUNTRY RELATIONSHIPS IN BRAZIL. The fullest description available of the relationship of the village to the open country in Brazil is given in Luiz Amaral's three-volume work on the history of Brazilian agriculture. According to this authority the Brazilian countryman infrequently goes to town and then only to the more or less obligatory Sunday Mass, on festive occasions, and for marriages and funerals. On Sunday morning everyone goes to the center. The laborers are up early preparing the horses for the *fazendeiro* and the members of his family to ride. The *agregados* and *camaradas* go on foot. Each Sunday morning one may see the numerous processions from the *fazendas* making their ways to the village. At the front of each goes the *fazendeiro,* followed by his wife, and the other members of the family, all mounted on horseback. Behind, afoot, come the workers, men in front, women following, and children bringing up the rear. With them they lug along, or carry on their heads, numerous parcels and bundles—eggs, fruits, vegetables, fowls, pigs, etc. Those belonging to the proprietor are carried as gifts for families who live in the village, mainly for the children's godmother at whose home the country

family will take lunch, and the children will stay when they
are in attendance at school. The burdens belonging to the
camaradas are made up of produce that is being taken in for
sale to the village merchants or in the market place.

Each person has the sacred duty of attending the last rites
for a deceased neighbor, so a funeral is another occasion on
which country people resort to the village or town center.
There is a custom prevailing which requires the *fazendeiro*
to stand treat at the *venda* or bar nearest the cemetery, whenever one of his retainers is buried. A rum called *cachaça*,
made from the juice of the sugar cane, is the drink. On these
occasions even the abstemious must partake, for it is a ritual.
In some cases excessive drinking takes place, and later on
one will see numerous persons lying by the wayside, sleeping
off the effects of the alcohol. For the most part, however,
Brazil's people are not heavy drinkers.

Visits of church dignitaries and the great religious holidays
are occasions when country people put in extended stays in
the village. These are the times when the *fazendeiros* open
their town houses, for their own use, to help shelter their
friends, and also to provide lodging for their most esteemed
camaradas.

A marriage between members of the *fazendeiro* class is
another event which brings about an influx of country people
to the center and the village to take on a festive appearance.
Ostentatious displays of food and sweets are brought forth
and everyone in the community, both the village and surrounding area, feels entitled to help himself. When a wedding
takes place each person must betake himself to the house
that serves as headquarters in order to "make an idea of those
who do not appear." From this house, which is that of one
of the godmothers in the event the *fazendeiros* concerned do
not have a town dwelling, the procession starts for the church,
and to it the organized double file of weary persons returns
after the ceremony. Heading the procession on its tortuous
journey is the bride in white and the "little father" who gives
her away. They are followed by the groom and the "little
mother"; then come other pairs of adults; and finally, the
children two by two, boy with boy, and girl with girl. Other

than on such occasions, rural people rarely go to the centers.[5]

Town-country relations in Brazil are not a one-way process. Inhabitants of the villages and towns also make a practice of visiting with their friends and relatives on the fazendas that surround the center. Unless the stay is an extended one, as it frequently is, Sundays are popular occasions for such visits, the townspeople going early to the *fazenda* and spending the entire day. Visiting back and forth between upper class families of the town and the *fazendas* is still very common. As yet townspeople have not affected "city airs" to any great extent, and so little town-country conflict has arisen on this score. The diffusion of the auto-bus is facilitating these visits.

People from the village also resort to the open country areas for commercial reasons. The village functions not only as a trade center to which country people come to buy and sell, but also as the headquarters of numerous peddlers who make regular visits to the surrounding *fazendas* and *sitios*. In former times, especially, the women depended upon these travelling *mascates* for dress goods, fineries, and other articles of conspicuous consumption. Today nearly every city, town, and village is the headquarters for some of these hawkers.

The Number of Communities in Brazil

The number of communities, rural and *rurban*, in Brazil, cannot be determined with exactitude. Nevertheless these relatively complete social units, more self-sufficient, too, in Brazil, than in the United States, certainly are very numerous. Undoubtedly every seat of a *município* or county is the nucleus of this type of a locality group; together with the families living in its trade, school, and church zones, it is entitled to be classed as a community. There are 1,574 of these, in addition to Rio de Janeiro. A few of them would rank as metropolitan communities, others have a small city as a nucleus. But from one-half to two-thirds of them would be classed as strictly rural, if the criteria in use in the United States were applied. . . .

[5] Cf. Luiz Amaral, *Historia Geral de Agricultura Brasileira*, São Paulo: Companhia Editora Nacional, 1939, Vol. I, pp. 39–41.

In addition to the *cidades,* or seats of *municípios,* many *vilas,* or seats of the districts, also would classify as nuclei of communities, a few as *rurban,* but most of them as rural. . . . In addition, many coffee *fazendas* and sugar *usinas* could qualify as communities in their own right, and there are also other population centers, not yet endowed with official political functions, which constitute the village nuclei of functioning rural communities. Taking all these facts into account it is estimated that there are at least 6,000 communities in Brazil.

THE IMPORTANCE OF THE NEIGHBORHOOD

The role of the neighborhood seems to be more important in Brazil than in the United States. This is to say that the areas of acquaintanceship are small; that the person's social relationships are confined mostly to a small circle of families living near one another; that contacts outside the small intimate circle of acquaintances are of relative unimportance; that many goods, services, and types of association which cannot be provided by or for a small cluster of families must be done without; and that the person and the family are closely identified with and bound up in the life of the immediate vicinity, and only remotely conscious of and rarely participant in the activities of larger and more complete areas of social interaction such as the community. The role of the neighborhood in Brazil is more comparable with that part it plays in the social organization of the South than with its function in other regions of the United States. Over much of Brazil, as in the South, social organization may be said to be in the neighborhood stage.

There is a rich variety among Brazil's neighborhood groupings. Generally speaking, each Brazilian *fazenda* must be considered as a neighborhood, although many of them are sufficiently large and so completely circumscribe the lives of their inhabitants that they rank as communities. This is especially true of the large coffee *fazendas* in São Paulo, and of the sugar *usinas* where the *colony* for the workers is large, a chapel and perhaps a school are present in the plantation's village nucleus, and where the bulk of all supplies is sold at the commissary at which the families are obliged to make their purchases. Certainly if these small social worlds performed the political functions they would rank as communities.

But most of the *fazendas* are smaller, mere nodules of settlement scattered over the Brazilian landscape. In each of these widely separated little localities lives a small cluster of families—those of the proprietor, his relatives, and a varying number of retainers, *agregados, camaradas, moradores* and *parceiros*. To the highly integrated group of families on the cattle *fazenda* Oliveira Vianna, Nelson Wernecke Sodre, A. Carneiro Leão and other Brazilian writers apply the name of "clan." This alone is considerable justification for considering it to be a neighborhood. As one passes through or over Brazil's vast interior he will observe thousands of small settlements. Each *fazendeiro*'s home and the six to fifty or even one hundred *casabres* (huts) clustered about it, is a center from which radiates a network of trails leading off in all directions. That some of them eventually attain the headquarters of another *fazenda* miles away indicates that these neighborhoods are not entirely unrelated; and that some of these trails fuse with others to make a more beaten way to the occasional village or town, demonstrates that they are not completely lacking in community attachments.

Neighborhood groups composed of "intruders," *sitiantes*, and other classes of the *povo*, who have not been brought under the influence and control of a *fazendeiro* and transformed into his *camaradas* and *agregados* are of almost endless variety. Sometimes a dozen or so families of these are clustered together in a mountain cove, or a considerable number of them may have strung their thatched cottages along the sea coast under the coconut trees, or they may have established a line village settlement in a favorable location along the natural levee of a stream, or one can find them grouped about in one of those small clearings in the forest which make one think that they are merely auger holes in the jungle.

Also to be classed as neighborhoods are the thousands of small hamlets and villages that are scattered throughout Brazil. In size and function they vary all the way from a few houses grouped in close proximity to a *venda*, or trading post, to villages serving as trading centers for considerable area and striving to get themselves elevated to the administrative category of *vilas,* which will give them the political function and make the seats of new districts.

WHY BRAZIL REMAINS IN THE NEIGHBORHOOD STAGE

In Brazil, as in the United States, the tendency is toward larger locality groups. Neighborhoods are losing part of their integrity and becoming fused into community units. The community is becoming more integrated, gathering strength, and coming to play a more important role in rural affairs. But this process as yet has not been carried as far in Brazil as in the United States. As mentioned above, Brazil still remains, for the most part, in the neighborhood stage of social organization. Even today the Brazilian rural community is still in an amorphous state reminiscent of that prevailing in Midwestern United States until about 1890, in the South until World War I. But whereas the open country church and the one room school have been primary elements in preserving neighborhood units in the United States, other factors have been responsible in Brazil.

Probably the most important of these is the system of communication and transportation. In general the roads, telephone lines, and other facilities for communication and transportation are still in their formative stages in Brazil. This is not to say that Brazil is in the "horse and buggy" stage. As a matter of fact this most valuable means of transportation has been almost entirely unknown in Brazil. The same is true of the wagon, which was almost entirely lacking until brought by German and Polish colonists in the nineteenth century, and still is entirely absent from most of the country. Except in the colonial parts of the South where wagons are used, and parts of São Paulo where there is an excellent system of railways and where gasoline-propelled vehicles are rather common, transportation in Brazil relies mainly upon the oxcart, the pack animal, the small boat or canoe, and man's head. The oxcart is most prevalent in the South; it gives way to the troops of pack animals as one passes North through Minas Gerais; and the human being comes to play his chief role as a beast of burden in the Northeast and North. In the Amazon Valley, in much of Mato Grosso, along the coast,

in southern Baia and in Espirito Santo small boats are the
most important element in the transportation system. Although members of the *fazendeiro* class frequently have cars,
especially in São Paulo, and there are even to be found localities in that state and in Minas Gerais where trucks make daily
collections of milk cans, as in Wisconsin, these are the exceptional cases. Throughout most of Brazil, reliance upon the
oxcart, the saddle horse, the pack mule, the small boat or raft,
and the head of man for transportation does much to keep
Brazil's locality group structure in the neighborhood stage.

The strong role of kinship is another factor that helps produce the same effect. For example, in many *municípios* of
Minas Gerais, an immense area formerly was held by one
owner in a tremendous estate or *fazenda*. Today, in many
cases, this vast terrain has been divided among numerous
descendants whose families maintain a very intimate neighborhood life among themselves. Not infrequently such a rural
clan will be in open conflict with the inhabitants of the town
or community center.

The retention of most of the essential services within the
household or in the neighborhood also is partially responsible
for the Brazilian rural community remaining in a relatively
amorphous condition. Household and *fazenda* enterprises
continue to process the great bulk of the products consumed
by rural people. For example, tens of thousands of grist mills
grind or pound the corn which forms such a significant element in the diet. As one passes through the rural sections of
the states from Minas Gerais south, he will see, every few
miles, one of these water-driven devices for grinding or pound-
ind corn kernels into meal. Each miller gives a sack of meal
for a sack of corn, and keeps the increase for his pay. As he
goes north he will see on each *fazenda* the sheds and vats in
which *farinha de mandioca,* or mandioca flour, the staff of
life from Baía north, is prepared. In other aspects the situation is similar—the Brazilian countryman is largely independent of the economic services offered by villages and towns.

This means that the relative unimportance of trade itself
is another factor helping to keep Brazilian rural society in the
neighborhood stage. When one leaves the sugar and coffee
estates he finds relatively little produced for the market. Con-

versely, few things are purchased. The level of living is mostly a function of what is both produced and consumed by the family itself. Sales of produce by many families are restricted largely to those carried in to market on the way to church, and purchases necessarily are limited to a few indispensables. Competition between trade centers, which does so much to expand the horizons of rural folk, remains in a retarded condition. The mail order house, whose catalogues have inspired so many new wants in North American farm families, is practically unknown. The displays of the *lojas Americanas* (American stores), which is the Brazilian name for the 5 and 10 cent emporiums, are confined to a few of the larger centers. For most of Brazil's rural millions the stimuli from such sources remain very much a thing of the future.

Class Structure and Locality Groupings

As in the plantation sections of our own Southland, there is a great difference between the locality group attachments of the upper, landowning classes and of the families who live and work on the estates. The former are sure to have contacts and attachments outside the neighborhood and local community, in the seat of the *município*, in the larger trade centers of the area to which airplanes make regular visits, and in the state capital. The latter are likely to live in a world whose horizon ends with the neighboring *fazendas* or at the nearest village or town. The world of the small farming classes who are crowded into the mountain coves, into badly cut-up areas, or onto other poor lands, is as restricted as that of the workers on the *fazendas*. The same is true of those assembled in small clearings in the palm forests of the North, strung along the coast amid the coconut groves, or settled along the natural levee of a river. In short, the landowning nobility are among the leading citizens of the state and nation, in whose affairs they participate actively, while the lower classes live, work, and die in locality groups of a very restricted size.

The Emerging Community

In conclusion one may well ask, What lies ahead? How will

the locality group structure of Brazil be modified as time goes on? A knowledge of the present structural pattern, and some of the factors in operation, gives the basis for venturing certain hypotheses relative to the changes in the near future.

As mentioned above, Brazilian rural social organization lacks certain of the elements that have contributed to the persistence of small locality groupings in the United States and have retarded the evolution of a strong, clear-cut, and closely integrated rural community. It may be said that Brazil has made comparatively little use of the one-room, open country school, with an attendance area that bears little or no relationship to the limits of other forms of human association. Thus the "little red school house" and all its sentimental attachments is not a divisive force in Brazilian rural society. Brazil's problem is to establish schools for its children, not to combine small, poorly taught, and poorly located one-room units into centralized schools rooted in the neighborhoods and serving the community; nor to remold those social monstrosities which have been foisted upon the public as "consolidated schools," in the name of progress, into units that can come to be functional parts of community groupings. In other words, the rural educational problems are neither those of our own midwestern and northern states, nor those of the South. As her schools are multiplied they are being located in town, village, and hamlet centers, frequently at the seat of a *fazenda* or *usina*. The attendance area of the school is not being drawn so that it cuts across the lines bounding other areas of association, but is being made to conform with them. This should contribute to the development of a well-defined, closely integrated rural community. Nor does the persistence of open-country churches maintained by a denomination long after an old population group has retreated before a new one, or constituting the rallying point for a nationality or language group that holds apart from the local community, or kept alive by the circuit rider who has substituted the automobile for the horse in making his periodic visits, retard the integration of the Brazilian rural community. Religious homogeneity, and the fact that the *matriz* in the village or town center is the mother church and servicing agency for all the chapels and *oratorios* on the surrounding *fazendas*, have already made for well-defined church communities. There is every opportunity for the areas of these to become those of the evolving rural communities.

Finally, the organization of the Brazilian *município* or county offers promise for the continued development of rather large, closely integrated, functioning rural and *rurban* communities. Of tremendous significance is the fact that the seat of a *município* is not permitted to draw apart from the open country, to encrust itself by separate incorporation. Where density of population is high, *municípios* small in area, and transportation fairly well developed, as in parts of southern Minas Gerais and São Paulo, the *município* already is a fairly well developed *rurban* community. This trend can be expected to continue, and the pattern will diffuse. Its pace will be determined by the extent to which transportation and communication facilities are improved, and education brings to the masses of the rural people new wants and instructs them in the productive skills and techniques essential for securing the means to fill them. As work becomes more efficient, and labor alone ceases to be the dominant element in the productive process; as regular work activities become necessary to keep pace with the Joneses and to comply with the minimum standards of the group; and as all of these in combination create more wants, greater productivity, and more trade, this larger community will become much more highly integrated as a functioning social group. In the future, Brazil may come near realizing Dr. Galpin's dream of what might be in the United States. A large share of the small *cidades* may come to be rather complete social and economic social centers for all the *sitios, fazendas,* hamlets and villages in the *municípios* which bear their names. These *rurban* communities then will consist of a town center plus a surrounding tributary zone lying within a radius of 10 or 15 miles of the center in which the institutions converge.

10 The Class Structure of Colombian Society

———————◆———————

SOCIETY IN Colombia is highly stratified. The differences between the social status of the small upper crust and that of
the great mass of the population are tremendous. The former
enjoy wealth and income, political power and prestige, educational training, culture, leisure, and positions of honor to a
high degree. Since the caste element is also strong (a position
at the apex of the social pyramid comes largely as a birthright
and not through the exceptional abilities and efforts of the
individual), there is little reason for any member of the elite
to question his own right to generous portions of the better
things of life. A wide chasm separates these favored few from
the great masses of the population who occupy the lower
positions in society. Undernourished, ill-clad, poorly housed,
disease ridden, often dissipated, frequently illiterate and
largely abandoned to their misery, these masses amount to
little in the economic, social, cultural, and religious life of the
country. Even though social relationships were greatly scrambled by the wars for independence, it is only in recent decades
that what may be considered as a genuine middle class has
begun to emerge in the larger cities and in some of the frontier zones.

Factors in the Traditional Pattern of Social Stratification

The factors involved in the traditional differentiation of the
population of Colombia into the two readily distinguishable

From T. Lynn Smith, *Colombia: Social Structure and the
Process of Development,* Gainesville: University of Florida Press,
1967, pp. 330–43. Copyright © 1967 by the Board of Commis-
sioners of State Institutions of Florida. Reprinted by permission of
the publisher.

classes, the *terratenientes* and the *campesinos,* are two: ownership of land and race. These have been inextricably bound
together ever since the conquest set in operation the forces
which have brought about the present situation. Some of the
old families who make up the elite of Colombian society trace
their origin to one of the white conquistadores who helped
seize control of this part of the New World. By right of conquest this handful of Spaniards set themselves up in their own
new administrative centers as a ruling oligarchy, exacted a
heavy tribute from the Indians who were portioned out in
encomienda as virtual serfs, rapidly took over the best lands
as private possessions on which to pasture their horses and
cattle, exploited the mines with Indian laborers impressed
through the institution of the mita and Negro slaves imported
from Africa, and established monopolies of trade. By the time
the encomienda system was abolished, more or less at the
expiration of the "two lives" for which the Indians were
commonly assigned, some of the conquerors had already established legal title to much of the most desirable land. As a
result most of the aborigines had no choice except to work
for the owners of the large estates on the owners' terms or to
flee into the most out-of-the-way and inaccessible retreats of
the Andean fastnesses. Something similar seems to have taken
place with those who resided in the occasional settlements of
white small farmers which were established in some parts of
the country.

The ease and rapidity with which the conquerors gained
for themselves and their descendants an impregnable position
at the top of the social heap was greatly facilitated by the
fact that the Indians had already developed settled habits,
agriculture, and nucleated settlements. Since the Spaniards
possessed the firearms which the natives lacked, the aborigines were easily reduced to the servile or semi-servile class of
laborers. Some were parceled out among the conquerors in
encomiendas, and some were forced to perform the even
more decimating work in the mines. But in any case they
were generally subject to the slightest whim of the master
class.

Since very few Spanish women entered the colonies, a few
decades were sufficient to give rise to a vast number of mes-

tizos, persons with white fathers and Indian mothers.[1] Under these circumstances, and since immigrants avoid the areas in which a handful of landlords wring a luxurious living from the blood, sweat, and tears of the enslaved masses, the increase of the white population was slow. As a result society quickly became differentiated into a small group of aristocrats at the apex of the social pyramid and the great servile masses at the base, with persons of anything resembling a middle-class status conspicuous by their absence. A few generations of forced labor and the lower classes were stripped of all possibility of bettering their own position, while the wealth of the masters enabled them to institutionalize their positions through the positions of *mayorasgos* and titles of nobility.

As a result Colombian society early became sharply differentiated into a two-class system. At the top was a small, wealthy, highly intelligent, landowning, white, aristocratic elite for whom nothing in this world was considered too good; and far below in the social scale was the mass of the population, humble, poverty-stricken, disease-ridden, uneducated, colored or mixed-blooded campesinos. As the cities have grown, especially during recent decades, hundreds of thousands of the latter have flocked into the centers and the bands of misery

---

[1] In rare instances the half-breed children of the conquerors succeeded in gaining acceptance as members of the upper classes, but probably very few of the numerous offspring of the *conquistadores* were as fortunate as Diego de Alcalá, one of the mestizo sons of Juan de Alcalá who accompanied Quesada from Santa Marta to the Savanna of Bogotá. It seems that Juan had four illegitimate children by an Indian woman of Bogotá, and that they were reared in his home. Two of the children, both girls, died in their youth, and the two boys were left in dire poverty when their father was killed in an expedition while fighting the Muzos. As early as 1559, less than a quarter of a century after the conquest, Diego was seeking to establish that he was his father's heir and entitled to share in the privileges of the conquering race. His claims were finally confirmed by The Real Audencia, but not until 1585, long after his father's encomienda had passed into other hands. At that time he was judged to be entitled to the protection of the king and named as a solicitor. Nothing is said of his brother whose lot no doubt was similar to that of thousands of other half-breeds who failed to attain the privileged status of the conquering whites. Cf. Raimundo Rivas, *Los Fundadores de Bogotá*, Bogotá: Imprenta Nacional, 1923, pp. 43–44.

that surround them. This migration, though, has done little or nothing to change the class system; it has merely transferred a part of them into a degraded urban proletariat who rank at the extreme bottom of the social scale. Now and then, however, one may encounter a former campesino whose position as a chauffeur, a mechanic, a mason, and so forth is enabling him to gain a status near the upper reaches of the lower-class category; and occasionally one is found whose efforts to gain a formal education may eventually enable him to rise into the middle class. Hence it is not impossible that during the years ahead substantial numbers of the former campesinos may join the foreigners and their descendants and the less fortunate part of the offspring of those of high estate in swelling the numbers of a growing middle class. Adequate study of this process, nevertheless, is still a thing of the future.

The Concept of Social Class

The term social class as it is used in the following pages has a very specific meaning. In the first place it denotes a number of persons in a given society whose economic, occupational, and socio-political levels and interests are closely similar. In the second place these individuals must recognize that they have a social and economic status similar to that of their fellows; they must be conscious of the fact that the fortunes of all those on their level are inextricably bound together, and thereby be impelled to make a common front with those on a comparable social level. The second part of this definition is intended to indicate that there is no social class, irrespective of similarities in levels of living, felt needs, and ambitions, unless a "consciousness of kind," a group solidarity, also has been established.

In order to arrive at such a concept of social class one must be cognizant of the fact that all societies are divided into various economic levels, occupational layers, and degrees of social prestige and political power and influence. The varying amount of wealth and income enjoyed or received by different people is closely related to the occupations they follow. It also is closely associated with the amount of respect they command from their fellows and the extent to which they are privileged to exercise power and authority in political and other social affairs. But the three scales are not perfectly correlated. A few occupations, such as those of clergyman or college professor, carry considerable social prestige and influence, even though the monetary rewards generally are rather meager; an old aristocracy may maintain its position at the top of the heap for several generations after the bulk of its wealth and income has disappeared; and it may take a long while for the newly rich family to be accepted into the "four hundred" or its equivalent in any given society.

As indicated above, "the consciousness of kind" is another indispensable characteristic that must be present before any given group of people may legitimately be designated as a social class. (In discussing this matter use will be made of three categories, upper, middle, and lower classes, although it is recognized that for many purposes it is better to carry the classification to finer degrees of precision.) Such a consciousness of kind is intimately linked with the three basic economic functions, namely those of the one who has and invests capital, those of the manager, and those of the laborer. As a general rule upper-class status is compatible only with the first of these, and in extreme cases even that function is denied to the drones who may have a strangle hold on the wealth and income of a society. Under exceptional circumstances, such as those that prevail in new countries which are dominated by a middle-class mentality (as has been true generally in the United States and Canada), the entrepreneurial and managerial functions may be exercised by members of the elite without serious loss of face and status in the select circles. At the other extreme, manual labor, toil with the hands, is the indelible mark of the lower classes, and the one which creates among their members the recognition of common interests and the bond of unity.

Most interesting of all is the social solidarity of the middle classes. It results from the exercise of all three of the basic economic functions. Access to or membership in the middle classes, or the mentality possessed by their members, demands that the rôle of the investor be assumed. But the capital involved is in small amounts and usually results from thrift and saving. Unlike the wealth of the upper classes it will not support any elaborate ostentation or any great display of conspicuous consumption. It is merely one of the less important sources of the income from which the middle-class family derives its support. In addition to performing the rôle of the investor on a limited scale, the middle class is also the managerial group par excellence. Not a little of the responsibility for the planning and the bulk of the execution of the details in all economic activities are in the hands of its members. Self-employment in the professions and in small businesses is highly important for them and their children. Generally the operators of family-sized farms are the backbone of such a class. But neither the fact that they are investors of capital nor their managerial responsibilities bring persons of the middle class to neglect and depreciate the skills involved in working with their hands. As a class they do not think of manual labor as bemeaning; nor do they tolerate the gross waste of time and money that would be required to maintain a number of lackeys at their beck and call in order that they might never have to soil their hands or "lower" themselves by some act involving manual labor. The person of middle-class status feels a strong bond in common with others who carefully guard the small investments they have built up, assume individual responsibility and self direction in most of their occupational activities, and esteem the dignity of human labor.

Class differences almost always become associated with the caste element although there is no indivisible link between the two. To the extent that free social circulation between the layers, to the degree that rising or falling from one stratum to another, is hindered by factors not directly related to the capacities of the individual members and the energies exerted by them, the class system partakes of caste characteristics. When through conquest, an old system of slavery, or any other means, readily distinguishable physical features, such as the color of the skin, come to be associated with class membership the caste features are likely to become especially strong and extremely difficult to eradicate. This creates no particular problem in a static society where most people accept for granted the estate to which they were born and are permitted to receive few if any stimuli encouraging them to seek a higher one. But it is fraught with serious consequences in terms of personal frustration and social conflict within a mobile society, such as that in the United States, in which the channels of social ascension now are open to those who possess the physical characteristics which once were the identifying marks of those of a servile group. Under such circumstances the scrambling of class and caste relationships may bring untold suffering and misery to millions of human beings, even though they may be making tremendous progress from the standpoints of material well-being, health and levels of living. As the Latin American countries, including Colombia, are swept into the maelstrom of the modern world, the shattering of old patterns and the crumbling of traditional attitudes are likely to produce a chaotic situation with respect to the relationships involving class and caste.

In addition to the nature of the several social classes which has just been considered, two other matters should be kept in mind by those who deal with the class system in any part of the world. The first of these is the fact that it is necessary to make a distinction between an *intermediate* social level and a genuine middle social class. There always are various gradations in the economic, occupational, and socio-political statuses, even, for example, among the laborers on a sugar-cane plantation where all with much reason may be categorized as belonging in the lower social class; or, to mention just one other case, among the farmers in a district monopolized by family-sized farming units, where all certainly pertain to the middle social class. The failure to distinguish what is merely a stratum intermediate between two others from a middle social class as such is responsible, of course, for much of the tremendous variation one finds between the estimates of two or more writers relative to the importance of the upper, middle, and lower social classes in a given society.[2] Fortunately, there have been exceptions to this rule, of which a

[2] For some examples of the great differences between the estimates of the relative importance of the different classes within the same societies, see Theo R. Crevenna (ed.), *Materiales para el Estudio de la Clase Media en la América Latina,* 6 vols., Washington: Pan American Union, 1950–51.

good example is Fals-Borda's study of the settlement of Saucio in Colombia. This perceptive sociologist sought to discover whether or not there were "strata within the peasant class in Saucio?" For this purpose he made use of a scale, based upon those developed by F. Stuart Chapin, William H. Sewell, and Louis Guttman; and this enabled him to indicate that among the 69 heads of households "excluding the *hacendado* who belongs to the terrateniente class" there were indeed four social levels among the humble inhabitants of the district he was surveying. The four levels or layers he identified and the relative importance of the households falling in each are as follows: upper, 19 per cent; middle, 17 per cent; lower, 42 per cent; and destitute, 22 per cent.[3]

The second basic consideration that should be kept in mind by those who attempt to study and describe any society is that there is absolutely no reason for one to expect to find representations of all the social levels or layers in the population of any given locality, department, or nation. Geologists certainly do not expect to find examples of all the earth's strata in any one given location, and there is no more reason why the sociologist should expect to discover all of the social classes at a given place at any particular time. Indeed, in Colombia and most of the other Latin American countries the traditional pattern has been the two-class society, in which the middle social classes have been conspicuous by their absence; whereas in the family-sized farming districts of the midwestern part of the United States, all of the major socio-economic levels are subsumed in one genuine middle social class. In practical terms this means that the pyramids customarily used for the graphic portrayal of the class structure of a given society may be entirely inappropriate.

The Middle Classes

Most of the moot points with respect to the class structure of Colombian society revolve about the question of the extent to which a genuine middle class is evolving in the major

[3] Orlando Fals Borda, *Peasant Society in the Colombian Andes,* Gainesville: University of Florida Press, 1955, pp. 160–61.

cities and in certain of the rural zones of the country. Unfortunately the specific studies needed in order to settle the issues are still to be made. It does seem evident, though, that in parts of Antioquia and in much of Caldas the rural population has developed many of the characteristics that entitle them to be classed as genuine members of the middle class, albeit their farms are too small to permit most of their operators to attain a status near the top of such a class. It will require a great deal of study before the basic outlines of the process involved in this development will be known, but some of the most pertinent factors seem to be the following: (1) this was the most remote and inaccessible section of Colombia, so that it was the one to which it was most difficult for influences from the outside to make their way; (2) the Indians in these mountain fastnesses were less "civilized," that is they were in a less developed stage of social organization than those in many other parts of Colombia, and hence they were more cantankerous about accepting the Spaniards as overlords than the ones who lived in the high inter-mountain valleys of the eastern range; (3) as a result more of them were slaughtered, driven back into the mountain fastnesses or the jungles, and the land left devoid of inhabitants; (4) mining and other nonagricultural activities occupied the attention of the population to a far greater extent than they did in most other parts of the country; and (5) during the nineteenth century, after the removal of royal restraints, a tremendous epoch of self-propelled colonization activities got underway, one in which the family itself carved out a farm and made a home in the wilderness with fair assurance that its members would be able to enjoy the benefits of their labors. But irrespective of whether these are the factors or whether the causes were different, the fact remains that hundreds of individual farm properties and thousands of other small enterprises have been developed by the enterprising Antioqueños. Considering that they have lived and worked in a country where the many social restraints have operated against the evolution of a genuine middle class, what has taken place seems all the more remarkable.

But the case of Antioquia and Caldas is unique. Elsewhere in Colombia there continued to be well-defined and widely separated classes of the elite and the lower orders, with hardly anything deserving of the designation middle class present to help fill the great void between the two. It is true that there are in cities like Bogotá, Cali, and Barranquilla large numbers of office holders, professionals, merchants, industrialists, and those engaged in other white-collar activities. However, one should examine the actual situation rather carefully before he jumps to the conclusion that all of these people constitute a middle class in the society. This is most true of the office holders and professionals; and apparently less the case with the merchants and small industrialists.

Consider first the fact that most of those in the swarm of minor officials who occupy posts in the national, state, and local governments are the sons, grandsons, and great-grandsons of persons who once occupied positions at the apex of the social pyramid in Colombia. The same is true of the host of lawyers, who make up the overwhelming majority of the professional men, and who must seek every opportunity to gain a small added stipend by performing notarial services, teaching, and so on, in order to support their families on the modest scale to which they have been reduced. "Self-made men" in Colombia are not entirely lacking, but they are not numerous. A count would probably indicate that the overwhelming proportion of those who may at first glance appear to be of middle class status, and whose descendants eventually may help form a genuine middle class, are members of proud old families.

In this connection the observations of Eduardo Santos, former president of Colombia and publisher of the great newspaper, *El Tiempo* of Bogotá, are very much to the point. He has written as follows. "Systems other than the liberal one are impossible in a country of the middle class, in which the aristocrats are tumbling from their exalted positions to very modest posts. Everyone recalls the grand families of a century ago whose descendants today are in the lowest positions in the bureaucratic scale. Those who dominated the Savanna with immense latifundia, and possessed enormous landed estates, presently humbly earn 80 pesos a month in an office of secondary importance."[4]

The reasons for this state of affairs are not hard to find. Until educational opportunities are extended to the masses, only an exceptional child here and there will succeed in lifting himself by his own bootstraps out of the illiterate, disease-ridden, malnourished, ill-clothed, poorly housed, poverty-stricken, landless mass which constitutes the bulk of the Colombian population. The fact that most of them are of more or less colored descent does not aid the prospects of the members of Colombia's lower classes. Added to this is the stern reality that the factors affecting vertical social mobility create a movement in just exactly the opposite direction to the principal currents of circulation within our own social pyramid.

This last statement calls for an explanation. In the United States and most countries of western Europe, the members of the upper-middle and lower-upper classes fail to reproduce themselves. One generation of them does not leave enough offspring to carry on the work performed by its members, and in addition the number of highly paid and responsible jobs is expanding fantastically. This creates a kind of a suction which carries many members of the middle and lower classes to positions considerably higher in the social scale than the ones occupied by their parents. It does much to generate an optimistic outlook on life within the society, the hope and expectation that one's offspring will enjoy a higher social status than that of the person himself. But in Colombia, as in most Latin American countries, there seems to be no differential fertility favorable to the lower classes. Upper-class families produce as many children, if not more, than those in less fortunate circumstances. Furthermore, of the children born, undoubtedly the upper classes succeed in safeguarding a larger proportion through the tender years of life than do the lower classes. As a result one of high estate leaves not one heir to assume a position in society more or less equal to that of his own, but a flock of sons all of them "to the manor born."

[4] *Una Política Liberal,* Bogotá: Editorial Minerva, S.A., 1937, p. 32.

As a matter of fact, since the generations come along about 25 years apart, a single member of the elite may live to see the time when three generations of his descendants (not infrequently as many as 100 persons) are struggling desperately to maintain positions on a high rung of the social ladder. If, as in Colombia, the original social position and wealth are based upon land, since the institutions of primogeniture and entailed estates have been abolished, a few generations are sufficient to pulverize even the largest holdings. If the actual legal and physical subdivision of the land among the heirs is not carried out the situation may be even worse. Then one more great property is added to the already large number of haciendas or fincas on which operations are paralyzed because the number of owners is legion and no one of them may operate since all the others have a claim on what is produced by his efforts. Such a state of affairs is conducive to anything except an optimistic outlook upon life on the part of the sons, grandsons, and great-grandsons of the important men of the country. Inexorable forces are pushing them down the social scale, making it increasingly difficult for them to maintain the appearances of the type of life to which they were born and which they came to regard as their right. Their actual levels of living may make it clear that they enjoy no more goods and services than a person of middle-class status, but their standards, the amounts to which they feel entitled, are far greater.

Eventually the descendants of many of these old families may be expected to contribute to the formation of a genuine middle class in Colombia, although not a few of them may be debased to the very bottom of the social scale. But the transition will not be easily nor quickly achieved, and many of the persons involved may become so demoralized that they will forfeit all chances for themselves and their children. Others will continue to use their connections to obtain minor positions in the bureaucracy; and in a highly familistic society, where the practice of nepotism is almost a sacred obligation on the part of successful politician or statesman, such employment becomes available to not a few. Many will resort to the liberal professions, especially the law which equips them for notarial work, teaching, and other activities involving use of wit and lacking the stigma attached to the trades, the most skilled labor, and much of commerce. Never under any circumstances short of almost absolute starvation will they consent to engage in any activities involving manual labor, at least in its traditional forms, for that would stigmatize them as acknowledging a mean origin and position. This attitude toward physical labor, the utter impossibility of viewing it as honorable and ennobling, a mind-set which they share with all other peoples whose formative processes were shaped by the large-landed estate and its accompanying servile labor force and two-class system of social stratification, is the thing which makes it most difficult for tens of thousands of present-day Colombians to become full-fledged members of a genuine middle social class.

Since 1943, tens if not hundreds of thousands of well-built and well-equipped dwellings and apartments have been built in new residential districts of Bogotá, Cali, Barranquilla, and the other major cities in Colombia. My contacts have been for the most part with those who practice law or medicine, with those who hold governmental positions, and with those in the universities. I have had very little opportunity to know those engaged in commerce and industry. This means that my information has been derived mostly from Colombians of Colombian parentage, and only slightly from the immigrants and their children. With very few exceptions, moreover, the Colombians I know who reside in what would be judged to be middle-class residential districts, in homes that our sociological scales would identify as dwellings of those of the middle class, are the descendants of those who were unchallenged members of the upper class. Furthermore, even today they seem to identify themselves with the elite, although probably to a lesser degree than was the case in 1943 and 1944. But it seems evident that this state of affairs cannot continue indefinitely, and that the connections between each generation of the offspring of such families and actual elite social status, even when the latter is limited to the standing of a grandfather or great-grandfather, is becoming more tenuous.

The findings of one recent study of the Bogotá entrepreneur shed a few rays of light upon the nature of the changing class structure of Colombia's great capital city.[5] Its author generalizes that these entrepreneurs are "well-educated, urban, and . . . from a predominantly middle class background, in a society that is mainly rural, has a low educational level, and an overwhelmingy large lower class."[6] His data were secured in interviews with 61 executives who headed 26 per cent of firms with membership in Asociación Nacional de Industriales, said to be roughly comparable with the National Association of Manufacturers in the United States. "In each case the person interviewed was the executive at the top of the personnel hierarchy in his particular firm."

One striking fact revealed by this study is represented by the finding that 41 per cent of his cases were foreign born, although the author correctly states that "Colombia has traditionally had a very low rate of immigration throughout the years."[7] Another is the indication that only five of the executives had fathers who belonged to the "working class," of whom four were "skilled workers," and that four of the five had fathers who were born in Europe and not in Colombia. Moreover, "in not a single instance had the entrepreneurs ever held any manual job in their previous occupational history."[8]

[5] Aaron Lipman, "Social Backgrounds of the Bogotá Entrepreneur," *Journal of Inter-American Studies,* Vol. VII (1965), pp. 227–35.

[6] *Ibid.,* p. 227.

[7] *Ibid.,* p. 331.

[8] *Ibid.,* p. 234.

11 The Structure of Rural Society in Colombia: The Case of Tabio

◆

[THESE EXTRACTS are from a sociological survey of the município of Tabio, a small county-like administrative subdivision of the Department of Cundinamarca, Colombia. The small village that forms the "head" of this small município is located about 32 miles to the north of Bogotá] in one of the numerous valleys that lead off the Savanna. It has an area of about 29 square miles, a good share of which lies in the fairly level valley bottom; but its limits extend to the divides on the surrounding mountains so that perhaps as much as one-fourth of the município is made up of steep mountain slopes. The small village which forms the seat of the município lies at approximately the same altitude as Bogotá, or about 8692 feet above sea level.

Settlement Patterns

The arrangement of the population on the land in Tabio represents a great departure from the village patterns of settlement which the Spaniards used in Europe, those which they found among the Indians who inhabited the Savanna of Bogotá, and those which they used in all their colonies from New Mexico to Chile. Today, in Tabio and throughout the Savanna, the form of settlement is that of the scattered farmsteads or isolated farms. There remain only a few survivals of the nucleated patterns which once existed. The data

From T. Lynn Smith, Justo Díaz Rodríguez, and Luis Roberto Garcia, *Tabio: A Study in Rural Social Organization*, Washington, D.C.: United States Department of Agriculture, 1945, pp. 6, 23–27, and 46–52.

gathered in the survey bring this out clearly. Of the 240 farm operators for which the records were sufficiently complete to allow analysis of this feature, only 26, or 11 per cent, resided within the village center. In the open country lived 13 operators of *haciendas* (over 50 fanegadas),[1] 119 operators of *fincas* (5 to 50 fanegadas), and 87 operators of *parcelas* (less than 5 fanegadas). Furthermore, the process of dividing and redividing the former estates of the original encomenderos among their numerous descendants has gone on without any well-defined rules and regulations until now the small plots have become subdivided in a haphazard manner that makes the isolation of one farm family from another about as great as is physically possible with holdings of the prevailing size.

Nor do the farm laborers live in the village center. In Tabio, as is so generally the case throughout Colombia, the permanent laborers on the haciendas and fincas either own or rent a small piece of ground on the outskirts of the larger farms. The slopes of the mountains surrounding the valley bottoms, whose more fertile soils are monopolized by the *hacendados* for their pastures, are the areas most frequently given over to the laborers as small holdings or as *estancias*. Here they live widely separated from one another, from the *casa grande* of the estate on which they work, and from the religious and market center, which forms the seat of the município. With proper planning, the holdings of these laboring classes could have been laid off in a line village arrangement, similar to those which border the Louisiana sugar plantations, with great social and economic benefits to the workers and to society in general. Only 5 of the 187 families of farm laborers lived in the village center.

Finally, the practice of having a home in town, to which to resort on Sundays and holidays, as well as the residence on the land, is not very prevalent in the município of Tabio. Only six families, five of the farm operators, and one of the laborers, had such a secondary residence in the pueblo of Tabio. Thus the scattered-farmstead mode of arranging the population on the land is fully as characteristic of this

[1] 1 fanegada equals about 1.6 acres.

município as it is of the typical rural community in the United States.

In this discussion of the settlement patterns in Tabio, a few words are necessary about the nature and functions of the village center itself. Like its North American counterpart, the Colombian village in general, and Tabio in particular, is chiefly a trade, religious, educational, and recreational center. It differs radically from the pattern so prevalent in Europe, Asia, and other parts of Spanish America, in which the village type of settlement prevails, and in which the nucleus is composed mainly of the homes of farmers who live in the village and commute to their fields in the surrounding area.

The services which are provided in the village for all the inhabitants of the município may be summarized as follows: First of all, there is the church whose tower dominates the pueblo. In it centers the entire religious life of the município. The colonial chapel, which surmounts a slight elevation on the northern outskirts of the center, serves more as an ornament than as a place to which worshippers resort with frequency; and the Sanctuary of Lourdes, on the foothills of the sierras that form the eastern limits of the município, is a place of pilgrimage not only for the people of Tabio but for hundreds of persons from the surrounding area. The chief occasion on which this temple is used is on the 15th of December, a day devoted to Our Lady of Lourdes. Each year on this day there is a great pilgrimage to this shrine. The festival is quite like the festivals of Spain, for the activities consist not merely of religious observances but also of numerous popular diversions and recreations. The country about the shrine fills with *toldos,* or stands, at which food and drink are dispensed to the pilgrims, and with musicians, dancers, groups of singers, and so forth. Other than on this special occasion, the religious life of the entire município centers in and about the main church in the pueblo.

Tabio is also an educational center, although as yet there remains much to be done in order to make its facilities adequate for the school population. Four public schools, each with 1 teacher and about 45 students, 2 of which are for boys and 2 for girls, are located in the village. The majority of the students who receive elementary education must attend these, for there are only two rural schools in the município, and these function for boys one day and for girls the next. Two parochial *colegios,* or secondary schools, each with one teacher, are located in the pueblo. These are the only secondary educational facilities available in the município. That for boys has an enrollment of about 40 pupils; that for girls, slightly more, or 45.

Economically, nearly the entire population of the município is dependent upon Tabio as the market in which to dispose of farm produce and in which to purchase salt, *panela,* drugs, and other necessities. Only in recent years has the larger market and manufacturing center, Zipaquirá, begun to bring the inhabitants of the northern part of the município of Tabio more closely within its sphere of influence. Of all the economic institutions in Tabio, the public market held in the plaza in front of the church every Thursday is by far the most important. On that day, at least one representative of every farm family must visit the pueblo, carry in and dispose of any produce it may have for sale, mingle with the throng in the plaza and in the *tiendas,* and make the necessary purchases. Other than the bargaining which occurs in the market place, certain of the most essential goods, along with soft and hard drinks, may be had in the tiendas. One fairly complete general store, or *almacen,* is in daily operation. On certain days the presence of a red flag in front of one of the houses indicates that fresh meat is for sale within. There are two small *boticas,* drug stores in the most literal sense of the word, and one small pension or hotel. There are no restaurants separate from the five general-purpose tiendas, *fondas,* or *assistencias,* which are found scattered about the village. Two small barber shops offer their services to Tabio's male population. There is no moving picture theater or other commercial recreational center.

Since Tabio is an independent município, and not merely a *corregimiento* dependent upon another pueblo, the Alcalde, police, and registrar all have offices in the center. There are also a telegraph station, a post office, and a bus station in the village.

Every Thursday, which is market day, a physician comes from one nearby município, and a dentist from another, and they offer their services to the people of Tabio. It seems strange that the município contains no lawyers.

Finally, the survey yielded data concerning the distance each farm family lived from the village plaza, the amount of time required to walk from the farm to the central square, and the type of road or way which gave access to the rural home. (See tables I, II, and III.) A particularly significant

Table I.   Distance of Tabio's Farm Homes from the Central Plaza

Distance in Kilometers[1]	Farm operators		Farm laborers		Total[2]	
	Number	Percent	Number	Percent	Number	Percent
Data lacking	4	1.7	0	0.0	4	1.0
Under 1 ,..............	22	9.1	21	11.2	43	10.1
1	18	7.5	19	10.2	37	8.6
2	38	15.8	39	20.9	77	18.0
3	19	7.9	18	9.6	37	8.6
4	10	4.1	13	7.0	23	5.4
5	27	11.2	18	9.6	45	10.5
6	5	2.0	8	4.3	13	3.0
7	18	7.5	7	3.7	25	5.8
8 and more	80	33.2	44	23.5	124	29.0
Total	241	100.0	187	100.0	428	100.0

1. 1 Kilometer equals 0.62137 mile.
2. The part-time farmers are included.

Table II.   Amount of Time Required to Travel on Foot from the Farm Home to the Central Plaza

Hours	Farm operators		Farm laborers		Total[1]	
	Number	Percent	Number	Percent	Number	Percent
Data lacking	4	2.0	0	0.0	4	0.9
Less than ¼	26	11.0	18	9.6	44	10.3
¼ to ½	17	7.1	26	13.9	43	10.0
½ to ¾	54	22.4	50	26.7	104	24.4
¾ to 1	8	3.3	14	7.6	22	5.1
1 to 1½	29	12.0	20	10.7	49	11.5
1½ to 2	37	15.1	29	15.5	66	15.4
2 and more	66	27.1	30	16.0	96	22.4
Total	241	100.0	187	100.0	428	100.0

1. The part-time farmers are included.

Table III.   Class of Road on Which the Farm Homes of Tabio Are Located

Class of road	Farm operators		Farm laborers		Total	
	Number	Percent	Number	Percent	Number	Percent
No data	3	1.3	0	0.0	3	0.7
Graded road ...	62	25.8	42	22.4	104	24.4
Passable for oxcarts	99	41.0	100	53.6	199	46.4
Trail for animals	75	31.1	42	22.4	117	27.3
Footpath	2	0.8	3	1.6	5	1.2
Total	241	100.0	187	100.0	428	100.0

observation is that one-third of the farm operators and one-fourth of the farm laborers live at least 8 kilometers (5 miles) from the village. Even at that, the operators, possessed of other means of travel than going on foot, enjoy a comparative advantage over the laborers in reaching the marketing, governmental, religious, and recreational facilities of the pueblo. To make the weekly visit to market and to attend Mass on Sunday, if the trip is made on foot, as is the rule among the lower classes, requires 2 hours or more to go in each direction on the part of 27 per cent of the operators and 16 per cent of the laborers. About one out of every four families in Tabio lives on a graded road that is passable in all seasons of the year. Nearly one half of them have a way passable for carts giving access to their homes, and nearly 3 out of 10 can get from their homes to market only by traveling part of the way over trails and footpaths. Tabio, being located in one of the level recesses leading off the Savanna of Bogotá, is much better serviced by roads and ways passable by wheeled vehicles than is the average rural community in Colombia.

Social Differentiation

The high degree of social homogeneity which prevails in the município is Tabio's most outstanding characteristic. As yet, social differentiation has made little progress; in fact, in many ways the social situation in the município is even more homogeneous than it was in the early colonial days.

RACE. . . . Only two races, the white and the red, are represented in Tabio. In colonial times these two varieties of the human species were set apart by a wide social chasm; today the process of fusion, which has already made considerable progress, continues with few hindrances. Thus, of the 321 couples interviewed in the survey, 144 (45 per cent) were cases in which both of the mates were mestizos. This indicates that the blending of the races already has made considerable progress. That it continues is demonstrated by the fact that 21 cases were pairs in which the husband was classified as white and the wife as mestizo, and 17 cases were those in which the mestizo husband had a white wife. However, 139 cases were those of white men mated with white women, showing that an important part of the white population has not mixed with the red and that the selective mating for color, which has prevailed for 400 years, continues unabated. Nevertheless, from the racial standpoint, the population is much more homogeneous than it was two or three hundred years ago.

RELIGION. In 1944 practically all organized aspects of aboriginal Indian religious beliefs and practices were nonexistent in Tabio. No visible evidences of Protestant religious activities exist, and Jews or other non-Christian faiths are not represented in the município. From what was once a sharply differentiated juxtaposition of Chibcha and Roman Catholic religious cultures, has developed the present condition in which the latter alone reigns supreme. Furthermore, there is little evidence of a religious syncretism, of the incorporation of Chibcha beliefs and practices into the external forms of Catholicism, such as that which is so prevalent in Brazil, Mexico, and other parts of Latin America. Religiously, Tabio is extremely homogeneous. That two of its citizens could engage in a serious debate or discussion, not to say conflict, over religious divergences, is almost unthinkable. The weather and politics remain, however, as topics of constant discussion.

LOCALITY GROUPS. There is a certain differentiation between the small village or pueblo, founded late in the sixteenth century, and the open-country districts of the município. In fact, it is in this respect that social differentiation in Tabio seems to have made the greatest progress. The village is strictly a trading, church, educational, administrative, and recreational center. Like those of Brazil and the United States, it bears the stamp "made in America" and cannot be considered in any respect as an "agricultural village" in the European or Asiatic sense of the term.

Some of the outlying *veredas* also could be classified as neighborhoods, for there is a network of intimate social relationships between the families who live in Río Frío Oriental, and also among those who reside in Río Frío Occidental. For example, the families of these neighborhoods lend one another farm implements, aid each other in cases of sickness and death, and generally practice a system of mutual aid. In fact, the case is not rare in which the adults of a family going elsewhere in search of temporary employment leave their small children with a neighbor for the months they are away. Elsewhere in the município, the neighborhood groupings are less well defined, but they are present nevertheless.

From what has been said in the two preceding paragraphs, the nature of the community structure of Tabio should be evident. The community consists of the village nucleus, on the one hand, and of the outlying open-country districts on the other. Economically, socially, religiously, politically, and recreationally, every farm home in the município is intimately connected with the village center. As in the United States and Brazil, many of these farms are homes clustered together into genuine neighborhood entities, which in turn are integral portions of the larger unit, the community.

The social solidarity which binds these families together into the community is partially that based upon division of labor and mutual interdependence, called by Emile Durkheim *organic solidarity;* but it is more of the type based upon similarity of function and belief, or of the type which that noted French sociologist designated *mechanistic solidarity.* As social differentiation proceeds, the former may be expected to become more important and the latter to decline.

OCCUPATION. Economic division of labor and occupational differentiation have made comparatively little progress in Tabio. The bulk of the population is still engaged in agriculture, and within agriculture there is comparatively little specialization by tasks and enterprises. Even transportation activities are not sharply set apart from those of agricultural production.

Except for the differentiation between the social classes, which has produced a small, elite leisure class, the bulk of the population perform the whole gamut of tasks involved in the planting, cultivating, harvesting, transporting, and marketing of the farm produce.

There is a small commercial and service personnel resident in the village, which is occupationally set apart from the farmers. But within commerce, there is relatively little specialization. The bulk of the trading is still done in the plaza on Thursdays and is an exchange between the campesinos themselves, between the country people and the buyers from outside who come to purchase the farm products, or between the agriculturists and the traders who come to display cloth, *alpargatas,* rock salt, tropical fruits, yuca, rice, *panela,* and other necessities which are not produced in the município. Between the small tiendas of the village, there seems to be no division of labor; they specialize in clientele rather than in the lines of goods offered for sale.

EDUCATION. Educationally, too, there is comparatively little differentiation. Even the two or three years of elementary schooling that distinguishes three-fifths of the population from the other two-fifths does not represent a difference of any great magnitude. Tabio still lacks the facilities and the personnel to provide much educational specialization.

POLITICS. Politically the inhabitants of the município are rather equally divided between the two major parties, conservatives and liberals. In most of the elections the former seem to cast a few more votes than the latter. This rather equal division politically is in sharp contrast to the situation in many other municípios, where the population is either solidly with the one party or the other. The communists and other minor political parties have little or no representation in Tabio, and there are no labor unions.

CONCLUSION. From the data presented above, it is evident that Tabio is an unusually homogeneous rural community. It consists of the village nucleus and the affiliated neighborhoods and families. Social solidarity is mostly of the mechanistic type, although to some extent its parts are bound together by the mutual interdependence that comes from specialization and division of labor. As times goes on, and especially as Bogotá exerts greater and greater influences upon this and the neighboring municípios, Tabio will come to be more and more dependent upon the organic type of solidarity. At the present each individual duplicates all the others in a considerable number of the most significant characteristics so that the community as a whole tends to be of the cumulative type.

Social Stratification

LAND AND SOCIAL STATUS. The class system of Tabio has its principal basis in the ownership and control of the land. The possessor of broad acreages automatically enjoys comparatively large wealth and income, he has great political prestige and exercises extensive political power, and he is entitled to expect from the members of the lower orders of society acknowledgments of his superior status in myriads of ways, some of them quite obvious and others extremely subtle. The large landowner is entitled to give orders; the lower classes must obey. This is the phenomenon generally designated as *caciquismo*.

The two most obvious layers in the class structure of Tabio are the *terratenientes* and the *campesinos*. The former, quite limited in number, are the owners of large acreages. Without any doubt they occupy the apex of the social pyramid. The campesino class is not so homogeneous, and it includes the bulk of the population. This class embraces not only the large mass of landless rural workers, who are permitted to occupy small estancias on the margins of the haciendas and fincas, but the bulk of the small landowners as well. In wealth and income, political status, level of living, and social privileges and obligations there is no great difference between the man who rents a small estancia and the one who owns a couple of fanegadas. Between the two and the terrateniente there is a social chasm. On the whole, though, the social differences in Tabio are less than they are in many parts of the Republic.

Within the class of campesinos there is considerable variation. The landless agricultural workers no doubt occupy the
bottom stratum of the social pyramid. Next come those who
own a fanegada or two. At the top of this class are a significant number who have acquired enough land to carry on considerable agriculture, maintain some livestock, and employ several workers. Some of these higher members of the campesino
class probably are the descendants of former terratenientes
who have been reduced to campesino status through the continued subdivision of the estates among the numerous heirs of
each succeeding generation. But some of them no doubt are
people who have made their way up the agricultural ladder
from a less enviable status. It would be interesting to know
the extent to which a family is able to keep its upper-class
status after it has lost its wealth, and also the vicissitudes encountered by the man rising from the ranks and attempting
to become an accredited member of the terrateniente class.

RACE AND SOCIAL STATUS. Although the ownership and control of the land form the principal basis of social stratification
in Tabio, social status has other important determinants as
well. One of these is race. There can be no doubt that the
white population occupies a higher average social status than
the mixed white and Indian, or mestizo class. Many of the
data gathered in the survey may be brought to bear on this
hypothesis. First, there is the indisputable fact that the whites
tend to occupy the position of farm operators, whereas the
mestizos, in much higher proportions, fall in the unenviable
category of farm laborers. (See table IV.) Headed exclusively
by whites are 50.7 per cent of the households of farm operators and only 32.5 per cent of those of the farm laborers;
headed exclusively by the mestizos are only 42.3 per cent
of the former and 57.8 per cent of the latter. These data
establish the fact that the white agriculturists of Tabio occupy
a higher position on the agricultural ladder than their fellows of the mestizo class.

In order to continue the analysis, a considerable number
of indexes of social and economic status were computed and
used for the purpose of comparing the 122 households of

Table IV.   Heads of Households and Their Mates Classified
According to Agricultural Position and Race

Race of head of household and mate	Farm operators		Farm laborers	
	Number	Percent	Number	Percent
White man and white woman	70	29.1	42	22.4
Mestizo man and mestizo woman...	61	25.3	70	37.4
White man and mestizo woman......	8	3.3	13	7.0
Mestizo man and white woman	9	3.7	5	2.7
White man without mate	25	10.4	7	3.7
Mestizo man without mate	19	7.9	19	10.2
White woman without mate	27	11.2	12	6.4
Mestizo woman without mate	22	9.1	19	10.2
Total	241	100.0	187	100.0

farm operators headed exclusively by whites with the 102
headed by mestizos; and for comparing the 61 farm-labor
households headed by whites with the 108 headed by mestizos. (See table V.) The conclusions to be drawn from this
table are clear. Almost without exception on all the indexes of
high social and economic status, the whites excel the mestizos, whereas on those indicative of low social and economic
status the mestizos are represented in the higher proportions.
Thus, in comparison with their white fellows, the mestizos live
at greater distances from the village center, on smaller tracts
of land. They own fewer livestock, and are less likely to possess wheeled vehicles. Their homes are smaller, of poorer construction, more likely to have thatched roofs, wattle and daub
walls, dirt floors, and to lack windows entirely. The homes of
the mestizos are also less likely than those of the whites to
contain such modern improvements as electric lights, running
water, and other plumbing; and they are more likely to depend solely upon the *cocina de fogón* for cooking purposes,
and to utilize the metate for grinding the flour which the
family consumes.

All these racial differences are more pronounced among
the category of farm operators than they are for the farm
laborers. The white family that has descended to the bottom
of the social ladder, to the class of farm laborers, lives little
better than its fellows of mixed white and Indian stock. Nevertheless, sufficiently pronounced are the differences among the

Table V. Comparison of White and Mestizo Farm Operators and Farm Laborers with Respect to Various Indexes Which Reflect Social and Economic Status

Index	Farm operators		Farm laborers	
	White	Mestizo	White	Mestizo
Operators residing in village ....Percent	11.5	5.9	4.9	1.9
Average distance of home from plaza ....Kms	5.2	6.2	5.4	5.1
Operators living on a road passable for wheeled vehicles ....Percent	87.9	58.7	75.4	75.0
Operators possessing a supplementary dwelling ....Percent	19.7	10.8	6.6	5.6
Operators with holdings of less than 10 fanegadas ....Percent	59.0	65.7	—	—
Operators owning their fincas or estancias .....Percent	90.2	88.2	72.1	72.2
Average riding, draft, and pack animals owned ....Number	1.3	1.1	.15	.22
Average cattle owned...Number	13.0	6.1	.87	.96
Average sheep and goats owned ....Number	7.4	2.2	1.2	.7
Average pigs and hogs owned ....Number	1.1	1.1	.93	.74
Average poultry owned ....Number	13.3	9.1	7.0	4.3
Operators possessing no wheeled vehicles ....Percent	91.0	95.1	96.7	99.1
Literacy among heads of households ....Percent	72.1	52.9	57.4	46.3
Average rooms per house ....Number	5.1	3.1	3.0	2.4
Homes with thatched roofs ....Percent	50.0	74.5	68.9	75.9
Homes with dirt floors ....Percent	46.7	75.5	78.7	82.4
Homes with wattle and daub walls ....Percent	39.3	69.6	65.6	63.9
Homes entirely lacking windows ....Percent	24.6	60.8	26.2	57.4
Homes that are ceiled ....Percent	73.0	51.0	60.7	41.7
Homes having electricity ....Percent	9.0	3.9	3.3	2.8
Homes having running water ....Percent	41.0	23.5	19.7	16.7
Homes having septic tanks ....Percent	3.3	0.0	1.6	1.9
Homes having indoor toilets ....Percent	13.9	3.9	3.3	0.0
Homes having estufas ...Percent	16.4	3.9	1.6	0.0
Homes having only cocina de fogón ....Percent	32.0	54.9	41.0	68.5
Homes having refrigerators ....Percent	1.6	0.0	0.0	0.0
Homes using metates....Percent	92.6	97.1	95.1	94.4

farm operators to make it evident that social stratification in Tabio is determined to a marked degree by racial factors.

RESIDENCE AND SOCIAL STATUS. There is also a definite tendency for the inhabitants of the pueblo to occupy a higher social and economic plane than those who live in the open-country portions of Tabio. In the first place, few of the farm laborers live in the cabecera of the município, only 5 of the 187 households. This indicates that when a family of farm laborers moves to the village it rarely continues to work in the fields. In the second place, the farm operators who reside in the center live on a much higher level than those who dwell in the fincas, and the nonagriculturists who make their homes in the village live much better than their fellows who dwell in the surrounding area. Thus of the 20 farm operators residing in the pueblo all are farm owners, and only 88 per cent of the 221 living in the open country are proprietors. Furthermore, of the 7 operators with farms of 200 fanegadas or more, 4 are included among the 20 who reside in the village. But the material gathered (table VI) brings out more clearly the sharp differences that exist between the farm operators who live in the center and those who reside on the farms, and also between the nonagriculturists dwelling in the pueblo and those living in the surrounding area. These data leave no doubt that the inhabitants of the village tend to occupy a higher social and economic level in society than do the persons residing in the open country.

Table VI. Comparison of the Farm Operators and Nonagriculturists Living in the Pueblo and in the Open Country with Respect to Various Indexes Which Reflect Social and Economic Status

Index	Farm operators		Nonagriculturists	
	Pueblo	Open country	Pueblo	Open country
Literacy among heads of households .... Percent	95.0	61.1	92.9	53.2
Average rooms per house .... Number	7.1	3.8	4.2	3.0
Homes having tile roofs .... Percent	70.0	19.9	78.6	22.6
Homes having thatched roofs .... Percent	15.0	65.6	7.1	62.9
Homes having dirt floors .... Percent	0.0	66.5	21.4	59.7
Homes having wattle and daub walls .... Percent	5.0	57.0	7.1	56.5
Homes having glass windows .... Percent	31.7	8.6	50.0	9.7
Homes having electricity .... Percent	25.0	4.5	35.7	3.2
Homes having running water .... Percent	80.0	27.1	85.7	25.8
Homes having indoor toilets .... Percent	35.0	6.3	32.1	4.8
Homes having only the cocina de fogón .... Percent	10.0	45.7	7.2	50.0

12 The Brazilian Family

———◆———

THE LARGE, aristocratic, patriarchal family always has been the most important of Brazil's social institutions. Rarely has this primary kinship group had to play a role secondary to that of the church, as so frequently has been true in Spanish-American countries; nor has its relative importance ever been seriously challenged by the school, as may be the case in a North American community. In colonial times such a large, closely knit group of relatives, acknowledging allegiance to the oldest living male, possessing many slaves, and carrying on the aristocratic tradition at its best, was the chief instrument employed in the occupation of Brazil. This was in sharp contrast to the colonization of Spanish America where the *conquistador* and the priest were largely responsible for establishing the Spaniards as a ruling caste and to the founding of the English colonies in North America where the community and the smaller, more equalitarian family were basic elements. As has been shown so well by Freyre's monumental work, the partriarchal form of social organization early obtained almost unlimited sway in Brazil. For centuries Portuguese America continued to be dominated by a few thousand casas grandes, seats of sugar engenhos and cattle fazendas, each of which was the fortress headquarters of a numerous clan.[1] Even today there remains much of this feu-

From T. Lynn Smith, *Brazil: People and Institutions,* third edition, Baton Rouge: Louisiana State University Press, 1963, pp. 459–461 and 472–481. Copyright 1946 and 1963 by Louisiana State University Press. Reprinted by permission of the publisher.

[1] Gilberto Freyre, *Casa Grande & Senzala* (Rio de Janeiro, 1938), pp. 19, 22, 134–135, *passim*. Cf. Nestor Duarte, *A Ordem Privada e a Organização Politica Nacional* (São Paulo, 1939); and Antonio Candido, "The Brazilian Family," in T. Lynn Smith and Alexander Marchant (eds.), *Brazil: Portrait of Half a Continent* (New York, 1951), Chap. XIII.

dal type of social organization, and this great family is the
institution through which the white or near-white upper class
maintains its control. Of course this patriarchal family has
little in common with the equalitarian family of the United
States and western Europe.

Freyre also has indicated that Brazil's patriarchal, aristocratic, and slavocratic family was not merely transplanted
from the mother country, but that many of its characteristics
and functions were acquired in the New World. This was
due in part to a complete change in occupation, for in Portugal a considerable number of colonists who eventually came
to head Brazil's rural clans had been neither rich nor agriculturists. Probably the commercial-minded Portuguese would
have preferred possessions which had already been more
highly developed by the native peoples so that they could
have devoted themselves to trading and commercial pursuits.
But physical conditions of the land and the cultural attainments of the inhabitants determined otherwise. "Live and
absorbent organ of Brazilian social formation, the colonial
family united upon a base of rich economic resources and
slave labor a variety of social and economic functions."[2]

It is significant that nearly all of the functions of the family
came to be performed in a distinctive manner in Brazilian
society. Consider first the primary function of the family—
the reproduction of the species. As has been brought out in
other places, very few of the colonists were women, and mating between the Portuguese men and the Indian women began
from the very first. The white men seem to have had few
inhibitions about increasing the numbers of their followers
and dependents by fathering the children of numerous
concubines. On the other hand, the Indian women may have
been excessively sensual and strongly attracted by the white
men. In any case, they were impelled to give themselves to
the whites by the patrilineal nature of native society. Says
Capistrano de Abreu, as quoted by Freyre: "The mixture is
explained by the ambitions of the Indian women to have children belonging to the superior race, for according to the ideas
current among them importance was attached to relationship

[2] Freyre, *Casa Grande & Senzala*, 22.

on the paternal side only."[3] Whatever the causes may have been, the fact is that very early the illegitimate children came to bulk large among the patriarch's retinue of companions and followers. They did their share to contribute to the power and prestige of the master of the big house. To the mores that were set in this colonial epoch must be attributed the fact that illegitimacy still swells the Brazilian population and that very little distinction is made between legitimate and illegitimate children.

The economic functions of the family also underwent elaboration and change. The casa grande became a self-sufficient little world of its own, producing and processing nearly everything used by the patriarch, the great family which he headed, the slaves, and the agregados. Says Oliveira Vianna: "Because of their extreme economic independence, . . . derived from their omniproductive regime, and owing to the extraordinary extension of their economic base, these small rural societies lived almost without relations with their neighbors . . . so that they formed truly autonomous nuclei, each having its own economy, its own life, its own organization."[4]

Contributions from the New World were especially great in foods, food habits, and culinary practices. Because of the importance of Indian women in colonial society and because every agricultural effort was devoted to the production of sugar cane and not a food supply, even the master class of Brazilian society soon was eating such foods as corn and mandioca prepared in the Indian way.

The patriarchal, aristocratic, slavocratic family, or clan, also acquired functions rarely thought of in connection with its equalitarian counterpart. Freyre includes political power and control among these. He points out that "the rural family, or better, the latifundium family" early battled and eventually was successful against the attempts of the Jesuits to establish a theocracy, "a holy republic of 'Indians domesticated for Jesus' like those of Paraguay," where the caboclos

[3] *Ibid.,* 59.
[4] F. J. Oliveira Vianna, "O Povo Brasileiro e sua Evolução," *Recenseamento do Brazil,* 1920, Vol. I (Rio de Janeiro, 1922), 291. Cf. Candido, "The Brazilian Family, 303–304.

would obey only the priests and there would be no in-
dividuality or autonomy of person or of family."[5] The Jesuits were expulsed and "in Brazil in place of the cathedral
or church more powerful than the king himself would be
substituted the casa grande of the engenho."[6] Each patriarch
maintained his own little army, composed of Indians and
mixed bloods, and eventually the casa grande became so
powerful that it could defy the state with impunity. Giving
shelter and protection to men wanted by the law was a common form of demonstrating this power. "Dom Pedro II,"
we are told, "attempted to limit the omnipotency of the proprietors of engenhos, frequently the protectors of assassins."[7]
The banditry that continues to plague parts of Brazil, especially the northeastern region, probably is intimately associated with political powers possessed by the patriarchs of
Brazilian rural clans.

Finally it is important to note the religious function of the
great family in Brazil. As suggested above, during early colonial times there was keen rivalry between the landed proprietors and Jesuits for political power. The landowners won, the
Jesuits were driven from Brazil, and the casa grande, not the
church, became the dominant power in the colony. As a result
Catholicism in Brazil became "a religion or cult of the family
more than of a cathedral or a church."[8] Against the counsel
of the Jesuits, "the other clergymen and even monks, big
and fat, accommodated themselves to the functions of chap-
lains, of teaching padres, of uncles, of godfathers to the children; to a comfortable situation as members of the family,
persons of the household, allies and adherents of the great
rural proprietors, in the eighteenth century many of them
living in the same casas grandes."[9]

[5] Freyre, *Casa Grande & Senzala*, 22–23.
[6] *Ibid.*, 134.
[7] *Ibid.*
[8] *Ibid.*, 22.
[9] *Ibid.*, 135.

Size of the Family

In Brazil the stereotype of the family has tended to include seven persons, two parents and five children. This contrasts greatly with that of a father, mother, and two children which, especially before the Second World War, was so widely used to portray the typical family in the United States. Furthermore, the statistical basis for the Brazilian stereotype has been fully as adequate as that for the one prevailing in the United States. Thus the 1920 census found that the population of 30,625,331 was living in 3,962,585 dwellings, an average of 7.7 persons per household, compared with one of only 4.3 in the United States at the corresponding date.

More recently the data for both countries have become far more adequate and reliable, but the same sort of differences persist, differences which emphasize that the family and household in Brazil continue to be large. Accordingly, some of the more pertinent information has been analyzed and is presented graphically in Figure I. This illustration, which shows the percentage of each country's population living in families or households of stated sizes, demonstrates that the

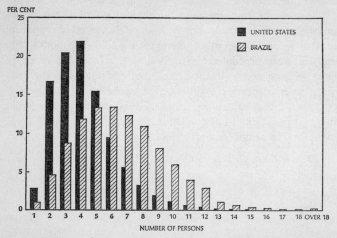

FIGURE I. Proportions of the populations of Brazil and the United States living in households of stated sizes, 1950.

average Brazilian is a member of a domestic group of six persons, whereas the average person in the United States is a member of one of only four persons. Furthermore, judging by these 1950 data and on a relative basis, one finds that the Brazilian is much more likely to be a member of a domestic circle of eight persons than the resident of the United States is to be included in one of six; the former is more likely to be included in a household of ten than the latter is to be in one of seven. Indeed, although households of ten or more persons have largely disappeared in the United States, considerable numbers of Brazilians still are living in those of eleven, twelve, and even more members.

The basic factor responsible for the large Brazilian family or household is, of course, the large numbers of children borne by Brazilian women. This has been discussed in Chapter VI, but in order to bring the matter into a still bolder relief, Figure II has been prepared. This graph shows for Brazil

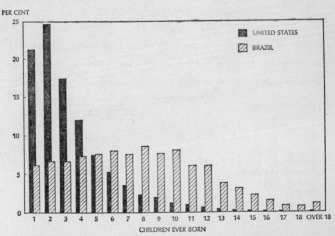

FIGURE II. Reported numbers of children ever born to women, ages 50–59, in Brazil and in the United States, 1950.

and the United States, respectively, the proportions of the women, aged 50–59 at the time of the census (who consequently may be considered to have completed their childbearing cycles) who reported that they had given birth to stated numbers of children. Any comment would be largely superfluous: the latest comprehensive statistical data fully support the widely held belief that the Brazilian family and household are large.

There are, of course, considerable variations with respect to the size of the family or household among the various segments into which the population may be divided. The census data, however, do not enable us to determine the nature and magnitude of many of these differences. They do indicate, however, that the tendency for the rural family to be larger than the urban, and the tendency for agriculturists to have larger families than those of persons in other lines of activity prevail in Brazil. See Table I. Nevertheless, one should note from observation of these data that the households of those engaged in public administration, in the liberal professions, and in commerce also are significantly above the average in size. Undoubtedly this is a reflection of the fact that

Table I.   Variations in Size of Household by Residence and Occupation of Head of Household, 1950 *

Residence and principal activity of head	Number of households	Persons per household
All residential areas	10,046,199	5.1
Urban areas	2,529,870	4.9
Suburban areas	1,200,498	4.8
Rural areas	6,315,831	5.3
Principal activity of head		
Agriculture, stockraising and forestry	5,405,224	5.5
Extractive industries	283,909	4.7
Manufacturing, construction and processing	1,064,105	4.9
Trade	546,618	5.3
Real estate, banking, credit and insurance	56,205	5.1
Services	468,563	4.6
Transportation, communication and storage	440,201	5.2
Liberal professions	45,917	5.3
Social activities	141,453	5.0
Public administration, legislation and justice	157,689	5.4
National defense and public security	117,175	5.0
Unpaid domestic service or attending school	900,907	4.0
Other activities or unknown	27,694	4.6
Inactive	390,540	4.5

*Compiled and computed from data in "Censo Demográfico," *VI Recenseamento Geral do Brasil, 1950,* I (Rio de Janeiro, 1956), 282–83.

the upper-class Brazilian family continues to be large and, in all probability, closely knit as well.

Composition of the Domestic Circle

The materials gathered in the 1950 census also make it possible to determine in a fairly acceptable manner the relative importance of the various elements that go to make up the Brazilian family or household. See Table II. Those who head the families, of whom the vast majority are men, make up almost one-fifth of the total, and their wives, along with the husbands of a part of the females who are heads of families, account for an additional 15 per cent. Children living at home with one or with both of their parents constitute more than one-half of all persons living in private households, and grandchildren, parents and grandparents, and other relatives of the heads are also present in considerable numbers (8.1 per cent of all). Servants living in the homes are not particularly numerous, but because of their presence in the households of those of the upper and middle socioeconomic classes, their "visibility" is especially great. The composition of households whose heads are in the ages 30–39 is not particularly different from that of households in general. See Table III. However, as is to be expected, the members of the nuclear family as such are of somewhat greater relative importance in the domestic circles of this particular type than they are in all households. Additional data on how the composition of the household varies with the age of the head are presented in Table IV, and finally, in order to show the importance of "broken families" of one kind or another, Table V has been prepared. In interpreting the materials in the latter, one must consider that only half of Brazil's widows (749,533 of a total of 1,496,539) were classified by the 1950 census as being heads of the households in which they resided. This undoubtedly is accounted for by the fact that the Brazilian family still retains to a high degree its function of caring for members, irrespective of age, who are unable to fend for themselves.

The materials in this section and the preceding one are or-

Table II. Persons Living in Private Households, Classified According to Their Relationship to Head of Household, by Sex, 1950*

Relationship to head of household	All persons Number	Per cent	Males Number	Per cent	Females Number	Per cent
Total	51,584,665	100.0	25,641,719	100.0	25,942,946	100.0
Head	10,046,199	19.5	8,827,218	34.4	1,218,981	4.7
Spouse	7,909,833	15.3	7,025	–	7,902,808	30.4
Child	26,891,483	52.1	13,850,238	54.0	13,041,245	50.3
Grandchild	1,040,949	2.0	526,566	2.1	514,383	2.0
Parent or parent-in-law	712,390	1.4	119,175	0.5	593,215	2.3
Grandparent	24,332	–	3,454	–	20,878	0.1
Other relative	2,417,547	4.7	1,143,006	4.5	1,274,541	4.9
Agregado	970,701	1.9	464,365	1.8	506,336	2.0
Roomer or boarder	854,624	1.7	463,604	1.8	391,020	1.5
Employee	707,931	1.4	232,676	0.9	475,255	1.8
Unknown	8,676	–	4,392	–	4,284	–

*Compiled and computed from data in "Censo Demográfico," VI Recenseamento Geral do Brasil, 1950, I (Rio de Janeiro, 1956), 280-81.

Table III. Composition of Brazilian Households That Are Headed by Persons Aged 30–39, 1950*

Relationship to head of household	Number of persons	Per cent of total	Number per household
Total	14,899,976	100.0	5.3
Head	2,804,288	18.8	1.0
Spouse	2,426,916	16.3	0.9
Child	8,146,748	54.7	2.9
Grandchild	12,322	0.1	–
Parent or parent-in-law	242,107	1.6	0.1
Grandparent	6,743	–	–
Other relative	613,758	4.1	0.2
Agregado	228,380	1.6	0.1
Roomer or boarder	206,811	1.4	0.1
Employee	206,578	1.4	0.1
Unknown	5,325	–	–

*Compiled and computed from data in "Censo Demográfico," *VI Recenseamento Geral do Brasil, 1950,* I (Rio de Janeiro, 1956), 282–83.

Table IV. Composition of the Brazilian Household in Relation to Age of Head of Household, 1950*

Age of head	Number of households	Persons per household		
		Total	Heads, spouses, and own children	Parents, grandparents, and grandchildren	Other relatives
Total	10,046,199	5.1	4.5	0.2	0.2
10–19	91,278	2.8	1.6	0.3	0.7
20–29	2,030,542	3.7	3.1	0.1	0.3
30–39	2,804,288	5.3	4.8	0.1	0.2
40–49	2,335,603	6.2	5.6	0.1	0.2
50–59	1,526,747	5.7	4.9	0.3	0.2
60–69	838,570	4.8	3.8	0.5	0.2
70–79	280,783	4.1	2.9	0.6	0.2
80 and over	87,979	3.5	2.5	0.6	0.2
Unknown	50,409	4.7	4.2	0.2	0.2

*Compiled and computed from data given in "Censo Demográfico," *VI Recenseamento Geral do Brasil, 1950,* I (Rio de Janeiro, 1956).

ganized from the standpoint of the two-generation or nuclear family. They indicate, however, that a considerable proportion of Brazilians have experience in three-generation households in the course of their formative years, and that much still remains of the old patriarchal family. Even in Rio de Janeiro one may find entire apartment houses occupied exclusively by an elderly couple and their descendants. The building may house ten or twelve familes of the children and grandchildren. In the rural districts an entire neighborhood will be made up of near relatives. Furthermore, not only is the Brazilian family of parents and children relatively large, but it remains closely tied into the larger kinship group headed by the patriarch of the clan.

Table V.   Heads of Brazilian Households, Classified According to Sex and Marital Condition, 1950*

Sex and marital condition	Number	Per cent
Total	10,046,199	100.0
Single males	965,954	9.6
Single females	282,056	2.8
Married males	7,493,760	74.6
Married females	172,753	1.7
Separated or divorced males	11,987	0.1
Separated or divorced females	9,382	0.1
Widowers	331,560	3.3
Widows	749,533	7.5
Unknown males	23,957	0.2
Unknown females	5,257	0.1

*Compiled and computed from data in "Censo Demográfico," VI Recenseamento Geral do Brasil, 1950, I (Rio de Janeiro, 1956).

Family Functions

In all societies the family is charged with the responsibility for performing certain necessary functions that are carried on not at all or only partially by other social institutions. These functions generally include (1) the reproduction of the race, (2) the care, sustenance, and rearing of children through the dependent ages, (3) the education and training of the young, (4) the induction of the members of the oncoming generation into the great society, and particularly establishment of their status in the various social groups, (5) recreation, (6) mutual aid and protection of members from enemies and dangers of all kinds, and (7) the care of the aged and other incapacitated members and kinfolk. Several observations may be made concerning the manner in which the Brazilian family is carrying on these essential functions.

REPRODUCTION OF THE RACE. The population of Brazil is multiplying at a very rapid rate. This means that the Brazilian family is performing this primary function in a manner that is equaled in few countries of the world. Nevertheless, the comparatively high rates of illegitimacy demonstrate that the family is not the exclusive agency for reproducing the race that it is in the United States and some other parts of the Western World.

It has been impossible for the present writer to determine the exact status of present-day Brazil with respect to illegitimacy, for the available data—and they are not at all recent—come only from Rio Grande do Sul, São Paulo, and the Distrito Federal, the most advanced portions of the nation. Even at that, it may be demonstrated that a considerable number of all Brazilians are born out of wedlock. The latest national summary is for the years 1931–1933 only, and those data are not very satisfactory. Of the 1,808,812 births registered by January 1, 1940, for that four-year period, 193,895 or 10.7 per cent were classed as illegitimate.[10]

Other fragmentary materials are available for a few of the states. For the state of Rio Grande do Sul data are available for the years 1910 to 1937, inclusive. Total births registered numbered 1,711,416, of which 173,814, or 10.2 per cent, were recorded as illegitimate.[11] For São Paulo data are at hand for the years 1930 to 1939, inclusive, and for 1942. In this most advanced of all Brazilian states the percentages of illegitimacy varied from 5.2 in 1930 to 8.4 in 1942, being 6.5 for the eleven years taken together.[12] In the city of Rio de Janeiro there were 34,620 births registered during 1940,

---

[10] *Anuário Estatístico do Brasil,* V (1939/1940), 121.

[11] *Anuário Demográfico do Rio Grande do Sul,* 1938, I, 80.

[12] The data are found in the *Resumo do Movimento Demógrafo-Sanitário do Estado de São Paulo,* for the years 1930–1942.

of which 4,573, or 13.2 per cent, were classed as illegitimate.[13] Most of the other states, especially those in the east and the north, do not include data on legitimacy among the demographic materials published, but Amazonas is an exception. Records completed up to January 1, 1940, contain this information for 2,108 births registered during the years 1930 to 1933, inclusive. Of this total, 432, or 20.5 per cent, were illegitimate.[14] Most of these births undoubtedly were registered in Manaus, the capital. Were the data available for the outlying areas, the proportion of illegitimacy probably would be much higher. It would also be high if the record for the states north of Minas Gerais were accessible. For example, the city of Bahia contained nearly 300,000 inhabitants in 1920. In 1922 there were 763 marriages recorded in the city and 4,617 births. More than one-half of the births, 2,432, or 53 per cent, were entered as illegitimate.[15] Prior to 1920 birth registration was confined mostly to a few of the larger cities in southern Brazil. The first issue of the *Annuario Estatistico do Brazil,* published in 1916, gave data on births for the years 1908 to 1912, inclusive, classified according to legitimacy, but only for the cities of Belo Horizonte, Curitiba, Rio de Janeiro, Florianópolis, Niterói, Pôrto Alegre, and São Paulo. During the five-year period the number of births registered in these seven cities totaled 196,286, a mere fraction of the actual number; of these, 36,395 (18.5 per cent) were classed as illegitimate. In the various cities percentages of illegitimacy were as follows: Belo Horizonte, 17.9; Curitiba, 11.1; Rio de Janeiro, 24.6; Florianópolis, 23.4; Niterói, 28.9; Pôrto Alegre, 22.4; and São Paulo, 6.9.[16] . . . .

CARING FOR CHILDREN. The high rate of reproduction and the numerous children mean that the care, sustenance, and rearing of children consume a comparatively large share of the time and economic resources of the family; at the same

[13] *Anuário Estatístico do Distrito Federal, 1941,* IX (Rio de Janeiro, 1942), 43.

[14] *Sinopse Estatística do Estado do Amazonas,* No. 4 (Rio de Janeiro, 1942), 26.

[15] Mario Ferreira Barboza, *Anuário Estatístico da Bahia—1923* (Bahia, 1924), 399.

[16] *Anuário Estatístico do Brazil,* I (1916), 402–403.

time the high mortality rates, especially through infancy, poor diets, poor housing, and so forth, would seem to indicate that there are many needed improvements to be made in child care. In the lower classes a high proportion of the children are on their own responsibility from a very tender age. However, any very satisfactory information on this subject belongs to the future.

EDUCATING THE YOUNG. Because of the lack of schools, the low percentage of children who are privileged to attend, and the shortness of the school period, Brazilian society must depend on the family for educating and training the young to a much greater degree than is general in Western society. Education acquired in this manner—by the boy's working with his father, the girl her mother, in the daily routine of living—is thorough. Rural Brazilians become excellent axmen, mule drivers, boatmen, craftsmen, fishers, hunters, and tillers highly skilled with the hoe. Millions of them are able to live in situations where the average citizen of the United States or Western Europe would perish of hunger and exposure. But education in the family contributes to maintaining the customary routine; it makes for very little change or progress. If the family lacks essential knowledge, habits, and skills, the deficiencies will be perpetuated generation after generation. Therefore, until Brazilian children can acquire a greater share of their mental equipment outside of the home, there is small chance for great progress in agriculture, health and sanitation, transportation, industry, or any other field which the industrial revolution has changed, or for change in rural mores.

ESTABLISHING SOCIAL STATUS. There has been little or no study of the subject, and so it is possible only from general observation to conclude that the Brazilian family is highly efficient in determining the position its members are to occupy in the classes and groups of the great society. In fact, since Brazilian society is rather highly stratified, with a strong tendency for social position to be inherited (the caste element) and relatively little vertical and horizontal social mobility, the accident of birth is almost all important as a determinant of which groups a man will belong to and what is to be his position on the social scale. This is not to deny that there is some shifting from one group to another, some rising and sinking, especially in the cities of southern Brazil. But it is intended to point out that the family determines for the great mass of Brazilians the groups to which they are to belong and their position in the class structure.

RECREATION. In recreation and all other social affairs the Brazilian family occupies a pre-eminent position. A very large part of all leisure time is spent in the company of the immediate family or near relatives. Even in Rio de Janeiro the married pair of middle- or upper-class status is obligated by the mores to dine at least once a week at the home of the husband's people and once a week with the wife's people. In the interior the visiting back and forth of relatives, both between those who live in the open country and between the farm people and their kinsmen in the towns and villages, is the chief type of social activity.

On occasion one may hear expressions of dissatisfaction by Brazilian leaders in educational and cultural affairs who indicate that family obligations prevent them from mingling socially as much as they would like with those of kindred interests. Moreover, for the visitor from abroad who is not fortunate enough to be "adopted" by one or more Brazilian families, the cohesiveness of the large kinship group may be a barrier that shuts him off from a satisfactory social relationship with his Brazilian fellows. As Hutchinson has emphasized: "The Brazilian social scientist usually has family responsibilities which are augmented by the network of extended family relationships which occupy most of the free time he has. This frequently makes it necessary to confine professional relationships to the working day only."[17]

MUTUAL AID AND PROTECTION. The highly segmented nature of Brazilian society, a revival of the feudal pattern of social organization, has made it necessary for the family to serve not only as the most important institution of mutual aid but also as the principal agency for providing protection for its members. This is especially true of the upper-class fam-

[17] Harry W. Hutchinson, *Field Guide to Brazil* (Washington, 1961), 37.

ily, the aristocratic possessors of the casa grande and the broad acreages surrounding it. The protecting arm of the patriarch is extended to all the members of his numerous clan; and the neighboring small farmer, along with the workers on the big estate, still finds it necessary to place himself under the protection of the master of the big house. Throughout much of Brazil local history continues to be written largely in terms of the feuds between one of these clans and another, but it is becoming more and more difficult for one clan openly to defy state and national governments.

CARING FOR THE AGED AND INFIRM. No one seems to have assembled data concerning the extent to which the Brazilian family serves as the social institution for caring for the aged and otherwise incapacitated members of society. However, from general observation it seems to have the principal part in this important social task. As one comes to know the rural communities and neighborhoods it is evident that a considerable number of the families are sheltering one or more grandparents, widowed sisters of the husband or wife, nieces or nephews, or other relatives. Many adopted children find places in Brazilian homes. A study would probably find that the Brazilian family continues to be highly important as an agency to care for the aged, the infirm, and for unmarried female relatives.

PART IV

—◆—

SOCIAL PROBLEMS, VALUES, CHANGE, AND DEVELOPMENT

Introductory Note

EVEN DURING an epoch of world-wide bewilderment and up-heaval, the societies of the various Latin American countries are distinguished for the variety of acute and chronic social or societal problems with which their leaders at all levels are forced to cope. Partially as a result of this and partly because of the recency with which they have been brought into the maelstrom of world-wide ideological, cultural, economic, and political tension, the pace of sociocultural change is very great in all of the countries of Latin America. Moreover, although particular events at specific times and places may seem to belie the fact, the process of development in all of its principal aspects (agricultural, industrial, economic, political, educational, and social) is going on at a rapid pace. To all of these features of societal perplexity, instability, change, and development, students of the modern period in Latin America must devote a great deal of attention. This section, therefore, is made up of selections which have a bearing on these problems.

To set forth a few of the salient facts about current social problems in Latin America, two fairly recent summaries are presented. The first of these, Selection Number 13, is an attempt to give in capsule form the nature and significance of six of what presently are recognized widely throughout Latin America as the major social problems afflicting the respective societies. It was prepared at the request of the organizers of the Sixth Latin American Sociological Congress held in Caracas, Venezuela, in 1961, presented in the original Spanish at the Congress, and published originally in the *Proceedings* of the same. The English text used here is a slightly enlarged and revised version of the same, as presented in a lecture at Louisiana State University. The second, Selection Number 14, was prepared at the invitation of Committee on

Foreign Relations of the United States Senate and presented at a session of its Subcommittee on American Republics Affairs on February 27, 1968. It was solicited for use as a part of the Hearings on the agricultural portions of the Survey of the Alliance for Progress, and, accordingly was restricted to some of the sociocultural aspects of agricultural problems in Latin America as a whole.

Many of the perplexities troubling Latin Americans of all social levels arise from the tremendous clash between traditional sociocultural values and those to which they are exposed as the world-wide process of the homogenization of society rapidly brings about a more equal distribution of the various cultural and social components throughout all parts of the world. Problems of this type had hampered the efforts of the various agencies of the United States government engaged in programs of technical assistance in Asia, Africa, and Latin America to a large extent as early as 1955; and that year three sociologists were invited to address the participants in the Sixth Conference for Agricultural Services in Foreign Areas, sponsored by the United States Department of Agriculture (in cooperation with the Land-Grant Colleges, and the International Cooperation Administration) and held in Washington, D.C., October 17–19. The general topic assigned was "Values Held by People in Latin America (or the Far East, or the Near East) which Affect Technical Cooperation," and T. Lynn Smith of the University of Florida, W. A. Anderson of Cornell University, and Afif I. Tannous of the U. S. Department of Agriculture presented papers for the respective great world areas. The three papers first appeared in the *Proceedings* of the conference, and then, in slightly revised versions, they were published as a group in *Rural Sociology*. This revised text is the one used as Selection Number 15.

Anyone who deals professionally with the problems afflicting Latin American societies and is involved in any of the attempts to mitigate them is almost sure to think of how some of the matters are handled in other parts of the world and to attempt in one way or another to promote social and cultural change and development. This in turn is likely to cause him to reflect about the ways in which such changes take place, and to use various expressions to denote the introduction in a given societal setting or certain operations that have proved successful in others. If he seriously studies the process involved it is entirely possible that he will develop some concern about the extent to which the attribution of volition to perfectly inanimate objects and even to pure abstractions is in vogue. This point in its relation to attempts to produce directed social change or development throughout Latin America was the core of the paper I presented in 1968 at the annual meeting of the Southern Sociological Society, and this is used as Selection Number 16.

Of all the changes and forces making for change throughout Latin America during the 1960's none have been more important and far reaching than the issue of agrarian reform and the mushroom growth of cities and towns. These two great aspects of sociocultural change also are the ones in which the development process has proceeded to the fullest extent. Accordingly six selections dealing with them are included in this volume. Three of them relate to agrarian reform and agricultural or rural development, and three to the process of urbanization. The first of those dealing with the changes and proposed changes in rural society, Selection Number 17, is the English text of a paper prepared for a Congress on "Les Problemes Agraires des Amériques." This meeting was organized by France's Centre National de la Recherche Scientifique and was held in Paris during October, 1965. The other two selections in this group, Numbers 18 and 19, are treatments of agrarian reform in Latin America as a whole and in Brazil, respectively. The first of these was prepared at the request of the editors of the *International Labour Review* and the second for a Conference on Brazilian Studies organized by and held at the University of Wisconsin.

The last three items in this section and in the volume embody attempts to set forth some of the more significant aspects of urbanization as that process is going on throughout Latin America. Of these Selection Number 20 is an attempt to present in summary form the most outstanding features of this cataclysmic transformation of Latin American societies. It was prepared by invitation and was published in a special issue (devoted to urbanization as a world-wide phenomenon) of the *International Journal of Comparative Sociology*.

Selection Number 21 is focused upon an analysis and description of the now rapidly changing functions of Latin America's cities. Finally, Selection Number 22 is a paper in which an attempt is made to show how the sociocultural values of Brazilian society have been affected by the sudden transformation of Brazil from a country that for over four centuries was overwhelmingly rural, agricultural, and pastoral, to one in which an urban mode of existence is the way of life of a majority of its people.

13 Current Social Problems in Latin America

———◆———

IT IS NECESSARY in the beginning of this discussion to emphasize that a social problem is not the same thing as a sociological problem. We sociologists have our technical problems of observation, classification, conceptionalization, etc., similar to those of any other science; and we also have the problems of measures and indexes, coefficients and tendencies, relationships and correlations in connection with our attempts to develop our science. But these are merely the technical problems with which a professional sociologist is confronted and not the problems of society as a whole. Genuine social problems, on the contrary, are society's problems, and the responsibility that the sociologist has in connection with their solution is similar to the responsibilities of the economist, the historian, the banker, the doctor, the lawyer, and other professional members of contemporary society. Thus first of all it is necessary to point out and to insist that a social problem is a problem of society as a whole.

There is still one additional prefatory word of caution that I desire to express. This is merely that there is a great deal of difference between the one who may observe, record, classify, analyze, and interpret the materials relating to unfavorable social realities, and one who is responsible for the existence of the social problems. Frequently, I fear, because sociologists are the ones to discover, analyze, describe, and publicize the nature of society's serious defects and short-

Lecture presented at Louisiana State University in Baton Rouge, on October 23, 1961. This is a slightly enlarged version of a paper delivered in the original Spanish at the VI Congreso Latinoamericano de Sociología and published in the Congress's *Memoria,* Vol. II, Caracas: Imprenta Nacional, 1961, pp. 305–319.

comings, they are credited with major responsibility for the existence of the social problems.

Definition of Social Problem

Let us next attempt to define rather precisely what is meant by a *social problem*. Of the two words involved, *social* is by far the easiest to dispose of. It merely denotes the collective aspects of life as distinct from the individual or the personal. An interplay of stimulus and response and a patterning of behavior, the essence of that which we designate as social, is, of course, present among others of those belonging to the animal kingdoms other than those classified as human; however, for our purposes it is best to limit social to the group activities of *homo sapiens*.

The other of the two words in the term is much more difficult. Any *problem*, personal or social, involves a perplexing situation or a troublesome question. It is a matter requiring action of some kind, something that simply cannot be ignored, which it is difficult to solve, to settle, or to handle in any other way. How can another world war, a catastrophe that probably would destroy civilization as we know it, be avoided? What can and should be done about the rapidly increasing numbers and proportions of aged persons in countries such as England, France, and the United States? Is mankind as a whole increasing more rapidly than it is possible for the food supply to be increased, and are we therefore facing the necessity of hanging out on our planet the sign "standing room only"? Are we rapidly destroying the thin layer of soil which covers the earth and upon which all of our lives depend, "plundering our planet"? In order to survive must we abandon our great metropolitan centers, and distribute ourselves in smaller communities throughout our countries? These are only a few of the questions troubling many people throughout the world as we move well along into the second half of the twentieth century.

Many social problems involve the idea of misconduct and maladjustment of one kind or another, activities thought to be detrimental to the wellbeing, or at least to the self-respect, of other members of the group. Prostitution, juvenile delinquency and crime—to mention only three—involve behavior generally considered as damaging to society; and ways and means for protecting and caring for abandoned children, the mentally deficient, and the mentally deranged frequently have developed largely because of a sense of shame produced by a comparison of the situation in one community, state, or nation with that in another.

Strictly speaking, if only one family in a community has a "problem" child a social problem might be thought to exist. If the case is an exaggerated one such a situation may indeed constitute a genuine social problem. However, it is much more definite if numerous families have "problem" children, and if the phenomenon is not confined to a few localities. Indeed, wayward children in large metropolitan centers, when organized into gangs, sometimes become a concern of people generally throughout the nation. The point I wish to stress is that for a social problem to be serious, it must arouse awareness and stimulate concern in a considerable portion of the members of the society, be it a neighborhood, a community, a state, a region, or a nation.

A social situation that is considered as a problem in one society is not necessarily so regarded in another. Probably the thousands of homeless waifs who thronged the growing cities of the United States during the second half of the nineteenth century were not considered as a serious social problem by the majority of the people who lived during that era. Even today, however, one cannot visit the world's major cities without finding many in which thousands of very young children appear to be confronting life strictly on their own. They seem to get enough food to keep body and soul together by begging a few small coins, shining shoes, carrying packages, or engaging in petty theft. They may be seen sleeping in doorways or on benches or newspapers in the parks. It is evident that they must live by their wits. Their chances in life appear to be very slim to many visitors from other parts. As yet, however, in many places such children appear to arouse relatively little concern on the part of the well-to-do and middle-class inhabitants of the cities in which they abound. The situation is rather generally taken for granted, and only a few ladies of uncommon humanitarian qualities seem to be trying to remedy it. Too few of those in a position to change the situation have been challenged, either in relation to their own personal welfare or by self-respect, to exert leadership in formulating and applying the necessary remedial measures. Therefore, the situation as yet poses no social problem for the societies directly concerned. It has not been defined by them as a social problem, and I must stress heavily that no phenomenon constitutes a social problem until it has been so defined by the members of the society concerned.

Once a social situation or condition, a social matter of any kind, is widely recognized and appraised as undesirable, corrective action is demanded as a matter of course. Then the problem actually arises because no tried and tested line of action is immediately evident. There may be several alternative ways of proceeding, none of which guarantees completely satisfactory results; or there may be an absolute impasse with no apparent course to pursue. Eventually, though, satisfactory solutions are found for some of the questions and they cease to be problems; others, however, seem to linger on for generation after generation, or to keep cropping up in one form or another every few years. Irrespective of what society we consider, it always is confronted with a multitude of perplexing matters, calling for action, and for which no tried-and-tested solutions are available.

The foregoing discussion leads me to the following definition: A social problem is a condition or a situation (1) of which a considerable share of the society's members are aware, (2) which they judge to be sufficiently out of line with their standards or such a threat to their well-being or self-respect that corrective action must be taken, but (3) about which the best course to pursue is highly perplexing and debatable.

The Identification of Social Problems in Latin America

Following this discussion of the nature and definition of social problems, let us next consider some of the conditions and situations in various parts of Latin America that have been identified and classified as social problems. In this connection some of the most penetrating observations and the most logical classification that has come to my attention is found in the work of one of Brazil's noted intellectuals, M. A. Teixeira de Freitas, based upon the social realities he encountered in connection with the 1920 census of population. Although made over forty years ago, and although there have since been some notable additions to the panorama of social problems in Brazil, the list prepared by this distinguished scholar still deserves careful consideration by everyone interested in Brazil. It also should prove highly suggestive for those in the other countries of North and South America. I myself find an invaluable reference in the twenty-seven unfavorable realities listed, which are as follows:

1. The excessive dispersion of the population which determines that a large part of the people live in complete social isolation, which is often accompanied by extreme physical and moral degradation.

2. The insufficiency, in some places, of religious participation, facilitating the moral regression provoked by other factors.

3. The lack, sufficiently general, of urban hygiene, and even of domestic and personal hygiene among some social strata.

4. Extreme misery among a part of the agricultural proletariat, subjecting this stratum of the population to the most precarious conditions of diet, dress, and shelter.

5. Frequent appearance of outbreaks of banditry.

6. The widespread abuse of alcohol.

7. The worst sanitary conditions in some zones, resulting from frequent recurrence of one or more of the greater maladies prevailing in the Brazilian interior (syphilis, lung troubles, digestive and intestinal ailments, leprosy, goiter, constipation, malaria and other fevers, grippe, etc.).

8. The exercise with impunity, in all parts, of the pernicious quackery of fetish doctors and charlatans.

9. The lack of medical and pharmaceutic assistance for the great mass of the rural population, and even in numerous centers of relative importance.

10. The injurious development of gambling.

11. Routine in the processes of work.

12. The blind, wasteful, and often unproductive and unnecessary devastation of the forests.

13. Deficient means of communication and transportation.

14. An insufficient number of cities, deserving of the title, as co-ordinating elements in the social and economic life.

15. Lack of technical and administrative organization in the great majority of agricultural undertakings.

16. Illiteracy among the mass of the rural population and even among a large part of the urban population.

17. Lack of the most rudimentary knowledge of practical life among most social classes.

18. Regression to illiteracy of the ex-students of the primary schools because the backwardness of social life does not provide them an opportunity to utilize the knowledge acquired.

19. Insufficient administrative assistance to the producing classes.

20. The corruptive action of motion pictures without the necessary censorship.

21. Extremely numerous cases in which landed estates are not divided among the heirs, unmarked, and lacking a legal title.

22. Great confusion in weights and measures.

23. The most rudimentary system of institutions of credit.

24. Irrationality in the administrative division of the territory.

25. Imperfect and deficient conduct in the administration of the municípios, resulting from the lack of knowledge of the boundaries, from extravagant cases of extra-territoriality of local governmental powers, and from the lack of co-ordination and combination of forces between the various municípios.

26. Lack of harmony and convergence in the undertakings of the various branches of public administration.

27. Deficient selection, discipline, stimulus and remuneration for the general body of public servants.[1]

I am certain that all of us will consider this a most formidable list of unfavorable social realities. Not all of them, however, can be labeled as social problems, in the sense in which earlier I defined the term. Many of them have not come to

[1] M. A. Teixeira de Freitas, "Educação Rural," *Revista Nacional de Educação*, Nos. 18–19, 1934.

be a concern to enough of the population to qualify; and for others, once the general public is sufficiently aware of their gravity, the course to follow in correcting the situation will be rather apparent.

Another important list of social problems in Latin America is the one contained in a 1945 publication of the Pan American Union, *Resoluciones, Acuerdos, Recomendaciones y Declaraciones de Conferencias Internacionales Americanas sobre Problemas Sociales.* This *bulletin* opens with a copy of the resolution on Social Problems adopted on the 30th of April 1923 at the Fifth Inter-American Conference which was held in Santiago de Chile. Because of the important role played by this resolution in the deliberations of subsequent conferences, and, through them, in helping bring so many unfavorable social realities through to the stage of social problems for which solutions have been found, it is well for us to review its six provisions.

The first of these recommended the inclusion, in the agendas of future Inter-American conferences, of study of international aspects of social problems. The second recommended that the nations included in the Pan American Union enact into law the principle, already in force in law in the United States, that human labor should not be considered as an article of commerce. The third, and somewhat lengthy, suggestion recommended that the various American republics should adopt measures to insure harmonious relations between capital and labor, and to provide for social welfare. It emphasized especially the need of developing legislation covering labor contracts, protection against occupational diseases and industrial accidents, and working conditions in general and especially those governing the employment of women and children. It likewise urged legislation dealing with housing, the home, health conditions and sanitation in offices, factories, and workshops, the encouragement of savings, and the development of credit systems for the masses. The fourth suggestion recommended the establishment, in each country, of social security systems, and especially of provisions relative to industrial accidents, sickness, and disablement. The fifth suggestion urged the various American states to establish technical divisions that would assemble pertinent statistical data, inspect working conditions, and exchange information with the departments in other countries. The sixth and final suggestion indicated the need for preparatory studies for the purpose of developing international treaties between the American republics relative to reciprocity in the treatment of workers or for establishing certain general norms to govern socio-economic policies.

Subsequently, the sixth, seventh, and eighth conferences, held in Havana, Montevideo, and Lima, respectively, adopted resolutions identifying as social problems conditions in each of the following areas: obligatory vacations for working mothers; conditions of the workers; food and drugs; the housing of workers; cooperation; the dignification of labor; the situation of intellectual workers; unemployment; kindergartens and nursery schools; immigration policies; living conditions of rural women; the Indian woman; freedom of association and expression for workers; and the protection of communities of Indians. The documents relative to all these are reproduced in the publication to which reference has been made.

Finally, the broad areas in which social problems presently are most acute and for which Latin American countries are seeking solutions may be identified by an examination of "The Charter of Punta del Este" through which in 1961 the American nations have agreed to establish an "Alliance for Progress within the Framework of Operation Pan America." This "Declaration to the Peoples of America," signed at Punta del Este Uruguay, August 17, 1961 pledges all countries signing it to work toward the following goals during the coming years, and the United States itself has guaranteed to "provide a major part of the minimum of twenty billion dollars, principally in public funds, which Latin America will require over the next ten years from all external sources in order to supplement its own efforts." Indeed the United States has committed itself to "provide from public funds, as an immediate contribution to the economic and social progress of Latin America, more than one billion dollars during the twelve months which began on March 13, 1961, when the Alliance for Progress was announced." One merely has to take note of the announced goals of this Alliance in order to be vividly aware of the range and scope of current social problems in Latin America. These stated goals are as follows:

To improve and strengthen democratic institutions through application of the principle of self-determination by the people.

To accelerate economic and social development, thus rapidly bringing about a substantial and steady increase in the average income in order to narrow the gap between the standard of living in Latin American countries and that enjoyed in the industrialized countries.

To carry out urban and rural housing programs to provide decent homes for all our people.

To encourage, in accordance with the characteristics of each country, programs of comprehensive agrarian reform, leading to the effective transformation, where required, of unjust structures and systems of land tenure and use; with a view to replacing latifundia and dwarf holdings by an equitable system of property so that, supplemented by timely and adequate credit, technical assistance and improved marketing arrangements, the land will become for the man who works it the basis of his economic stability, the foundation of his increasing welfare, and the guarantee of his freedom and dignity.

To assure fair wages and satisfactory working conditions to all our workers; to establish effective systems of labor-management relations and procedures for consultation and cooperation among government authorities, employers' associations, and trade unions in the interests of social and economic development.

To wipe out illiteracy; to extend, as quickly as possible, the benefits of primary education to all Latin Americans; and to provide broader facilities, on a vast scale, for secondary and technical training and for higher education.

To press forward with programs of health and sanitation in order to prevent sickness, combat contagious disease, and strengthen our human potential.

To reform tax laws, demanding more from those who have most, to punish tax evasion severely, and to redistribute the national income in order to benefit those who are most in need, while, at the same time, promoting savings and investment and reinvestment of capital.

To maintain monetary and fiscal policies which, while avoiding the disastrous effects of inflation or deflation, will protect the purchasing power of the many, guarantee the greatest possible price stability, and form an adequate basis for economic development.

To stimulate private enterprise in order to encourage the development of Latin American countries at a rate which will help them to provide jobs for their growing populations, to eliminate unemployment, and to take their place among the modern industrialized nations of the world.

To find a quick and lasting solution to the grave problem created by excessive price fluctuations in the basic exports of Latin American countries on which their prosperity so heavily depends.

To accelerate the integration of Latin America so as to stimulate the economic and social development of the Continent. This process has already begun through the General Treaty of Economic Integration of Central America and, in other countries, through the Latin American Free Trade Association.[2]

Six Important Current Social Problems

In the remainder of this lecture we shall attempt to describe briefly the nature of six of the most important current social problems with which the Latin American societies are confronted.

HEALTH. Matters related to the health of the population long have been of great concern throughout Latin America. During the past twenty-five years remarkable strides have been made in improving health and sanitary conditions, accompanied by precipitous declines in the death rates and rapid upsurges in the growth of population. Especially important has been the control of infectious and contagious diseases, and of anything against which injections and vaccinations prove to be effective. But the need for additional and more effective measures along many lines is widely recognized and urged by all the educated classes in the population. However, the control of many of the important causes

[2] "Declaration to the Peoples of America," Alliance for Progress (Official Documents Emanating from the Special Meeting of the Inter-American Economic and Social Council at the Ministerial Level), Punta del Este, Uruguay, August 5 to 17, 1961, pp. 1–2.

of death involves the safeguarding of water and milk supplies, much more widespread general education, changes in diet, changes in the care and feeding of children, sanitary improvements on a large scale, and many other things that are difficult and expensive. Even if there were general agreement on the objectives, various proposals of pooling community, state, and national resources in order to achieve those ends would prove to be unacceptable to important segments of the population. Despite the remarkable progress that has been made and that continues, questions related to health remain among the big social problems throughout Latin America.

ILLITERACY. This item should certainly figure prominently in any list of current social problems in Latin America. According to the results of the most recent censuses, most of them taken in 1950 or thereabouts, the proportions of illiterates among those 10 years of age and over—that is in the age levels after people are mature enough to have learned to read and write—range from lows of 14 per cent[3] in Argentina, 21 per cent in Costa Rica, 24 per cent in Cuba (1953), and 28 per cent in Panama, to highs of 57 per cent in the Dominican Republic, 60 per cent in El Salvador, and 65 per cent in Honduras. In Brazil the corresponding figure is 52, in Paraguay 32, in Ecuador 44, and in Colombia (1938) 44. These proportions are high, some of them extremely high, in a world in which a fundamental knowledge of reading, writing, and of somewhat complicated arithmetical calculations has come to be numbered among the basic necessities of life.

Throughout Latin America there seems to be a widespread dissatisfaction on the part of governmental officials, educators, leaders in business and finance, and the best-informed persons of all classes with the existing situation. Among the masses, too, general discontent with their own meager educational attainments and the prospects of schooling for their children is becoming more and more evident. Furthermore, there is on the part of an ever-enlarging part of the population

[3] Among those 14 years and over, the data are for 1947.

a fierce determination to bring about improvement in the educational showing of their country.

Many of the efforts that are being expended and the solutions being attempted have not as yet solved the problem of which the societies have become aware. Mexico's rural missions, Brazil's rural education campaign, and the national efforts attempted in Panama and elsewhere to get everyone who is able to read and write to pledge that he will teach another person to do so in the course of a year, certainly do much to advance the cause of general education in the various countries. But few persons, even among those who are engaged in the programs, seem to think that they are the ultimate answer to the problem. Satisfactory systems of general universal primary education are still to be devised, and the expansion of secondary educational facilities remains as a colossal task to be undertaken. In brief, the problem of illiteracy remains as one of the more important social problems in Latin America.

LATIFUNDISMO AND MINIFUNDISMO. These twin brothers which so stoutly oppose progress in providing social and economic well-being for the masses in Latin America are almost always classed as among the most important current social problems in Latin America. They are the raison d'être for the movements for agrarian reform throughout the Americas. . . .

In some countries, of course, such as Brazil, Bolivia, and Peru, *latifundismo* is considered as the all-important defect in the relations of man to the land, whereas in such Andean countries as Colombia and Ecuador *minifundismo* shares much of the opprobrium. Widely recognized is the fact that in many areas the bulk of the best lands are held in a few hands, while the great majority of those who live from agriculture are landless workers. In areas in which ownership is widespread, as along the Andean slopes in Colombia and Ecuador, the plots are far too small to produce even a minimum subsistence for the families who own them; hence the problem of *minifundismo*. In the areas of the large estates the general rule appears to be for the best land to be devoted merely to pastures for livestock with agriculture relegated to the steep slopes of the mountains, or, worse still, to be

deliberately withheld from any productive purposes whatsoever. Indeed, throughout Latin America, the term *latifundismo*
generally connotes a large area of idle land, or a large tract
deliberately withheld from productive purposes. Especially
acute is the problem—widely recognized and condemned by
the responsible officials of the ministries of agriculture and
other informed leaders—when the lands in the zone surrounding a great city such as Rio de Janeiro are concentrated into
latifundia and the production of essential foodstuffs for the
urban population is forced farther and farther away from the
centers of consumption.

With the phenomena of *latifundismo* and *minifundismo*
known and decried by many, including during the twentieth
century increasing numbers and proportions of the rural workers, it is not strange that various solutions are proposed.
Whatever the content of these proposals, and they are of
great variety and highly different quality, they come to be
dubbed almost universally as agrarian reform. Measures
proposed range all the way from merely seizing the large
estates and subdividing them among the workers, to the establishment of *ejidos,* as in Mexico, to the purchase of the
land and development of it into family-sized farms, owned
and operated by politically stable, middle-class farmers, as
once was the dream of Dr. Miguel López Pumarejo and some
of his associates in Colombia. But any proposal that is made
soon arouses opposition and unites those of the most diverse
philosophies to help block its success. In most of the countries, anything approaching a satisfactory solution remains a
thing of the future. *Latifundismo* and *minifundismo* remain
among the most important social problems in Latin America.

RURAL-URBAN MIGRATION. A fourth problem under consideration is that of the mass movement of rural workers to the
rapidly growing towns and cities of Latin America. Involved
in this are a host of specific problems, including the shortage of hands (at prevailing wage rates and with present
methods of production) in the rural areas; housing; health,
sanitary, transportation, and educational problems in the
towns and cities; and the shortage of dietary staples, food
riots, and mass political disturbances and pressures upon
legislative bodies in some of the cities. Most rural employ-

ers loudly deplore the loss of workers to the urban centers, and many leaders in the cities, and especially the government officials, tend to think that their problems would be greatly eased if the flow of people from the rural districts could be stopped. Frequent, very frequent, indeed, is the suggestion that many of those who have already migrated should be returned to the areas from which they have come.

But few of the migrants evidence any desire to leave the towns and cities. Instead they are prone to encourage relatives and friends in the country to join them in the urban districts. We probably shall see in most Latin American countries a speeding up of the movement, rather than a tendency for it to slow up.

Few Latin American countries are likely to attain the level of economic production and the levels and standards of living to which they aspire, until far larger proportions of their populations are steadily and remuneratively engaged in manufacture, transportation, commerce, and educational activities in the urban centers. What would life in the United States today be like, had all of those who have been born in our rural districts since 1900 remained on the farms?

THE SUBURBS. The serious social problem which Latin Americans designate as the *problema de los suburbios* is relatively new in the Latin American countries. Nevertheless today it is the principal preoccupation of many of the leaders in the Latin American countries and it is much in the thoughts of all those who are seeking to improve the social and economic conditions of the Latin American peoples. It already is a matter of which the great majority of the population is aware, which is considered to be intolerable, and for which as yet no adequate solution has been devised. Instead year after year it is a problem that is increasing in magnitude and complexity.

Let us consider, for example, some of the data supplied by *La Mision de Lima* in the year 1958.[4] Already at that time in a band surrounding Peru's capital 200,000 persons were congregated in 80 unhealthful slums. This was characterized as a complex human and social problem affecting the

[4] As reported in *El Comércio* of Lima, May 30, 1958.

capital principally, but which was beginning to extend to all of the coastal cities, and already was serious at Arequipa, Chiclayo and the industrial zone of Chimbote. The movement of rural people to Lima, in search of a better life and especially by the desire for better housing, was given by the reporter as the principal cause for the establishment of these suburban slums. These suburbs, in turn, were described as mere aggregations of hovels, in districts lacking water, sewage facilities, and electricity, where a promiscuous population estimated at 200,000 formed "a belt of hunger and unhealthfulness, of illiteracy and a subhuman existence, of beings hardly integrated into the civilized life of the cities. The rapid growth of population assumes its most tragic aspects in these zones. Thousands of children sleep on the ground, along with their parents, with no other covering than the clothing they wear. Many of them are unexpected and even uncared for guests, since they arrive in households where there is no father and where they constitute during their infancy a terrible burden upon the mother, who, with a baby in her arms, finds it difficult to obtain work." The source cited indicates that these slums surrounding Lima are made up of those who have invaded and are squatters upon lands belonging to the state, the county, and to private owners. In these belts the poor build such shelters as they can, using everything from bricks and cement, to adobes, poles, mats and pieces of tin. Collectively they oppose all attempts of the government to move them to other places where they might be settled under more advantageous conditions. "These slums which have been established on the hills and other lands surrounding Lima do not differ in their organizational patterns from those of native Indian communities."

The belt of slums surrounding Lima is not exceptional. As the author has already done, each of you may encounter similar belts of "suburbs" surrounding a major part of the cities of Latin America. He has in his possession, for example, the documentation describing such a social problem at Bogotá, Rio de Janeiro, Recife, Bahia, Caracas, Cali, Barranquilla, and many other important cities. For present purposes, probably, it is sufficient to call attention to the case of Bogotá, capital of Colombia. *La República* of Bogotá for June 8,

1958, informs us that in the capital of Colombia, that "100,000 persons lack services," "150 clandestine subdivisions seek them [water, sewage disposal, electricity]," and that on "June 15 there will be a meeting of the representatives of these *barrios.*" The story goes on to say that the representatives of the 150 districts on the periphery will request the extension of water mains, sewage lines, electric lines, and telephone lines, in addition to such things as the establishment of market places, the alignment of streets, etc. The districts affected by the lack of such basic services are generally designated as "clandestine" were built up outside the urban perimeter of the capital. There the enormous influx of persons seeking to escape the violence in the rural districts have produced in recent years an enormous congestion that has broken over the limits of the city to extend in an uncontrolled manner into the surrounding areas.

In these sections the lack of water, lack of food, lack of schools, etc. create problems that demand an immediate solution. The people themselves are not to be blamed because they are forced to live beyond the city's limits, and the budget of the city is not sufficient to provide for the services in the 150 barrios involved. Hence, these suburbs of Bogotá, along with those of Lima, of Recife, of Santiago, and of dozens of other major centers in Latin America, today constitute major social problems for the societies in which they are located.

THE GROWING GAP BETWEEN THE STANDARD OF LIVING AND THE LEVEL OF LIVING. During the last fifty years a veritable revolution has taken place in the expectations of the masses of the population throughout Latin America, and this has been accompanied by substantial increases in the average amounts of goods and services actually consumed by the people. However, the rise in expectations, in what the sociologist and the economist call the standard of living, has been more rapid than that in actual consumption practices, or the level of living. As a result, since 1910, and especially since 1935, the gap of the spread between the two has become much more pronounced. The masses throughout Latin America now aspire by the millions to the ownership of small parcels of land, to a voice in political affairs and to a way of life more comparable with that they see enjoyed by the more favored classes in their own society and that which they have been told prevails in some other parts of the world. But this is also to say that it has been easier for politicians to promise than to fulfill, for agitators to arouse than for statesmen to satisfy, for the people to aspire than for them to attain, and for the standard of living to rise than for the level of living to go up to a comparable degree. As a result the gap between the actual plane of life of the masses in Latin America and that on which they feel entitled to live is much greater that it was fifty or even twenty-five years ago.

To put it rather briefly, social and economic ferment and a demand for change has become the order of the day, and there is little or no attempt nor even desire to distinguish between the elements in the old order that have worked to the advantage of the masses and those that have been responsible for their woes.

The revolution of expectations discussed here is a recent development. Even in the early 1930's the bulk of the people in most of the Latin American countries lived in highly rural communities, where, because of poor facilities for communication and transportation and the low educational level, they were almost completely sealed off from contact with people in other parts of the world and even from association with their fellows in nearby sections of their own countries. They were in great part illiterate and landless agricultural workers, living as had their ancestors for many generations in huts and hovels, poorly clad and fed and generally completely docile in the hands of the numerically small landowning class and their representatives. Except in Mexico and for a few sporadic outbreaks in widely separated sections in other countries, when they did resort to arms it was as soldiers in the personal armies of local aristocratic chieftains and not in any way as a part of a rising in which the masses sought to overturn their masters and the system they represented.

Reams of paper could be filled with discussions of the many forces and factors which have played a part in generating the social ferment presently at work throughout Latin America and the increased gap which this has engendered between the level of living and the standard of living. But even in a short article such as this some of these forces and factors should be listed. Those which in the judgment of the present writer deserve high priority in this respect are as follows: (1) the development and extension of modern means of communication and transportation, including those that link one country with another as well as those that help unite the various sections of a given country; (2) considerable headway in developing what eventually may become a system of universal elementary education in each of the countries; (3) greatly increased contacts between Latin Americans and the inhabitants of other parts of the world; (4) the enactment in all of the countries involved of substantial social legislation pertaining to hours of work, minimum wages, job security, paid vacations, sick leave with pay, severance pay and the rights of labor to organize; and (5) an increased tendency to substitute an appeal to the electorate and the vote for the military coup as the means of transferring power from one regime to another.

The problems occasioned by the enormous population growth and the rapid development of an urbanized society in Latin America are numerous but not insoluble. It is however the ever-widening gap between the actual level of living and the standard of living that poses the greatest challenge in Latin America during the second half of the twentieth century.

14 Current Problems of Agriculture in Latin America

[AT THE INVITATION of Senator J. W. Fulbright, Chairman of the Senate Committee on Foreign Relations, I appeared on February 27, 1968, at the hearings on the Alliance for Progress, being conducted by the Subcommittee on American Republics Affairs. My assignment was to comment upon a statement which had been prepared by Professors William C. Thiesenhusen and Marion R. Brown of the University of Wisconsin, and to present some of my own materials.]

1. POPULATION PROBLEMS. I fully support the highly significant statements by Professor Thiesenhusen and Brown relative to population trends and problems in Latin America. Indeed it is with difficulty that I restrain myself from entering into a lengthy exposition of this subject, since, among other things, recently at the request of The Select Commission on Western Hemisphere Immigration I completed a study of *The Growth of Population in Central and South America, 1940 to 1970.* My own conclusions are fully in accord with the materials in the study prepared for this Subcommittee, except that they indicate the lowest annual rate of increase of population to be 1.3 per cent for Uruguay, whereas my own figure for that country is substantially higher, or 1.8 per cent.

My friends from the University of Wisconsin also are correct in insisting upon separate consideration of the changes in the population and the labor force in the rural and agri-

---

Reprinted from "Statement of Prof. T. Lynn Smith on 'Problems of Agriculture,'" in *Survey of the Alliance for Progress: Hearings before the Subcommittee on American Republics Affairs of the Committee on Foreign Relations, United States Senate,* Washington: U. S. Government Printing Office, 1968, pp. 18–26.

cultural sections of the various countries. To supplement what they have said on this subject, the Senators may be interested in a couple of additional points. First, my own studies show that of approximately 71,000,000 people enumerated in Brazil's census of 1960, more than 7,000,000, or about one person out of ten, personally had moved from the rural districts to urban places during the decade ending in 1960. Moreover, there is nothing to indicate that this exodus has slowed appreciably since 1960. Second, I wish to present a few of the results of a study of depopulation in Colombia recently completed and submitted as a master's thesis at the University of Florida by Professor Carlos Escalante of the Colombia's National University. This careful analysis of changes during the intercensal period 1951 to 1964 showed that almost 20 per cent of all of the county-like political subdivisions called *municípios* had fewer inhabitants in 1964 than they had thirteen years earlier.

Professor Escalante also sought to bring his data to bear upon another of the significant topics discussed by Professors Thiesenhusen and Brown, namely, the effect of mechanization (or motorization) of agriculture upon the need for workers in the agricultural districts. Admittedly, the procedures he had to use were rather crude and inadequate, but he was able to demonstrate that there was no correlation between the introduction of tractors for use on the farms and the increase or decrease in the rural population. In some areas the adoption of this source of power was accompanied by a falling off in the numbers of people in the rural districts, but in others exactly the opposite was true. Professor Escalante explained this as follows: in those sections in which the land was actually being used for the production of crops, the substitution of the tractor and attached implements for the traditional hand tools and hoe culture resulted in substantial displacement of workers. But, on the other hand, in the extensive areas, including large segments of the most fertile and most favorably located lands, the introduction of the tractor actually meant a superimposition of tillage and the growing of crops upon the traditional rudimentary pastoral economy of the nation. The result was a substantial increase in the need for workers, and hence a significant increase in the population.

2. A CURIOUS "INVERSION" OF LAND-USE: PASTURES IN THE VALLEYS AND CULTIVATED FIELDS ON THE HILLSIDES. Professor Escalante's reasoning leads me to inject here a comment upon the history of agriculture in Spanish America which I personally consider to be of primordial importance in gaining an understanding of what presently is taking place to the South of the Rio Grande. At the time of the conquest of America, Spain was not an agricultural country, but one in which the livestock interests ruled supreme. The conquistadores quickly seized the best lands, the fertile plains which the native Indians were cultivating foot by foot in order to grow the crops of corn, potatoes, beans, and other crops on which their livelihood depended, and transformed these into pastures for their horses and cattle. The pigs which functioned as the commissaries for the bands of explorers and conquerors also served as the spear points of the attacks upon the Indians' cornfields and potato patches. This forced the natives to "abandon" their traditional fields, which in keeping with the King's orders, made them legally eligible for assignment to members of the expeditions. In this manner in many densely populated areas the Spaniards quickly took over for their own pastoral activities the larger portions of what had been the cultivated lands of the Indians, and the subjected natives were forced to make their plantings on the steep slopes (which never should have been cultivated), in the coves, and in other out-of-the-way places not wanted by the overlords. In many places such as the great Savanna of Bogotá, the extensive coastal plains along the Caribbean, and the fabulously fertile Cauca Valley, this merely meant putting into "cold storage" the best lands in the country; and since the close of the Second World War some of them again are being used to grow crops. However, in Peru, where the Incas had spent thousands of years applying advanced engineering skills and enormous amounts of labor in terracing the precipitous mountainsides and perfecting an irrigation system to water their almost vertically superimposed fields, the results were tragic to the extreme. These European masters made no at-

tempt to expand the agricultural base of the civilization; but their herds quickly destroyed large parts of it. Almost from the moment when their livestock were allowed to range about at will, here and there a few stones were loosened from one of the retaining walls of the terraces, some of the canals became blocked at various places, and the waters began spilling out of their prepared channels and down the mountainside. Today we see the results—a major part of the great engineering achievements of the Incas have been irredeemably destroyed by the gully erosion on a horrendous scale.

3. THE CONCENTRATION IN THE OWNERSHIP AND CONTROL OF THE LAND AND THE PROBLEM OF LARGE, POORLY-MANAGED FARMS, PLANTATIONS, AND RANCHES. The process just described whereby, in many of the most densely populated parts of the New World, the Spaniards seized the cultivated lands of the Indians and converted them into pastures for livestock was largely responsible for another of the great agricultural problems which Drs. Thiesenhusen and Brown have called to our attention. This is the high degree to which the ownership and control of the land is concentrated in the hands of the members of a few affluent families. Indeed, this maldistribution of the property rights to the land, which existed almost unchallenged for over 400 years, has been since 1950 the most burning issue in Latin America. (In Mexico the upheaval began about 1917.) It is the central feature of the agitation, proposals, plans, and programs for what most Latin Americans persistently designate as "Agrarian Reform."

In talking about this topic I limit my remarks to those parts of the subject that pertain strictly to what may be denoted as the *"hacienda system."*[1] Moreover, for the most part I

---

[1] I use this term generically to include, along with the hacienda systems of the vast majority of the Latin American countries, the *estancia system* of Argentina, Uruguay, and southern Brazil; the *fundo system* of Chile; and the *fazenda system* of most of Brazil. In all of them the use of large amounts of land, the employment of relatively little operating capital, inputs of management so parsimonious as to be almost nonexistent, and lavish use of servile, unskilled laborers are central features. I do not include the large plantations which are devoted to the intensive use of land for the production of coffee, cotton, sugar-cane, etc.

shall merely list the basic features, leaving discussion of them to come later if it is desired. These are as follows:

a. The concentration of the ownership of the best located and most fertile lands in the hands of a few affluent and powerful owners.[2]

[2] I must stress that in most of the countries this is even greater than is indicated by the data presented by Professors Thiesenhusen and Brown. I, myself, was one of the first, and perhaps actually the first, to apply the conventional techniques in this type of analysis of data for the Latin American countries. The procedure is to take the materials from the census classification of farms according to size and to calculate the proportions of the land in the farms which are above a stated minimum in size. If each farm, ranch, or plantation were operated by its proprietor, and if each owner had one and only one farm, expressions such as "From 5 to 10 per cent of the landowners in Latin America control from 70 to 90 per cent of the agricultural land," would mean almost exactly what they say. The fact that not all of the farm operators are owners or farm managers, however, is of no great consequence in dealing with Latin America. There, as in the United States (except on southern plantations which still use the sharecropping system, and on the holdings of banks, insurance companies, etc.), and quite unlike the situation in Great Britain, the size of the landholding is essentially the same thing as the size of the farm.

The other difficulty involved is much more serious. The assumption, which necessarily is implicit on the part of those of us who make the computations, that each large proprietor has one and only one estate results in a gross understatement of the actual degree of concentration in the ownership of the property rights to the land. Actually, in the compilations of data in the censuses of agriculture, a given proprietor who owns two or more tracts of land which do not adjoin one another, or which extend into two or more of the county-like municípios, is counted not once but as many times as the number of farms, ranches, plantations, recreational places, etc., included in his holdings of real estate. That this introduces serious error into our computations of the extent to which a few upper-class families own and control the land in Latin America I am certain, but the amount of this distortion I am unable to determine. Permit me to indicate, however, that during the years from 1935 on I personally have visited several hundred of the largest landed estates in the area extending from northern Mexico to central Chile and central Argentina. Generally this has been in the company of the proprietors themselves. My memory is stocked with recollections of these rich experiences, and my journals are replete with details about the haciendas and plantations visited. It may be that during those years I actually was on the grounds of some large rural establishment in which that tract of land was the

b. In Spanish American countries most of the large landowners do not live on their estates. Instead they reside in the national and provincial capitals and visit their ranches and plantations only at rare intervals. In Brazil, however, traditionally the owner of the large estate has had his principal mansion and his seat of operations on the land; but even there as sugar-cane plantations, coffee plantations, etc., have come to be owned by "family corporations," fewer and fewer planters are living on their fazendas and *usinas*.

c. Very few of those who manage the large farms and ranches for their absentee owners have had any training in modern agriculture and animal husbandry. Likewise not many have any particular managerial ability. Often they are merely members of the humble laboring class who have been left in charge. As a result agricultural activities in many parts of Latin America suffer acutely from the lack of proper amounts and quality of management.

d. For the reasons already enumerated, production for the market, or the commercialization of agricultural and pastoral enterprises, has hardly begun in many of the potentially most productive portions of Latin America.

e. The predilection in the hacienda system is for a kind of rudimentary cattle ranching, rather than the growing of crops. Indeed the powerful cattlemen who exercise great control in national affairs often practically suppress crop enterprises and even the farrowing and fattening of pigs. Moreover, as Drs. Thiesenhusen and Brown have stressed, even if improved breeds of livestock are introduced, often this is accompanied by little or no effort to better the pastures.

f. The status of the workers in the hacienda system, who collectively make up the bulk of the rural population and until very recently at least, the majority of the national population in most of the countries, traditionally has been of a servile or semi-servile type. The relationships between master

---

only one owned by its proprietor; but if such were the case neither my memory nor my journal now enables me to recall that fact. On the other hand, both my memory and my journal are crammed with information about cases in which the owner of the estate I was visiting also possessed one, two, three, or even more, large holdings in various parts of his country.

(or his major domo) and man have been those which gave
the noun *peonage* to the English language; and as is rather
generally the case throughout the world and all through the
span of history, wherever haciendas and other large estates
monopolize the land severe exploitation of the workers is a
part of the system.

4. DEFECTIVE LAND SURVEYS AND TITLES. Most Latin American countries are severely handicapped in their efforts to
solve their agricultural problems by the defective systems used
in surveying the boundaries of farms and ranches and record-
ing the titles to the same.[3] Briefly stated the surveys are both
indefinite and indeterminate, and most of the markers used
are impermanent. The result in many of the countries (such
as Brazil and Colombia) is quarrels, conflicts, and protracted
lawsuits on a scale comparable to those which eventually
forced Daniel Boone and many of his contemporaries to move
on west to Missouri. The property lines run from stone to
stone. They follow this or that watercourse or dry wash.
Frequently they are described as following the divide between
two streams. And often the land of Mr. A is described as
bounded on one side by the property of Mr. B, while con-
versely B's land is described as being bounded in part by Mr.
A's land. In the deeds it is almost universal practice to state
the area and then to qualify it by adding the words *"mas o
menos"* or more or less. All of this is complicated to the extreme by plagues of squatters (simple country folk who seek
some place in which they can make small crops of corn,
beans, manioc, potatoes, yams, and so on, with which to feed
their families) who infest extensive areas in Central America,
Colombia, Venezuela, Ecuador, Brazil, Peru, and some of
the other countries.

In order to illustrate the seriousness of this problem let me
mention a few specific facts. First, the seriousness of this
problem was the reason I was sent to Colombia in 1943 by
the U. S. Department of State at the request of Dr. Miguel

[3] The practices still being used in the transfer of portions of the
public domain to private ownership, are about the same as those
employed in our own country before the genius of Jefferson gave
us our official "checker board" system.

López Pumarejo, the director of Colombia's national credit agency (The Caja de Credito Agrario) and brother of Alfonso López then serving his second term as President of Colombia. Second, during the first three years of its existence, a period ending in June 1965, Colombia's new Agrarian Reform Institute retrieved for the public domain, through exercising the right of eminent domain to lands illegally being held in estates of 2,000 hectares or more in size or merely by the "owners" surrendering lands without the institution of lawsuits, a total of 1,327,225 hectares.[4] Third, I wish to refer to a case in which the problem of clouded titles was solved, as given in the words of Dr. Hilgard O'Reilly Sternberg, Brazil's most accomplished geographer, now a professor at the University of California (Berkeley):

> Take, for instance, the matter of clear-cut titles of ownership. A profitable lesson can be learned from what is perhaps the most successful of all large-scale pioneering settlement ventures in Brazil—that carried out by a railroad and colonization company in northwestern Parana state. In order to guarantee future purchasers clear title to the land, the enterprise bought up all titles presented—even if it meant acquiring the same tract five or six times.[5]

Fourth, and finally, let me mention the case of Brasília. Today there is in the courts of Brazil the largest case in that nation's history. According to the *Correio da Manha,* one of Brazil's leading daily newspapers, of April 23, 1961, there were scattered throughout Brazil some 40,000 plaintiffs all claiming to be owners of parts of the land on which the new capital city had been built. Together they were demanding an indemnity of 120 billion *cruzeiros* (about $425,000,000).

5. WASTEFUL INEFFICIENT METHODS OF FARMING. The continued reliance upon antiquated ways or techniques of farming certainly deserves mention in any list, however brief, of the current problems of agriculture in Latin America. Drs. Thiesenhusen and Brown have pointed to some of these, and

[4] INCORA, *1964: Third Year of Agrarian Reform in Colombia,* Bogotá: Imprensa Nacional de Colombia, 1965, p. 3.

[5] "Brazil: Complex Giant," *Foreign Affairs,* January, 1965, pp. 303–304.

I desire to supplement what they have said. Let me begin by indicating that as we meet here this morning, when mankind is well within the portentous portals of the nuclear age, tens of millions of Latin America's farmers still are relying upon ways of preparing seed beds, caring for the crops, taking the harvest, and transporting things on the farm and from farm to market that are in no way more advanced than those used in Babylonia during the days of Hammurabi. At that time those using the fertile flood plains of the Tigris and Euphrates, and also the agriculturists in the Valley of the Nile, were already at the stage in which they were adding to the strength of their arms by the use of a crude wooden plow, the lumbering ox, and practical applications of the principle of the wheel. A comparable degree of modernization of agricultural procedures has not yet been attained by perhaps as many as one-half of all the Latin Americans who depend upon agricultural activities for a livelihood.

I classify man's ways or methods of securing products from the soil into six major categories,[6] namely: (a) river-bank plantings, or the system in which the woman saves some seeds and presses them with the ball of her foot into the soft, spongy mold she finds on the banks of a falling stream; (b) felling and burning, or what I have designated sometimes as "fire agriculture," in which a seed bed is prepared by felling and burning a portion of a forest, and then seeds are dibbled into the soft, pliable, ash-covered spots between the charred stumps and logs merely with the use of the big toe, a digging stick, or in most advanced stages of the system, with the aid of a crude hoe;[7] (c) hoe culture; (d) rudimentary

[6] For descriptions of these and analyses of their roles in Brazilian and Colombian societies see, T. Lynn Smith, *Brazil: People and Institutions,* third edition, Baton Rouge: Louisiana State University Press, 1963, Chapter XV, and T. Lynn Smith, *Colombia: Social Structure and the Process of Development,* Gainesville: University of Florida Press, 1967, Chapter 5.

[7] The persistence of this highly integrated system of farming certainly is a major problem in vast portions of Brazil, in all of its neighbors from Paraguay on the south to Venezuela on the north, and also in many parts of Central America. The procedures involved are as follows:

a. At the beginning of the dry season the humble countryman

plow culture, a complex involving a plow made of a forked stick, oxen or water buffaloes as draft animals, and even the principle of the wheel (as applied in a clumsy oxcart) as its key components; (e) advanced plow culture, characterized by the metal plow, the use of horses or mules as draft animals, the four-wheeled farm wagon, etc., which the families of some of us and our neighbors knew and used in the family-sized farming districts of the United States until about 1920; and (f) mechanized or motorized farming with the tractor and its associated implements and machines as the central components of the most advanced system man has devised for cultivating the soil. Because of the difficulties those of us who deal professionally with agricultural matters have about terminology, perhaps I should stress that the first two of these types or systems are ones in which there is *no tillage or cultivation* whatsoever, for we like many others almost instinctively tend to think of tillage or cultivation and the growing of crops as denoting exactly the same thing.

---

selects a favorable site in the virgin forest or almost equally mature second growth.

b. With his ax he spends four or five months felling the trees growing on an acre or so of ground.

c. As the signs indicate that the rains are about to commence, he fires the entire lot of fallen timber, and even follows through to some extent by piling and burning some of the limbs and branches not consumed in the first enormous bonfire.

d. With the big toe, or a digging stick, or in rare instances a hoe, he dibbles into the ash-covered terrain, in spots between the stumps and charred logs, some seeds of corn, beans, rice, and other staples.

e. He may or may not use some of the unburned limbs of the trees to construct a crude fence about the plantings, and he generally will use his machete to cut down a time or two the suckers which shoot up from the trunks of the trees.

f. When the crop is mature he takes the harvest.

g. If the forest does not hasten to restore itself he may plant another crop in the clearing, but often the next year and almost always by the second the hardening of the ground, weeds, and new growth forces him to select another favorable location where he repeats the process, leaving the "old field" to revert to forest.

h. After 20 or 30 years have passed the second growth generally is high enough and heavy enough to enable another "farmer" to use the land for the purpose of securing from nature a few pecks of corn, rice, beans, or manioc.

Varieties b and c in this series, or "felling and burning" (*rozar* in Spanish and *derrubadas e quemadas* in Portuguese) and hoe culture, respectively, compete very closely for the dubious distinction of being the system by means of which Latin American societies presently are doing most to destroy the natural resources of their countries, needlessly waste the life blood of the rural masses of their populations, and forego the opportunities to develop a sound agricultural basis for their burgeoning urban mode of existence.[8] Type a, the most primitive one of all, presently does not rank in importance with either felling and burning, or hoe culture, but even it still persists in many places throughout the Amazon Basin; and one of its variations, plantings made in the beds of intermittent streams when the water ceases to flow, are part of the way of life in Brazil's vast, problem-stricken Northeast. The most advanced type of agricultural technology possessed by the Spaniards and Portuguese in 1500, i.e., rudimentary plow culture, still competes to some extent with felling and burning and hoe culture in many parts of Latin America; and advanced plow culture is found in sections of south Brazil, southern Chile, and a few other scattered localities in which immigrants of European origin settled during the nineteenth century. Elsewhere, efforts to transplant this highly important method of farming have met with slight success, possibly because an experienced "plowman" and horses as draft animals rarely, if ever, figured in the "experiments." Finally, mechanized or motorized farming presently is doing much to enable agriculture in selected parts of Latin America to enter the twentieth century. In this case, in contrast with the oft-

[8] Consider in connection with this statement, for example, the fact which emerges from an analysis of the results of Colombia's first census of agriculture taken in 1960. In that important country, one which in many ways may be considered as the nation most nearly representative of the 20 in the group, only seven years ago fully 75 per cent of all the heads of households who were dependent upon agricultural activities for a livelihood had to rely exclusively upon themselves, their wives and their children as the sources of power used in growing and transporting their products. They had neither draft animals, pack animals, or mechanical power of any kind to aid them in their work. T. Lynn Smith, *The Process of Rural Development in Latin America,* Gainesville: University of Florida Press, 1967, pp. 45–47; and Smith, *Colombia,* pp. 208–211.

repeated and on the whole severely disappointing attempts to transplant advanced plow culture into Latin American settings, everyone recognizes that the system as a whole must be introduced. Thus the endeavors always include, along with the tractor, its many attachments, the implements and machines constructed expressly for use with it, and an experienced mechanic.

6. DEFECTIVE TYPES OF FARMING. To the members of a Subcommittee whose distinguished membership includes three Senators from states that are entirely or partially within our fabulously productive "corn belt" I take especial pleasure in presenting my next point. Let me start by saying that I have observed carefully during a period of more than 25 years in areas extending from the Rio Grande to Patagonia, and I have searched diligently through thousands of books, monographs, articles, etc., dealing with agriculture and animal husbandry and other aspects of life and labor in Latin America; but I have been unable to find a single case in which corn has been used for the purpose of fattening beef cattle.[9] Almost the

[9] The arguments now used in various parts of Latin America to discount proposals for feeding corn to livestock are essentially the same as those presented to me in Colombia as early as 1943. At that time, Dr. H. V. Geib then agricultural attaché at the American Embassy and I, in my capacity as advisor to the Colombian government on matters pertaining to colonization and the subdivision of landed estates, tried to interest our Colombian associates to attempt a pilot project involving the corn-hog-beef cattle combination of enterprises for use in the area near the city of Villavicencio which is located at the base of the Andes almost due east of Bogotá. Then as now the lands involved were eminently suited for the growing of corn, and even two crops of that cereal per year; then as now Colombia suffered from a severe shortage of pork products; and then as now a substantial portion of the tough, leathery tissue which passed for beef in the nation's great capital city came from rangy cattle from the enormous grassy plains which lie to the east of the Andes. There they were kept to an age of six years, then brought in to the luxurious pastures at the base of the mountains for a seventh year on grass, and finally driven for ten days on the long, hard climb up and over the crest of the cordillera and down to the outskirts of Bogotá where they were slaughtered. Our proposal never really received any serious consideration, for it was contended, first, that all the corn was needed for human consumption and that none of it could be spared for use as feed for livestock; and, second, that it was not wise to

same can be said about the failure to use this economically "golden" grain for fattening hogs, although I do know a few areas in Central America in which swine are allowed to "hog down" the corn as well as the plantains that are grown for that specific purpose. I consider this, which in effect means the lack of the demonstrably most effective *combination* of Latin America's three traditional farm enterprises (the growing of corn, the farrowing and fattening of swine, and the production of beef cattle), to be an outstanding example of agricultural "underdevelopment" in the 20 countries we are considering. It is my considered opinion that Argentina's marvellous pampas are fully as capable of supporting a prosperous

---

promote a substantial increase in the production of corn because that would glut the market and ruin the price of the commodity.

As the paragraphs in this paper were being written I have been reading an interesting discussion of the possibilities of expanding greatly Brazil's exports of corn and of reducing the tremendous year-to-year fluctuations in the same. The latter recently have been as follows:

Year	Tons
1961	4,447
1962	6
1963	699,206
1964	62,315
1965	559,675

This discussion appears in the October, 1967, issue of the *Correio Agro-Pecuario*, an important farm journal published monthly in São Paulo, the great industrial and agricultural capital of South America. For one who has been concerned with the matters involved for more than a quarter of a century, the following extracts in translation from that discussion have a familiar ring: "Some people speak of the disadvantage to a country of exporting the corn it produces when it could be used as feed and transformed into meat and milk to a much greater advantage. To this [. . . the director of the agency involved] replies that the nation's agriculture has not yet attained a stage of development which makes it possible to produce corn at a cost sufficiently low to justify its use as a feed on a large scale. A complex of factors is involved in this which it is difficult to analyze in a few lines. We shall merely give an example. The growing of cattle in confinement necessitates the best of feeds, but corn, which is one of them, cannot be produced cheaply because as yet the domestic market will not bear the costs of expanding its culture and of establishing it on a technical basis."

corn-hog-beef cattle type of farming as is Illinois, Iowa, Kansas, or Nebraska; and that there are numerous other extensive areas throughout South America, Central America, and Mexico which, although not as richly endowed with fertile soils and favorable climate as Argentina, likewise would benefit tremendously by a proper combination of the three farm enterprises which comprise the "hard core" of this type of farming. It will be a happy day for many of the countries we are considering when in the words of Thomas Nixon Carver, one of the most distinguished economists ever to fill a chair at Harvard University, "Owing to the practice of allowing hogs to fatten on the droppings of the corn-fed cattle pork came [comes] to be, in a measure, a by-product of the beef-producing industry."[10] or when (in the words of the man of

---

[10] *Principles of Rural Economics,* Boston: Ginn and Company, 1911, p. 104. The steps in the development of the most effective combination of farm enterprises the world has ever known, i.e. the corn-hog-beef cattle type of farming which blankets the "corn belt" of the United States can be stated very simply; and at the same time we can indicate which of these also have been taken in Latin America, and which of them have not yet entered into the systems of agricultural production in any of the 20 countries which make up that richly endowed section of the world. These are as follows:

a. The discovery near the close of the eighteenth century, and especially early in the nineteenth century that fantastically large crops of corn could be produced on the rich soils of Ohio, Kentucky, and other areas to the west of the Appalachians. In Latin America the growing of large crops of corn on highly fertile land was widespread at the time of the conquest.

b. The lack of any "remunerative market" for that corn, and even the suppression of the efforts of many enterprising individuals to transport it to eastern markets in the form of liquid spirits. The lack of a remunerative market for corn continues to be the case in immense sections of Latin America, particularly those somewhat remote from the cities.

c. The ingenuity of Felix and George Renick, recent migrants from Hardy County, Virginia, who had settled in the Scioto Valley of Ohio, who hit upon and applied the idea "for the first time conceived in this country, of fattening large herds of cattle with their luxuriant crops of maize, and *marching* their grain to distant marts in the shape of beef." (*Report of the Commissioner of Patents, for the Year 1849,* Part II "Agriculture," Washington: Office of Printers to the Senate, 1850, p. 299.) I have been unable to dis-

letters and the authority on animal husbandry who recently attempted a definitive study of pigs and history) the caption of a photograph showing beef cattle and hogs together in a pasture in Argentina, or Brazil, or Colombia, or one of the other countries can truthfully read: "The base of corn-belt feed lot profits—hogs following steers."[11] And especially when one or more agricultural experiment stations in Latin America will have data, similar to those painstakingly assembled at the Iowa State Agricultural Experiment Station, which show that "in 120 days of feeding, an average pig, following two steers, picked up the equivalent of 312 pounds of corn."[12] I make these statements even though I am fully aware that the feeding of livestock in the United States is moving into a stage in which it no longer is advisable, in many cases, to feed corn in the kernel or on the cob directly to beef cattle, or to depend solely upon the gastric processes of the steer to pre-

cover a case in which anything like this has been done in any one of the 20 countries under consideration.

d. The discovery perhaps at numerous places that corn which had been eaten by beef cattle, spent a day in the digestive organs and tracts of bovines, and then dropped by them was ideally prepared for use by hogs, was applied in a systematic manner to produce a symbiotic relationship between the growing of corn, the fattening of beef cattle, and the farrowing and fattening of swine. This *combination* of enterprises, permit me to repeat, is by far the productive type of farming in the United States. Obviously, since even now in Latin America corn is not used for the fattening of cattle, no such type of farming has ever evolved in or been transplanted to any of the Latin American countries. They have had for over four centuries all of the components: maize itself originated somewhere in the area from Mexico to Peru; the raising of cattle for beef has always been the chief interest of those who own and control the bulk of the best land in the Latin American countries; and hogs served as the commissaries of the expeditions of the explorers and conquerors, the effective means whereby the Spaniards uprooted the Indian agriculturists from their traditional fields and forced them to seek out-of-the-way and marginal lands for their plantings of corn, potatoes, beans, etc. All that has been and that continues to be lacking is the proper *combination* of the enterprises.

[11] Charles Wayland Towne and Edward Norris Wentworth, *Pigs: From Cave to Corn Belt,* Norman: University of Oklahoma Press, 1950, p. 11.

[12] *Ibid.*, p. 211.

pare corn for consumption by pigs. At a few favored locations in Latin America undoubtedly it would be advisable to attempt these most advanced features of animal husbandry. In extensive areas, however, and especially those removed from markets, lacking adequate transportation facilities, and where the farmers do not possess sufficient capital, the transplantation of the system which prevailed in our great "corn belt" from about 1820 to 1960 is greatly to be desired.

Finally, I have been unable to discover anywhere in Latin America a close symbiotic relationship between the growing of rice of the "paddy" or irrigated type and the production of beef cattle. I mention this because, as far as I have been able to determine, in Louisiana the only effective way so far found to control the problem of "red rice" is to plant that grain only in alternate years and to have beef cattle graze the fields heavily in the "off years." Much to my dismay, however, on a recent visit (for an entirely different purpose) to Cali, Colombia, I was informed by my friend, Dr. Victor Patiño, who probably is Colombia's most accomplished agricultural scientist, that the production of rice in the fabulously fertile Cauca Valley is on the verge of extinction. The reason? The problem of "red rice." Senator Morse, in view of what I have said about the absence of these two examples (the corn-hog-beef cattle and the rice-beef cattle combinations of enterprises), I hope you and the other members of the Subcommittee will think that I have some reason for mentioning defective types of farming as one of Latin America's serious agricultural problems.

The following material is included as an addendum because it seemed especially pertinent to the work of the Subcommittee. This is a list I helped prepare of the most important *needs* of Latin American agriculture. It has never been published.

These statements of the basic agricultural needs in Latin America were formulated by a team of social scientists appointed to take stock of the ways in which the Inter-American Institute of Agricultural Sciences, one of the dependencies of the Organization of American States which has its headquarters in San José, Costa Rica, could serve better the needs of the various Latin American countries. The members of

the team were Dr. José Marull, noted Chilean agricultural
economist, then Director of Programs and Planning for the
Institute (chairman); Ingeniero Antonio Pérez Garcia, Vice
Director of the Puerto Rico Agricultural Extension Service;
and T. Lynn Smith, Graduate Research Professor of Sociology of the University of Florida. They spent two months
in 1961 making the survey and presenting the report to the
conference which evaluated the program and made recommendations for the future work of the Institute. The list of
needs which follows represents the collective and unanimous
thinking of all three members of the team:

B. MAIN AGRICULTURAL DEVELOPMENT NEEDS AND PROB-
   LEMS FOUND IN LATIN AMERICAN NATIONS

   4. The needs listed in this section fall into two categories:
      a. Those clearly felt and expressed by large numbers
         of the officials and others who were interviewed, and
      b. Those mentioned occasionally in the interviews and
         which, upon reflection, the members of the team are
         unanimous in considering to be highly important.
   5. In the first category the following may be listed:
      a. More and better trained personnel. This is especially
         acute in the fields of agricultural economics, rural
         sociology, and agricultural extension work, includ-
         ing home demonstration work.
      b. More adequate financial support for national agri-
         cultural institutions and agencies (Ministries of Agri-
         culture, Agricultural Colleges, Agricultural Credit
         Agencies, etc.).
      c. Desire that IAIAS and other international organiza-
         tions give strong backing locally to national pro-
         grams and activities.
      d. Expansion and integration of agricultural research,
         extension work and teaching activities.
      e. Desire that the IAIAS provide personnel to help staff
         and other services to help carry on national pro-
         grams.
      f. The wish for assistance in the solution of a variety

of problems that best can be described as a need for more effective management of institutions, organizations, farms, etc.

g. Necessity of improving the lot of the rural workers and their families. This includes education, health, housing, diet, wages, land reform and community development.

h. The need for improved systems of marketing and agricultural credit.

i. The need for some international agency, such as the IAIAS, to assemble, collate, and make available data and information on a variety of problems which many of the nations have in common, such as those of volcanic soils, irrigation, drainage, and range and pasture management.

j. Desire that available research findings be presented in such a form that they may readily and immediately be applied in the solution of local problems.

6. The second category of needs includes the following:

a. Need for acute concern about present debility of local governmental units and activities.

b. Need for much greater opportunities for agricultural education at the secondary level.

c. Need for fuller understanding of the nature and philosophy of agricultural extension work and for a fuller appreciation of the contributions that extension can make in economic and social development programs. (Mere graduation with the degree of Ingeniero Agrónomo is not adequate preparation for an extension worker.)

d. Need for an appreciation of hard and skilled work on the part of all elements in a society in order to bring about economic and social development.

e. Need to transform the educational institutions into the type which are controlled by their faculties and which stress professional and technological training and self discipline on the part of the students.

f. Need to develop, in Latin American institutions, graduate training programs for large numbers of specialists in all of the sciences related to agriculture.

g. Need for well planned and balanced national agricultural policies based upon detailed knowledge of local resources and problems.

h. Need for stronger and better organized Ministries of Agriculture, Colleges of Agriculture, Extension Services and national research agencies.[13]

[13] *Report of Review Team in Social Sciences,* pp. 2–3.

15 Values Held by People in Latin America which Affect Technical Cooperation

———◆———

LET ME OPEN the discussion by commenting briefly upon what I believe to be the dominant element in our own mentality, in the values of those of us who are called upon to work either at home or abroad with persons from other lands. Let each of us ask himself: Do we North Americans wear a particular type of "spectacles" which gives a special slant to the values and ideas we encounter in other countries or among students and others who come to this country to work with us? Personally, I believe that we do. We tend to see everything, to evaluate everything, through a pair of "middle-class glasses." Few of us can ever acquire the mentality of one who was "to the manor born"; and it is even more impossible for us to accommodate ourselves to the outlook of one near the level of mere creature existence that prevails among the bulk of the population in so many parts of the earth. I would maintain further that the overwhelming importance of middle-class activities has been the major factor in making this country what it is, and that a middle-class mentality is our most distinguishing characteristic.

Since definitions and descriptions of the middle class and middle-class status are so numerous and varied, perhaps I should state specifically my own thinking on the matter. For me, the middle-class person is the one who exercises all three of the basic economic functions. As exemplified by the operator of a family-sized farm—the one who has done most to give form and substance to the national characteristic

---

From *Rural Sociology,* Vol. 21, No. 1 (March, 1956), pp. 68–75. Reprinted by permission of the publisher.

I am discussing—he is at once a capitalist on a small scale, a manager and entrepreneur, and a laborer. Part of the return from the combination of enterprises in his farm business is interest on the capital he has invested in the farm or that he uses for operating expenses; another part is that which he has earned by his managerial activities; and still another is wages for the labor he has performed on the farm. It follows—as night follows day—that such a person will esteem and appreciate the rights of private property. He will not be heard claiming that property is stolen from the masses. Nor, knowing so well the time, energy, and trials and tribulations involved, will he belittle the contribution that management makes in the productive process. Finally, he will affirm the dignity of human labor and constantly seek its conservation through the adoption and perfection of labor-saving devices. For him, work with the hands can never be a stigma denoting a servile or semiservile status. He will be horrified upon observing the extravagant manner in which labor is expended (literally "thrown to the birds") in those societies in which the middle-class mentality is not dominant. Let me repeat, our mind-set of middle-class ideas constitutes a particular pair of spectacles through which we view life and labor in other parts of the world.

Great Variation in Value Systems

Turning now to our assignment, the first fact to be kept constantly in mind is the tremendous variation to be encountered with respect to the values held by those with whom we will deal in various parts of Latin America. It is inevitable that such would be the case. Twenty separate and distinct countries are involved. Each of these has its own geographic setting and particular set of natural resources. No two of them received from the native Indians, the European conquerors, the African slaves, and the later immigrants (including in several important sections liberal contingents of Asiatics) precisely the same social and cultural heritages. The differences to be observed between some of the Spanish-American countries, such as between Nicaragua and El Salvador, Colombia and Ecuador, Bolivia and Chile, or even the more extreme differences such as those between Mexico and Argentina or Honduras and Uruguay, do not, of course, approach in magnitude those between gigantic Brazil and one of the Spanish-American countries. Nor are they comparable to those between Haiti and Brazil or Haiti and any part of Spanish America. Nevertheless, there are considerable differences in each case.

Many of the significant ideas or stereotypes encountered in one nation differ substantially from those found in the neighboring countries. Furthermore, within each of the countries, much variation also must be expected. In the realm of values, as in so many other respects—as one moves from the German, Polish, and Italian settlements, in southern Brazil, to the coffee fazendas of São Paulo, to the cattle ranches of Minas Gerais and Bahia, to the sugar plantations of Pernambuco, and to the settlements along the Amazon—it is almost like moving from one world to another. And, in Colombia, the mental luggage of the population in Nariño seems entirely different from that of the sturdy inhabitants of Antioquia and Caldas, or even from that of other parts of the republic such as Boyacá or Magdalena. Likewise, the mind sets of the whites, Indians, and mestizos who live on the high mountain slopes seem poles apart from those of the Negroes and mulattoes who dwell in the lowlands along the coast and in the hot, humid valley bottoms. Finally, of course, the values held by the members of the old established families, the members of the small elite class, have little in common with those of the peons and *colonos* on the large estates, or even with those of the small holders and squatters who vegetate in some of the valleys and on the coastal plains. Beyond doubt, great variation should be expected, for it surely will be encountered by the worker who moves about at all in the area to the south and east of the Rio Grande.

Values Associated with the Class System

Probably the set of values prevailing throughout Latin America with which a thorough familiarity is most important for those who work in Spanish America or in Brazil, or with persons coming from those countries, is that relating to the class system. From the very first, the Spaniards and the Portuguese who sought their fortunes in the New World were thoroughly imbued with the idea of securing others to work for them, on their lands and in their mines. As is well known, in attaining this basic objective they were eminently successful. From Mexico to Chile and Argentina, through the force of their superior arms and military tactics, the Europeans quickly established themselves as a small elite of overlords, living in luxury on the fruits of the toil of the natives they impressed into labor gangs, received in encomienda as virtual serfs, or captured and enchained as slaves. Probably the distinctions between these three categories—impressed laborers, Indians held in encomienda, and slaves—are more apparent than real. Their actual status, the bonds in which they were held, the oppressions to which they were subjected, and the creature existence to which they were reduced differed little from those of the Negro slaves early imported from Africa to fill the gaps in the labor force. The result was largely the same throughout most of the Latin-American area. Society became sharply divided into a small group of aristocrats at or near the apex of the social pyramid and a great mass of servile or semiservile workers at its base. The few families in the former category quickly made themselves the possessors of broad acreages of the best lands; and the immense numbers in the latter class were forced to eke out a bare existence by tilling small subsistence tracts of the poorer lands in the few hours per week in which they were not required to work on the estates of the masters. Conspicuous by its absence in those agricultural societies was anything resembling a category of operators of family-sized farms, a substantial middle class to fill the vast chasm between the upper and the lower strata of the social pyramid. This statement is true if we are referring to the Spanish-American colonies in which the conquerors established themselves in new administrative centers from which, as absentee landlords, they exercised dominion over the conquered masses and the imported slaves on the plantations or in the mines; and it also is true if we are referring to colonial Brazil in which the aristocrats established their mansions and seats of power in the midst of their great holdings, from whence they exercised their princely prerogatives over vast dominions and a host of slaves and dependents. A few generations of forced labor sufficed to strip the members of the lower class of all possibility of bettering their own position, and to institutionalize the exalted status of the masters.

Thus, Latin-American society early became differentiated into a small, wealthy, highly educated, white elite for whom nothing in this world was considered too good, and a mass of humble, poverty-stricken, disease-ridden, illiterate, colored or mixed-blood agricultural laborers. Although hundreds of thousands of the most demoralized segments of the lower class recently have flocked into the rapidly growing towns and cities, this has not radically changed the class system. It has merely transformed a part of the lower class into a degraded urban proletariat. However, the fact that many thousands of European immigrants have settled in Latin-American cities—such as Buenos Aires, Santiago, Havana, Rio de Janeiro, and São Paulo—has done much to develop a genuine middle class in them; and the same is true in certain rural districts such as southern Chile, southern Brazil, and some parts of Argentina, to which the immigrants have been attracted.

Disrepute of Manual Labor

Naturally such a system of social stratification generated and perpetuated many basic values with respect to human behavior and social relationships. Most important of all are those which became and have remained almost universally accepted with respect to human labor and toil. Throughout Latin America, work with the hands, manual labor of almost any type, any activity that has been the work of slaves or peons, is looked upon as the stigma of servile or semiservile social status. Anyone not resigned to life as a member of the lower classes must avoid it as he would the plague. Possibly, the more precarious one's claim to a position somewhat above that of the masses, the more certain must he be to abstain absolutely from any such bemeaning activity.

Such ideas deeply embedded in the mores, and universally held, are, of course, almost impossible to eradicate. A visiting high official from the United States who himself drives a few spikes on a new railroad, for example, and places the members of his entourage in the position that they must do the same, makes no dent on the prevailing system of values. He merely exposes the Latin-American officials who are accompanying him to the ridicule of the people, and, perhaps, to the likelihood of defeat at the polls. Such values, too, constitute an immense barrier to the transmission to Latin-American farmers of the agricultural skills, techniques, and systems—the "know how" of which we hear so much—that have made the North American farmer the envy of so many in other parts of the world. I know, for example, a large area in Colombia in which merely the application of elementary principles of seed selection would probably more than double the production of potatoes, the staple crop. When I expressed this idea to a friend of mine, a university graduate, owner of one of the large estates or haciendas in the area, he countered with a statement about the waste involved in planting the large potatoes. To this I replied, of course, that the seed potatoes should be cut into sets for planting. Following other objections to the effect that some of the parts would lack eyes—and, therefore, one who cut the potatoes would be unable to get a stand—I offered to give a demonstration of how it was done in some of the principal potato-growing sections of the United States. Some potatoes were brought and I showed him how to cut them. He then sent for his brother, who was serving as the administrator of the hacienda, in order that I could give the latter the demonstration. Following this, the brother sent for the *mayordomo*, or overseer, and had me show once more how to cut the potatoes. Finally, the *mayordomo* called in two peons and I repeated the process for them. In the end, each of the peons cut a few potatoes as I looked on; but not until the level of the actual worker was reached had anyone except myself taken the knife in hand!

The fundamental problem that such ideas about manual labor pose in relation to our technical coöperation with Latin Americans is, of course, how the performance of the ordinary tasks on the farm can be made socially acceptable to others than those definitely known and admitted to be of lower-class status. If this basic hurdle can be surmounted, everything else will be relatively simple.

Lavish Use of Labor

Closely related to the idea that manual labor is bemeaning is the one which views labor as being of so little value or consequence that it may be expended with the utmost abandon in the productive process. In Brazil, particularly, but also in many other parts of Latin America, one eternally hears the cry of *"falta de braços"*—literally "the lack of arms," which we would call the "lack of hands." So universal has been this complaint over the past 400 years that I have come to refer to it as Brazil's theme song. But, by my standards or yours, there is anything but a shortage of labor in Brazil and other parts of Latin America. Labor is the one thing in the production process that is expended lavishly. Except in pastoral activities, land certainly is not used extensively. The system of large estates in charge of administrators—or even in the care mainly of overseers or *mayordomos*—and visited only occasionally by the absentee owners insures that managerial activities are reduced almost to the absolute minimum. Capital is used so sparingly that even the most rudimentary tools or implements, not to mention work stock or other sources of power, are largely lacking. Men and women work for the most part almost with their bare hands; and the amount of human toil that goes into the production of a ton of sugar, a bag of coffee, a sack of beans, a bushel of wheat or corn, or a unit of any other product, in most parts of Latin America, is almost beyond belief. Thus, prevailing ideas and practices relating to labor and its role in the productive process insure that the volume of the product can never be large enough to divide into any substantial shares for all those who have a hand in producing it. Ultimately, of course, these ideas determine that the level of living for all except a few members of the elite must be very low, much nearer the mere level of creature existence than many of us who have come to appreciate some of the finer qualities of the humble inhabitant of the rural districts of Latin America like to think is necessary. Here, too, is a basic value of utmost importance in connection with technical coöperation.

Descent in the Social Scale and the Pessimism
It Engenders

Also closely related to the nature of the class structure throughout Latin America, at least as it appears to me, is what may be styled a mind-set of resignation, a deep-seated pessimistic outlook on life, a widespread acceptance of the idea that things which work perfectly well in the United States, Canada, or one of the European countries are bound to fail in Brazil, in Colombia, or elsewhere in Latin America. I do not mean to say, of course, that all inhabitants of the Latin-American countries are overburdened with such a set of ideas, but I do wish to indicate that this type of thinking is widespread among persons of the classes with whom we deal. Probably it is much more prevalent than should necessarily be the case, and it is something that those of us who work with Latin Americans should be prepared to face. The sociological basis for this pessimistic thinking is a bit involved, but I hope you will bear with me while I sketch my ideas on the subject. In so doing, I shall contrast the situation in Latin America with that in the United States.

As is well known, in our own country there is a pronounced tendency for the number of children per family to decrease as one moves up the social scale. Probably the old refrain "the rich get rich, and the poor get—children" is about as accurate a piece of biosocial generalizing as has ever been produced in this nation. To a very considerable extent those who have occupied the well-remunerated positions of authority and responsibility in our economy, those in the upper middle-class and lower upper-class have failed to produce enough children to replace themselves. In sharp contrast, those farther down the social scale have produced far more than needed to keep their numbers constant. Coupled with this has been a rapid expansion of our social and economic system accompanied by the development of many, many more highly desired positions in our business and industrial worlds. All of this, along with the peculiar advantages of our educational system, has made for a rapid ascent of the social ladder by millions of our citizens. As a matter of fact, we confidently expect our children to occupy a higher level in society than that of their parents. And I suggest that this set of conditions is the basic explanation of the optimistic outlook on life that characterizes our people.

Consider on the other hand how the same factors work in the Latin-American countries: With few exceptions, their societies have been based almost exclusively on an agricultural and pastoral economy, much of it of an elementary or almost primitive type. (Probably more than half of all the people in Latin America today are gaining their livelihood through a system of agricultural techniques or a system of farming that is more primitive than that the Egyptians were using at the dawn of history.) Until the time of the Second World War, the development of new important positions in commerce, transportation, and industry was negligible in comparison with the population. One generation finds little more room in the upper ranges of the social scale than was open to the one preceding it. At the same time, there still are no differentials in the birth rate corresponding to those in the United States and much of Europe. Those of wealth and position have fully as many children, if not more, than those in the lower classes. (And at all levels the rate of reproduction is exceptionally high, as evidenced by the fact that the birth rate today throughout Latin America is about double that which is producing such a rapid upsurge in the population of our own country.) In addition, members of the upper classes undoubtedly save far higher proportions of their children from the ravages of disease and malnutrition than the impoverished and uninstructed masses. The age at marriage is low and the generations come along with remarkable rapidity. As a result, the proud head of a well-known family leaves not just one or two descendants to take over as he passes on. Before he dies, he may be surrounded by a hundred or more children, grandchildren, and great-grandchildren all struggling desperately to maintain appearances indicative of the rank to which they were born. If the family wealth is in land, as most generally is the case, less than a century may serve to pulverize the largest holdings; and if the legal division is not made, as frequently it is not, operations may soon be paralyzed because of the impossibility of getting working arrangements between hundreds of co-owners spread through four or five generations. All of this sets up forces exactly the opposite of those making for rapid ascent of the social scale in the United States. In Latin America the pressures are from the top, and they are pushing large numbers of people down. In any Latin-American city one can find thousands of persons who appear on the surface to be of middle-class status. As compared with middle-class people in the United States, their incomes are no higher, their work in the professions and white-collar activities of one kind or another is little different, their homes are no better, and their level of living no higher. But these Latin Americans are the descendants of grandfathers or great-grandfathers who once constituted the elite of those societies. They are by no means content with the discrepancy between the level to which they were born, and on which they feel entitled to live, and the one they perforce must occupy. In spite of all they can do, things do not work out as they should for most of them, and each generation finds life more difficult. I believe we have here the explanation of the widespread idea that it is hopeless to try many new undertakings in Latin America. In any case, the pessimistic outlook is a value that must be dealt with in attempts at technical coöperation.

Latin Americans as Generalists

Another point to be kept in mind is that the educated Latin American with whom we come in contact is sure to be less of a specialist, much more of a generalist, than his counterpart in the United States. The Latin American in a coöperative venture will have at least a superficial acquaintance with many fields of knowledge, will know something of the activities in many lines of endeavor with which you and I are entirely unfamiliar. We might very well envy the breadth of his knowledge and culture. On the other hand, his ideas in any particular specialty are likely to be found wanting in many respects which we regard as fundamental. His wider range of ideas is, of course, the result of the educational system in which he has participated and of the multifarious activities in which he engages as an adult. Rare indeed is the educated Latin American who can or does make a living holding only one job at a time or following a single occupation or profession year after year; and one of the first things learned by one of our specialists sent to work in Latin America, let us say one of our agricultural scientists or technicians, is that he too must become a generalist. Irrespective of his field of specialization, if he is to be successful in his work, the major part of his time must be devoted to problems and activities that would be considered far outside his proper realm of work in the United States.

Belief in the Futility of Long-Range Plans

Finally, in concluding these remarks, I shall mention another idea so widespread throughout Latin America that it must be considered among the basic "facts of life" for those of us who work with Latin Americans. This I shall style as a deep-rooted belief, almost fatalistically entrenched, in the futility of any undertaking of a long-range nature, in the certainty that accomplishments must be achieved quickly or all is in vain.

Such an idea is, of course, the inevitable conclusion to be derived from intimate, firsthand experiences with the political processes in the various Latin-American countries. From the very first the concentration of land ownership and control, the system of large estates, the separation of society into the small class of elite and the mass at the bottom of the scale, absenteeism (with the large landowners residing in state and national capitals), and political control by the favored few, have placed local and departmental government in a strait jacket. Through constitutional provisions which prohibit the residents of the *municípios* or counties from levying any tax on the land, the members of the upper classes have deprived the rural masses of the population from using the tried and tested method of pooling local efforts in order to provide the services they need. Land is an asylum for the capital of the absentee landlords, and the people in the rural communities must suffer from want of schools, protection for life and property, health and sanitary services, roads and bridges, etc. As a result, local leadership and responsibility are practically nil. Everything must come from the national capital and the federal government. Hence, inevitably, the Latin Americans with whom we deal are those currently basking in the favor of the regime presently in power. If there is a revolution of the Latin-American variety, or any other change in government, they quickly will be numbered among the "outs," and their places will be taken by the kinfolk and other political allies of the leaders who have gained control.

As is well known, coups and revolutions go on with almost clocklike regularity throughout many of the countries. But even if there is no violent overthrow of a regime, there is no assurance of security of tenure in the various governmental positions. Changes in the cabinet bring with them overturns in personnel almost as drastic, in many cases, as those that accompany the ousting of one faction by another through the process that is referred to, in connection with Latin-American countries, as a revolution. The seething intrafactional strife is ever present in the national capitals; it is the principal activity of large numbers of the upper classes; and it results in numerous changes. In many of the countries, it is almost impossible to find an upper-class man past the age of 40 who is not ex-minister of agriculture, of education, of hacienda, or of one of the other departments. In one country that I have visited periodically for the past twelve years, sometimes as frequently as twice a year, I have yet to find the same man as minister of agriculture on two consecutive visits. In the various divisions of the ministry the changes are almost as rapid, and it is rare to find anyone who has been in the same post for as many as five years. Frequent change is regarded as inevitable.

The Latin-American student who comes to the United States on some kind of grant from his government cannot be reasonably sure that he will continue to receive the funds he is counting upon for the period of his study. The head of a department who pays a visit to this country may not be head when he gets back in a few months. The minister who comes may not be minister long after his return. The technician who arrives for further training may have little chance to apply his learning in the post from which he took leave. The certainty of many quick and drastic changes is the one thing on which they can all count.

Out of all this comes the conviction that the thing to do is something which will produce tangible results in a hurry. If the accomplishments are those that will be apparent only after 15, 10, or even 5 years, very few can afford to take the risk. Nor can one put the stamp of approval on the work of a predecessor by familiarizing himself with previous plans and policies and trying to advance them. Each man must start anew and draw up a fresh set of projects. He must seek ways and means of making monumental achievements during his short time in office. A few lucky ones may have the ink dry on their blueprints before they have joined the numbers of the "ex's." But few can be so foolhardy as to give more than lip service to long-range plans and programs.

In conclusion, let me state specifically that I have concentrated upon the problem aspects of the subject in this presentation. Omitted from consideration are the hundreds of values we share with the Latin Americans as a result largely of our common European heritage.

16 Possibilities and Pitfalls in the Transplantation of Sociocultural Traits, Complexes, and Systems, with Special Reference to Latin America

———◆———

THIS PAPER IS a modest endeavor to contribute something of value in connection with one of the most important problems of our epoch, namely, that of accelerating the process of development in the so-called "developing" societies. No challenge facing our generation is more difficult than that of promoting this to the degree that it will come to rival "directed social change" in what are incongruously designated as "developed" societies. This brief exposition is directed specifically to the possibilities available to those who seek to "modernize" the rural and agricultural way of life in Latin American countries, and also to some of the pitfalls which may bring to naught many of the best-intentioned plans and programs for agricultural development in the areas between the Rio Grande and "The Horn."

The data and analyses presented are the results of many years of intensive probing, both by means of pragmatic, empirical observation and by devoting many hours to attempts to formulate significant inductively derived concepts, classifications, relationships and generalizations.

Many years of study have been devoted to the general aspects of the subject now focused upon, and since 1965, ef-

Presented at the annual meeting of the Southern Sociological Society, Atlanta, Georgia, April 11, 1968.

forts to gain fuller understanding of this specific aspect of sociocultural change has been one of my major concerns. Nevertheless, only within the last twelve months have I begun to set down in a systematic form the results of these endeavors, and this present paper actually is the first occasion on which I have ventured to present any of them to a group of my fellow professionals.[1] In doing so, I limit myself to six specific cases, ranging from what I believe is the simplest possible to one of the more involved and complex, all of them ones with which I personally have had considerable professional involvement. Four of these are drawn from the somewhat experimental activities of Colombia's able sociologist, Orlando Fals Borda,[2] and the others, the two most complex ones, are those which I, myself, long have been trying to understand. They are as follows: (1) the introduction of a modern fungicide into a neighborhood in a cultural area which hitherto had lacked any effective means of dealing with "blights" of one kind or another; (2) a demonstration that wells could be dug on the hillsides, far above the level of the nearest stream, to supply water for household purposes; (3) efforts to get simple, unschooled small farmers to make use of the scythe, in replacement of the sickle, in the manual tasks of cutting forage crops, harvesting wheat and other grains, and cutting weeds; (4) endeavors to substitute the metal turning plow, equipped with a mold board, for the antiquated wooden plow, made from the forked branch of a tree, of the type used by the ancient Babylonians and Egyptians; (5) attempts to bring about the combination of Latin America's three great traditional farm enterprises (the growing of maize or Indian corn,

[1] Much earlier and less systematic endeavors along the same lines, however, are evidenced by a part of the analysis in my "Sistemas Agrícolas," *Revista Brasileira de Geografía*, Ano IX, No. 2 (Abril-Junho, 1947), pp. 159–184; and "Agricultural Systems and Standards of Living," *Inter-American Economic Affairs*, Vol. III, No. 3 (Winter, 1949), pp. 15–28.

[2] As presented in *Facts and Theory of Sociocultural Change in a Rural Social System*, Monografias Sociológicas No. 2 Bis, Bogotá: Universidad Nacional de Colombia, 1960, and as gained by repeated personal visits to the locality group (the *vereda* of Saucío, Cundinamarca, Colombia) in the company of Fals Borda himself, on most occasions, and that of his father on others.

the farrowing and fattening of pigs and hogs, and the production of beef) into a genuine corn-hog-beef cattle type of farming, which I personally consider to be the most effective and efficient one ever developed by mankind; and (6) the mechanization or motorization of agriculture, or the introduction and promotion of the most modern and complex ways of extracting products from the soil.

The Term Transplantation and Possible Alternatives

Before we concentrate our attention upon several specific attempts to transplant sociocultural traits, complexes, and systems from one society to another, it is deemed advisable to consider briefly the full meaning of the substantive I have decided to employ to designate the process. In other words, I am asking you to bear with me while I comment upon what not infrequently is disdainfully referred to as "the mere semantic" aspects of the topic. Were it not for the fact that with increasing frequency I am encountering graduate students and sociology instructors who lack any clear and concise concepts of such standard terms as society, culture, variable, group, social class, social mobility, and so on, perhaps I would not have the temerity to raise some of the issues which follow.

Only after considerable careful deliberation have I decided to employ transplantation to denote the process whereby specific traits, complexes, and systems, which are discovered or developed by one society, or part of a society, are successfully incorporated or integrated into another. Among the various alternatives considered and rejected for one reason or another are all of the familiar terms such as *diffusion, borrowing, migration of traits,* and *adoption* (or *acceptance*) *of new practices,* along with *acculturation, assimilation, integration* and other of the more inclusive terms. At the very root of my deliberations has been the matter of volition itself, and precisely who and what is capable of exercising it. Are we justified in making use of the forms of expression which seem to attribute this fundamental power to a statistical index (such as the gross national product or the Dow-Jones average of prices on the stock market), to cultural forms of any kind, or even to the most refined computer systems? Is it possible for sociocultural traits themselves to move from one place to another, or from one location in social space to another? Or is at least one person an indispensable part of the process (as in the case of Robinson Crusoe and the movement of some cultural features from one geographic site to another) and two or more people (at least one "giver" and one "receiver") essential in all but an infinitesimally small proportion of all social and territorial mobility on the part of cultural entities? I myself am unable to ascribe volition to any environmental feature, even to the whole or parts of the man-made environment which properly is designated as culture; and for this reason reject the designations of diffusion, transmigration of culture, or even acculturation, for the process I am studying.[3]

In the case of the terms *borrowing of culture* and the currently popular *adoption* (or *acceptance*) *of new practices,* however, the situation is somewhat different, is it not? Is it not implicit in each of the terms that someone, some human being, is exercising the volition, doing the borrowing or making the adoption? If so, why did I choose not to use one of them?

Unfortunately, in my own case, at least, one of the questions mentioned above still complicates the issue. Is it possible to have a *borrower* where there is no *lender?* Can there be an *adopter* or a *receiver* if there is no *giver?* Or an *acceptor* if there is no *promoter?* Or to what extent is it more valid to speak of the borrowing of culture or the adoption of improved practices than it would be to think, in connection with the game of football, of a forward pass from a star quarterback to himself? Just how far do we get if we as sociologists devote years of work to the socio-psychological (and perhaps in some cases, individual-psychological) acceptance or adoption of this or that practice, if we never attend to the study of the sociocultural system into which the new entity is being ac-

[3] The renowned anthropologist with whom I was privileged to study at Harvard University (1930–31), Roland B. Dixon, wisely chose *The Building of Cultures* (New York, Charles Scribners' Sons, 1928) as a title for his great book. This, however, was in sharp contrast to his contemporaries and especially his successors in that field of study.

cepted, the one in which it originated, and the process of transferral involved? Indeed, is it not possible that the entire process much more closely resembles that involving physicians and surgeons who are making "transplants" of livers, hearts, and other human organs than of any other model we might choose? Also, in passing, should we not ask ourselves if the tendency of sociocultural systems in the "underdeveloped" countries to reject "transplants" from economically more developed societies may not be even greater than that of the human body to do so with respect to transfers of organs from closely comparable beings? Be this as it may, the term *transplantation of sociocultural entities* seems to be less objectionable, when evaluated in the light of the many legitimate questions that may be raised with respect to the most suitable designation for the process we are studying, than are any of the other names in use. Hence it is the one that has been chosen for use in this and other of my discussions of the transfer of sociocultural traits, complexes, and systems from one societal body to another.

At least six separate and distinct parts seem to be essential for the makeup or composition of the process as a whole. These are as follows: (1) the discovery, invention or genesis and development of a specific sociocultural entity (idea, procedure, combination, seed or plant, tool or implement, machine, apparatus, and so on) in a given location; (2) the exercise of imagination on the part of one or more human beings to the end of generating an idea that this entity would have utility if it were transferred to another location; (3) the selection of a specific site in physical space and in social space to which the trait, complex, or system is to be moved, or in which it is to be duplicated; (4) the preparation of the "seed bed," if agricultural designations are used, or the readying of the patient for the operation (the "transplant"), if medical terminology is preferred; (5) the actual transportation of the sociocultural item (by human beings individually, or by use of any of the various means of communication) from the original sociocultural "field" or "body" to the new one, and performance of the complete "operation" involved in any "transplant"; and (6) the care, nourishment, encouragement, and protection of the sociocultural item in its new location and environment.

If anyone wishes to remonstrate against the highly telic nature of the process of transplantation as I am attempting to portray it, I can only concur with the objection. However, I would stress that it is no more extreme in this respect than are the terms more conventionally used by those who have devoted attention to one or more aspects of the general process we are attempting to analyze. Consider, for example, the "old reliables," such as "cultural diffusion" and "the migration of traits and symbols." Actually, neither of these does or can take place independent of human agents, although in both cases, it is not essential for the actual transportation of the sociocultural item involved to be a planned, purposeful act. With respect to "borrowing," however, both consciousness and telesis would seem to be essential; and certainly this is true with respect to "the adoption of new practices," or the "acceptance of improved practices," to which many sociologists have devoted great attention in the course of the last 25 years.

From what has been said in the above paragraphs, I hope it is crystal clear that I regard the transplantation of sociocultural traits, complexes, and systems as being strictly analogous with the transplantation of rice, tomatoes, or petunias, in the plant world, and of the "transplants" of organs such as livers, kidneys, and hearts, in the animal realm. Furthermore, I think efforts in this line of "directed social change" require attention to all features of the process fully as much as is the case with the successful transfer of plants from nursery to field or garden, or of organs from one body to another. For example, as indicated below, many of the hundreds of unsuccessful endeavors to introduce simple metal turning plows in various parts of Latin America seem to have been roughly comparable with the inadequate and frequently disappointing efforts of many amateur gardeners to transfer trees and shrubs to locations in the yards surrounding their homes. Moreover, from what I have been able to learn, I am inclined to conclude that the "rejection phenomenon" in the transplantation of sociocultural complexes and systems is about as general and severe as it is in the widely publicized "transplants" of hearts and other organs from one human body to another.

The Introduction of Fungicides and Sprayers

The ease and rapidity with which the use of fungicides and a mechanical pump for applying them were adopted in the settlement of Saucio, located in the high uplands of the department of Cundinamarca, Colombia deserves careful consideration. This district is inhabited almost exclusively by humble rural folk, largely unlettered, and tradition-bound, whose low levels of living, rustic way of life, and chronic problems are fairly representative of those of tens of millions of people who inhabit the rural parts of the densely populated Andean areas extending from Venezuela to Bolivia. Moreover, a thorough analysis and description of the population, the social organization, and the way of life of the families in this semi-community are readily available in one of the most thoroughgoing sociological studies ever made of a Latin American society.[4] The essentials of the experience upon which our attention should be focused are given succinctly by the proponent, Dr. Orlando Fals Borda, in the following paragraph:

"For various seasons the peasants had been experiencing losses in their potato crop due to blight. Then some well-to-do farmers learned of fungicides and spray pumps, tried them, and liked the results. Their local neighbors and workers also observed the results, perceived the advantages (dramatized visibly when plants in one field survived due to the innovation in treatment, while those in an adjacent untreated plot died promptly), and proceeded to adopt the new technique. The first sprayer was introduced in about 1940; in 1950 there were five pumps, although many more farmers used them through rentals and borrowings; in 1958, 27 owned sprayers were counted. There is little question that a significant variation in potato cultivation has taken place, that the innovation

[4] See Orlando Fals Borda, *Peasant Society in the Colombian Andes*, Gainesville: University of Florida Press, 1955.

was well received, and that its diffusion is considerably under-way."[5]

A few reflections about this and the other cases will be presented in the concluding section of this paper. At this point, I merely want to observe that the practice and equipment involved offered a solution to a critical new problem which was imperiling the production of the crop on which the majority of the small farmers depended for their cash incomes and for food for their families. There was in the settlement no deep-rooted traditional practices for use as alternatives to the fungicides and sprayers. No activities in which the *campesinos* had developed great skill were forced into disuse by the changes. The proof of the efficacy of the new practice was conclusive and readily observed by all. The innovations offered no apparent threat to the continued existence of the old sociocultural system, the old way of life. Rather, it eliminated a dire threat to the survival of the same. Finally, the introduction of the fungicides did not entail any evaluation of the relative merits of two or more possible solutions for the problem. Prayer alone seemed to be the only alternative available to Saucio's people. In brief, this seems to be an example of the least complicated sociocultural transplantation one may expect to find. It enables us to generalize that many of the greatest possibilities for success in efforts at directed social change probably are to be found at this elementary level, one in which a set of new practices is incorporated into an old system in order to cope with crises that have arisen. If there were no crises, if the deterioration were slow and gradual, the innovator probably would have slight success in an endeavor of this type.

The Transplantation of the Art of Well Digging

Another of Fals Borda's "experiments" also resulted in rapid adoption of the recommended practice, once he had succeeded in the difficult work of persuading one of the farmers to make the trial. This, however, was a practice to which there was an alternative, a way of meeting the felt need that

[5] Fals Borda, *Facts and Theory*, pp. 16–17.

had been in use since time immemorial, so that the favorable judgment on the part of those adopting the practice involved weighing the relative merits of the old and the new procedures. Fals Borda's own summary of the happenings is as follows:

"Ever since she bought her farm about forty years ago, the woman of one household had to carry water from a pond by the railroad tracks, a fifteen-minute walk. The family had never thought of digging a well by the house; in fact, it was believed that there was no underground water. However, as a participant-experiment, her son was encouraged in September, 1957, to try for a well. He started digging while his neighbors watched in tense skepticism. One month later, water was found. Amazed friends came to the farm to inspect the well and to inquire how it was made. One day after this farmer struck water, a neighbor started to dig his own well; a week later, two more commenced to work; three others in the area had their wells dug within the next four months, and two purchased mechanical pumps to raise the water. It is evident that the farmers discarded an ancient belief in regard to underground water and adopted an innovation quite speedily."[6]

As we reflect about this case, and the opportunities for sociocultural transplantations offered by its parallels, let us first keep in mind a traditional belief of Saucio's campesinos. As I well know from my conversations with Fals Borda and other talks with my friends in Saucio, the humble inhabitants of this part of Colombia believed that any well would have to attain a depth of several hundred feet, one going down to the level of the stream in the bottom of the valley before any water would seep into the excavation. This, in turn, is fairly typical of much folk "wisdom," and even of the logical patterns some of us use in our graduate schools, in which answers to various questions are secured by reasoning deductively from some *one* known principle to the complete neglect of other related factors. Our humble friends in Colombia's uplands knew that "water seeks its own level"; but they had had little or no experiences with any forms of capillary at-

[6] *Ibid.*, p. 17.

traction, for even the use of wicks in kerosene lamps, samo-vars, or other kinds of lighting equipment was not known to them. In this case, at least, they did not even apply the old adage that "circumstances alter cases."[7]

Once the demonstration was made, however, there was absolutely no desire on the part of the families of the area to retain the old way of getting water for household purposes. No doubt this was largely because the carrying of water was conceived of there, as elsewhere, as being pure drudgery. I have yet to learn about any case, in Colombia or out of it, in which the women take pride in such work, or in which men will assume the major responsibility of carrying the water for the house. Likewise, as in the previous example, there was no apparent threat to the prevailing sociocultural system or way of life by the adoption and use of the improved means of getting a water supply for the home.

The Attempt to Substitute the Scythe for the Sickle

The third of Fals Borda's "experiments" to which we attend is offered as an example of the pitfalls rather than that of the opportunities in relation to the transplantation of socio-cultural traits, complexes, and systems. It is deemed especially significant because rarely does any "agent of change" have such a perceptive mind, such comprehensive knowledge of the "underdeveloped" society involved, or such thorough rapport with the people of the communities in which he works, as has been true of Colombia's most accomplished sociologist and the situation in which he has worked. His own statement of the trial, its results, and his analysis of the reasons for the failure are as follows:

[7] In connection with the erroneous logic involved in the example of folk "wisdom" to which we are referring the following case from another part of Latin America is not entirely lacking in signifi-cance: "I remember once to have been conversing with the Presi-dent of one of the inland provinces about Steam Navigation, and on telling him that many of the English Steam-boats were now en-tirely constructed of iron, he did not say he did not believe me, but simply remarked 'that in Brazil, when iron was put into water, it always sank.'" George Gardner, *Travels in the Interior of Bra-zil . . .* , London: Reeve, Benham, and Reeve, 1849, p. 102.

"In the first place, there are negative assessments that are fully justified for technical, or objective, reasons. The farmers distinguish what can be damaging or prejudicial to them; thus they reject apparently useful innovations. Such was the case with the writer's experimentation with the scythe in 1956. After one year and a half of continued trials with a number of Saucites, it became evident that the scythe could not displace locally the rudimentary sickle for the harvesting of grain. The terrain; the kind of seed; the nature of weed growth; the weather in relation to tying, shocking, and stacking; the system of threshing; all conspired to curtail the local efficacy of the scythe as a grainharvesting implement. The sickle remained while the farmers handed down their decision against the innovation. This decision was sound from the technical viewpoint."[8]

Our own interpretation of the reasons for the negative assessment is considerably different from that given in this quotation. In this case, as explicitly stated in what Fals Borda has said, the objective was to replace the "core" component in a highly integrated sociocultural system with an alternative that someone from outside the community thought was superior or more efficient. It also represented, in effect, and this I want to stress with all the power at my command, an attempt to revive a *lost art*. It was typical, I fear, of many of the endeavors of those of us who attempt to better life and labor in other sections of the world in that it actually involved an attempt to implant elsewhere instruments, skills, and practices which no longer are effective, functional parts of the societal fabric in which we ourselves live and work. In the trial under consideration, I doubt that Fals Borda, even aided and abetted to the extent possible by me and by others with whom he consulted, was able to establish a fair test of the relative efficacy of the scythe and the sickle. Also I confess that now, by "hind sight," I am able to recognize some of the difficulties which I was not astute enough to anticipate when the trial was first proposed. Presently I am inclined to think that the extreme differences between the *art* of handling the sickle and that of wielding the scythe was a major factor

[8] Fals Borda, *Facts and Theory*, p. 19.

in causing the failure, and that the endeavor itself is indicative of the extreme difficulty of transplanting any *one* key
component of a given sociocultural system into a similar role
in another. I now consider it extremely difficult if not impossible to transplant successfully merely one or two parts of
any highly integrated system.

Let me stress that this test of the scythe and the sickle in
Saucio was essentially the matching of a living art against a
lost art. The campesinos of the neighborhood had learned the
art of using the sickle from childhood on, and they were
about as adept and dexterous in plying that light, carefully-
sharpened little instrument as it is possible for a man or a
woman to be. Their skills in this respect reminds me of those
with which the campesinos of Mexico and Central America
handle the machete. On the other hand, by the 1950's in the
United States, where Fals Borda learned about the scythe,
the use of that cutting tool long had been practically a lost art.
I, myself, for example, although regularly required to use it
(in the period from about 1910 to 1925) to cut weeds for the
pigs, alfalfa for horses and cattle, and so on, never learned to
swing it in a skillful manner; and my efforts to sharpen one
of the blades were even less satisfactory. Even my father, who
tolerated my crude endeavors, and those of my brothers, was
by no means expert with this tool. Indeed, its extensive use was
on its way out when he was a youth. In fact, in all my life, I
personally saw only one man who knew the art of wielding
the scythe, and he was my father's oldest brother. As I reflect
about the "generation-gap" which separated the ability to
manipulate England's once advanced harvesting instrument,
as represented by that between men who lived and worked
before the invention of the mechanical reaper and those of
us who were coming of age in the early 1920's, I gain a much
greater appreciation of the sociocultural significance of what
many British writers have incorporated into their books on
agriculture and rural life.[9]

[9] Consider, for example, in connection with the use of the scythe,
the following generalization by T. Hennell (*Change in the Farm,*
Cambridge: The University Press, 1936, p. 101): "It is not very
hard to handle a scythe after a fashion, but there is great skill in
using it well. A feeble old man who is master of it will do better

Efforts to Introduce the Use of the Simple Turning Plow

In a number of important parts of Latin America (including south Brazil, southern Uruguay, Argentina, and southern Chile) European immigrant farmers readily have transplanted their advanced plow culture to rich new areas in Latin America. Before tractors and the associated implements were somewhat readily available, Japanese farmers who settled in Brazil also showed alacrity in substituting horse and mule-drawn steel turning plows for the traditional hoe culture to which they had been habituated in their homeland. Elsewhere, as in Colombia, the long series of efforts to introduce the simple turning plow in replacement of the old wooden "rooting plow" of the type used by the ancient Egyptians largely have come to nought. In my book-length study of Colombian society[10] I have referred to some of these endeavors, and their lack of success, along with some mention of possible explanations of the failures. There brief mention is made of one of the most recent of these attempts, that of Fals Borda to contribute to the well-being of his campesino friends in Saucio by going to the trouble and expense of securing some old-fashioned plows from tradition-bound sections of the United States and having his friends try them out. When Fals Borda first mentioned his project to me while he was still a graduate student at the University of Florida I responded eagerly and urged him to go ahead with the venture. At that time neither of us was wise enough to realize that the undertaking actually consisted of trying to implant one of the components of one highly integrated complex sociocultural system into another. We gave little or no attention to the fact that successful use of the turning plow depended upon hundreds of

___

work, and with less effort, than the most athletic novice; nor is it easy for a hand who has accustomed to one type to adapt itself to another." For minute descriptions of the use of the sickle and the scythe in the reaping of wheat, barley, oats, and rye, see Henry Stephens, *The Book of the Farm*, Edinburgh and London, 1851, Vol. II, pp. 328–354.

[10] T. Lynn Smith, *Colombia: Social Structure and the Process of Development*, Gainesville: University of Florida Press, 1967, pp. 220–224.

things other than the plow itself, including horses or mules as the source of the power, properly constructed and balanced harnesses, finely adjusted systems of double-trees, single trees, clevises, and so on, and most important of all a plowman who had served an apprenticeship of many years. As a result, much to the disappointment of all, the endeavor failed completely. Fals Borda's own summary of the pitfall is as follows: "The first steel plows easily broke, and later models were defective. . . . Therefore, the farmers assessed these innovations negatively."[11]

The Transplantation of the Corn-Hog-Beef Cattle Type of Farming

Apparently I have been almost alone in attempts to transplant the most successful type of farming in the United States, the combination of the corn, hog, and beef cattle enterprises characteristic of the great "Corn Belt" of the United States from about 1830 to 1960, to any of the Latin American countries. So far my efforts have been unavailing, but I have not entirely abandoned hope.

As early as 1943, in Colombia, and as late as 1968 in Peru, I have endeavored to implant the idea of pilot projects in which an endeavor would be made to bring about a combination of these traditional Latin American enterprises on some of the farms of those countries. At first my efforts doubtless were very naive, and perhaps they continue to suffer from that defect, but I shall continue to seek for ways and means in which this idea may be given a fair trial. Irrespective of that, however, in 1944 I endeavored, along with the agricultural attaché at the American Embassy, to persuade the director of Colombia's Caja de Crédito Agrario and the director of the Departamento Nacional de Tierras to use such a base for a colony of farmers to be established at the base of the Andes near Vilavicencio. In that area there were great expanses of territory, then used merely as pastures, eminently suited for growing corn. Then as now Colombia was acutely short of hams, bacon, lard, and all other pork products; and

[11] *Facts and Theory,* p. 20.

then, as now, much of the beef for the Bogotá market came from the herds of rangy cattle which grazed on the immense natural pastures of Colombia's great eastern plains. These cattle were kept to an age of six years on these plains and then moved to the base of the mountains, for a seventh year on grass, before they were driven for about eight days up the steep mountain trail and over the crest of the eastern cordillera to the slaughter pens at Bogotá. Our proposal was never given a trial, but even so in the brief memorandum I left with the officials with whom I had worked when I left my two-year assignment as advisor on colonization and settlement, the following paragraph (in its English translation) constituted one of the major points.

8. THE SELECTION OF SITES FOR COLONIES. Colonies should be located only in areas where there is every possibility of their being able to develop a diversified system of agriculture on a paying base. Some of the better sites to select would be those suitable for dairying near the larger cities; others near the base of the Andes in the Llanos or in northern Antioquia where cattle could be intercepted on the way to market, fed home-produced corn, and a genuine corn-hog-beef cattle combination established. In general, only the very most favored areas should be considered for the first colonies.[12]

The record shows that the lack of success with this recommendation did not cause me to abandon hope that some time somewhere in Colombia such a combination of enterprises might be established. For example, in June, 1946, I was requested to stop in Colombia (while on my way to Rio de Janeiro to teach at the University of Brazil) to confer with officials of the national government and those of the Departamento of Santander about their plans for the establishment of new agricultural colonies in the Carare zone of Santander. The second item on our lengthy agenda was entitled "Sistema de Cultivos" and a translation of the full text of minutes dealing with the item is as follows:

Based on his experience in the United States, Dr. Smith recommended that the most important "sistema de cultivos"

[12] T. Lynn Smith, "Colonization and Settlement in Colombia," *Rural Sociology*, Vol. 12, No. 2 (June, 1947), pp. 128–139.

would be the combination of corn, pastures, cattle and hogs. The objective of this system is to shorten the period of fattening for cattle to no more than 18 to 20 months by feeding them on corn. He also suggested that in the beginning, perhaps, it would be best to purchase lean cattle for fattening, rather than for each farmer to produce his own. This could be done easily since many lean cattle are moved down the Magdalena River from the plains of Bolivar to the markets on the coast. The representatives of the Department of Santander expressed themselves in favor of the sistema de cultivos recommended by Dr. Smith, but they suggested that at the same time the colonists ought to grow cacao, manioc, fruits, beans, and other crops that would not entail the use of the plow, a thing that would be difficult at first because of the thick woods that cover the land. Dr. Smith indicated that he also approved such a diversification of crops.[13]

Offhand it seems easy and simple for farmers in any given part of Latin America to begin use of the corn-hog-beef cattle type of farming, since all three of the components are tried and tested in all of the countries, and only the combination itself is new. Corn originated in the New World and was being grown abundantly over most of what is now Latin America in the days of Columbus. Hogs were introduced by the first bands of explorers and conquerors, and, indeed were the means by which the native Indians literally were "uprooted" from their traditional corn fields and potato patches so that their lands legally could be incorporated into the grazing estates of their new white masters. And the growing of beef cattle has been the major rural enterprise of the large Spanish American landowners who have owned and controlled the bulk of the most fertile and best-located land from colonial days to the present. The manner in which most of the Spanish American societies are dichotomized, however, makes the undertaking far more difficult than might first seem to be the

[13] From a Memorandum in my personal files entitled "Proyecto de Colonización de la Zona del Carare: Memorandum Sobre los Puntos que Deben Tratarse en la Reunión del 21 de Junio con los Enviados de la Gobernación y del Consorcio Industrial de Santander" and "Conversaciones con el Doctor Smith Sobre Colonización del Carare" prepared in the Instituto de Fomento Industrial in Bogotá and dated June, 1946.

case. So far none of the affluent has seen fit to add the corn and hog enterprises to his cattle ranching activities in the close type of symbiosis required, and the campesinos perforce must operate much too close to the survival level for them to aspire to the substantially enlarged agricultural operations that would be essential. Nevertheless the experience of farmers in the great corn belt of the United States from about 1830 to 1960 is such that this particular type of farming seems to offer a great opportunity for those who operate the farms and ranches throughout many portions of Latin America, and especially those in which the land is exceptionally well suited to corn culture. I continue to hope that the day will come when some governmental agency, some colony of immigrant farmers (such as the Dutch or the Japanese in Brazil), some of the descendants of European farmers in Argentina and Uruguay, or some agricultural missionaries in almost any of the countries will accomplish the breakthrough that I envision.

[The sixth item mentioned above, the transplantation of mechanized farming, is treated in selection number 17, which follows.]

17 Improvement of the Systems of Agriculture in Colombia

———◆———

WILL IT BE possible for Colombia quickly to replace systems of agriculture that are antiquated, inefficient, and frequently degrading with modern ones that are efficient and which will enable the masses of her agriculturists to lead a more human and dignifying type of life?* The future of that nation depends to a high degree upon the answer to this question. If by chance at the present time the average farmer in Colombia were equipped with the knowledge and practices pertaining to agricultural and pastoral enterprises more or less equal to those possessed by Canadian farmers in the provinces of Ontario and Saskatchewan as early as 1910, then the Latin American country we are considering already would be a model of social and economic development worthy of imitation by all of the so-called underdeveloped countries. I feel perfectly justified in making such generalizations in spite of the fact that I observed highly perfected systems of agriculture in various parts of Colombia, such as the magnificent sugar-cane plantations in the Cauca Valley, the splendidly mechanized cotton plantations in Tolima and other parts of the upper Magdalena Valley, the extremely modern establishments for dairying on the Savanna of Bogotá, and the large agricultural units recently developed in the Department of Meta and on the northern coastal plains.

Nevertheless I also have seen thousands and thousands of

From T. Lynn Smith, *The Process of Rural Development in Latin America,* University of Florida Social Science Monographs No. 33, Gainesville: University of Florida Press, 1967, Chap. 4. Reprinted by permission of the publisher.

* The original text of this paper in Spanish was presented to the Colloque Internationale sur les Problèmes Agraires des Amériques Latines, Paris, October 11–16, 1965.

fincas (or small to moderate-sized agricultural units) and hundreds of *haciendas* (or large estates usually devoted almost exclusively to rudimentary pastoral activities) in the most densely populated portions of the nation on which the prevailing systems of agriculture are very similar to those used in Biblical times or even in the days of the Egyptians. It is very easy to ascertain the fact, which later will be demonstrated in some detail, that there presently are in Colombia approximately one million farmers, that is the overwhelming proportion of all of her agriculturists, who are completely lacking any agricultural implements other than the ax and the hoe. They also have no power whatsoever, either of animals or machines, except that of their own hands. With such systems of agriculture it is evident that human labor is wasted to an appalling degree. Furthermore, keeping pace with this abysmal deficiency in the traditional practices is the lack in the agricultural system of the Colombian farmer of an adequate and efficient input of the all-important managerial factor.

The Nature of a System of Agriculture

The concept of system of agriculture or agricultural system as used here requires an exact definition although its general connotations are rather self-evident.[1] Like any other system, a system of agriculture is an arrangement or organization of component parts into a functioning whole which distinguishes such a unity from a mere aggregation. Thus the significance of the word system in the concept is the same as that which it has in connection with other concepts such as organic system, astronomic system, weather system, and so on. Simultaneously, in order to distinguish the system of agriculture from all others, we must indicate that it is a body of practices, cultural traits, customs, ideas, skills, techniques,

[1] For more complete explanations of the concept and a classification of its principal types or varieties, see T. Lynn Smith, *The Sociology of Rural Life*, 3rd ed., New York: Harper and Brothers, 1953, Chapter 14; and T. Lynn Smith, *Brazil: People and Institutions,* 3rd ed., Baton Rouge: Louisiana State University Press, 1963, Chapter XV.

prejudices, habits, implements, machines, animals, scientific knowledge, seeds, and so forth, used by the members of a specific society in order to secure agricultural and livestock products from the soil. Moreover, this part of the social order is highly institutionalized, so that among the farmers of any given region or community the acceptable methods of preparing the seed bed, cultivation, caring for livestock, harvesting, and transportation are highly standardized; and in general the social and cultural values of the community are oriented in the direction of preserving the traditional forms of life and labor.

The system of agriculture should be thought of in terms sufficiently broad to include all of the scientific knowledge, skills, practices, implements, machines, domesticated animals, and so on, which have a part in agricultural and pastoral activities and in rural transportation. Thus the system used by a village of Indians in the Colombian jungle may have as its central components the digging sticks used by the women of the tribe and a complex of magical and religious practices designed to promote the germination of the seeds and to foster the productivity of the soil; whereas that in vogue in a large sugar-cane plantation in the Cauca Valley, or a big cotton plantation in Tolima, may consist of a highly intricate combination of practices that have stood the test in many parts of the world, well-established scientific principles, and the most modern machines and implements, that is of components that had not even been conceived of 50 years ago.

In passing, it also is important to recognize that the acquisition of the fund of knowledge and the richness of the procedures which enables the modern agriculturist to magnify the gifts of nature and to bring forth an abundance of agricultural and livestock products is the greatest development in the history of civilization. Only to the extent to which the control of the natural processes brought about an increase in the quantity of food and fiber produced by a given man was it possible for human energy to be directed to other branches of industry, commerce, transportation, communication, science, philosophy, the liberal professions, services, and so on, which have led us to the nuclear age.

The Six Principal Systems of Agriculture

Some time ago I classified the various systems of agriculture into the six following fundamental types: (1) river-bank plantings; (2) "fire agriculture"; (3) hoe culture; (4) rudimentary plow culture; (5) advanced plow culture; and (6) mechanized farming.[2] Of these six systems only three are of any particular importance in Colombia, namely, "fire agriculture" and hoe culture (sometimes supplemented by a feeble addition of some of the elements of rudimentary plow culture), which are the traditional ones used by the rural masses; and mechanized farming, which represents the wave of the future. Fals Borda in his fundamental study, the most important contribution to date to the study of Colombia's systems of agriculture, makes no mention of river-bank plantings nor of advanced plow culture.[3] However, although the first of these is lacking in the department of Boyacá, it still persists on a small scale among the Indians who live along the streams in the remote parts of the Amazon Basin far removed from the heavily populated parts of the country. But the system in which the fundamental components are the metal turning plow, the use of horses as draft animals, and the four-wheeled farm wagon (this is to say the combination which lead to the high stage of development in countries such as England, France, Germany, Holland, Canada, and the United States) never found a place in Colombian society, and it seems impossible to bring about the radical change in the social system that would be required to accomplish the introduction

[2] A general analysis of the systems of agriculture is presented in Smith, *The Sociology of Rural Life*, Chapter 14; and a study of the roles of each of the types in Brazilian society is given in Smith, *Brazil*, Chapter 15.

[3] Orlando Fals Borda, *El Hombre y la Tierra en Boyacá*, Bogotá: Ediciones Documentos Colombianos, 1957, Chapter IX. (The original in English entitled *A Sociological Study of the Relationships between Man and the Land in the Department of Boyacá, Colombia* was submitted in 1955 in partial fulfillment of the requirements for the Ph.D. degree in sociology at the University of Florida.)

of this advanced plow culture.[4] In any case for purposes here, the important thing is to attend to the three systems of agriculture that are designated as "fire agriculture," hoe culture, and mechanized farming.

The Improvement of Traditional Systems

The Colombian campesino remains tied to antiquated procedures that waste his labor prodigally and there are slight prospects that he will be able in the near future to make any radical changes in his routinary and inefficient systems. In the torrid zones, the rural families continue caring for their subsistence plots, that is of the patches of plantains, bananas, manioc, yams, and so on, in their *conucos,* aided solely by the ax and the machete. They do not cultivate the soil in any sense of the word; in the system they use there is no necessity for digging, moving, or turning the earth. Their present system of agriculture is the traditional one called *rozar* ("fire agriculture") that is so well described in Libro IV, Título XII,

[4] It is highly interesting to study the attempts, commencing in the days of the struggle for independence, of Englishmen, Frenchmen, persons from the United States, and even Colombians themselves, to transplant to Colombia the turning plow and other basic features of this system of agriculture. See, for example, Charles Stuart Cochrane, *Journal of a Residence and Travels in Colombia . . . ,* London: Henry Colburn, 1825, Vol. II, pp. 5–6 and 188–189; William Duane, *A Visit to Colombia in the Years 1822 & 1823,* Philadelphia: Thomas H. Palmer, 1826, pp. 407–408; P. L. Bell, *Colombia: A Commercial Handbook,* Washington: Government Printing Office, 1921, pp. 163, 177, 199, and 221; and Orlando Fals Borda, *Facts and Theory of Sociocultural Change in a Rural Social System,* Monografías Sociológicas No. 2 Bis, Bogotá: Universidad Nacional de Colombia, 1960, p. 20. The experience reported by Fals Borda in his studies of Saucio probably is more or less typical of these attempts to introduce the turning plow as an implement without, at the same time, transplanting the many complementary elements upon which its successful use depends. Be this as it may, among the campesinos of Saucio "The first steel plows easily broke, and later models were defective in the angle and bladecatching mechanism." *Ibid.,* p. 18. (A few of the essential features that were lacking in these trials are: the necessary clevises, double trees, adequate harnesses, well-trained teams of horses or mules, and, most important of all, a plowman who had had several years of apprenticeship, preferably during his youth.)

Ley XXII of the Laws of the Indies, which reads as follows: "Whereas in the district of the villa of Tolú, of the province of Cartagena, there are large expanses of unproductive land, and of great and very dense forests which have no value or use other than that of farming or agriculture, by felling, burning, and clearing the woods, and their quality is such that only during the year in which the forest is felled and burned do they plant and replant the maize, which is called a new *roza*, and at least the next year and for twenty subsequent years they are of no further use. . . ."

In the densely populated temperate and cool zones, where the bulk of the rural population lives, the system of agriculture is one that involves the cultivation of the land. But in these areas as a general rule the small farmers depend almost exclusively upon hoes, the digging stick, and the machete, that is upon agricultural implements whose use is totally dependent upon human energy. Only a few of them are in economic circumstances which permit the use of a mule as a pack animal. Furthermore, due to the high degree to which the components of a system of agriculture are interdependent and the large extent to which the campesinos are bound by their cultural heritage and their traditional social values, it is extremely difficult to bring about improvements in their agricultural practices. The proponents of various theories of directed social change, for example, should pay particular attention to the results of the efforts of Fals Borda to introduce new implements among his campesino friends in the Saucio district. Here are the exact words used in his report: "The farmers distinguish what can be damaging or prejudicial to them; thus they reject apparently useful innovations. Such was the case with the writer's experimentation with the scythe in 1956. After one year and a half of continued trials with a number of Saucites, it became evident that the scythe could not displace locally the rudimentary sickle for the harvesting of grain. The terrain; the kind of seed; the nature of weed growth; the weather in relation to tying, shocking, and stacking; the system of threshing; all conspired to curtail the local efficacy of the scythe as a grainharvesting implement. The sickle remained while the farmers handed down their decision against the innovation. This decision was sound from the technical viewpoint. In a similar manner, resistance against the modern combines, that appeared in Saucio for the first time in 1955, was justified for at least one good objective reason: The machines did not separate efficiently the weed from the wheat; and, consequently, the harvest was damaged."[5]

Very explicit and exact statements may be made with respect to the extent of the persistence of antiquated systems of agriculture among the masses of Colombia's campesinos, since in the year 1960 the national government completed the first agricultural census to be made in that country. Presently we already have available the national summaries of these data, sources of information that have made obsolete all of the partial estimates prepared for earlier years. According to the extremely valuable information collected in this census, the total number of *explotaciones agropecuarios* (or of farms and subsistence tracts taken together) in 1960 came to 1,209,-672, of which 781,717 (or 65 per cent) relied exclusively upon human energy. This is to say that two-thirds of all the agricultural and pastoral units in the country, from the *conucos* and subsistence *estancias* of the resident laborers on the fincas and haciendas to the great estates containing more than 2,500 hectares apiece, completely lacked any draft animals, horses, mules or burros for riding or packing. They also had no tractors or motors of any type. See Table I. Moreover, there are departments in which this proportion is as high as 95, 96, and 97 per cent. . . .

It should be indicated that even these statistical materials are not truly indicative of the extreme degree to which the Colombian campesinos remain dependent upon the hoe, the machete, the ax, and fire in their agricultural enterprises. First, although the great majority of those who own the large estates and the moderate-sized fincas do not live on their properties, there still are many more dwellings on the farms and subsistence tracts than there are explotaciones agropecuarios themselves. Thus the census gives 1,309,942 as the total number of dwellings on the agricultural and pastoral units, a figure 100,270 greater than the number of explo-

[5] Fals Borda, *Facts and Theory of Sociocultural Change*, pp. 19–20.

Table I.   Numbers and Proportions of the Explotaciones
Agropecuarias in Colombia Reporting No Power Except
Manpower Being used by Size, 1960*

Size of explotaciones (in hectares)	Number of explotaciones	Explotaciones dependent solely upon manpower	
		Number	Per cent
Less than 0.5	165,652	144,236	87
0.5- 0.9	132,419	96,059	73
1- 1.9	191,347	131,054	68
2- 2.9	117,005	75,630	65
3- 3.9	92,001	56,216	61
4- 4.9	58,181	34,739	60
5- 9.9	169,145	94,579	56
10- 19.9	114,231	60,849	53
20- 29.9	44,049	23,362	53
30- 39.9	26,500	14,204	54
40- 49.9	16,240	8,792	54
50- 99.9	39,990	21,872	55
100- 199.9	22,317	11,711	52
200- 499.9	13,693	6,233	46
500- 999.9	4,141	1,536	37
1,000-2,499.9	1,975	551	28
2,500-over	786	93	
Total	1,209,672	781,716	65

*Source: Compiled and computed from data given in Departamento
Administrativo Nacional de Estadística, "Resumen Nacional (Segunda
Parte)," *Directorio Nacional de Explotaciones Agropecuarias (Censo
Agropecuario), 1960*. Bogotá: Multilith Estadinal, 1964, p. 56.

taciones. Furthermore, the number of dwellings should correspond roughly to the number of agricultural and pastoral
families who live on the farms and subsistence tracts; but it is
regrettable that the data available do not permit a cross classification of the number of families living on the *explotaciones*
who lack completely any draft and pack animals or motorized
equipment. Second, as is well known, there are many thousands of peons and other agricultural laborers who do not live
on the land itself but in clusters of huts (*rancherias*), hamlets, villages, towns, and cities of all sizes. The number of
such families who do not live on the explotaciones, but who
gain their livelihood by working on the farms and ranches
must be approximately 200,000; and we may be certain that
at least 95 per cent of them have neither animals nor motor-

ized equipment for use in their work. Thus it seems reasonable to estimate that there are about 1,500,000 Colombian families who are dependent upon agriculture and stock raising. Of these about 75 per cent or 1,125,000 families must rely exclusively upon their own hands, aided only by the hoe, the ax, the machete, and fire.

The Mechanized System of Agriculture

There are substantial reasons for believing that the mechanized system of agriculture, based upon the tractor and the modern implements associated with it, is the doorway through which Colombian farming will enter the twentieth century. As a matter of fact, there are a few parts of the country in which the cultivation of the soil is abreast of the possibilities of the second half of that century. Among all of the factors related to the revolution in Colombia's systems of agriculture, this is to say to the great process of development now underway, two are of primary importance: (1) as a general rule until the close of the Second World War the lands best suited for cultivation in Colombia (because of their topography, fertility, and location with respect to the cities) were held almost unused in the extensive and rudimentary pastoral estates of a few powerful landowners; and (2) the mechanized system of agriculture is an entirely new cultural complex, largely lacking links with traditional ways, so that its use demands the simultaneous introduction and employment of its thousands of components. (In sharp contrast to the many futile attempts to introduce the simple turning plow and the advanced plow culture system of agriculture, no one is tempted to try fitting a few features of mechanized farming into the antiquated ways of rudimentary plow culture.)

The pattern in which for a period of 400 years the lands most suited for farming were monopolized by the Spanish overlords and their descendants for pastures for their livestock while the plantings of the Indians and mestizos were crowded off into out of the way places and up onto the steep mountainsides has been documented elsewhere.[6] Here we are

[6] See, for example, T. Lynn Smith, "Land Tenure and Soil

limited by space to a reference to two of the most important observations pertaining to the obstructive nature of the pattern under consideration. One of these items is from the highly important report of Manuel Ancízar, secretary of the famous Codazzi Commission and it was written more than a century ago. It refers to the situation on the Savanna of Bogotá, by far the largest and most important area of level land in the high, cool and densely populated zones of Colombia. In literal translation, it reads as follows: "From Bogotá to Zipaquirá it is ten granadian leagues of level road, whose greater part has the same floor which the good Bochica left us when he drained the great lake whose bed constituted the beautiful plain upon which the innocent Chibchas lived and worked. They, according to what we are told by the chroniclers of the conquest, were cultivating palm by palm the entire plain: we have converted it into pasture for fattening livestock, that is to say, we have taken a step backwards, since grazing is the first step in civilization, which is not truly developed except by agriculture. In the ten leagues of plains mentioned, only the pueblo of Cajicá presents its lands carefully cultivated and planted, being preserved there, as in the other pueblos of the indigenes, the primitive type of agriculturist in contrast with our lazy industry of stock raising."[7]

Inasmuch as cultural complexes and social systems are highly resistant to change, the third citation has been made for the purpose of indicating that the monopolization of the best lands for a rudimentary pastoral industry had taken place long before the perceptive work of Ancízar was done. It is a statement by one of the last of the Viceroys of the New Kingdom of Granada, who also was Archbishop, a man who held power during the decade ending in 1789, and in translation it reads as follows:

"One sees the most fertile valleys, whose abundance pleads for the hand of man, more to harvest than to labor; and nevertheless they are found to be empty without a single in-

Erosion in Colombia," *Proceedings of the Inter-American Conference on the Conservation of Renewable Resources,* Washington: U. S. Department of State, 1948, pp. 155–160.

[7] Manuel Ancízar, *Peregrinación de Alpha,* Bogotá: Arboleda & Valencia, 1914, pp. 12–13.

habitant, at the same time that the rough, sterile mountain-sides are peopled by criminals and fugitives, persons who have fled society to live without law or religion. It is sufficient to delineate a small map of the population of the Kingdom in order to appreciate the confusion and disorder in which these men of the mountains live, electing of their own choice and without the intervention of the Government nor of the local judges their places of retreat, the more remote from the pueblo and its church the more pleasing to them [the mountain people]. Except for the few cities of the first class which hardly merit second class rating from the mere appearance of their unhappy buildings or third class rating of pure name from the memory of their ruins and remains; except also for some Parishes which recently have been established on better lines, all the other population centers are merely small collections of miserable *ranchos, chozas,* and *bujíos,* which constitute only the twentieth part of the inhabitants attributed to the respective places. This comes from the old and deep-seated liberty of fleeing from one to the other to live at their expense without fear of apprehension in their infamous and vile undertakings. Men designated as fairly well off are those who from the lack of measures designed to prevent the concentration of [the ownership of] land in the hands of a single person, have succeeded in acquiring at ridiculous prices immense holdings in which they regularly hold as serfs the less well-to-do. The former preserve more firmly their possessions through the income which they receive from their broad domains; but the latter, who make up the great majority of the free inhabitants, constitute strictly speaking a migratory, floating population who, forced by the tyranny of the land owners, move about with the facility conceded to them by the small amount of their household goods, the slight value of their huts, and the lack of love for the fonts in which they were baptized. They have the same in the place they die as in the one in which they were born, and in any place they find the same as they left. They eat little with considerable grossness, but they are not so temperate in drinking. They are always ready and willing for games, dances, and functions, inclined to laziness, to which the fertility of the land contributes, a little work sufficing to supply their few necessities.

Their children, educated in this school, go on imitating faithfully their parents; they continue propagating always the same thoughts and the same conduct and rusticity, and in spite of the general increase in population, they only increase the number of such useless vassals, who with great strides are precipitating themselves in the same barbarity as the first inhabitants."[8]

Turning our attention to the present and to the interest that some of the large proprietors are taking in monoculture of various types, such as the cultivation of sugar cane, cotton, and rice, a few of the most important tendencies may be indicated. It is well to start this by mentioning that for a long while, especially since 1947, Colombia has been undergoing the destruction and ravages brought about by great political divisions and struggle, or the tremendous blood bath resulting from the so-called "violencia" of civil war and banditry, and the general lack of security for life and property. From the sociological point of view the nation is undergoing the torment of all the tensions and conflicts of a chaotic condition in which one general social system is losing its force, leaving the society involved on a course that is unpredictable and seemingly beyond control. Nevertheless, even in the situation prevailing, much headway is being made in the development of a modern system of mechanized agriculture. The fact has already been mentioned that the vast majority of the best land is readily available for cultivation as quickly as and to the extent that a few large and powerful landowners develop a concern about plants and cultivation. Also highly important to mention in this connection is the abundance of petroleum in Colombia, for export as well as for all domestic needs. Moreover, there are in that country immense beds of coal and large deposits of iron ore, and it already has a domestic steel industry well capable of satisfying the needs of the factories

[8] "Relación del Estado del Nuevo Reino de Granada, que hace el Arzobispo de Cordova a su sucesor el Exemo. Sr. Don Francisco Gil y Lemus, Año de 1789," in José Antonio García y García, ed., *Relaciones de los Virreyes del Nuevo Reino de Granada,* New York: Hallet and Breen, 1869, pp. 215–216. It should be indicated that some of the successors of the Archbishop declared that His Excellency's judgments were a little extreme. Cf. *ibid.,* pp. 452 ff.

that could make the agricultural machinery. In summary everything points to substantial changes in the traditional systems of agriculture in which human labor is wasted to such a staggering degree.

Today one who visits the Savanna of Bogotá, the Cauca Valley, the plains of the upper Magdalena, the areas near Villavicencio and Florencia on the great plains to the east of the Andes, the Caribbean coastal plain, and so on, no longer will be surprised by the absence of tractors, modern plows, and all of the other implements and machines involved in a system of agriculture that is in line with the social values of the second half of the twentieth century. In the rice plantations and even in some of the wheat fields he can see combines for harvesting and threshing the grain, in place of the sickles and the animals circling the threshing floors which prevailed until very recently. If he goes to one of the cotton zones, such an observer may even see small airplanes taking part in the work of dusting the growing plants.

When we did our sociological study of the município of Tabio during the years 1943 and 1944 my Colombian associates and I found no tractors whatsoever in this small arm of the Savanna of Bogotá. On the basis of interviews with all the heads of agricultural families in the município, those of the farm operators as well as those of the farm laborers, we found that: "Only 27, or 11 per cent, of Tabio's farm operators possess steel plows. Another 174, or 72 per cent, have only the wooden plow with its crude steel point. The remaining 40 possess no plow of any type, but through the various systems of compañia in vogue some of their farms probably have the plow applied to the soil. However, a considerable amount of the land is never stirred by any means except the hoe. Of the farm laborers, only one family possesses a steel plow, and only 55, or less than 30 per cent, have wooden plows. Through the various partnership arrangements some of the others, too, may have some use made of these animal-drawn instruments on their small estancias. But it is fair to say that for the most part the pan coger yielded by their small subsistence plots is extracted solely by hand labor."[9] Twenty

[9] T. Lynn Smith, Justo Díaz Rodríguez, and Luis Roberto

years later, in one of the periodical visits subsequently made to the município, almost as soon as the boundary of the county-like unit was passed, a tractor was seen working in the field; and the 1960 census of agriculture enumerated a total of 39 that were owned by farmers in the small administrative subdivision.

Unfortunately other studies that would indicate with exactitude the nature of the systems of agriculture prevailing in Colombia 20 years ago are lacking, but notes I made daily in visits to various parts of the Republic in the years 1943, 1944, and 1945, indicate that only now and then does one encounter any entries pertaining to tractors or other modern agricultural machinery. For example, in the course of a visit (February 26, 1944) to one of the haciendas owned by a prominent family in Pasto, we recorded that the proprietor, who was president of the Agricultural Society of Nariño, possessed a tractor and that it was one of the two in the entire department. (. . . there were 263 tractors in the department in 1960.) Similarly there are the notes made on the occasion of a visit (October 17 and 18, 1943) to one of the haciendas of the Ministério de Economia in the Samacá Valley, in Boyacá. There we saw tractors at work on preparing for planting to wheat level lands on the floor of the valley that had been devoted exclusively to pastoral activities for almost 400 years. But these cases are the exceptions: as a general rule in the hundreds of fincas and haciendas that we visited, from the department of Magdalena on the north to Nariño on the Ecuadorian border, we found no implements whatsoever that had anything to do with the mechanization of agriculture.

At present the data are vastly superior. As has been indicated above the reports of the agricultural census taken in 1960, the first comprehensive enumeration made in Colombia, are a treasury of important information about the subject. Already indicated is the fact that there are approximately 1,300,000 families living on Colombia's farms, ranches, and subsistence plots, and that this total does not include other hundreds of thousands of families whose livelihood is di-

García, *Tabio: A Study in Rural Social Organization*, Washington: Office of Foreign Agricultural Relations, 1945, pp. 36–37.

rectly dependent upon agricultural work even though their dwellings are in population centers of various sizes. Since the census gives a total of 15,361 tractors on Colombia's farms, it may be calculated that there is approximately one tractor for each 85 families residing on the explotaciones agropecuarias.

It is reasonable to suppose that there would be a close association between the size of the agricultural units and the degree to which the tractor and complementary implements are used; and this proposition can easily be confirmed from an examination of the materials presented in Table II. Thus the number of dwelling units (which should correspond rather closely to the number of families) per tractor is 2,177 for the smallest of the size categories, whereas it is only 4 per tractor on the estates containing more than 2,500 hectares.

It also is possible to indicate with some precision the extent to which the mechanization of agriculture varies from department to department. . . . This variation is tremendous, or from only one tractor for each 503 dwellings or families in the rugged terrain of Antioquia to one tractor for each 20 dwellings in the department of El Valle del Cauca. Mechanized farming likewise has developed slowly in the cool and heavily populated uplands of the departments of Santander, Boyacá, and Nariño, while it is keeping pace with the rhythm of change in El Valle del Cauca, in departments such as Atlántico (on the Caribbean coastal plain), and in Meta (to the east of the Andes). Furthermore, in the departments which include parts of the plains in the upper Magdalena Valley, that is in Tolima, Huila, and Cundinamarca, where cotton is king, and on the Savanna of Bogotá (also in Cundinamarca), the adoption of modern methods for cultivating the soil is making rapid headway. Finally, in other portions of the northern coastal plain, or more specifically in the departments of Magdalena, Córdoba, and Bolívar, the tractor presently is being used extensively in the radical transformation of large areas traditionally devoted to grazing into huge plantations of cotton, sugar cane, and rice.

Other useful information relating to the distribution of tractors and of the system of agriculture of which these form the core or integrating feature, may be secured from a study of

Table II.   The Relationship Between the Size of the Explotaciones Agropecuarias and the Number of Households per Tractor in Colombia, 1960*

Size of explotaciones (hectares)		Number of dwellings	Number of tractors	Number of dwellings or households per tractor
Less than 0.5		154,599	71	2,177
0.5-	0.9	112,628	150	751
1.0-	1.9	171,641	353	486
2.0-	2.9	113,327	208	545
3.0-	3.9	94,823	214	443
4.0-	4.9	62,199	148	420
5.0-	9.9	194,738	762	256
10.0-	19.9	142,691	1,054	135
20.0-	29.9	58,676	728	81
30.0-	39.9	36,369	600	61
40.0-	49.9	22,822	477	48
50.0-	99.9	59,228	1,920	31
100.0-	199.9	37,637	2,242	17
200.0-	499.9	27,670	2,540	11
500.0-	999.9	11,191	1,705	7
1,000.0-2,499.9		6,516	1,380	5
2,500.0-over		3,187	799	4
Total		1,309,942	15,361	85

* *Source:* Compiled and computed from data in Departamento Administrativo Nacional de Estadística, "Resumen Nacional (Segunda Parte)," *Directorio Nacional de Explotaciones Agropecuarias (Censo Agropecuario), 1960,* Bogotá: Multilith Estadinal, 1964, pp. 56 and 59.

the extent to which these machines have found places for themselves on the fincas and plantations of the various municípios or counties into which the departments are subdivided. See Table III. These materials enable us to see that in the year 1960 more than half (58 per cent) of all the municípios in the country had at least one tractor in use on its farms. . . .

Finally, it is interesting to note exactly in which municípios the mechanized system of agriculture is most advanced. In this connection the most striking case of all is that of the município of Palmira in the department of El Valle del Cauca, seat of the famed sugar-cane plantation called "La Man-

Table III. Number and Proportions of the Municípios in Which There Was One or More Tractors, by Departments, 1960

Department	Total number of municipios	Municipios in which tractors were reported	
		Number	Per cent
Total	824	480	58
Antioquia	102	39	38
Atlántico	21	21	100
Bolívar	43	43	100
Boyacá	123	34	28
Caldas	47	24	51
Cauca	33	19	58
Córdoba	21	21	100
Cundinamarca	114	74	65
Huila	33	27	82
Magdalena	30	28	93
Meta	13	12	92
Nariño	49	27	55
Norte de Santander	35	13	37
Santander	75	31	41
Tolima	43	33	77
Valle del Cauca	42	34	81

*Source: Compiled and computed from "Resumen Nacional," *Directorio Nacional de Explotaciones Agropecuarias (Censo Agropecuario), 1960,* Bogotá: Multilith Estadinal, 1962, pp. 23–91.

uelita," whose agricultural enterprises in 1960 were making use of more tractors than those in the entire areas of six of the sixteen departments into which Colombia is subdivided. See Table IV. Even the agricultural producers of the small município of Candelaria in El Valle del Cauca, with an agricultural population of only 10,855, were using at the time of the census of 1960 more tractors (349) than those of the famed department of Antioquia, with an agricultural population of 964,710 and only 341 tractors. Table IV gives the data for the 40 municípios in Colombia in which the farmers of the small political subdivision involved were using at least 75 tractors.

Table IV.   The Number of Tractors and the Resident Agricultural
Population of Each Municipio for Which 75 or more Tractors Owned
by the Productores on Explotaciones Agropecuarias Were Reported in 1960*

Municipio and department	Number of tractors	Resident agricultural population
Palmira, Valle del Cauca	501	21,482
Espinal, Tolima	403	12,414
Candelaria, Valle del Cauca	349	10,885
El Cerrito, Valle del Cauca	313	8,261
Agustín Codazzi, Magdalena	295	6,916
Armero, Tolima	278	6,951
Guamo, Tolima	270	19,808
Aracataca, Magdalena	204	10,475
Villavicencio, Meta	190	12,289
Pradera, Valle del Cauca	182	7,986
Tuluá, Valle del Cauca	181	18,148
Caloto, Cauca	150	14,236
Purificación, Tolima	149	19,581
Guacarí, Valle del Cauca	146	6,002
Jamundí, Valle del Cauca	141	14,081
Monteria, Córdoba	138	48,076
La Dorada, Caldas	138	4,037
Florida, Valle del Cauca	135	6,593
Miranda, Cauca	128	6,443
Tunja, Boyacá	128	20,889
Valledupar, Magdalena	126	32,267
Ibague, Tolima	123	31,898
Ambalema, Tolima	118	1,113
Lérida, Tolima	114	4,142
Ginebra, Valle del Cauca	99	3,818
Cucutá, Norte de Santander	98	16,853
Ciénaga, Magdalena	97	25,469
Santander, Cauca	94	19,577
Flandes, Tolima	92	3,086
Cali, Valle del Cauca	91	14,601
Buga, Valle del Cauca	86	8,663
Corinto, Cauca	85	11,916
Pasto, Nariño	81	29,416
Robles, Magdalena	79	10,140
Ortega, Tolima	78	19,528
Carmen de Corupa, Cundinamarca	78	7,942
Alvarado, Tolima	77	5,352
Piedecuesta, Santander	77	9,235
Campo Alegre, Huila	75	5,536
Corozal, Bolívar	75	17,379

* *Source:* Compiled and computed from "Resumen Nacional,"
*Directorio Nacional de Explotaciones Agropecuarios (Censo
Agropecuario), 1960,* Bogotá: Multilith Estadinal, 1962, pp. 23–
91.

Conclusion

In conclusion, we should see in the rapid development of the mechanized system of agriculture in Colombia the portents of even greater changes in the traditional and dominant social system than those that have occurred during the last two or three decades. The skilled worker who is trained to handle tractors, other machines, and modern agricultural implements is a very different human type than the peon, *arrendatario,* or *conuquero,* of the traditional fincas and haciendas. The skilled and demanding activities of the worker who drives and keeps in working order the tractor, truck, and so on, require specialized training in which mental activities and the capacity to take responsibility and make decisions are indispensable. Often such an employee must know more about machinery and mechanics and even the processes of agriculture than the landowner, the administrator in charge of the finca, and any kind of a driver, overseer, or gang boss. These comments are intended to indicate that by itself the transformation of a few large pastoral estates into mechanized plantations is putting in march vast changes in the mentality, aspirations, and power of some of the *campesinos.* There should follow pressures for a genuine agrarian reform on a large scale to bring about a substantial redistribution of the property rights to and control of the land. It may be, at long last, that Colombia will accomplish the long-time objectives of some of its important leaders of a middle class of owners of family-sized farms and a social system that is similar to those of such countries as England, France, Denmark, Switzerland, West Germany, Holland, Canada, and the United States.

18 Some Salient Features
of Agrarian Reform
in Latin America

————◆————

IN THE COURSE of the last century and a half many absorbing
and disturbing issues have commanded the attention of those
in positions of power and influence throughout the Latin
American countries; but the current almost universal concern
about agrarian reform is in a class by itself in the degree to
which simultaneously it has come to monopolise the attention of affluent and educated Latin Americans and has become the major hope of the masses. As has been stated by
one of the most perceptive Latin Americans of our day:
"Never was a reform so discussed and debated, in Brazil or
outside of it, as the agrarian."[1]

The accuracy of this generalisation by an author who is
one of those most conversant with the present situation in all
parts of the half continent we call Brazil, in the 19 other nations in the Latin American group, in the newly emerged nations of Africa, and in others of the "underdeveloped" countries could easily be documented with mountains of evidence.[2]
At the present time, though, it is sufficient to indicate that as
plans and proposals take form in measures and activities, interest in agrarian reform waxes and debate over specific proposals and accomplishments intensifies. Thus in the press and
in reviews of all types, on television and on radio, in political

From *International Labour Review,* Vol. 91, No. 4 (April,
1965), pp. 321–336.

[1] J. V. Freitas Marcondes: "Reforma agrária à luz das clen-
cias sociais", in *Sociologia,* (São Paulo), Vol. XXIV, No. 4, Dec.
1962, p. 273.

[2] For a few of the most pertinent sources see T. Lynn Smith:
Agrarian Reform in Latin America (New York, Knopf, 1965).

gatherings at all levels and in the halls of the parliaments there is a lavish flow of words having to do with the nature and purposes of agrarian reform, plans and proposals for accomplishing its objectives, and the extent to which the laws enacted and the programmes of the agencies that have been established are attaining the ends for which they were created. This goes on, with the specific topics being determined largely by the stage of development of the programme in the respective country, in all parts of gigantic Brazil, in Bolivia and Colombia, in Cuba and Venezuela, in Chile and Ecuador, in Costa Rica and Peru, and all the rest. Even in Mexico, where with much reason the past tense may be used in speaking of agrarian reform accomplishments, the reorientation of objectives and the revision of measures continue to absorb the attention of many of the highest officials and most accomplished analysts.[3]

With popular interest in the subject running high, persons seeking governmental office at the local, provincial, and national levels find proposals for agrarian reform, or for modifying programmes that are being attempted, to be important planks in their platforms; officials in the ministries of agriculture and other governmental departments become aware that the ways and means of modifying the prevailing relationships between man and the land are among their own chief preoccupations; and social scientists in the universities, in various research agencies, and in governmental service discover that they cannot remain aloof from the issues. Nowadays they must give substantial attention to the study of land tenure, the distribution of land ownership and control, the antiquated and ineffective systems of agriculture that still devour the energies of the population in many sections, the development of social legislation that will promote the welfare of agricultural labourers, and the problems of community development. Even the heads of the military establishments, with increased

[3] See, for example, Ramón Fernández y Fernández: "La reforma agraria mexicana: Logros y problemas derivados", in *Boletín de estudios especiales* (Mexico City, Banco Nacional de Crédito Ejidal), Vol. VIII, No. 93, July 1957, pp. 211–220; and Victor Manzanilla Schaffer: *La reforma agraria* (Mexico City, Departamento de Asuntos Agrarios y Colonización, 1964).

frequency, are getting involved publicly in the issues revolving about agrarian reform.

Perhaps, though, the best perspective on the current role of agrarian reform in Latin American affairs is obtained by a thoughtful reading of the two following extracts. The first of these contains the words of Dom Helder Camara, Roman Catholic Archbishop of Rio de Janeiro, and is part of an address he made on 27 February 1963 over a television station in Washington, D.C.:

> I am not speaking as a Brazilian addressing Americans but as a man talking to other men. . . . The Alliance for Progress is dead, however much I should hope for its resurrection. The main reason for its failure seems to be the following: it was necessary to establish close co-ordination between the help from the Alliance and the basic reforms, but unfortunately the rich in Latin America talk too much about reform and label as Communists all those who try to enforce it. This is easy to understand: the rich in Latin America go on holding 80 per cent. of the land on the continent. Often they control parliament and have the intensity of their idealism and hope in the future gauged by the bank deposits kept in their names in the United States and Europe. Unfortunately, the rich in your country also create problems: President Kennedy could be a witness to that.[4]

The second is the most pertinent part of the solemn pledge made by all of the Latin American countries except Cuba in 1961 in the Charter of Punta del Este, popularly known as the Alliance for Progress. The signatories of the Charter agree—

> To encourage, in accordance with the characteristics of each country, programs of comprehensive agrarian reform leading to the effective transformation, where required, of unjust structures and systems of land tenure and use, with a view to replacing latifundia and dwarf holdings by an equitable system of land tenure so that, with the help of timely and adequate credit, technical assistance and facilities for marketing and distribution of products, the land will become for the man who works it the basis of his

[4] From a press release issued by the Brazilian Embassy, Washington, D.C., 27 February, 1963.

economic stability, the foundation of his increasing welfare, and the guarantee of his freedom and dignity.[5]

Background and cause of the current outburst of interest in agrarian reform

For anyone deeply concerned about the social and economic welfare of those who till the soil in various parts of the earth, there is much food for thought as to why the current eruption of interest in agrarian reform throughout Latin America should be taking place now. Why did this particular outburst take place early in the second half of the twentieth century rather than about 1800, 1850, 1900, 1920, or even 1940? One does not need to delve much into the writings about Latin American societies by historians, economists, sociologists, and other scholars before it becomes evident that, judged by present standards, most of the indicators of an acute need for agrarian reform have been present throughout Latin America for at least a century and a half. These include, of course, the two-class society with its high degree of concentration of ownership and control of the land; the prodigal waste of the labour of the landless masses, who are paid scarcely enough to enable them to satisfy the mere creature-needs of life; the high degree to which the most fertile and accessible lands in the valleys and on the plains are devoted to rudimentary pastoral activities or left unused entirely while the cultivated fields of the peasants have been confined to the steep slopes of the mountains or to other marginal areas; the considerable extent to which land is an asylum for capital; and the prevailing illiteracy and miserably low levels of living of the rural masses. Moreover, it is easy to find that from time to time and place to place able exponents of substantial changes in the distribution of land ownership and other essential features of agrarian reform have appealed to their compatriots to put measures into effect that would enable the masses of their countrymen to rise above the serf-like existence to which they have long been subjected. Prominent in

[5] This is the complete text of paragraph 6 of Title I of the Charter.

the list of such exponents are names such as José Bonifacio de Andrade, Tavares Bastos, A. P. Figueiredo, and Joaquim Nabuco in Brazil; and Salvador Camacho Roldán and (more recently) Alfonso López in Colombia.[6]

As events turned out, though, neither the revolutionary forces in Europe and the United States and Canada, nor those which produced drastic changes in two of the Latin American countries, nor even the calls of foresighted statesmen in nations such as Brazil and Colombia made any general and substantial impression throughout Latin America. Thus late in the eighteenth century the extreme and bloody revolution in Haiti which brought about a profound agrarian reform, involving the complete liquidation of the aristocratic, landowning class of masters, the freeing of the slaves, and the wholesale redistribution of rights to the land, produced no tendency towards emulation in the Spanish and Portuguese colonies. Even though the ferment for independence was going on at the time, with revolts and rebellions soon to break forth, the Haitian experience seems to have had relatively little influence elsewhere in Latin America. Similarly, more than a century later when, after several years of civil war, Mexico's internecine struggle brought about a deep-cutting agrarian reform, there seems to have been relatively little repercussion elsewhere in Latin America. It appears that most of the educated Latin Americans of those two periods, those who alone were cognizant of what was taking place in Haiti and Mexico, considered them as horrible examples of what should be avoided at all costs. The fact is that even during the 1930s, when Portes Gil and Lázaro Cárdenas were effecting wholesale redistribution of landownership in Mexico, such measures enjoyed no popularity among the members of the upper classes elsewhere in Latin America, a small group who owned the land, ran the governments and the economies, and managed the channels of communication; and the great masses of the population in most of the countries, illiterate agricultural labourers who were still in a servile or semi-servile condition and who had practically no contacts with persons other than

[6] Cf. Smith, op. cit., passim; and José Arthur Ríos (editor): *Recomendações sobre reforma agrária* (Rio de Janeiro, Instituto Brasileiro de Acção Democrática, 1961), pp. XI–XVII.

those from the small neighbourhoods in which they lived—
these humble people never even became aware of the fact that
a bitter struggle for "land and liberty" was going on in another country called Mexico. Neither did the relatively few
members of the upper classes nor the great numbers of persons in the lower classes throughout Latin America make any
particular endeavour to extend to the Americas the agrarian
aspects of the Russian Revolution or those of the "Green
Rising" that swept through Europe after the close of the First
World War.

The crucial fact is, of course, that prior to 1920 there were
relatively few contacts between Latin Americans and their
fellows in other parts of the world, and even less between the
inhabitants of a given Latin American country and the people of the others, except, of course, between people living in
immediately adjacent nations such as Argentina and Uruguay
or Honduras and El Salvador. Moreover, the Latin Americans who did come to know Europe or the United States—
practically none went to Asia—were drawn almost exclusively
from the more affluent families. During the opening quarter
of the twentieth century, in sharp contrast with the situation
since 1950, there were no large numbers of Latin American
students in the universities in Europe and the United States;
the aeroplane, the radio and the automobile were not bringing
about millions of social contacts between persons in one country and those in another; international organisations and
agencies were not responsible for the visits of thousands of
Latin Americans to other parts of the world and the stationing
in Latin America of large contingents of experts and technicians from other parts of the earth; and the concerted efforts of various organised groups to promote ideologies of one
type or another in the various Latin American countries were
merely in a stage of incubation. In brief, prior to 1925 few
factors were operating to produce a confrontation between
the traditional Latin American values and standards and those
which formed integral parts of the social systems prevailing
in other parts of America, in Europe and Asia. Or, if the
ideas and values did reach Spanish America and Brazil, as
for example those of central importance in the French Revolution, their realm of influence was limited to the drawing-

rooms of the intellectuals, and they almost never got down to the level at which they could have any particular influence upon the life and labour of the masses of the population, who still remained almost hermetically sealed off in tens of thousands of small, self-sufficient and isolated neighbourhoods and communities. All of this means, in summary, that prior to 1950 it was possible for social systems based largely upon feudalistic patterns and values to persist almost without challenge throughout the huge, highly rural expanses which made up the bulk of the territory and contained a large majority of the people in Latin America.

Before proceeding with the analysis it seems essential to comment briefly upon the nature of the social and value systems that have been mentioned above. Essentially, with some variations which limitations of space do not enable us to analyse here, mankind has produced only two basic social systems for giving form and meaning to the great rural societies which have dominated world history until recent times and to the rural portions of those societies in which the urban pattern of living has gained the ascendancy. One of these highly integrated social systems or entities has the large landed estate as its core and principal determinant; and the other has the family-sized farm as the central component and moving force of the complex. Each of these prime features and determinants, in turn, gives rise to and perpetuates a series of other significant components or characteristics, all of which contrast sharply with their counterparts in the opposing or competing system. Thus the large landed estate, with its close association with slavery, feudalism, peonage, and all other types of servile and semi-servile status for the masses of the families involved in the system to which it gives rise, inevitably produces other social and economic correlates. These include: (i) a two-class society, with a small élite at the upper extreme and a huge mass of impoverished, largely dependent people at the other, the two being separated by a vast void in all parts of the range that would correspond to middle-class status; (ii) a low degree of vertical social mobility; (iii) an overwhelmingly strong tendency for social position to be inherited (the predominant importance of caste); (iv) low average levels of intelligence among the population; (v) limited development of the personalities of the masses; (vi) social relationships of the "order and obey" type, or in other words domination by the élite and rigid subordination of the masses; (vii) great value placed upon routine, with the workers compelled to adhere strictly to the performance of a limited number of tasks in the manner prescribed by the omnipresent "driver", overseer, or *mayordomo;* (viii) low average levels and standards of living; (ix) the omnipresent obsession that manual labour is bemeaning and degrading; and (x) slight stimulus to the development of regular work habits and little stimulus towards or reward for habits of thrift and saving.

Quite the opposite are the basic characteristics of the social system which is brought into being and perpetuated in a rural society in which farms of substantial size are operated by the great majority of all the families who depend directly upon agriculture for their livelihood. In such a social system almost the entire rural population enjoys a middle-class social status, few or no families at all can claim an aristocratic standing and there are comparatively few if any persons who by the accident of birth are condemned to a lifetime of poverty, insecurity and general inferiority. In such a rural social system the moderate social gradations which are present within the middle-class strata preclude the development of caste to any considerable extent, while at the same time there is an intense vertical social circulation up and down the limited social scale, so that each individual tends to rise or sink to the level that is most in accord with his own personal abilities, potentialities and efforts. Children born within such a social system are conditioned almost from birth in ways which prepare them to perform simultaneously the roles of manager, proprietor and manual labourer, with the result that well-rounded personalities are developed and the average level of intelligence (or the ability to adapt to new situations) becomes very high. Where family-sized farms are the moving force in a rural society, persuasion, leadership and voluntary co-operation stand out (in contrast to the patterns of order-and-obey, domination and subordination and caciquism which prevail where plantations and other large estates monopolise the land). Competition for excellence in the performance of farm tasks, the improvement of techniques and implements, the amounts and qualities of products, and so on, gives zest to rural life in the family-sized farming districts and results in miracles of production and distribution. Especially worthy of consideration is the fact that of the billions of agriculturists who have peopled the earth, and even the billions that have lived on the land during the past two centuries, only among the few millions, the handful, of farmers who have been so fortunate as to populate the family-sized farming areas of Western Europe, the United States and Canada, are to be found the inventors and perfecters of almost all of the agricultural implements and machines which now make possible the most highly efficient and productive systems of agriculture the world has ever known.[7] In such a middle-class social system, of course, the search for improvement and change stands in sharp contrast to the emphasis upon routine in the other. Likewise the high average levels and standards of living, the insistence that work with the hands is honourable and uplifting, and the habits of thrift and saving, which characterise the rural social system that has family-sized farms at its core, give a rich form and substance to rural living that is forever

[7] For the role of the family-sized farms in the development and perfecting of agricultural implements and machines see T. Lynn Smith: "El desarrollo de unidades agrícolas medianas", in *Boletín uruguayo de sociología,* Vol. I, No. 2, 1961, pp. 39–47. The major exception to the general responsibility of family-sized farming systems for the development of agricultural machinery of all types is, of course, the basic role played in recent decades by agricultural engineers and their associates at agricultural experiment stations. However, to an overwhelming degree these experiment stations themselves developed and progressed as a function of the family-sized farming areas of a very limited extent of the earth's surface. Indeed, with minor exceptions, there are still no tractors, ploughs, disks, harrows, combines, milking machines, hay loaders, cream separators, and so on, that were developed in and for plantations and other large estates; when these large-scale farms become mechanised, which still has happened to only a small part of those that prevail throughout the world, it is by the adoption and use of large numbers of the pieces of equipment that were perfected in family-sized farming social systems, and not by the application of implements and machines which had their origin and development in systems of large estates, that is in societies in which the bulk of the farm population is confined to the status of agricultural labourers.

lacking when large-scale agriculture and the two-class system it engenders are permitted to determine the pattern of life in the countryside.

That the dominant social system throughout rural Latin America has been and continues to be the one based upon great landholdings is well known. Likewise it is hardly necessary to document the continued importance of many of its features such as the two-class system, the princely positions of the large landowners, and the value systems which supply consistency to the social system involved and give ethical rightness and sanction to the behaviour patterns of the members of the upper class and to the relationships of domination and subordination between master and man. But these features are precisely those that would suddenly come to be considered as archaic, feudalistic and intolerable as Latin American societies were thrust into intimate contact with those of Western Europe and the United States following the close of the Second World War. For example, one of the most brilliant Brazilians of all time, responsible during the Vargas régime for drafting the bulk of Brazil's labour legislation, a man fully attuned to the thinking of his contemporaries, could voice praises of the latifundium such as the following, in volumes that went through edition after edition in the 1930s and 1940s:

> . . . we have been from the beginning a nation of latifundia: among us the history of the small farm can be said to go back only a century. All the long colonial period was one of the splendour of the immense landed estate. In this period it alone appeared and shone; it alone created and dominated; it is the central theme interwoven throughout the entire drama of our history for three hundred fecund and glorious years.[8]

But today, only a few decades later, one will seek in vain for any publication by a Latin American of any intellectual standing which glorifies the large estate. Universally *latifundio* and *latifundista* are terms of opprobrium. Nowadays one en-

---

[8] F. J. Oliveira Vianna: "O povo brasileiro e sua evolução", in *Recenseamento do Brazil, 1920,* Vol. I (Rio de Janeiro, Imprenta Nacional, 1922), p. 282.

counters on every hand the most severe denunciations of the large plantations. A brief extract from one recent example will suffice. In his attempt to gain understanding of and sympathy for the 1964 revolution which ousted President Goulart and brought President Humberto Castelo Branco to power, the dean of Brazilian social scientists and writers, himself one who had glorified the old-style sugar-cane plantation in his classic *Casa Grande e Senzala*, had the following to say:

In some areas, such as in the sugar-cane plantation districts, the land serves only to provide what it can for industry, with the most archaic and anti-economic methods of production, by means of a poorly paid agrarian labour force and a rural population held as pariahs by the landowners. Not a few of these proprietors are absentees from the land which they have long owned and have little contact with their semi-serfs, who live, it is well to repeat, in the condition of pariahs, while the urban workers and also the employees of commercial establishments and banks and the public employees in the cities during recent decades have benefited from the legislation protecting labour and promoting social welfare. It was a situation in which the greater part of the rural population of Brazil was used on the rudest work on plantations and farms, on the estates of men with a mentality quite different from that which years ago characterised the relations between the landowners and their labourers, when the former really were, most of them, a rural gentry: not only proprietors deeply attached to their estates but masters attentive to the needs of their workers in accordance with the patriarchal forms of association.[9]

In the last analysis, it is the change in values, of which this example is representative, that is chiefly responsible for the fact that the recent sudden outburst of concern about agrarian reform throughout Latin America came when it did.

Indicators of the need for agrarian reform

From time to time the present writer has drawn upon his knowledge of Latin American societies and social movements

[9] Translated from Gilberto Freyre: "La lucha no es de clases", in *Life en Español*, 11 May 1964, pp. 25–26.

in an endeavour to set forth the reasons why leaders throughout the various countries consider agrarian reform as absolutely essential. The list thus derived of specific indicators of this need always includes such items as the following: (i) *latifundismo,* or the prevalence of immense tracts of unused or poorly utilised land, estates that not infrequently are deliberately withheld from productive purposes; and, closely associated with this, *minifundismo,* or the proliferation of minute subsistence tracts, far too small to provide for the modest needs of the humble families which own or rent them; (ii) any high concentration of ownership and control of the land even though the units of production may be large commercial plantations; (iii) high proportions of farm labourers in the agricultural population; (iv) low production per worker; (v) low average levels and standards of living; (vi) widespread illiteracy, malnutrition and poor health among rural people generally; and (vii) a high degree of social stratification, or the existence of the two-class system discussed above.[10]

Perhaps, though, the need for agrarian reform has never been stated more eloquently than it was by President Alfonso López of Colombia on 24 July 1935 in a message to Colombia's Congress. This was in defence of his Government's early programme for improving the conditions of those who worked the land. Consider the following few extracts from that message:

> In dealing with these landowners the Government intends to follow no policy other than that of insuring favourable and humanitarian conditions for the working class—day labourers, "renters", and peons—and of preventing the continuance of certain feudal forms in the labour contracts and in the relationships between the owners of the land and the workers. . . . There are still regions in Colombia in which the *campesino,* day labourer or "renter", not only lacks guarantees and security in his work but must endure systems of punishment and contributions imposed by individuals, contrary to the provisions of our laws. . . .

[10] Cf. Smith, op. cit., passim; and idem: *Current social trends and problems in Latin America,* Latin American Monographs No. 1 (Gainesville, University of Florida Press, 1957), pp. 30–34.

The security of the hired labourer should be no less concern to the State than that of security of private property. . . . If the agricultural proprietors and operators find it to their advantage to be governed merely by the law of supply and demand in the labour market, being free to employ cheap hands and dismiss the more costly ones, they must accept the consequences of this mechanical economy with all its excesses. The miserable, uprooted, wandering masses who go about from one place to another in search of work, without finding it on favourable conditions, will always be disposed to listen to the voices of the agitators who play upon their instinctive desires for usurpation and awaken them to the unjust contrast between their economic condition and that of the landowners. The *campesinos* seek stability, not revolution. They aspire to have a plot of land of their own, where they can rear a family without fear of having to return to vagabondage and misery. The proprietor can give it and he does so in the majority of cases; but he cannot resign himself to being deprived of the feudal and supreme right to take it back again, to destroy it if he wishes, to destroy the results of years of toil, even though he must pay for doing so. The bad feeling and the disturbances which some time ago appeared on some large coffee plantations were born of similar causes. Before the eyes of the workers whom the master had dismissed were burned the huts that had been erected under such difficulties by the "renters" and their families, and the excessive cruelty of this act of dispossession was not mitigated by the fact that they had been paid for their improvements.[11]

Finally, it seems essential to mention that most of the 16 paragraphs in the introductory section of Cuba's Executive Order of 17 May 1959 state that country's need for agrarian reform in terms of the indicators that have been given above. This order declares that "it has become urgently necessary to rescue the great majority of the rural population of Cuba from the state of poverty in which it has traditionally struggled"; that in Cuban agriculture "frequent use is made of the sharecropping agreement and the system of ground rents"; that "the great majority of the farms now being cultivated are

[11] The text of the presidential message translated here is given in Marco A. Martínez: *Régimen de tierras en Colombia*, Vol. I (Bogotá, Mundo al Día, 1939), pp. 16–17.

being worked by persons who do not own the land"; that in the agricultural census "the extreme and undesirable concentration of land ownership in a few hands also became evident . . . 1.5 per cent. of the owners possess more than 46 per cent. of all the farm land in the country . . . some owners possess several very large farms"; that "70 per cent. of the farms occupy less than 12 per cent. of the nation's farm land"; that in large farms "there is a detrimental failure to utilise the natural resources"; and that "it is unanimously agreed that the existence of large landholdings . . . not only runs counter to the modern concept of social justice but constitutes one of the factors that shape the underdeveloped, dependent structure of the Cuban economy".[12]

The objectives of agrarian reform

More than a century ago A. P. Figueiredo of Recife, Brazil, stated lucidly and succinctly the proposition that now figures to an overwhelming degree as the basic objective of agrarian reform in the various countries of Latin America. After describing in detail the conditions prevailing on the estates of the "modern feudal barons" of north-eastern Brazil, he indicated that "for such a state of affairs there are only two effective remedies: the first is a return to the old forms of absolute government, which invests the central power with extraordinary control; and the second is to create immediately, at the expense of current feudalism, a middle class that will permit the constitutional government to proceed normally". But, continues Figueiredo, "we would never recommend, in order to correct a temporary problem, the restoration of those ancient obstacles, whose destruction has cost rivers of blood of all civilised peoples. Therefore it is necessary to resort to the second alternative, which is the creation of a middle class".[13] Since 1950 this basic objective of creating a rural middle social class composed of the operators of family-sized farms has gained legal expression in most of the Latin American coun-

[12] See *Land reform law* (Havana, Office of the Prime Minister, 1961), pp. 4–5.

[13] A. P. Figueiredo: "Pernambuco: revista retrospectiva", in *O Progresso* (Recife), Vol. I, 1846, p. 298.

tries that have put agrarian reform laws into effect, and it figures in the proposals and projects for legislation in most of those that have not yet acted.

Thus in Colombia article 50 of the Agrarian Social Reform Act (No. 135 of 1961) states that: "In its colonisation projects as well as in those involving the subdivision of estates and the consolidation of small parcels, the Institute [the official agency created to administer the agrarian reform programme] shall seek preferentially the creation of 'family-sized farms'." Moreover, this law specified that the family-sized farm "must fulfil the following conditions: (a) that the size of the tract . . . shall be sufficient, if utilised with a reasonable degree of efficiency, to provide to a normal family an income sufficient to cover its living expenses, to meet the payments on the purchase or improvement of the land, if this is involved, and to permit the progressive improvement of the dwelling, the farming equipment, and the general level of living; (b) that the said size normally shall not require for its use with reasonable efficiency more labour than that of the proprietor and his family".[14]

Essentially the same basic objectives are being sought in Venezuela, where the programme of agrarian reform is already benefiting by several years of fruitful experience. The 1960 Venezuelan *Ley de Reforma Agraria* in article 2, paragraph *b,* "guarantees the right of every individual or group of people who are suited to work in agriculture or stockraising and who lack land or have insufficient amounts of it to be given the ownership of lands that are suited for economic utilisation", and paragraph *e* of the same article guarantees "to favour and protect in a special way the development of the small and medium-sized rural properties and the agricultural co-operatives so that they shall come to be stable and efficient. For this purpose, the right of the small family-sized farm is established in accordance with the norms relative to gratuitous grants contained in this Law".[15]

Equally specific are the stated objectives of the more im-

[14] See *Carta agraria* (Bogotá, Caja de Crédito Agrario), No. 81, Jan. 1962, annex.

[15] *Ley de reforma agraria* (Caracas, Publicaciones Nacionales, 1960), pp. 3–4.

portant and influential of the Brazilian groups who have struggled with the basic problems of agrarian reform in that huge and extremely heterogeneous country. One of these, after a week of intensive discussion and study, stated explicitly that "agrarian reform is not essentially a change in the régime of property, although it cannot be accomplished without such a change". Rather, because it "seeks the creation of a rural middle class, an agrarian reform should place major emphasis upon a régime of properties distributed in accordance with this criterion".[16]

Bolivian formulations of the objectives of agrarian reform have been complicated to a considerable extent because the problems of the relationships of man to the land are intertwined with those relating to the huge Indian population and also by the largely *ex post facto* nature of her agrarian reform. Nevertheless the essentials have been expressed by José Flores Moncayo as follows: "Fundamentally the agrarian reform proposes to elevate the levels of the indigenous [Indian] economy so as to liberate the country from illiteracy, poverty and fear; to place within the reach of the Indian the right to property which will add to the personality of the human being, giving him opportunities to shape his own destiny within the social order"; and "it was necessary to adjudicate the rights of ownership to the Bolivian *campesinos* because merely to concede to them the use of the land would have been to sanction the uncertain and precarious tenancy which was used by the *latifundistas* to destroy their landholding traditions."[17]

Perhaps the stated objectives of the "new phase" of agrarian reform in Mexico are the most important expressions of the determination throughout Latin America to develop and strengthen a rural middle class composed of the operators of family-sized farms. These are based upon the experience of half a century in dealing with the realities of reform endeavours. One of the most authoritative statements of such objectives is to be found in a recent brochure by Victor Manzanilla Schaffer of the national agency responsible for Mexico's on-going programme of improvement in the social

[16] Ríos, op. cit., pp. 61–62.
[17] José Flores Moncayo: *Derecho agrario boliviano* (La Paz, Editorial Don Bosco, 1956), pp. 234–236.

relationships of man to the land. Briefly, those at present in charge of directing Mexico's activities expect that "through the attainment of the objectives set forth a complete social transformation of our country will be accomplished with the elevation of the masses of our population into middle-class producers and consumers".[18]

The techniques of agrarian reform

If the various Latin American countries achieve the major stated objectives of their agrarian reform laws and projects, they will necessarily have to devise and put into effect a wide range of specific techniques and measures that will produce: (1) a much broader distribution of the ownership and control of the land; (2) the substitution of modern, efficient and productive ways of getting products from the soil for the labour-devouring, ineffective and frequently bemeaning methods at present widely in use, and especially the revision of prevailing systems of farm management, so as to increase greatly the input of management in the average farm enterprise; and (3) the development of comprehensive and realistic programmes of community development, including substantial local concern with, financial support for, and administration of, schools, health programmes, services for the protection of life and property, the construction of local roads and bridges, agricultural extension activities and farm credit facilities, and so forth.

It is unlikely, though, that any of these, except the first, will receive any substantial place in the agrarian reform programmes of most of the countries in the near future. Therefore, for all practical purposes, the techniques of agrarian reform of immediate concern are those having to do with the redistribution of property rights to the land. Such measures, though, require specific means for national governments (or in Brazil, the state governments) to regain their rights to substantial portions of the land that has been alienated, for it would be deceptive to maintain that adequate agrarian reform

[18] Manzanilla Schaffer, op. cit., p. 73; see also Fernández y Fernández, op. cit., pp. 211–220.

measures could be put into effect merely by operations on the public domains presently in existence. Even in Bolivia, Brazil, Colombia, Venezuela and other countries in which there still exist huge expanses of unoccupied territory, genuine agrarian reform will require substantial changes in the areas presently settled. Therefore, the utmost importance is to be attached to the ways in which the State regains the title to substantial parts of the arable and pasture lands within its limits. These in turn are of considerable variety.

CONFISCATION

The confiscation of the lands which members of a ruling clique had gathered into their hands during a long period in which they held power has supplied some of the countries with extensive portions of the most fertile and best-located land for use in their national programmes; and the seizure of estates owned by foreign interests has provided large acreages for similar use in others. In still others, if the constitutions are modified to provide that payments for lands expropriated may be made with "long-term, low interest, non-negotiable bonds", as is sometimes proposed, the galloping inflation rampant in some of these countries may make "expropriation" in them tantamount to confiscation.

EXPROPRIATION

Most Latin American leaders consider expropriation, as exemplified in the laws and agrarian reform projects, to be the chief way in which the State will secure the ownership of the land that is used in the programmes. There is, however, considerable disagreement with respect to the legal bases for expropriation, and the manner of paying for the land that is taken. All aspects of this subject are greatly complicated by the rampant inflation that is almost chronic in many of the countries. Rarely in practice or theory does full remuneration at cash or market values figure in the programmes and proposals; it is much more common to make use of some percentage of the value, generally greatly understated, at which the property has been returned for tax purposes. In Mexico a doctrine of "unaffectability" has prevailed, which is highly pertinent to the topic of expropriation. In brief it exempts from expropriation certain portions of the landed estates, segments selected by the landowners themselves. However, at the present time serious consideration is being given to substantial modifications in this policy[19]; and there seems to be no tendency in other countries to adopt the doctrine. If a substantial tax were placed upon land in the various Latin American countries and the proceeds used to support the educational, health and other programmes that are so badly needed, the value of the land would be reduced considerably, perhaps to a ratio to its productivity more nearly comparable with that which prevails throughout Europe, the United States and Canada. This, in turn, would make the problem of financing agricultural reform measures through expropriation very much less difficult than it actually is.

LIMITS TO THE AMOUNT OF LAND THAT MAY BE OWNED

In Europe, Asia and parts of Africa the placing of ceilings upon the amount of land that may be owned by one individual or one family is one of the principal instruments of various agrarian reform programmes. The same device under the name of "the 500-acre limitation" is one of the chief features of Puerto Rico's endeavours. Among the 20 Latin American countries, however, little or no attention has been given to this possibility; and at present there is little evidence that it will figure to any extent in the future.

The principal device Latin Americans are using in their efforts to increase the number and to strengthen the position of middle-class operators of family-sized farms in the various countries is the establishment of highly supervised and minutely directed groups of agriculturists on segments of what once were large estates. These groups are very costly in relation to the number of families benefited. In addition, it seems

[19] Manzanilla Schaffer, op. cit., passim; and Fernández y Fernández, op. cit., passim.

to be difficult to get any substantial part of the managerial functions actually transferred from the personnel in charge of the projects to the farmers themselves. The present writer does not expect any comprehensive results to come from the multiplicity of colonisation projects presently in operation or being planned and presently monopolising the funds expended on agrarian reform programmes.

In conclusion, perhaps it may be justifiable to mention briefly three specific measures for agrarian reform in Latin America which seem greatly needed but to which, at the present time, there seems little likelihood that any particular attention will be given. The first of these is the adoption of a system of surveys of the remaining public domain that will result in property lines that are definite, determinate and permanent. Many of the Latin American countries need ways and means of bringing method and order into the occupation of the public domain, and the adoption of such a system could form a highly important part of a genuine agrarian reform programme.[20]

The second is a suggestion so prosaic in nature that it is generally passed by with complete disdain, to say the least. Nevertheless the present writer continues to insist upon its importance for use in the United States and, especially, throughout Latin America. It requires merely the establishment of an agency that would acquire the ownership of large estates when they are for sale and then resell the land in tracts of from about 25 to 200 hectares in size to persons who have the funds or the credit to pay for a family-sized farm.

The third and final suggestion or recommendation is the imposition of a substantial tax upon land, with the proceeds going to pay the costs of local governmental activities such as elementary and secondary education, health and welfare programmes, the protection of life and property, and the construction and maintenance of local roads, trails and bridges.

[20] On this point consult T. Lynn Smith: *The sociology of rural life*, 3rd ed. (New York, Harper, 1953), Ch. 11; idem: *Brazil: People and institutions,* 3rd ed. (Baton Rouge, Louisiana State University Press, 1963), Ch. 12; idem: *Sociología rural* (Maracaibo, Universidad del Zulia, 1963), pp. 89–93.

In addition to solving once and for all the problems of *latifundismo*, or of large, slightly used or entirely idle expanses of land, and the widespread tendency for land to be an asylum for capital, such a measure could help immensely in the solution of most of the other problems of comprehensive agrarian reform. Indeed, if properly planned so as to make use of the principle of homestead exemption and graduated rates, and if used in conjunction with a comprehensive plan of supervised farm credit and other features of an adequate agricultural extension service, it could within a decade exert a profound influence upon all facets of life and labour throughout the rural districts of Latin America.

19 Agrarian Reform in Brazil

———◆———

AGRARIAN REFORM is one of the principal themes of life in contemporary Brazil. In the press, on television, over the radio, in the halls of the state legislative assemblies and in those of the national congress, there is a lavish outpouring of words and phrases about agrarian reform. The need for, the objectives of, and possible ways of bringing about changes in the agrarian socioeconomic system now prevailing in the largest nation of the southern hemisphere all enter into the discussion. Naturally, under such circumstances many of Brazil's most able and objective social scientists have recognized that they must give questions relating to land tenure, the distribution of property rights in the land, the size of agricultural holdings, the often antiquated systems of agriculture, and rural community development their most serious attention. Naturally, too, politicians at all levels and of all ideological and political persuasions find that a call for agrarian reform is a popular plank for use in their platforms, and demagogues greedily seize upon such a theme for the purpose of helping to forward their own selfish ends. All of the nation's presidents since 1950, this is to say from Getúlio Vargas to João Goulart, have given the problem of agrarian reform a high priority among the subjects for their pronouncements; almost all the members of Congress have helped to swell the refrain; and clergymen of all levels, from parish priests to archbishops and cardinals, have participated actively in conferences, seminars, and other endeavors designed to promote and give guidance to programs of agrarian reform. There are even reports that wealthy speculators are buying up large expanses of land with a view to making huge profits when it is expropriated.

Originally published as "Agrarian Reform in Brazil," in *Luso-Brazilian Review*, Volume I, Number 2, pp. 3–20. Copyright © 1964 by the Regents of the University of Wisconsin.

Under these circumstances it is not strange that an outstanding Brazilian sociologist and lawyer could generalize that "never was a Reform so discussed and debated, in Brazil or outside of it, as the Agrarian."[1] Or that he could point to a bibliography recently published by the Instituto de Ciências Sociais of the University of Brazil which listed 1,164 publications on agrarian reform and related subjects.[2] Or that he could estimate that in Brazil alone over 300 agrarian reform projects have been introduced in the legislative bodies of the states and the nation. . . .

It is hoped that what has been said will indicate that the cry for agrarian reform is one of the dominant notes in the chorus of discontent currently convulsing Brazilian society. Moreover it may be asserted categorically that measures for improving the relationships of man to the land, for bringing into action more productive and efficient ways of extracting products from the soil, and for securing a more equitable distribution of the results of agricultural and stockraising enterprises, all figure among the chief hopes of those who are attempting to solve the nation's host of chronic and acute ills. In this respect agrarian reform probably is surpassed only by the almost magical belief in industrialization with which most sectors of the population are imbued. All of this appears to be true in the camps of those who seek to develop Brazil in the ways of modern, democratic western societies, and also in the ranks of those who are making every effort to hinge Brazil's fortunes to those of the Soviet Russia, Communist China, and Castro's Cuba. In the following discussion of agrarian reform in Brazil, three principal aspects of the subject are included: first, an enumeration of a few of the indicators that are used to demonstrate the need for agrarian reform; next, a brief discussion of the major objectives of genuine agrarian reform; and finally, an indication of some of the measures or techniques that may be employed to assist in bringing about substantial progress in attaining the goals of agrarian reform.

Before beginning a consideration of these specific matters,

[1] J. V. Freitas Marcondes, "Reforma Agrária à Luz das Ciências Sociais," *Sociologia*, XXIV, No. 4 (Dec., 1962), p. 273.

[2] Instituto de Ciências Sociais, *Bibliografia sôbre Reforma Agrária*, Rio de Janeiro: Universidade do Brasil, 1962.

however, it is well for us to have in mind that Brazil, along with the other Latin American countries, has solemnly pledged to carry out the various objectives of Charter of Punta del Este, commonly known as the Alliance for Progress. Moreover, the Brazilian delegation to the Punta del Este conference had a major role in phrasing the provision in Title II, Chapter II, section 2, which states categorically that "National development programs should incorporate self-help efforts directed to: . . . The more effective, rational and equitable mobilization and use of financial resources through the reform of tax structures, including fair and adequate taxation of large incomes and real estate. . . ." Finally, and without this any promised agrarian reform is little more than pure mockery, Brazil is committed (Title I, 7) "to eliminate adult illiteracy and by 1970 to assure, as a minimum, access to six years of primary education to every child in [her part of] Latin America."

Indicators of the Need for Agrarian Reform

The conditions or indicators which reveal the need for agrarian reform included in this paper are those frequently mentioned by Brazilians. To a considerable degree they correspond with those the author has concluded are the most useful for this purpose, but the list given is by no means the same as the one he would use in discussing the matter of agrarian reform in general. Naturally some persons in this audience and many in Brazil would prefer to revise the enumeration presented by deleting some of the items and perhaps by adding others that are not mentioned at this time. To this the author would have no particular objection, except in the case of some such as *latifundismo,* and the concentration of the ownership and control of the land in general, which are the first to be mentioned here and which figure in almost every Brazilian discussion of the need for agrarian reform. Furthermore, it should be indicated that all of the items enumerated are highly intercorrelated with one another, since they all are central elements in essentially the same social system. Indeed some of them may be mere reflections of others in the list. Nevertheless for the present diagnostic purposes they are deemed sufficient.

1. LATIFUNDISMO. In Brazil *latifundismo* generally has a special connotation, closely equivalent to that it is given in some other Latin American countries, such as Colombia, and which is not the same as the one it has in other important parts of the hemisphere. Only in recent years, as the debate over agrarian reform has waxed in volume and importance, has there been any tendency in Brazil to refer to a highly developed coffee *fazenda* or sugar-cane or rice plantation as a latifundium. The general rule has been and continues to be to restrict the use of this term to denote the large landed estate which, perhaps with premeditation, is maintained in complete idleness or at least in a very low stage of productivity. As the writings of A. P. Figueiredo[3] published slightly more than a century ago indicate, there occasionally has been an eloquent plea for the use of the land tax as a means of mitigating the obvious disadvantages of *latifundismo*. Until the recent imposition of a tax of 5 per mil upon the land by the state of São Paulo,[4] however, such efforts have been merely cries in the darkness. The powerful land-owning families have seen to it that there always has been a clause in the nation's constitutions specifying that the right to levy a property tax on land is reserved to the state (which is also to say that it is forbidden to the *municípios* or counties).[5] Since the large landowners, usually absentees, have maintained rather fully effective control of the state governments, this has meant that, with the single recent example in São Paulo just mentioned, land has remained untaxed. As a result the ownership of land is in effect an asylum for capital. Economic pressures are lacking that would force the economic use of the soil. Even the zones about many of the large centers of consumption vegetate in idleness, and in 1963, as when Figueiredo wrote in

[3] Cf. the citations to the works of this author and the translation of significant extracts from them in T. Lynn Smith, *Brazil: People and Institutions,* 3rd. ed., Baton Rouge: Louisiana State University Press, 1963, pp. 325–327.

[4] J. V. Freitas Marcondes, *Revisão e Reforma Agrária,* São Paulo: Instituto dos Advogados de São Paulo, 1962, pp. 69, *passim.*

[5] See, for example, article 19 of the Constitution of 1946, the one presently in force.

1846, "Agriculture is encircled by a barrier that cannot be surmounted by the man of slight means. . . . And what is this barrier? It is the large landed estate, the terrible entity that has ruined and depopulated Ireland, the plains of Rome, and many other countries." Then the brilliant thinker and lucid writer whose words we are translating got down to specific cases in the following paragraphs, which deserve to be broadcast throughout Brazil and the other parts of Latin America. It would be well if they were required reading for every technician from the United States who might possibly have anything to do with a technical assistance program in any part of Latin America.

"The culture in which our population should be occupied and which one day will give us a middle class and establish the validity of our representative system, as we have already demonstrated, is not that on a large scale, which demands large amounts of capital, and which here is carried on by slaves; but it is culture on a small scale, which can be perfomed by the father of a family and his sons, aided at the most by a few hired workers during the periods of planting and harvest. But the lands which are advantageous for small-scale farming, because of the nature of the soil, the availability of springs and creeks, and nearness to centers of consumption and exportation, are not those of the far-distant *sertões*, nor those of the rolling, sunburned plains (*catingas*) which have been reduced almost to sterility by the imprudent activities of the cotton planters. The lands [best suited for family-sized farms] are those near the seacoast: in our provinces they are in the region occupied by the *engenhos* [old-style sugar-cane plantations]. This region which extends along the entire coast of our province and to a depth of ten, twelve, and even fifteen and eighteen leagues, is, as is well-known, divided into plantations or estates whose dimensions vary from one-fourth of a league square to two, three, and even four or five leagues per side. Here because the culture of the sugar cane requires a special type of soil, which is not found in all parts of the area, it follows that in addition to the cane fields, the necessary woods, and the lands needed for the cattle and for the fields of mandioca, indispensable for the feeding of the slaves, the majority of the *engenhos* contain huge extensions of unused lands, lands that would be eminently suited for small farming, and which, if they were cultivated, would suffice to supply an abundance of mandioca flour, beans, and corn for the entire population of the province, for the neighboring provinces, and even for export.

But the owners refuse to sell these lands, or even to rent them. If one is wealthy, then he can buy an *engenho;* but if his means are slight and he wishes to buy a few acres of land, he will not find them: this is what produces the unproductive population of the cities, the class of those seeking public employment which increases daily. This is what causes the crimes against property to become more frequent and what daily impoverishes the country, since the number of consumers is growing whereas that of the producers either remains constant or at least increases more slowly. But, say the large land-owners, we are far from refusing poor people the land they need to cultivate; let them come and for a modest charge, or even gratis, we will give them not merely land to plant but also timber with which to construct their homes. This is true, but these favors which you landowners bestow upon them continue only at your pleasure. At any moment you may, either because of your own capriciousness, or because they refuse to vote for your candidates in an election, or because they fail to carry out any order you may give them, eject them without recourse. How can you ask them to plant, if they have no certainty of being able to harvest? What incentive is there in this for them to improve the land from which they may be expulsed at any moment? On your lands they enjoy no political rights, because perforce their opinion must be in accord with your own; for them you are the police, the courts, the administration, in a word, everything; and, except for the right and the possibility to leave you, these unhappy beings are in no way different from the serfs of the middle ages.

. . . In order that he [a large landowner] can dispense with parts of his lands . . . it is necessary for his neighbors to do the same and for government to become sufficiently strong that it can protect all of them against possible aggressions.

But in order to obtain a result of this kind, there is only one effective means: to restrain all of them, simultaneously, by an external force; and this force we find in the direct taxation which is authorized in our constitution, and in

the general property tax which we have already proposed
in other pages of this periodical and whose advantages we
have already demonstrated. If it were gradually extended
throughout the province this land tax would force the large
landowners to get rid of the lands which are of no use to
them. These lands, subdivided among numerous individuals, would be the source of a middle class of small farmers
who would augment in great scale the production of the
nation and contribute greatly to the government and the
maintenance of public order. Then, with all of its sons occupied productively and advantageously, Brazil could
issue a call for the excess of the industrious populations of
Europe to whom it could offer work and secure means of
existence. Other than this, any attempts at colonization are
absurd."[6]

The lengthy extract just translated should receive particular
attention, not merely in connection with the nature of *latifundismo* (our chief purpose at the moment), but also in connection with various other sections of this paper. Especially
important for our consideration of the objectives of agrarian
reform is Figueiredo's emphasis upon the formation of a
middle social class of agriculturists, and for our thinking in
relation to the techniques of agrarian reform is his proposal
for the use of the general property tax.

2. A HIGH DEGREE OF CONCENTRATION OF OWNERSHIP AND
CONTROL OF THE LAND. Merely because huge landed estates
are not allowed to vegetate in idleness in the manner that
would qualify them as latifundia in the Brazilian sense does
not mean there is no need for agrarian reform in areas where
large landholdings dominate the rural scene. As a matter of
fact a high degree of concentration in the ownership and
control of the land, if viewed from the world point of view, is
probably the most generally recognized indicator of the necessity for agrarian reform. Certainly it is one the author would
place first in importance, a conclusion which was reached
upon the basis of comparative study of two sharply contrast-
ing social systems in the United States some years before he
had had the privilege of visiting either Brazil or most other

[6] Translated from A. P. Figueiredo, "Colonisação do Brasil,"
O Progresso (Recife), Tomo I (1846), pp. 634–637.

parts of Latin America. In one of these social systems, which dominates rural life in the Midwest and many other sections of the United States, the family-sized farm is the central element in the system; in the other, which is all important in many parts of the Southern Region, the large plantation is the nucleus of the social system which has generated so many of our nation's major social, economic, and political problems.

That there is a high degree of concentration in the ownership and control of the land in most sections of Brazil is easily demonstrated. Thus, on the basis of 1950 census data, it is apparent that not more than one out of four of the Brazilian families which are dependent upon agriculture and livestock for a livelihood is headed by a person who could be classified as a farm operator. This is true even when the considerable number of the heads of rural families which are merely squatting upon the land they use are included with the farm operators. This means that at least 75 per cent of Brazil's agriculturists fall into the unenviable category of mere farm laborers, a matter which is discussed below. Furthermore, of the minority who may be classified as farm operators (owners, renters, managers, and even squatters), almost one-fifth have the use of farms that are less than 13 acres in size, and 75 per cent have tracts that are less than 125 acres. Collectively this group, which makes up three-fourths of all Brazil's farm operators, has the use of only 10 per cent of the land in the nation's farms. On the other hand, the 0.5 per cent of the operators whose farms contain above 6,250 acres have the use of more than 36 per cent, and the 0.1 per cent with estates containing above 25,000 acres have control of almost 20 per cent of all the land in Brazilian farms. Furthermore, in the decade between the 1940 and the 1950 censuses, the trend was towards an increase in the concentration of ownership and control of the land by the few.[7] Therefore, despite the fact that inheritance is a powerful factor in bringing about the subdivision of land in Brazil, its effects are more than offset by those of other factors, and the tendency is for the need for agrarian reform in that country to become more rather than less acute as one decade succeeds another.

[7] For detailed data on this trend see Smith, *Brazil*, pp. 330–337.

3. HIGH PROPORTIONS OF AGRICULTURAL LABORERS IN THE AGRICULTURAL POPULATION. The presence of the large estate ipso facto means that a large proportion of the heads of rural families are doomed to spend their lives at the very bottom of the rural social pyramid. In Brazil, as elsewhere, unskilled laborers rank at the bottom of the socioeconomic scale, and the ones whose work is in agriculture are the very lowest of the lowly. In addition, a high proportion of Brazil's farm workers are migratory, a fact that makes their social status and the roles which perforce they must play even less enviable than otherwise would be the case. Naturally, a high proportion of laborers in the agricultural population is merely a reflection of an extreme degree in the ownership and control of the land, which was discussed above; but even so the mere fact that at least three out of four of the heads of Brazilian families who live from agriculture fall into this category is a strong indicator of the need for substantial agrarian reform in Brazil. Furthermore, this need will continue until the vast majority of those who now gain a precarious living through the sale of their poorly executed and badly applied labor, or their descendants, either can ascend the agricultural ladder and become farm operators or can find remunerative employment in non-agricultural activities.

4. THE PREVALENCE OF MINIFUNDIA. In many areas there is an acute need for agrarian reform even though a majority of the heads of the agricultural families may technically fall into a category of farm owners. This is the case when the bulk of the plots of land are so small that they cannot produce sufficient food and fiber to meet even the creature needs of those who live from farming and stockraising. The existence of hundreds of thousands of minute, badly shaped, and poorly tilled farm units is only slightly less disadvantageous for society and disastrous for those who live from the soil than is the concentration of the ownership and control of the land. In a word, *minifundismo* on any substantial scale is another of the indicators of the need for agrarian reform.

Fortunately Brazil is not handicapped by *minifundismo* to a degree which even remotely corresponds to the situation in such Andean countries as Ecuador, Colombia, and Venezuela. Nevertheless, as indicated above, one out of five of her

farm operators is using tracts of land that contain less than
13 acres; and it may be stated without fear of refutation
that in many sections in South Brazil which were colonized
by peasants from Germany, Italy, Poland, and other parts of
Europe, the continued subdivision by inheritance of farms
that never were large by any criterion is rapidly bringing the
problem of *minifundismo* to the fore. Already this problem
is sufficiently serious to indicate a considerable need for
agrarian reform.

5. LOW PRODUCTION PER WORKER. In Brazilian agriculture
the production per worker is very low, a fact that has been
documented by so many economists and governmental officials that it is not necessary to devote space at this point to a
statistical demonstration of the same.[8] This low production
per worker, in turn, probably is merely a reflection of the
socioeconomic factors engendered and perpetuated by the
concentration of ownership and control of the land and the
latifundismo mentioned above. Of the various factors involved, however, the following deserve specific mention: (1)
the paucity of agricultural skills possessed by the laborers;
(2) the extremely small input of management in the productive processes involved in Brazilian agricultural and livestock
enterprises, a deficiency that is inevitable wherever the necessary capacities are not "built in" each person who tills the
soil so that they may be applied by him to every square yard
of the soil, all of the plants in each stage of their development,
every farm animal irrespective of where it may wander, and
every piece of machinery and equipment regardless of the
part of the farm to which it may be taken; and (3) the lack
of propulsions leading to regular work activities on the part
of those who live from agriculture. All of these features are
prominent parts of the systems of agriculture in use in most
parts of Brazil. Indeed in that country, where more than one
half of the entire population is directly dependent upon agriculture, the ways used in extracting a living from the soil by at
least one half of the agricultural population are more wasteful of human energy and more inefficient in general than were

---

[8] One who lacks such data can find no better place to start than
one or more issues of the *Survey of the Brazilian Economy* issued
annually by the Brazilian Embassy in Washington, D.C.

those employed by the Egyptians at the dawn of history. The persistence of this complex of factors which results in low productivity per worker, the wasteful and inefficient combination of the factors of production, and even the bemeaning of a high proportion of those who live from the soil are eloquent testimony of the need for agrarian reform.

6. LOW AVERAGE LEVELS AND STANDARDS OF LIVING. Man's knowledge of the earth on which he lives and of the processes of agricultural production is sufficient to make possible a far more abundant output of goods and services than is enjoyed by the populations of most parts of the world. In Brazil the aspirations of the people and also the amounts of goods and services actually consumed are not as abysmally low as they are in some other parts of the earth. Moreover in recent years, and we may add frequently in quite unrealistic ways, the aspirations of the common people have risen spectacularly, whereas the rise in the actual level of living has been of modest proportions. As a result, the gap between the level of living and the standard of living, or what your speaker designates as the "zone of exasperation," has widened drastically. Probably this problem is not as acute in most rural sections as it is in the urban districts, but even in the agricultural areas it is one that demands attention. Indeed throughout the interior of Brazil the poorly directed aspirations and the prevailing low levels of living point to a need for substantial modifications in the land system, the system of agriculture, the availability and functioning of educational institutions, the role and vigor of local governmental institutions, and various other aspects of a genuine agrarian reform.

7. EXTREME DEGREES OF SOCIAL STRATIFICATION. In all societies in which a system of large estates has dominated the social, economic, and political aspects of life, the class system has come to be one in which there is a handful of elite families at the apex of the social pyramid, and a great mass of impoverished, uneducated, unskilled, and slightly productive workers at the base of it. Until late in the nineteenth century, when many thousands of European peasant families were settled in the states of Rio Grande do Sul, Santa Catarina, and Paraná, Brazil's almost exclusively rural society contained little or nothing in the way of a middle class of farmers to fill

the broad gap which existed between her small stratum of the elite and her huge mass of slaves and other servile or semi-servile workers. A society so constituted is certain to develop all of the indicators of the need for agrarian reform, as these are evaluated in terms of the values prevailing in the world during the second half of the twentieth century, and Brazil is no exception to the rule. Even if it were the sole indicator available, the existing system of social stratification in most of Brazil's vast territory would point strongly to the need for agrarian reform.

This listing could be extended almost indefinitely, for wherever any considerable degree of concentration prevails in the ownership and control of the land (and even if this control be in the hands of the state), low productivity and a whole host of other social and economic ills are certain to abound. This is especially true in areas such as most of the states in the Brazilian confederation in which the absence of the general property tax enables land to become an asylum for capital and the problem of *latifundismo* to grow to almost inconceivable dimensions. The seven items listed, though, should serve present purposes for indicating that there is great need for agrarian reform in Brazil. However, in order to demonstrate that such thinking is not merely that of one person, and the thoughts of a non-Brazilian at that, it may be useful to list the indicators of the need for agrarian reform that have been formulated by the most noted writer in the Brazilian lay Roman Catholic group. These are as follows:

1. A high proportion of illiterates and the consequent general lack of culture.
2. Poor sanitary conditions and high indexes of mortality.
3. Low agricultural production and over-population.
4. Low levels of marriage and family organization.
5. Absence of or an extremely low rate of technical progress.
6. The destruction of the soil, and in general the poor titles to the land.[9]
7. Defective distribution of landownership.
8. Serious smothering of the civic consciousness because of the debility of municipal [county] life, and more re-

motely through the general weakening of a democratic life.
9. Lack of leadership.
10. Low degree of vertical social mobility and a high degree of geographic mobility.
11. Technical and legal deficiencies in the register of titles to the land.[9]

The Objectives of Agrarian Reform

The objectives of the agrarian reforms proposed by Brazilians of various classes, philosophies, professions, and sections of the country vary to an extreme degree. Many of the landless agricultural workers, whose cupidity is appealed to by some of the revolutionaries, undoubtedly believe that agrarian reform means simply the confiscation of the large estates and their division among the laborers. For these people agrarian reform signifies essentially the same as did the measures put into practice in Haiti during the French Revolution, or the ideas promoted among the ex-slaves in the South following the Civil War in the United States (as expressed in the slogan "forty acres and a mule"), or the unfulfilled dreams of the peasants who supported the Russian Revolution. At the other extreme one encounters influential groups in Brazil who maintain that merely the mechanization of agricultural production is all that is needed in order to designate the changes as an agrarian reform.

Much more general and representative, however, are the thoughts that were at the core of the "guide lines" or *diretrizes* formulated early in the 1950's by the members of the Comissão Nacional de Política Agrária, with then Minister of Agriculture João Cleofas as chairman. This commission was established by Getúlio Vargas in compliance with the plank in his presidential platform which had promised agrarian reform. The members of this commission, after stressing that

[9] Gustavo Corção, "Conceituação da Reforma Agrária," (mimeographed), presented to the Simpósio sôbre Reforma Agrária, organized by the Instituto Brasileiro de Ação Democrática, Rio de Janeiro, April 17–22, 1961. For a report of the proceedings of this symposium see José Arthur Ríos (ed.), *Recomendações sôbre Reforma Agrária,* Rio de Janeiro: Instituto Brasileiro de Ação Democrática, 1961.

article 147 of Brazil's constitution provides that "the use of property is to be conditioned by social well-being" and that "the law shall promote a just distribution of property with equal opportunity for all," specified the following objectives for agrarian reform in Brazil:

The fundamental objective of agrarian reform in Brazil is to provide opportunity to become landowners to those who work on the land, so as to prevent the proletarianization of the rural masses and to eliminate the effects of an uneconomic and antisocial use of the land. Simultaneously with the subdivision of the latifundia and the grouping of minifundia, the agrarian reform shall also seek to valorize man and the land, so as to insure for all work that will make possible an honorable existence.[10]

When in 1952 the author was in Brazil serving as advisor to this Brazilian Commission of Agrarian Policy, there seemed to be almost unanimous assent to the proposition that the primary objective of agrarian reform was improvement in the quality and the well-being of the inhabitant of rural Brazil. This in turn involved the valorization of man, and along with this, an improvement in the productive capacity of the land and the perfection of the institutions that govern man's relationships to the land. Later, in 1956, when the author lectured on the subject of agrarian reform in all of the principal centers from Belém to Rio de Janeiro, he formulated the three principal objectives of agrarian reform in the following words:

(1) A genuine agrarian reform should effect substantial improvement in the abilities, capacities, and performances of those who cultivate the land to bring them more in line with human potentialities.

(2) Any worth-while agrarian reform should result in a substantial increase in the amount of agricultural and livestock products secured from a given amount of land and the efforts of those who work it.

(3) A real agrarian reform should result in the replacement of wasteful, inefficient, bemeaning, and stultifying

[10] Comissão Nacional de Política Agrária, *Diretrizes para uma Reforma Agrária no Brasil* (mimeographed), Rio de Janeiro: Comissão Nacional de Política Agrária, 1952, p. 1.

ways of producing agricultural and livestock products by methods of agriculture that are efficient, that husband human energy, and that may be considered as uplifting, dignifying or ennobling to those engaged in agriculture and stock raising.[11]

Then, following a discussion of each of these propositions, he rephrased the basic objective of agrarian reform as that "of getting a nation's agricultural and stock-raising activities highly concentrated in the hands of a middle social class of farmers." Moreover, to accomplish this he indicated that it would be essential to attain the following lesser objectives:

1. The control of the land, as owners or as renters on long-term leases, must be placed in the hands of those who actually till it. This means the elimination, on the one hand, of any class of permanent agricultural laborers, by whatever name such workers may be called, and likewise the elimination of privileges of a category of landlords through which they have virtual powers of life and death over the workers who toil on their estates.

2. Through education, training, and experience, the ordinary man who works the land must be developed into a person who is capable of exercising with considerable facility the functions of the manager or entrepreneur and those of the capitalist or property owner, as well as those of the agricultural laborer. Each farmer must come to combine in his own personality all the attitudes, skills, and habits that go with the performance of the three basic economic functions of which the economist writes, namely that of the capitalist, that of the manager, and that of the laborer. In brief, this means teaching, encouraging, and enabling each future agriculturist to develop all the qualities, skills, characteristics, attitudes, and habits of the middle-class farmer.[12]

Because of this background it was gratifying to the author, to say the least, when the participants in the Symposium of

[11] T. Lynn Smith, "Reforma Agrária," *A Lavoura* (Rio de Janeiro), Ano LIX (Sept.-Oct., 1956), pp. 7–8; and T. Lynn Smith, *Current Social Trends and Problems in Latin America,* Gainesville: University of Florida Press, 1957, p. 34.

[12] Smith, "Reforma Agrária," pp. 7–8–9; and Smith, *Current Social Trends and Problems,* p. 37.

Agrarian Reform which was held in Rio de Janeiro, April 17–22, 1961, agreed upon and stated precisely the objectives of agrarian reform summarized in translation in the following sentences. For this group "Agrarian Reform is not essentially a change in the regime of property, although it cannot be accomplished without such a change." Rather, because it "seeks the creation of a rural middle class, an Agrarian Reform should place major emphasis upon a regime of properties distributed in accordance with this [middle-class] criterion." As the editor of the proceedings summarized in general terms, "an Agrarian Reform of the democratic type is, then, a combination of political, cultural, and economic measures which should be employed where the indicators of a defective agrarian structure are observed as the cause of a sub-human condition of life. This combination of measures should bring about immediately an elevation of the human level and the dignification of the rural populations; and it should also produce, as a consequence, an improvement in the general political, cultural, and economic level of the population where it is applied." Finally the group maintained that "an Agrarian Reform of the democratic type, in a country such as [Brazil], although not consisting exclusively of an alteration in the laws governing rural property, cannot fail to provide a revision in those statutes that will alter the relationships between the agricultural classes and make it possible for large numbers of persons to become landowners."[13]

Techniques of Agrarian Reform

This discussion is already pressing hard upon the limits of time and space that were prescribed when the invitation to prepare it was extended. Therefore, this section is limited strictly to the recommendations the author made to the Brazilian government in 1952 as he was terminating his short assignment as advisor on agrarian reform. Also it should be specifically indicated that the portion of his recommendations which dealt with the settlement and alienation to the public

[13] Rios, *op. cit.*, pp. 61–64. For another excellent statement of similar objectives see Freitas Marcondes, "Reforma Agrária à Luz das Ciências Sociais," p. 281.

domain are not included; they are somewhat lengthy and many might think they are inappropriate in a discussion of agrarian reform. It should be emphasized, however, that the recommendations made in 1952 appear to your speaker to be fully as timely and as pertinent now as they were when first made more than a decade ago.

Five specific proposals were made for improving the situation in the areas already settled. These are as follows:

a) 1. To require each *município* to maintain at least one public secondary school with a minimum of five full-time teachers.

2. To authorize the *município* to place *ad valorem* a tax upon all real estate within its confines, and to levy a minimum tax nation-wide of 1 per cent per annum with the receipts collected in each *município* remaining there, and being dedicated to the support of the school or the schools mentioned in No. 1. In assessing and collecting this tax, the minimum amount on any piece of property shall be Cr$50, but above this amount the homes and farms which are occupied by their owners shall be exempt from taxation up to the value of (Cr$50,000? Cr$100,000? or Cr$150,000?).

3. To establish a fund to be used by a designated agency (Bank, Ministry?) for the sole purpose of purchasing, when they are for sale, estates of 1,000 hectares or more in size and selling them to those who have the means to buy in lots of from 10 to 200 hectares in size. In administering this agency, no person or group of closely related persons should be permitted to purchase more than 200 hectares of contiguous land.

4. To provide for the expropriation of such large estates, in areas near the centers of consumption, as may remain uncultivated or largely unused for more than five years after the above policies have been adopted and have begun building up economic pressures designed to force the productive use of the land.

5. To levy a tax of 1 per cent per annum *ad valorem* on urban real estate with the proceeds to be dedicated to the construction of a road system that will connect the major centers of consumption with the principal producing areas now in existence or that may be developed.

Later on in the memorandum containing these recommendations, the following brief discussions of each of them were given:

b) The valorization of the rural Brazilian, as is clearly stated in the *Diretrizes* prepared by the Commission, is the ultimate objective of any agrarian reform program worthy of the name. Therefore it should be the first and the last thought in any efforts at framing and putting into effect the various specific measures which all taken together will constitute a genuine program of agrarian reform.

If and when the masses of the rural population of Brazil are valorized, the effects will be visible to all in the form of a more adequate diet, improved housing, better clothing, reduced illiteracy, efficient methods of extracting a living from the soil, and a rich and satisfying community life. Then, for example, Brazil will cease to be a country in which there are many more chauffeurs to care for the cars of the well-to-do than there are teachers in all of the secondary schools of the nation.

What are the steps and measures needed to bring about such a valorization of the ordinary rural Brazilian? And how are those related to an agrarian reform? The specific procedures are many; and taken together they themselves will constitute a thoroughgoing agrarian reform.

In order to enter into the discussion, I start with rural education but in so doing it should be kept in mind that this is merely one facet in the entire complex which involves diet, health, efficiency of work, improved transportation, and all the rest.

In brief the bulk of Brazil's agriculturists need to become acquainted with modern and efficient ways of extracting a living from the soil. They must learn to farm. And this can only come about if there is a far greater emphasis upon education in general, and agricultural and mechanical education in particular, throughout the length and breadth of the country. Changes are involved that will result in a much more sparing use of labor in the productive process and far greater use of draft animals and machinery. The primitive and wasteful systems of *derrubadas* and *queimadas,* and the labor-devouring hoe culture, must be replaced by ones in which the labor of the ordinary man enters into combination with that of considerable horse power and well-designed implements in the processes of preparing the soil, planting the crops, controlling the weeds, taking the harvest, processing the products, and transporting the materials to the market. Brazil can and should improve the efficiency of her rural producers to the point at which no more than 40 per cent of her population produce food, fiber, and raw materials sufficient for her entire population and a large volume for export as well. This, however, can only be done if the bulk of her rural people are members of the middle class, themselves exercising all three of the principal economic functions (capitalists on a small scale as the owners or renters of family-sized farms; entrepreneurs who themselves plan and conduct the several enterprises in their respective farm business; and laborers who themselves with the aid of the members of their families do the bulk of the manual labor required in carrying on their agricultural activities), and are spurred onward by the high standards of living that a thoroughgoing educational system can instill.

1. I recommend that the first specific step in the program of agrarian reform be the addition of one more requirement to the list of those now in force with respect to becoming or remaining a *município*. In brief, each *município* in order to remain as such should be required to establish and maintain at least one public secondary school with not less than 5 full-time teachers. Such schools should offer instruction in the usual subjects such as language, literature, mathematics, geography, history, etc., and in addition should provide elementary courses in general agriculture, mechanics, and home economics. It definitely is not the thought to establish agricultural schools in which the instruction will be different from that in other secondary schools, and whose graduates will not be eligible to enter universities for further training. It is my thought that instruction in agriculture and mechanics and home economics be thought of as a part of the general education necessary for the ordinary citizen.

It should be noted that I have not commenced with elementary schools, and that I have not even mentioned them. This is deliberate. In one way or another, I am convinced, Brazil must develop a system of universal elementary education if she is to endure life in the society of modern nations. However, the valorization of man envisioned in this memorandum cannot be accomplished by elementary education alone. Boys and girls at the elementary school level are not sufficiently mature. Only a thorough secondary training, theoretical and applied, for the majority of the rural population, one that will fit them to be genuine members of a middle class, with the skills and mentality that accompany such a status, can accomplish our objectives. Of course the same kind of a device as the one recommended for pooling local efforts in order to secure facilities for secondary education also would prove the most suitable one for supporting the right kind of nation-wide system of public elementary schools.

2. How can the ordinary Brazilian *município* meet this new obligation? How can from 8,000 to about 40,000 rural people in one small part of the national territory secure the money needed to secure a building, furnish the supplies and equipment, provide janitorial and other services, and pay the salaries of at least five well-trained and full-time teachers?

This problem is not essentially different from that which has confronted other rural people in all parts of the world, and which has been successfully solved by those in many countries. Briefly, a way must be provided whereby all of the people in the *município* are required to make an annual contribution of a significant part of their productive efforts which in turn are used for secondary educational purposes. In countries which have secondary schools readily available for all of the children, the average person is required to contribute substantially to their support. In an agrarian society there is one tried and tested way through which this may be accomplished, one sure means of pooling local efforts needed for the maintenance of such educational (and other essential social) services. This is the general property tax levied upon the value of the land and other real estate within the limits of the district (*município*) served by the school. It is for this reason that as a second specific step I recommend that the necessary constitutional change be made so as to empower the *município* to levy a general property tax, and that a minimum of 1 per cent nation-wide be established, with the proceeds in each *município* being dedicated to the maintenance of its school or schools.

In order to establish assessed values for purposes of taxation it will be necessary for each *município* to elect a tax assessor who shall have the duty of placing a valuation upon each piece of real estate in the *município*. Each *município* shall also have a board of three members to whom individual property owners may appeal for readjustment of the values placed upon their holdings in the event there appears to be too high a valuation placed upon the property of any owner. However, it also should be stipulated that whenever property is expropriated for public uses the indemnity paid the owner shall in no case be more than twice the assessed valuation of the property.

This property tax, with the homestead exemption proposed, will be an effective way of ending *latifundismo* in Brazil. For the proprietor who is making efficient use of his land, the payment of the tax will require merely a small portion of his income or profit. But for the one who is speculating in land or deliberately withholding it from productive uses, it will prove unbearable. For him the general property tax will prove the equivalent of a capital levy. Through it he will be forced either to put the land to productive uses, or to see it "eaten up" by the taxes. There is no more effective device available for ending the problem of vast, unused areas near the large cities. In a country such as the United States, in which the general property tax is high, and in which it has been used to pool local efforts to build roads, maintain schools, organize local government, etc., the problem of the latifundia has not been able to arise. Merely putting an end to it in Brazil would greatly stimulate agricultural production, especially in the areas near the large population centers.

The degree of autonomy for the *município* called for in these measures may cause some concern to many well-informed persons. There is no doubt that, in many *municípios,* federal and state inspection may be necessary to help safeguard the funds. However, the fact that the money is collected locally and disbursed within the *município* is in itself one of the best insurances against waste and dishonesty.

3. (This was disposed of by a reference to p. 323 of T. Lynn Smith, *The Sociology of Rural Life,* 3rd. ed., New York: Harper and Brothers, 1953).

4. Purposely I have refrained from saying very much about expropriation. This is because this subject already appears to be receiving the attention it deserves. I would warn, however, that expropriation alone, unaccompanied by the measures that will instruct in modern agricultural methods and farm management, could easily become a device that would worsen rather than improve the situation. I

repeat that learning to farm by methods other than the *derrubadas* and *queimadas* or the labor-devouring use of hoe culture is absolutely essential if the bulk of the rural population of Brazil is to benefit by any *reforma agrária*. If any extensive tracts of land are expropriated I recommend that they be opened for settlement by homesteaders in the same manner as that recommended for the *terras devolutas*.

5. The present distribution of investments in Brazil is dangerous, especially to the classes that are benefiting most and have most to lose. Much too large a proportion of the national income is going into the construction of apartment houses and other buildings in Rio de Janeiro, São Paulo, and the other cities, and far too little of it into the improvement of the ways of supplying the great populations that are assembling in them. On the other hand, the farmers in some of the rural districts must see their products rot because they cannot get them to the markets. This makes improved transportation facilities absolutely essential. The device recommended would make those who benefit most pay a part of the cost, and also would serve as a brake upon the dangerous trend that is under way. This should constitute an integral part of agrarian reform.

In closing the author desires to repeat that in his considered judgment these recommendations of ways and means of bringing about genuine agrarian reform in Brazil are fully as urgent and timely, and perhaps even more so, than was the case in 1952. Indeed, he doubts seriously that any genuine agrarian reform in Brazil can be attained without the imposition of a heavy tax upon the land. This tax must be so heavy that land no longer can be an asylum for capital, that *latifundismo* in the Brazilian sense will involve heavy economic penalties in place of the economic rewards presently sustaining the system, and that the states and *municípios* will have ample funds for financing essential services, and especially the educational institutions which alone can valorize the masses of Brazil's inhabitants. Please let me repeat once again: it is my firm conviction that levying and proper use of the land tax is the first indispensable step in all of the measures designed to achieve the ownership of the land by a middle social class of farmers.

The situation probably cannot long remain as it is, and there seem to be two chief alternatives to our own suggestions for a genuine agrarian reform program: (1) The confiscation and division of the large estates among the landless laborers. This certainly would not worsen the situation of the individual rural families, but it would be chaotic. It probably would not be substantially more beneficial to the nation as a whole than was the Haitian agrarian reform of almost two centuries ago. (2) The confiscation and direct transformation of Brazil's coffee *fazendas,* sugar *usinas,* rice and cotton plantations, and large cattle ranches into state farms, comparable to the confiscation and transition recently effected in Cuba. In this case the rural masses would have to abandon any hope of becoming landowners themselves. However, their new masters undoubtedly would seek to increase their effectiveness as cogs in the productive machine by stern measures designed to improve the educational status, the health, the housing, the food, and the clothing of the workers and their families. But of course, it would be as impossible for them, as it is for Marxists in other parts of the world, to get an adequate input of management in the process of agricultural production; and for many years to come Brazilians would have to live with acute shortages of agricultural and livestock products as well as the repressive measures of a totalitarian regime.

20 Urbanization in Latin America

DRASTIC CHANGES are the order of the day throughout the twenty Latin American countries, with the process of urbanization as a cause and also as an effect occupying a central position in the tremendous modifications that are underway. For centuries Mexico and Brazil, Peru and Venezuela, Costa Rica and Colombia, and almost every one of the other countries, were predominantly rural with economies based largely upon agricultural, pastoral, and collecting activities. Now from the Rio Grande to Cape Horn the peoples of Latin America and most of their leaders of all ideological orientations feverishly are seeking in urbanization and industrialization the solutions for their chronic personal and collective ills and their rapidly mounting host of new acute social and economic problems. In this article attention is directed to several of the more important aspects of the tempestuous shifts from rural to urban ways of life on the part of the most rapidly increasing portions of the world's population.

The Growth of Cities and Towns

Fortunately for our purposes Brazil, which alone contains one-third of all the people in the twenty Latin American countries, had well-executed censuses in the years 1940, 1950, and 1960. Together these provide a substantial and fairly reliable basis which one may use for taking stock of the more essential aspects of the growth of cities and towns. The most publicized aspects of the phenomenal urban growth in gigantic Brazil are, of course, the almost fantastic expansion of

From *International Journal of Comparative Sociology*, Vol. IV, No. 2 (September, 1963), pp. 227–242. Reprinted by permission of the publisher.

the cities of Rio de Janeiro and São Paulo. As late as 1920 there were no more than 1,250,000 persons in the area in and about the city of Rio de Janeiro, an extremely limited portion of Brazilian territory which now constitutes a metropolitan community of over five million inhabitants. In 1900 the city of São Paulo had only 240,000 residents, and a remarkable growth of the city brought this figure up to 579,000 by 1920. In 1960, however, as capital of a state having a population of almost thirteen million inhabitants, of whom two-thirds were urban, São Paulo is the greatest industrial center in all of Latin America. Its built-up areas have expanded far beyond the boundaries of the *município* in which it is located, a political subdivision of the state which alone contained 3,288,000 residents in 1960, to make it the core of a metropolitan community of more than five million inhabitants. Thus São Paulo, as well as Rio de Janeiro, has the right to dispute with Buenos Aires and Mexico City the distinction of being the largest city in Latin America and the second largest in the western hemisphere.

One must stress, however, that the dizzy pace at which these two huge metropolitan centers are growing is merely indicative of the upsurge of urban development throughout the nation. In this connection it is important to note that in 1940 only 31.2 per cent of Brazil's 41,236,000 inhabitants were classified in the urban (including suburban) category, whereas by 1950 36.2 per cent of its 51,944,000 people was so classified, and by 1960 45.1 per cent of a total of its 70,967,000 was placed in that category. Such changes were possible only because the bulk of extremely rapid additions to Brazil's population was accounted for by the growth of urban centers. . . .

Another enlightening set of information about the burgeoning of cities and towns in Brazil is presented in Table I. This consists of the data showing the number of population centers in size groups ranging from 2,000 to 5,000 inhabitants to those having above 3,000,000 residents. One could hardly ask for more striking proof of the phenomenal increase that is taking place in the number and size of Brazilian cities and towns. By 1960 31 of Brazil's cities had populations of 100,-000 or more, whereas as late as 1940 the center occupying the 31st place in the rank order (Bauru, São Paulo) had only 32,796 inhabitants; by 1960 73 of her cities had passed the 50,000 mark in population, whereas only twenty years earlier only 22 had done so; and by 1960 there were in Brazil 405 cities of 10,000 or more residents in comparison with only 166 such places in 1940. All of this was part of a pattern of change over a twenty-year period in which the nation's population increased by 72 per cent, that classified as urban rose by 148 per cent, and the number of places with populations of more than 2,000 almost exactly doubled.

Table I.   Numbers of Towns and Cities in Brazil According to the Sizes of their Populations, 1940, 1950 and 1960

Number of inhabitants	*Number of places*		
	1940	1950	1960
Total	900	1174	1799
More than 3,000,000	0	0	2
2,000,000 – 3,000,000	0	2	0
1,000,000 – 2,000,000	2	0	0
500,000 – 1,000,000	0	1	4
250,000 – 500,000	3	3	4
100,000 – 250,000	5	8	21
50,000 – 100,000	12	19	42
25,000 – 50,000	19	44	80
10,000 – 25,000	125	145	252
5,000 – 10,000	177	258	378
2,000 – 5,000	557	694	1,016

Mexico, the second most populous nation in the Latin American group, also is one in which recent census data are most adequate for present purposes. This is highly important since if one has information about her 35 million people to go along with those for Brazil's 71 million, he already has accounted for fully one-half of all Latin Americans. In this context it is important to note that as Mexico's population rose swiftly from 16,552,722 in 1930, to 19,653,552 in 1940, to 25,791,017 in 1950, and to 34,923,129 in 1960, her urban population shot upward from 5,540,631 in 1930 to 17,705,118 in 1960. As a result, the number of Mexicans residing in places of 2,500 or more inhabitants, who made up only one-third of the national population in 1930, actually outnumbered those living in villages and the open country by 1960. Most striking of all, of course, is the growth of Mexico City and its satellites which now comprise a metropolitan community of more than five million persons. The Federal District alone, although now too small to contain Mexico's great metropolitan conurbation, experienced a population growth of 1,292,912 (or 74 per cent) between 1940 and 1950, and another of 1,820,434 (or 60 per cent) in the decade 1950–1960. Of the 4,870,876 persons enumerated in the Federal District by the 1960 census, almost two million had been born in other parts of Mexico and 83,000 abroad, so that those native to the District comprised only 58 per cent of its inhabitants. As a result of the mushrooming of Mexico City and its satellites, the proportion of Mexico's people who resided in the Federal District rose from 11.8 per cent in 1950 to 14.9 per cent in 1960.

This strong tendency for Mexicans to concentrate in their national capital was matched on a lesser scale by rapid growth of the smaller cities which are the capitals of its various states. Merely between 1950 and 1960 Guadalajara skyrocketed from a place of 377,016 inhabitants to one of 736,800, Monterrey from a city with a population of 333,422 to one having 596,939 residents, and Puebla from a center in which 211,331 persons lived to one in which 289,049 human beings had their homes. Also by 1960 Mexico's category of capitals having 100,000 or more inhabitants included Mexicali (174,540), Mérida (170,827), San Luís Potosí (159,980), Chihuahua (150,430), Aguascalientes (126,617), and Morélia (100,828).

For Argentina, third most populous of the Latin American countries, the data at the time this article is written are far less adequate than those for Brazil and Mexico. Censuses taken in 1947 and 1960, however, will provide a wealth of information of the process of urbanization in Argentina, once the materials for 1960 are published in the necessary detail. Even as matters stand there can be no doubt but that the tendency for people to crowd into cities and towns, plus a comparatively high rate of natural increase in the urban centers themselves, continues to produce a rate of growth of the urban population that is far higher than the one for the rural. This is especially important since in Argentina the urban population long has outnumbered the rural and as early as 1947 almost two-thirds (63 per cent) of all Argentines were classified in the urban category. By 1960 probably at least 75 per cent of the people in this country were urban and as yet the process of urbanization showed no likelihood of slowing or coming to a halt.

The most spectacular aspect of urban growth in Argentina is, of course, the phenomenal concentration of population in her great sprawling capital, Buenos Aires, and the broad band of densely populated suburbs and satellites surrounding it. Understandably between 1947 and 1960 practically none of the growth of this great metropolis took place within the limits of the national capital itself (it grew from 2,966,816 inhabitants in 1947 to 2,982,580 in 1960), since long before 1947 the city had burgeoned many miles into the surrounding portions of the Province of Buenos Aires. . . . [The] 17 civil divisions (*partidos*) of the Province which are grouped about the capital in the shape of a big half moon more than doubled in population during the 13-year intercensal period, increasing from approximately 1,741,000 to about 3,697,000. Some of the most striking population gains involved are those registered in such *partidos* as La Matanza, from 98,000 to 403,000 (309 per cent); Merlo, from 20,000 to 100,000 (400 per cent); Almirante Brown, from 38,000 to 135,000 (241 per cent); Moron, from 110,000 to 344,000 (212 per cent); Quilmes, from 123,000 to 318,000 (318 per cent); and San Martin, from 270,000 to 541,000 (93 per cent).

At the time of writing only fragmentary preliminary returns are available for most of the other Latin American countries which took censuses of the populations in 1960 or soon thereafter. For this reason it still is too early for one to undertake definitive comparisons of the comparative rates of growth of urban and rural areas during the decade that has just elapsed. Nevertheless one may be sure that the tendency of population to concentrate in the cities and towns of Colombia, Peru, Venezuela, and all the rest is fully as marked as it is in Brazil, Mexico, and Argentina; and that probably it was even more pronounced between 1950 and 1960 than it was between 1940 and 1950.[1]

These statements are strictly in accord with the data for the four of the countries for which recent materials are available. Thus between 1950 and 1960 the urban population of the Dominican Republic increased by 81 per cent and the rural population by only 29 per cent, a differential even greater than that between 91 per cent and 34 per cent registered for the period 1935 to 1950. Similarly between 1950 and 1960 the urban population of Panama mounted by 54 per cent, and the rural population by only 22 per cent, a difference substantially greater than that between the comparable increases of 34 per cent and 25 per cent taking place during the decade ending in 1950. Likewise in El Salvador between 1950 and 1961 the percentage increases of the urban and rural populations were 45 and 29, respectively, whereas those for the period 1930 to 1950 were 43 and 25 per cent. Finally, in Peru between 1940 and 1961 the urban population registered a gain of 118 per cent, and the rural population one of only 38 per cent. As a result for the most part of the flocking of people from the rural districts into the cities, by the time of these latest censuses Lima and its suburbs made up a metropolitan community of more than 2,500,000 people, Santo Domingo contained almost 370,000 inhabitants, Panama City was a place with almost 275,000 residents, and San Salvador had become a city of nearly 250,000 persons. By 1961 Lima was almost three times its size in 1940, and merely in the years since 1950 San Salvador, Panama City and Santo Domingo doubled in population. When the data become available it will be seen that similar phenomenal increases in number of inhabitants have been taking place in

[1] For the materials on the comparative rates of population growth in rural and urban areas during the intercensal periods ending in 1950 or thereabouts in the ten countries for which such comparisons are possible, see T. Lynn Smith, *Latin American Population Studies*, Gainesville: University of Florida Press, 1961, pp. 78–82. With very few exceptions these indicated that the rate of growth of the urban population was at least double that of the rural population, and in the case of Venezuela (1941–1950), an increase of 79 per cent in the cities and towns was accompanied by a decrease of 1 per cent in the rural districts.

Montevideo, Havana, Santiago, Caracas, Bogotá, Quito, La Paz, Guatemala City, San José, Managua, Tegucigalpa and Asunción, as well as in dozens of other large cities which do not enjoy the distinction of being national capitals. Almost overnight Latin America, until recently so rural, agricultural, and pastoral, is becoming a great world area in which the urban elements in the population outnumber the rural.

"Urbanization"

Urbanización throughout Spanish America and *urbanizacão* in Brazil, both of which the present writer translates as "urbanization", are widely used in a technical sense to denote the work of planning and constructing the physical parts of a city. This is to say that *an* "urbanization" is a subdivision or other area in which aligned streets have been laid out, public squares and parks have been provided, streets and sidewalks have been paved, storm sewers and sewer systems have been constructed, and central water systems and lighting systems have been installed; and it is also to indicate that, except for a broader use of the term by a few sociologists and economists, both *urbanización* and *urbanizacão* almost always are employed in Spanish and Portuguese in the limited sense indicated. As a rule throughout Latin America the public improvements that are designated as "urbanization" are concentrated in the central portions of a city and the surrounding sections, many of them very densely populated, are practically devoid of facilities. Perhaps the difference between "urbanized" and "non-urbanized" areas, in the Latin American sense, is best expressed in the following translation of the distinction as used in Brazil for census purposes. This states that "an urbanized area is considered as that part of the territory that is served, or due to be served, by public improvements, as well as that included in the planned zone of expansion, including that along the highways. Considered as a non-urbanized area is that constituted of groups of buildings or dwellings in which there is a predominance of huts or rude dwellings constructed without obedience to any plan, outside the area of aligned streets, without legal rights of occupation (i.e. huts erected by squatters), and not served by public facilities."[2]

Some extracts from a recently approved Peruvian law, the *Ley de Remodelación, Saneamiento y Legalización de los Barrios Marginales*,[3] designed to *provide* for the "urbanization" of the large and populous *barriadas*, or slums, that have sprung up in the zones immediately about all of Peru's important cities, also illustrate the connotations of the term. Thus the "Presentación" in its opening paragraph states that the law has a social objective, but that no gift or "give away" is involved. It was born of a reality and represents the compliance with a pledge that had been made. It came about because of the tremendous upsurge of population in Peru, etc., and it "seeks to solve the problems of the most unfortunate families and of those who have established themselves on the vacant lands which border on the *urbanizaciones*." Similarly in promulgating the law the President of Peru indicated that it was intended to "transform and improve these population centers in their *urbanistic* and sanitary aspects, as well as in the juridical condition of their inhabitants . . ." Finally, Article I of Title I, which states the objectives and purposes of the law, reads as follows: "Declared to be of public necessity and utility and in the national interest is the *remodelación, saneamiento* and legalization of the *Barrios Marginales* or *Barriadas* existing in the urban and sub-urban areas of the nation's territory. The process, for the purpose of transforming the *barrios marginales* into *urbanizaciones* for the people and for social purposes, shall be governed by the dispositions of this Organic Law, whose application and execution is entrusted to the National Housing Corporation, created by Law Number 10,722."

The key concepts, which it has been deemed advisable to leave in their original Spanish forms in the above translation, are defined specifically in Article 4 of Title I as follows: (a)

[2] Alberto Passos Guimarães, "As Favelas do Distrito Federal," *Revista Brasileira de Estatística*, XIv, no. 55 (1953), 259. Cf. Louis J. Debret, José Arthur Rios, Carlos Alberto de Medina, and Helio Modesto, "Aspectos Humanos da Favela Carioca", *O Estado de S. Paulo, Suplemento Especial*, April 13, 1960, p. 7.

[3] Lima: Senado de la Republica, 1961.

"Barrio Marginal or *Barriada,* a zone of land belonging to the state, the municipality, the community or to private owners which lies within the political and administrative limits of those population centers which are (national or departmental) capitals, or within the suburban or rural areas surrounding them, in which by invasion and legally marginal dispositions relative to property rights, with or without authorization from the municipality, and upon lots that have been distributed without reference to any officially drawn and approved plans, groups of dwellings of any kind of materials have been constructed, such a zone lacking in one or more of the following services: drinking water, drains, lighting, foot paths, streets passable by wheeled vehicles, etc."; (b) *"Remodelación,* to adapt a *barrio marginal,* in accordance with pertinent technical studies, to the basic norms of planning so as to give to it at least the essential *urban* conditions and characteristics"; and (c) *"Saneamiento,* the execution of the works necessary for the drainage of the soil, the canalization of irrigation and drainage streams, the elimination of brush heaps, the burning of garbage, and the installation of water and sewer systems. By extension it includes the construction or improvement of the ways of transit, as well as the establishment of public and private electric lighting."[4]

It has been deemed worthwhile to present the above translations not merely for the primary purpose of making clear the connotations of the terms, urban, *urbanización,* and so forth in Spanish America, but also in order to suggest some of the bases for the generalization that "urbanization" is not keeping pace with urbanization throughout Latin America. The mere fact that "the problem of the suburbs" is now generally recognized as one of the chief social problems afflicting the populations of all of the countries from Mexico to Argentina and Chile alone is eloquent testimony to the validity of this proposition.[5] Moreover, the recent publication of com-

---

[4] Italics are not in the original Spanish text.
[5] On the problem of the Latin American suburbs, see T. Lynn Smith, "Los Problemas Sociales de la Actualidad en la America Latina," in Asociacion Venezolano de Sociologia, *VI Congreso Latinoamericano de Sociología, Memoria,* Caracas: Imprenta Nacional, 1961, II, pp. 315–317.

prehensive data for Brazil relating to "The Process of *Urbanização* and the Deficiency of Public Service or Those of Collective Utility in the Seats of Municípios," makes possible for that great country a fairly adequate analysis of the situation, one that probably does not differ in essential respects from that in most of the other Latin American countries. The materials are given as of December 31, 1954, and it is stated that:

> Even leaving out of consideration the small towns and villages, which in general are of less importance demographically, and taking into account only the seats of municípios (counties), there is to be observed an accentuated deficiency of public services and those of collective utility in the interior of the nation. According to data published by the Section of Urbanistic Activities of the former Ministry of Education and Culture, the following was the situation on December 31, 1954: of the 2,399 seats of municípios existing in Brazil, 1,080 had no pavement whatsoever, 1,354 had no systems for supplying drinking water, 1,939 lacked systems for disposing of sewage, and 349 were without the benefits of electrical illumination . . .
>
> Furthermore in some of the capitals the situation was no better: there were no mains for drinking water in Rio Branco, and no sewage system in this same city nor in Boa Vista, Teresina, Maceió, or Cuiabá.[6]

The call for improvement made in this report, or perhaps the greater recognition of some of the basic prerequisites for life in urban aggregations, are making for much greater efforts to provide the essential facilities and services under consideration. Thus, according to the 1960 issue of Brazil's *Anuário Estatístico*,[7] by the close of the year 1958 47 per cent of the seats of the municípios were served by water mains and 34 per cent had sewer systems, and these proportions are substantially higher than those for 1954.

The fact that water mains and a sewer system are present

[6] Alceu Vicente W. de Carvalho, *A População Brasileira,* Rio de Janeiro: Conselho Nacional de Estatística, 1960, pp. 108–110. The cities enumerated are the capitals of the territories of Acre and Rio Branco and of the states of Piauí, Alagôas, and Mato Grosso, respectively.

[7] Rio de Janeiro: Conselho Nacional de Estatística, 1960.

in a given city does not indicate, of course, that all of the homes or even a majority of them receive the benefits of the same. Relative to this point some of the data for the great city of Rio de Janeiro are enlightening, and were comparable facts available for Lima, Bogotá, Caracas, and dozens of other great Latin American population centers, the picture would be essentially the same. The 1960 census indicated that there were a total of 630,390 domiciles in the urban and suburban portions of the state of Guanabara, i.e., in Rio de Janeiro minus its important suburbs which are situated in the state of Rio de Janeiro; and the 1960 issue of the *Anuário Estatístico* gives the total number of water connections in the state, as of December 31, 1958, as 284,693. Of the latter, 84,168 were measured by meters and 200,525 were merely simple faucets. These data make it clear that the majority of the families residing in Brazil's great former capital secure the water they use for household purposes from taps which serve more than one dwelling. Similarly the *Anuário Estatístico* for 1960 indicates that as of December 31, 1959, 233,641 buildings in the state were connected with sewer systems; and on this basis, after making liberal allowances for apartment buildings of one kind or another, one may infer that probably less than one-half of the residences in Rio de Janeiro are equipped with modern facilities for disposing of the wastes from human bodies and other sources. In this connection one should indicate that the 1960 census also indicated that 70,353 of the dwellings, or the residences of 337,412 persons, were located in the city's noted *favelas* or slum districts, where by definition "urbanization" is almost completely lacking.

A recent valuable sociological survey of Rio de Janeiro's *favelas* provides a wealth of detail to substantiate the conclusions one would draw from the type of statistical data just presented. Thus the perceptive authors of this report[8] state that "from the sanitary point of view the *favelas* appear to us as suburbs embodied in the heart of the city; and some even resemble certain parts of the rural zone with their extremes transplanted into the heart of the nation's capital." Upon the

[8] Debret, Rios, Medina, and Modesto, *op. cit.*

basis of their thoroughgoing studies of those who dwell in the hundreds of thousands of hovels that cover the hills within Brazil's famed and picturesque metropolis, the sociologists who conducted the studies concluded that "with rare exceptions water is the number one sanitary problem of the *favelas*. Water not only for the bath, a general problem in many of Rio de Janeiro's middle-class and even upper-class residential districts; but water to drink, water for the minimum necessities of the human being. In the *favela* of Escondidinho, for example, near the Laranjeiras-Rio Comprido tunnel, if the persons who live on the hill-top want water to drink, they must descend flights of stairs having 352 steps, and then cross a stretch of steep hillside in order to get it, a kilometer away, in the Rua Almirante Alexandrino." In general the data supplied by the same team of researchers relative to the facilities, or lack of them, in this great city, justifies one in concluding that the absence of hygienic ways for disposing of bodily wastes and garbage create a problem that is only slightly less than that arising from the difficulty of getting water.[9]

No comparable studies are available for other Brazilian cities, but the same type of statistical information given above may be secured for most of them. For illustrative purposes a few of the basic facts having to do with the situations in two vastly different states, Ceará in the North, and Rio Grande do Sul, the southernmost state in the Brazilian confederation. The census of 1960 reported a total of 582,739 dwellings in the state of Ceará, of which probably about 195,000 were in the urban areas. However, the *Anuário Estatístico* for 1960 gave for December 31, 1958, the figure of 20,433 (12,599 with meters) as the number of water connections and one of 29,486 as the number of buildings having facilities for disposing of human wastes (22,188 with septic tanks and 7,299 with connections to sewer systems). In the entire city of Fortaleza, having 355,000 inhabitants in 1960, there were in 1958 only 4,500 water connections, 21,973 buildings linked with septic tanks or cesspools, and 6,827 connections with sewers. On the other hand in the state of Rio Grande do Sul,

[9] *Ibid.*, p. 25.

with a total of 1,026,778 dwellings reported by the 1960 census, of which probably about 410,000 were in urban areas, the essential facilities were much more prevalent. Thus the *Anuário Estatístico* for 1960 gave the following totals for December 31, 1958: water connections, 236,666, of which 116,146 were metered; and buildings connected with facilities for disposing of wastes, 77,919, including 67,238 connections with sewer systems. Porto Alegre, the capital, was responsible for 65,832 of the water connections and 25,635 of the sewer connections. Thus these materials indicate not only that "urbanization" fails by a large measure to keep pace with urbanization in Brazil, but that the width of the gap between the two varies tremendously from one part of that nation to another. In an even broader perspective the materials for Brazil, along with those for the other Latin American countries, emphasize the tremendous problems all of the countries are facing as huge segments of their rapidly mounting populations suddenly abandon life in the countryside and crowd into the cities and towns and the broad "zones of misery" which surround almost all of them.

The Functions of Latin American Cities

As urbanization proceeds throughout Latin America, the functions of her cities are changing drastically in a direction which makes them more similar to the cities of Europe and the United States and Canada, and even more like those which were in existence at the dawn of history. . . . Detailed studies of the roles played by cities in their respective societies, however, have challenged few if any sociologists throughout Latin America, a neglect that is matched only by the almost total lack of concern about such matters that have characterized their fellows in the United States and Europe. Even so a somewhat careful study of the materials for Brazilian capitals, supplemented by some examination of the pertinent materials for the more important Spanish American cities enables one to set forth a few pertinent observations on the subject.[10]

[10] For some discussion of the nature of the data on the general subject of analysis that may be undertaken, see T. Lynn Smith,

The function of cities are legion; and to some extent every one of the Latin American cities performs almost all of them. Trade and commerce, manufacturing and transportation, recreation and education, financial and personal services, construction and maintenance, administration and protection, religious and cultural activities, and residence as such, are some of the more important things which constitute the reasons for the existence of cities in Brazil, Mexico, Argentina, and all the other nations; but it would be possible to extend greatly the list of the functions that the cities perform for the society of which they form a part. In addition one may wish to subdivide the categories listed above into many varieties, even though he makes no attempt to exhaust the possibilities in this respect. Thus among familiar and important examples of such a classification one could mention heavy and light manufacturing; retail and wholesale trade; air, rail, sea, river, and highway transportation; and national, state, and local government. Of course some of them overlap, as is the case, for example, of educational and cultural activities, or protection and administration. Moreover, the importance of the several classes varies from time to time, for as mentioned above, the functions of Latin American cities in the second half of the twentieth century are vastly different from what they were during the first quarter of the same century, not to mention the preceding three or four centuries for which most of these cities have been in existence. Today there is far more specialization on the part of individual cities and division of labor between various cities than was the case as late as 1925. São Paulo and Monterrey have specialized to a considerable degree in the performance of certain specific functions; Mexico City, Rio de Janeiro, and Buenos Aires play much more general roles; and places such as Oroya, Barranquilla, Viña del Mar, and Brasília, which are highly specialized in heavy industry, transportation, recreation, and administration, respectively, have still to develop to an important degree more than a single function.

Cities in Latin America, as elsewhere, may be classified into

"The Functions of American Cities," in T. Lynn Smith and C. A. McMahan, *The Sociology of Urban Life*, New York: Dryden Press, Inc., 1951, pp. 97–103.

those which specialize in one, two, or three basic functions (uni-, bi-, tri-functional centers and so on) and those which are multifunctional in the strictest sense of the word. Of course since all of the functions are essential to the type of western civilization prevailing throughout Latin America, each of the cities performs to a greater or lesser degree every one of them. However, some Latin American cities concentrate largely upon one, two, or three of them, whereas others perform to a high degree six or more of them.

That European cities during the medieval period were largely market towns, or market towns and administrative strong points, is well-known. It is possible, however, that cities such as Havana, Fortaleza, and Recife, may be almost as highly specialized in the trading function as were the market places of earlier centuries, or as some modern places in the United States such as Dallas, Salt Lake City, Miami, and Kansas City, Missouri.

Fortress cities, that is to say strong points developed and maintained largely for protective purposes, or placed on trade routes so as to facilitate the exacting of tribute, are another well-known type of medieval urban centers; and the colonial fortress of Cartagena on the north coast of what now is Colombia is a more recent example of a place that specialized to an extreme degree in the protection feature. At present, however, such Brazilian cities as Natal and Florianópolis, well may claim distinction in this respect, along with San Diego, San Antonio, and Norfolk, in the United States.

Manufacturing and industrial centers are a recent development, even more recent in Latin America than in Europe and the United States. For the most part since the colonization of America the self-sufficiency of the large landed estates (*fazendas* or *engenhos* in Brazil, and *haciendas, fundos, estancias*, etc., in Spanish American countries), the very small scale on which transforming activities were carried on, and the limited amount of exchange, caused most processing of raw materials to take place in the rural districts. Nowadays, however, São Paulo, Monterrey, Paz del Rio, Volta Redonda, and some of the suburbs of Rio de Janeiro, of Mexico City, or Buenos Aires, are about as dependent upon manufacturing as are Birmingham in England or its namesake in Alabama.

Since 1500 Spanish American cities seem to be the ones that have specialized to the greatest degree in the performance of administrative and other governmental functions, and as residential centers for the members of the upper classes of their respective societies. Therefore, until the recent revolution in the functions of Latin American cities, places such as Paris, Rome, London, Stockholm, Berlin, and Washington, hardly rivaled, in this respect, the degree of specialization exhibited by such capitals as Lima, Caracas, Bogotá, Quito, and Santiago. Within the last decade Brasília has been added to the list, and it now stands in a class of its own in the degree to which the governmental and administrative functions are the raison d'être for its existence.

From the earliest times, cities have developed at favorable locations on the seacoast and on rivers where conditions made it necessary and possible to construct port facilities. Except in such cases as those of Havana, Cartagena, Montevideo, and Buenos Aires, however, this factor was relatively unimportant in the development of Spanish American cities until late in the nineteenth century. When Brazil's ports were opened to trade shortly after 1800, though, Rio de Janeiro, Salvador (Bahia), and Recife began to flourish, and later on Porto Alegre, São Luis, and Belém came to be of importance as ports.

The preceding paragraphs are designed to suggest that for centuries the functions of Latin American cities were extremely limited. Throughout the possessions of Spain the conquistadores who seized the lands and subjected the natives founded hundreds of new towns and cities. Almost all of them were built according to the exacting plan specified in the *Laws of the Indies* and they were also remarkably similar in the social and economic roles that they played. For the most part they were merely administrative and residential centers and seats of garrisons from which the white overlords exercised their dominion over the surrounding territory in which the villages and other settlements of their Indian, mestizo, and Negro vassals were located. Very few of the Spanish towns and cities relied to any extent upon the commercial function, and manufacturing was almost entirely lacking. Such transforming industries as were present in the colonies were located for the most part on the estates in the rural sections. Very few cities were important as ports, and the great majority were transportation centers only in the sense that from them radiated numerous trails that were traversed by pack trains of mules and burros.

Brazilian cities during colonial times differed from the Spanish American counterparts in two fundamental respects: they were built in a planless manner, quite different from the carefully drawn blueprint used in the Spanish settlements; and for the most part the members of the small, elite upper class lived in mansions on their estates and were not congregated in the towns and cities as was true throughout Spanish America. Except for a few ports, however, the functions of their cities were fully as limited, if not more so, than those in the Spanish colonies.[11]

For a full century after most of the Latin American countries gained their independence early in the nineteenth century, the functions of their cities changed very little. They continued to be for the most part merely residential, administrative, and political centers. By then, though, it was much easier and much more frequent for the Indians, mestizos, Negroes, and mulattoes to establish residence in the centers themselves or in their outskirts. A dozen or so cities emerged as important seaports, and the construction of railroads brought about an increased importance of transportation and commerce in many of the others. When the twentieth century opened, Buenos Aires, Rio de Janeiro, Havana, and Montevideo were among the capitals in which trade and transportation had become the principal functions, and throughout Latin America there was a strong tendency for

[11] For some discussions of the nature and role of early Brazilian cities, see Richard M. Morse, in *From Community to Metropolis*, Gainesville: University of Florida Press, 1958; and José Arthur Rios, "The Cities of Brazil" in T. Lynn Smith and Alexander Marchant, *Brazil: Portrait of Half a Continent*, New York: The Dryden Press, 1951, pp. 193–194.

places which had little or no administrative role to gain in importance. Rosario, Valparaiso, Barranquilla, Recife, and Callao may be mentioned as representative of this latter group.

Table II.   The Principal Functions of Brazilian Cities as Indicated by the Relative Importance of Major Occupational Categories, 1950.

| City | Percentage of the urban male labor force employed in: | | | | |
	Manufacturing and construction	Commerce	Transportation, communication and storage	Public service	Defense and public security
North					
Manaus	27	22	17	9	5
Belém	23	20	22	4	10
Northeast					
São Luis	28	20	20	6	4
Teresina	29	19	10	8	8
Fortaleza	24	25	14	5	8
Natal	21	17	14	4	23
João Pessoa	26	19	15	9	8
Recife	30	22	13	4	7
Maceió	36	17	14	6	6
East					
Aracaju	30	17	16	7	8
Salvador	28	20	16	5	7
Belo Horizonte	30	16	12	7	7
Vitoria	18	20	20	10	7
Niterói	26	15	17	7	11
Rio de Janeiro	23	16	10	7	10
South					
São Paulo	47	16	8	3	3
Curitiba	37	14	10	5	10
Florianópolis	21	17	14	10	14
Orto Alegre	30	20	12	6	9
West Central					
Cuiabá	32	15	10	11	10
Goiania	30	14	11	11	6

* Computed from data in "Censo Demográfico," *VI Recenseamento Geral do Brasil, 1950,* I (Rio de Janeiro, 1956), 204–251.

In the decades that have passed since the close of the First World War, manufacturing as a basis for urban existence in Latin America has gained considerable importance. As indicated above, in this connection the names of São Paulo and Monterrey come to mind whenever industrialization in Latin America is mentioned. Medellín is in about the same category. However, by 1950, Buenos Aires, Havana, Santiago, Lima, Mexico City, Porto Alegre, and Bogotá all were places in which manufacturing and transforming industries led all other categories in supplying jobs for their breadwinners.

For the cities which serve as state capitals in Brazil it is possible to present more detailed information with respect to the relative importance of several of the more important functions as reflected in the occupations which supply employment for the male members of their labor forces. See Table II. Eventually it may be possible to compile comparable summary information for various Spanish American countries.

Ecological Patterns

In order to conclude this brief treatment of urbanization in Latin America, a few comments relating to the ecological patterns of Latin American cities are offered. In general, even though a few noteworthy studies of the social ecology of these cities have been made,[12] relatively little is known about the ecological patterns that prevail in the cities of Mexico, Central America, the Island Republics, and South America. It is certain, of course, that in the towns and cities of this important part of the world various types of social phenomena tend to cluster in particular parts of the urbanized area, and that truly symbiotic relationships prevail between many

[12] Among the materials dealing with the social ecology of Latin American cities are the following: Theodore Caplow, "The Social Ecology of Guatemala City," Social Forces, 28 (December, 1949), 113–133; Floyd Dotson and Ota Dotson, "Ecological Trends in the City of Guadalajara, Mexico," Social Forces, 32 (May, 1954), 367–374; Asael Hansen, "The Ecology of a Latin American City," in E. B. Reuter (ed.), Race and Culture Contacts, New York: McGraw-Hill Book Company, 1934, pp. 124–142; Harry B. Hawthorn and Audrey Hawthorn, "The Shape of a City: Some Observations on Sucre, Bolivia," Sociology and Social Research, 33 (Nov.-Dec., 1948), Norman S. Hayner, "Mexico City: Its Growth and Configuration," American Journal of Sociology, 50 (January, 1943), 295–304; Norman Hayner, "Oaxaca, City of Old Mexico," Sociology and Social Research, 29 (Nov.-Dec., 1944), 87–95; Philip M. Hauser, (ed.), Urbanization in Latin America, New York: International Documents Service, 1961, passim; and T. Lynn Smith, Brazil: People and Institutions, 3rd. ed., Baton Rouge: Louisiana State University Press, 1963, Chapter 21.

of the social, cultural, economic, and political elements that are found in a given section. The nature of these clusters, however, and of the relationships between their components are still largely unknown.

No doubt the rental value of urban real estate is fully as important as a factor in producing the ecological patterns prevailing throughout Latin America as it is in bringing about the natural areas that are found within cities in the United States and Europe. This is to say that the amount that families can pay for housing serves as a sieve to sort them into socioeconomic categories and to place those of similar status in specific parts of a city. As a result one always finds exclusive residential districts for the wealthy, other areas occupied almost entirely by families of middle-class position, working-class sections, slums, and various other types of residential areas. But the arrangement of these areas seems to be vastly different in Brazilian and Spanish American cities than that which is commonly found in the urban centers of the United States, probably largely because of differences in intra-urban transportation facilities and the differences in the relative importance of the upper, middle, and lower social classes north of the Rio Grande and to the south of it. Thus almost without exception in the United States the most exclusive residential districts are on the outskirts of a city, and the term suburb generally denotes a far better than the average residential district; whereas in Latin America in general the most exclusive residential districts are near the center of the city, and the term *suburbio* is far from having any salutory connotations.

Likewise in much-studied Chicago and other cities in the United States, the cheapest rents, the most unsatisfactory housing, the largest concentrations of anti-social behavior, and so forth, are highly concentrated in the disorganized zones which surround the central business districts. This is inevitable where a growth pattern prevails that is transforming one-time residential sections into extensions of the commercial area. But all of this is quite different in most parts of Latin America in which the worst slums are by no means common in the hearts of the cities. Instead the area surrounding each of the "urbanized" portions of a city constitutes a thick band of hovels and huts whose inhabitants are living under the most precarious conditions. As indicated above, these are the densely populated portions of the built-up area which have not yet been "urbanized" through the alignment of streets, the extension of water mains, the provision of electricity, and the development of facilities for disposing of garbage and wastes from the human bodies. Perhaps the Latin American image of urban ecological patterns is most adequately expressed in the following succinct paragraph which the author used to introduce his fundamental study of the *favelas* of Rio de Janeiro:

In all urban centers there generally are sections which are distinguished from the others by the almost complete lack of public improvements and by the uncomfortable conditions in their dwellings. As a rule, these districts in which the poorest layers of the population live form the periphery of the cities, and they constantly spread to greater distances from the centers of greatest activity, carrying along with their human agglomerations, with greater or less mobility, to the degree that the urban expansion becomes more intense. The social groups of high economic levels generally are located in the central districts, or in proximity to them, whereas those lacking resources live on the outskirts.[13]

[13] Guimaraes, *op. cit.*, p. 250.

21 Urbanization and
Socio-Cultural Values
in Brazil

———◆———

In the 1960's Brazil is experiencing a socio-cultural upheaval unrivaled in its history except perchance by that which accompanied the almost simultaneous freeing of the slaves and downfall of the monarchy (1888–89); and urbanization, both as a cause and as an effect, is the central feature of the current socio-cultural revolution. On the one hand a series of powerful factors in transforming a nation that, for more than four centuries, was overwhelmingly rural, pastoral, and agricultural into one in which various kinds of urban activities predominate; and on the other hand living in the cities and towns is remaking completely the personality of the typical Brazilian, the groups in which he is enmeshed, the social strata into which his society is divided, the cultural influences which impinge upon him and his family, and the values by which he lives. Frequently, very frequently indeed, the falling apart of the old ways of life is producing social, economic and political problems of appalling magnitude.

Volumes might be written about the forces which almost overnight are transforming Brazil from a highly rural into a predominantly urban society. Here we must be content with the mere mention of some of the more important ones such as: (1) the growth of population at a rate that is almost unprecedented in any large and substantial parts of the earth's surface; (2) the promotion of industrialization as a hoped-for cure-all for a host of the nation's chronically acute social and economic problems; (3) frantic efforts to promote the volume of exports accompanied by endeavors to limit

---

Presented to the XXI Congress of the International Institute of Sociology, Madrid, Spain, October, 1967.

the amount of imports; (4) the development of modern systems of communication and transportation; (5) the establishment to some extent of more adequate educational facilities at all levels; (6) and the gradual abolition of servile and semi-servile labor arrangements in the rural districts. These factors, along with many others that might be listed, and the rapid homogenization of Brazilian society and culture in general, are producing a mass movement of people from the rural areas to the urban centers. This is to say that with few, very few, exceptions, the huge numbers of persons born and reared in Brazil's rural communities are not swarming along the frontier in the conquest of the tremendous sections of the country that are still to be settled; rather they are flocking into cities and towns of all sizes and adding to the rapidly multiplying numbers of those already living in urban places and in the huge bands of misery called "suburbs" which surround all of them.

It definitely would be a mistake, though, as it would be in most other socio-cultural equations, to assume that the chain of causation is operating only in the one direction. The fact that the Brazilian population is coming to be one that is predominantly urban itself is operating as a moving force or *cause* to reshape drastically the structure, processes, and values of Brazilian society along lines and into patterns that are radically different from those prevailing in 1900, 1920, or even 1940. Nowadays, for example, Gilberto Freyre, maximum authority on Brazilian society and culture, stresses the vast differences between life and labor on the present-day sugar-cane plantation and those on the large estates of the patriarchal society which he idolized in his classic *Casa Grande e Senzala*.[1] Likewise one who knew such cities as Rio de Janeiro, São Paulo, Recife, Belo Horizonte, Bahia, Porto Alegre, Fortaleza, and Curitiba in 1920 can find very few similarities between those places as they were at that time and the metropolitan centers they are at present.[2]

[1] Gilberto Freyre, "La Lucha no es de Clases," *Life en Español*, May 11, 1964, pp. 25–26.

[2] For more of the facts, a fuller discussion and bibliography of works related to the topics discussed in this paper, see T. Lynn

The Magnitude and Rate of Urban Growth

Fortunately Brazilian census data are of a nature and quality that makes it relatively easy for anyone familiar with modern demographic techniques to gauge rather accurately the degree and rate of urbanization in Brazil. As late as 1940 the population of that nation was only slightly more than 41 million of which a mere 36.5 per cent was classified as urban. During the decade ending in 1950, the total population rose by 26 per cent, a very rapid rate, to a figure of almost 52 million. In this ten-year period, though, the rural exodus already was getting well under way, so that the urban-suburban population increased by 46 per cent, or more than 5.9 millions, whereas the much larger rural population grew by only 17 per cent, or 3.8 millions. Then between 1950 and 1960, in a phenomenal spurt of growth, Brazil's population rose by more than 19 millions, or by 37 per cent, with more than 13 millions of the total being accounted for by the increases in urban places and less than 6 millions by the growth of population throughout the vast rural expanses of the nation. On the relative basis during this decade the increase of 17 per cent in the rural population was accompanied by one of 70 per cent in the number of inhabitants of urban centers. Since the census of 1960 was taken it is likely that the growth of population in Brazilian cities and towns has outstripped that in the rural areas to an even greater extent than was the case between 1950 and 1960; and it is likely that in 1965 the proportion of all Brazilians classified as living in urban centers had moved up from the 45 per cent registered in 1960 to at least 50 per cent.

The mushrooming of population in specific cities and their environs offers evidence of the fact that the Brazilians whose

Smith, *Brazil: People and Institutions,* third edition, Baton Rouge: Louisiana State University 1963, Chapters III, IX, X, and XX and *passim;* T. Lynn Smith, "Urbanization in Latin America," *International Journal of Comparative Sociology,* Vol. IV, No. 2 (Sept. 1963), pp. 227–242; and T. Lynn Smith, "The Giant Awakes: Brazil," *The Annals of the American Academy of Political and Social Science,* Vol. 334 (March, 1961), pp. 95–102.

powerful, landowning, aristocratic families for centuries resided on their baronial estates, and whose great masses lived in almost hermetically sealed little rural neighborhoods and communities, are now caught up in the mad swirl of urban life. Thus, the highly publicized growth of São Paulo and Rio de Janeiro is almost fantastic. As late as 1920 there were no more than 1,250,000 people in Rio de Janeiro and the surrounding area about the Guanabara Bay; but by 1960 the great complex made up of the central city and its satellites formed a metropolitan community of about 5 million inhabitants. Moreover, this represents such a change from the older patterns of life that the residents of the "bed-room towns" surrounding New York City and other cities in the United States, who think they have difficulties in getting from where they sleep to where they work and back again, all within a twenty-four hour period, would have much to learn if they were to trade places with their fellows in Rio de Janeiro's teeming suburbs. São Paulo, which disputes with Brazil's former capital for the prestige that goes with being the nation's largest city, had only about 240,000 residents in 1900, and, after twenty years of spectacular growth, no more than 590,000 in 1920. By 1960, though, as capital of a state of about 13 million people and the hub of the greatest industrial complex in all of Latin America, the conurbation of which it formed the core had at least 5 million inhabitants, and the figure continued to mount at a dizzying pace.

It should be stressed, however, that neither São Paulo nor Rio de Janeiro is the fastest growing of Brazil's large cities. That distinction belongs to Belo Horizonte, capital of the immense and populous state of Minas Gerais, whose growth, as measured by the increases in the municipio or county in which it is located, amounted to 67 per cent between 1940 and 1950 and 93 per cent during the decade ending in 1960. These proportions may be compared with corresponding increases of 66 and 72 per cent in the municipio of São Paulo; but they are not comparable with those of only 34 and 39 per cent, respectively, for the two decades in the former Distrito Federal, since many of Rio de Janeiro's most rapidly growing districts actually are beyond the limits of the state of Guanabara in the surrounding portions of the state of

Rio de Janeiro, and not in the enclave itself. As a result of the huge increases of population in many of the most densely parts of metropolitan Rio de Janeiro ordinarily are not taken into account by those who give the figures about the rise and rate of growth of this huge conurbation. Moreover, in considering the extent to which urban realities presently are impinging upon the behavior and cultural patterns of the Brazilian people, the population increases in other major cities during the ten-year periods ending in 1950 and 1960, respectively, must be taken into account. These include the following, with the first number of the pair of figures representing the growth between 1940 and 1950 and the second that between 1950 and 1960, and with the data in each case being for the municipio in which the city is located: Curitiba, 28 and 100 per cent; Fortaleza, 50 and 91 per cent; Porto Alegre, 45 and 63 per cent; and Salvador (Bahia), 44 and 57. Of these cities, by 1965 Recife no doubt already had passed the one million mark; Belo Horizonte and Porto Alegre, and possibly Salvador, will have done so before 1970; and Fortaleza will not be far behind in reaching the point at which it will represent an aggregation of more than a million poorly equipped people, mostly drawn from the sub-rural zone of the great Northeast, who will be struggling with the realities of life in a great urban complex in which jobs in industry are conspicuous by their absence.

The Necessity for Drastic Changes in Socio-Cultural Values

The transplantation of millions of Brazilians from extremely rural surroundings to great, densely inhabited, and poorly supplied urban agglomerations is producing far-reaching changes in almost every facet of Brazilian life, labor, and culture. This is true even on the part of the members of the affluent families, although to a far lesser extent with them than in the case with the millions of humble folk who themselves were reared in the patterns of traditional relationships between master and man, patron and retainer, of a great rural society in which a few families owned and controlled the land. The latter now find themselves entrapped in the situation of trying to carry on their own lives and to bring up their own children amid surroundings in which the politicians fall far short of performing satisfactorily the roles of the patrons. Their family relationships and the patterns of mutual responsibilities on the part of kinfolk are badly scrambled. In their new surrounding their traditional folkways are fraught with great danger to health, money in considerable amounts is found to be essential for survival, new wants arise to confront them on every hand, the ability to read and write and make arithmetical calculations is now a necessity of life, and so on. In the time and space available, it is, of course, impossible to analyze in detail any of these or to develop the implications they have for the revolutionary changes they are bringing in the patterns of living and the socio-cultural values of the masses of Brazil's people. However, it seems essential to list some of the things involved, although the items selected are by no means all of the significant ones, nor a representative sample of them, and the list may not even include all of the more important features.

Consider first some of the changes in dietary patterns which accompany the aggregation of huge populations in cities and towns. Even though many of the migrants themselves may be content with, or actually prefer, a daily ration of beans, rice, manioc, dried beef, and so on, their children quickly develop a taste for other things and feel deprived if they cannot have a more varied diet. As a result they demand such things as fresh meat, potatoes, fresh vegetables, fruits of various kinds, dairy products, and a host of other foods, most of which are more costly than the staples of the traditional rural diets. Furthermore, now that the Japanese cultural heritage has gained a strong foothold in the areas surrounding the city of São Paulo and rapidly is being diffused to other adjacent states, many of the items in the newer dietary patterns are available in the markets.

The changes in dress likewise are drastic. Bare-footed persons, dressed only in tattered shirts and pants, or in something resembling cotton blouses and skirts, are hardly in keeping with the standards of appearance that prevail in the central districts of large, modern cities. Thus, even if there were no city ordinances prohibiting shoeless people from moving about in down-town areas, and even if there were no rules forbidding those without coats from riding on the street cars and buses, the weight of public opinion would bring about a mode of dress more in keeping with urban patterns than are the norms to which the migrants were accustomed in the districts in which they originated; and which, we may add, are norms that become deeply rooted in Brazilian rural values and cultural patterns during the centuries in which slavery and other systems of servile and semi-servile labor were the general rule. One does not need too much sagacity in order to discern that Jeca Tatú (the listless, poverty-stricken country man) may be a splendid type for literary themes as long as he lives a life of abandon in the countryside; but when he and his fellows bestir themselves and swarm into the cities, he somehow loses his appeal for members of the literary guild.

Changes in housing are no less significant. Hundreds of thousands of those who flee the rural districts to make their abodes in Rio de Janeiro, São Paulo, Belo Horizonte, Recife, Brasília, and dozens of other important cities and hundreds of smaller ones, find work on the construction projects that are multiplying great apartment houses and less pretentious dwellings almost as if by magic. Not infrequently such workers and their families actually live in the unfinished structures which they are helping to build; but much more commonly they call home the huts and shacks which they throw up in the suburban slums which ring the cities, or in inconvenient and undesirable areas within some of them such as places along damp river bottoms, on the mud flats that are washed by the incoming tides, and on high hillsides. It would be difficult to imagine a greater contrast in housing facilities than that for example between the elaborate new apartment houses in Brasília and the replicas of their rural homes which the members of the construction labor force have built in the "free city" just outside the limits of the new Federal District; or that between the apartments that line many of the avenues of Rio de Janeiro and the famed *favelas* high on the hillsides which overlook the city and in which large numbers of the construction workers reside. More important for present purposes, though, is the revolution in values that is triggered by such contrasts in the minds of many of the migrants and especially in those of their children. All of this is intensified by the ferment of political life in which politicians of all political hues vie for the votes of the masses, and perhaps even more by the slum-clearance projects undertaken by state and municipal governments by means of which some of the lower-class families actually come into possession of houses in which there are floors and windows, which have masonry walls and roofs of tile, and in which running water and toilet facilities have been installed.

The items mentioned so far, each of which may appear at first to be insignificant, when multiplied by the millions of persons actually involved, and multiplied again by the interactions between those of a given social class and also those between the members of the different social classes, add up to a tremendous amount of pressure for fundamental changes in the socio-cultural value system of Brazilian society. So far, though, we have mentioned only a few of the foci which help make up the general matrix of the process of adjustment and development. Limitations of space preclude further elaboration of this line of thought, but it may be stated categorically that the institutional framework involved in each of the following aspects of society also is deeply involved in the remodeling of socio-cultural values that the process of urbanization is bringing about in Brazil: family and kinship patterns, privileges and obligations; formal educational activities at the elementary, secondary, and university levels; political and administrative structure and power, both in the bases upon which they rest and the forms in which they are expressed; levels and standards of living; the organization of labor and the roles of the unions in national and state affairs; social and welfare legislation and activities of all types; the nature and use of leisure time, and recreational behavior of all kinds; and even in religious affiliations, beliefs, and practices, of which the upsurge of the Pentecostal denomination or sect may be mentioned as a striking example.

Some Examples of the Changing Socio-cultural Values

In order to conclude this brief exposition, a few examples may be given of the manner in which the changing sociocultural values are affecting contemporary Brazilian society.

1. THE EXPANDING "ZONE OF EXASPERATION." As Brazil's population has flocked into her cities and towns in the years since the close of World War II, a veritable revolution has taken place in the expectations of the masses of the population, or in what sociologists and economists call the standard of living. This seems to have begun for the most part in the cities of Rio de Janeiro, São Paulo, and other important places in southern Brazil. Rapidly, however, it has spread to the urban centers in all parts of the half continent encompassed within the boundaries of the nation we are considering and it has even been disseminated into most portions of its widespread rural territory. All of this, of course, is part and parcel of the change in socio-cultural values which we are discussing and of the more general process of the homogenization of society of which it forms a part. Furthermore, to a considerable extent the rise in expectations or standard of living, that is the amounts of goods and services which the populace think themselves entitled to enjoy, has been matched by actual increases in the things they have been able to get and consume, that is their level or plane of living. Nevertheless for various reasons it has been far more difficult to produce and distribute equitably a greatly expanded volume of goods and services than it has been to stir up on the part of the masses a desire for vastly greater amounts of such items. As a result the difference between the two, which may be called the area of frustration or the zone of exasperation, has become much broader; and, we may add, thereby the explosive potential of Brazilian society has been greatly magnified.

2. THE EDUCATIONAL CRISIS. The revolution in sociocultural values that has been produced by a "great leap" of Brazilian society from a pastoral and agricultural base to an urbanized and to some extent industrialized mode of existence has reached a crisis stage in many areas, but in none is the present situation more critical than in that of education. By this the present writer is not referring primarily to the rampant development of "the political university" with all of its ramifications, from student strikes to the ousting of professors who differed ideologically from those who controlled the

Ministry of Education and other ruling cliques, serious as this has been during the last decade. Rather he is thinking mainly of the need for formal education in considerable amounts by all of those who are needed to man a great industrial plant, and to build and operate a system of communication and transportation such as is requisite for existence as an important nation in the Nuclear Age. He has in mind the trained people necessary for a commerce and trade that will promote and serve the interests of the people and the nation rather than to suck the life blood from them. He is preoccupied about the type and amount of education that will prepare properly the personnel needed in governmental service, in the service activities, in the construction industry, in the professions and sciences, and even, to the extent of four or five per cent of the entire labor force, for functions in the educational institutions themselves. Now that Brazil has set her hopes upon industrialization and urbanization as the answer for her host of chronic and acute social and economic problems and has cast her lot in this direction, she has not much choice in the matter. It would appear that she must either build quickly the necessary educational system or that she will fail dismally in her attempts to reach the goals she seeks. Already her socio-cultural values are such that she cannot continue with a system of elementary education in which only a little more than half of her children ever see the inside of a school, and those who do attend cannot secure more than two, three, four, or five years of such training, depending upon the state and the part of the state in which they live. Now she can no longer limit her secondary school opportunities to those who live in or can be sent to board in the larger towns and cities, mostly on the seacoast. She will never come into her own as a great nation as long as approximately one-half of all her municipios or counties lack any schools whatsoever other than those elementary levels. The present ambitions of her leaders cannot be realized without a radical change of the situation in which in a population of over 80 million people only about one million students are enrolled in schools that compare roughly with junior and senior high schools in the United States. Finally, to carry on in a family of urbanized and industrialized nations, Brazil no longer can exist with the system of higher education bequeathed by the socio-cultural values that typified bygone days in which higher education was for a handful of the offspring of the affluent old families who sought degrees in medicine and law. The road she must follow calls, among other things, for hundreds of technical high schools where there now is only one, for thousands of students in colleges of engineering where now there are dozens, for years of hard work at full-time study where now there are brief endeavors of part-time students, for hundreds of thousands of full-time university professors where now there are only thousands of part-time teachers, and for the immediate building of large facilities for graduate study where now there is very little deserving of such a name.

3. THE LAG IN URBANIZAÇÃO RELATIVE TO URBANIZATION. A third, and for present purposes, final implication of the change in socio-cultural values intimately linked with urbanization in contemporary Brazil is the tremendous lag in what Brazilians call urbanização in comparison with the upsurge of urbanization itself. In order that this statement may not be construed as an example of very blurred thinking, it should be indicated that in Brazil, except in the words and writings of a handful of sociologists and economists, the term *urbanização* denotes the work of developing some of the physical aspects of the cities, such as aligned streets and sidewalks, public squares, water mains, sewer systems, and lighting systems. Definitely it does not embrace all of the various features of the development of towns and cities such as are inherent in the English word *urbanization*. If viewed in this light considerable significance should be attached to the statement that urbanização in Brazil is lagging greatly in comparison with urbanization; for this is to say that large parts of the great urban communities that are springing up are almost completely lacking streets that are laid out and aligned, not to mention paved and equipped with curbs and sidewalks; that major proportions of the dwellings have no water connections, and that the families living in them must carry all the water they use for drinking and culinary purposes from spigots some distance away; that sewer connections are limited to the houses in selected portions of the urban ag-

glomerations, and that vast numbers of homes have no facilities whatsoever for disposing of bodily wastes as well as garbage, kitchen slop, and so on; and that the benefits of electricity are entirely lacking or confined to those supplied by a rudimentary and dangerous string of wires. All of this is related to the matters involving education just discussed and to the host of scarcities of all types, from personnel trained and equipped for most essential jobs to staple foods and municipal funds, which could be included if time and space allowed. As it is, however, it serves as a fitting conclusion to this brief discussion of the changing socio-cultural values which accompany, as effect and also as cause, Brazil's present mad rush into an urbanized stage of existence.

22 The Changing Functions of Latin American Cities

THE FUNCTIONS of the city are legion; and to a certain extent every city in Latin America performs nearly all of them. Trade and commerce, manufacturing and processing, communication and transportation, government and public administration, educational and cultural activities, religious and ceremonial observances, financial and personal services, servicing and repair, and recreation and welfare work, are a few of the better known categories. This list does not include, however, residence per se which is one of the principal raisons d'être of cities in general. Moreover, even these better known urban functions can be subdivided into many varieties and classes, without in any way being exhaustive. Familiar examples are wholesale and retail trade; motor, rail, water, and air transportation; light and heavy manufacturing; and national, provincial, and local government and administration. In addition some of them tend to overlap, as in the cases of educational and cultural activities, or government and protection. Finally, the absolute and relative importance of any one of the functions, or of any particular combination of them, varies greatly from one city to another and in the same city from one time to another.

One of the most significant classifications of cities is that based upon the number and complexity of the fundamental functions which they perform. Those which existed at the dawn of history were multi-functional in the strictest sense. They seem to have performed almost all of the social and economic functions necessary for life in that remote past;

Prepared for presentation at the International Congress of Americanists, Buenos Aires and Mar del Plata, Argentina, September 3–11, 1966, and published in *The Americas,* Vol. XXV, No. 1 (July, 1968), pp. 70–83. Reprinted by permission of the publisher.

and the same was true of the fortress cities of the early Roman state. In sharp contrast with these are the extremely limited functions of the cities which developed during the Middle Ages, as symbolized by the houses and shops of the tradesmen which were huddled at the base of the hill or cliff on which the castle was built. Protection was at first the fundamental function of the village or town, gradually supplemented by trade and commerce. In more recent times in Spanish America, Cartagena of the Indies, long the world's greatest fortress city, was during the entire colonial period one of the most highly specialized urban centers that man has built. As is stressed below, however, the functions of colonial Latin American cities were extremely limited, and the major concern of this paper is with the diversification that has taken place as a strong fever of urbanization has suddenly seized the twenty countries involved.

By some queer aspect of sociological and anthropological reasoning that it is difficult to explain, it seems that the study of the functions of cities has offered little or no challenge to the scientists working in those fields. Is it because so many of us are preoccupied with matters which belong largely to the study of psychology and even to the psychology of the individual? Is a societal entity or group par excellence, such as the city, actually outside the scope of our professed concern? In any case the failure for any of us to focus attention upon the functions of Latin American cities is almost total.

The absence of such effort certainly cannot be attributed to the lack of basic data nor to the difficulty of making significant first-hand observation. Any perceptive observer, equipped with a sound sociological frame of reference, may gather highly pertinent and useful materials by bare observation alone; and if he will take the trouble to examine the great quantities of statistical information gathered and published in recent decades, he will discover a rich mine of quantitative information bearing directly upon the subject. Most useful of all, for the various cities of Latin America, are the facts about the labor force. These, for example, enable one to ascertain the absolute and relative importance of the workers who are classified in the principal industrial and occupational categories such as trade and commerce, manufacturing, transportation, and so on, a sound basis for many significant and highly pertinent inferences.

It should be mentioned, however, that the appropriate use of these quantitative data involves making large numbers of compilations and computations. I, myself, have devoted considerable time to the analysis of the materials for Brazil and Colombia, although I also have worked with data for some of the cities in other countries.[1] As more of the materials from the demographic censuses made in 1960 and subsequent years become available, I hope to expand considerably this phase of my research.

Before we concentrate our attention upon the current revolutionary changes in the functions of Latin American cities, two essential preliminaries must be handled. The first of these is to sketch briefly the functions of those cities during the colonial epoch, or from the time they were founded (largely in the sixteenth century) to about 1825 when most of the colonies had gained their independence; and the second is to outline the nature of the changes in their functions during the national period up to about 1935 or 1940.

The Functions of Latin American Cities During the Colonial Period

During the long colonial period the functions of Spanish American cities were extremely limited. Founded in accordance with carefully planned specifications they were closely similar in their ecological features and much alike in the roles they played in colonial society. In a word they were locations for the residences of the Spaniards from which these

[1] For a summary of the results of my studies of the functions of Brazilian cities see T. Lynn Smith, *Brazil: People and Institutions* (3rd ed.; Baton Rouge: Louisiana State University Press, 1963), Chapter XXII; and for a few of the more significant features of the functions of cities of the United States see T. Lynn Smith and C. A. McMahan, *The Sociology of Urban Life* (New York: The Dryden Press, 1951), pp. 97–103, and Joseph S. Vandiver, "Urbanization and Urbanism in the United States," *International Journal of Comparative Sociology,* IV, No. 2 (Sept., 1963), 272–273.

overlords exercised their dominion over the lands, peoples and mines in their particular part of the possessions of the Spanish Crown. Administrative centers and military posts or garrison towns best describes the raison d'être of the hundreds of new towns in which the Spaniards lived. Almost all of them were founded in the sixteenth century, and all except the very first ones were platted in accordance with the detailed plans and specifications set forth in the *Laws of the Indies*. Moreover, the learned jurists who formed the Council of the Indies sent out, over the Spanish sovereign's signature, decree after decree intended to maintain a rigid separation of the races in the colonies. The Spaniards were required to have houses (and later "inhabited" houses) in their towns and forbidden to have any buildings (and later even to spend the night) in any of the Indian villages.[2] Very early rings of huts of the mestizos and other outcasts sprang up on the outskirts of some of the Spanish towns, not too different from the "bands of misery" which have grown up like mushrooms or toadstools adjacent to most contemporary Latin American cities. However, the presence of these miserable segments of humanity did little to affect the basic functions of the cities involved.

Nor were most of them to change their social and economic functions very much throughout the whole colonial epoch. Practically none of them developed as centers in which manufacturing and processing furnished a significant number of jobs for the breadwinners of the family. The few feeble attempts actually made along these lines, such as the making of a crude brown sugar, the production of syrup and molasses, the spinning and weaving of cotton and woolen textiles, and so on, took place on the haciendas and other large landed estates. The few powerful owners of the large properties involved lived in the cities, of course, but the rest of the urban residents functioned only as consumers of the few products involved.

Likewise trade and commerce were insignificant among the occupations of those who lived in the Spanish American cities

[2] Cf. T. Lynn Smith, "Some Neglected Spanish Social Thinkers," *The Americas*, XVII, No. 1 (July, 1960), 37–52.

during the centuries of Spanish domination. Given Spain's colonial policies it could not have been otherwise. These seem to have had two principal objectives: (1) to make the colonies into producers of gold, silver, and precious stones; and (2) to limit their consumption of manufactured goods strictly to those produced in Spain, shipped in convoys from Spanish ports, and destined for a few strongly fortified seaports, of which the principal ones were Vera Cruz, Cartagena, and Callao. Even certain types of agriculture, such as the planting of vineyards and the growing of tobacco, were strictly limited or prohibited altogether.

The effects of concentration upon that part of mining which involves precious metals and stones, including those relating specifically to the functions of cities, have been summarized by one highly perceptive Spanish American as follows:

. . . Spanish Americans saw themselves excluded from industry, foreign trade and agriculture to a high degree, by the innumerable monopolies and prohibitions of the colonial regime. Mining, reduced to that of gold and silver, was the cardinal element of riches. But mines of gold and silver enriched no one except their proprietors, few in number and exempt from genuine social activity by the extreme ease with which they made their fortunes. Gold travels to all parts in small and valuable bars; it does not stimulate the building of roads, agriculture, the arts, the growth of population, schools, etc.; it concentrates enormous fortunes in the hands of a few who live in the comfortable cities; it leaves the mass of the proletariat in misery, idleness, ignorance, and stagnation; it favors social inequalities; and it is a powerful stimulant to gambling, ostentatiousness, sterile luxury, dissipation, laziness, and all similar vices and consequences.[3]

The throttling of trade and commerce which effectually blocked the development in Spanish American cities of some of the most important functions was accomplished by several

[3] José M. Samper, *Ensayo sobre las Revoluciones Políticas y la Condición Social de la Repúblicas Colombianas* (*Hispano-Americanas*), (Paris: Imprenta de E. Thunot y Cie, 1864), pp. 114–115.

specific policies, including: (1) the prohibition of manufacturing in the new world; (2) the exclusion of the ships of all nations but Spain from the ports in the colonies; (3) the establishment of the *Casa de Contratación* in Seville with a monopoly on trade and shipping to the fortress ports in the western hemisphere; and (4) the restriction of shipping to the convoys sent out once a year.

Samper bitterly compared the effects of these deadly restrictions on commerce to the puerile and ineffectual work of the Holy Office of the Inquisition.

> But the work of the fiscal inquisition was a different matter. In the view of the *Santo oficio fiscal* every piece of dinnerware from England, every bottle of wine from Bordeaux and every box of spaghetti from Genoa were scandalously heretical.[4]

For present purposes the basic importance of all this is the fact that trade and commerce were insignificant as bases for urban life in Spanish American cities all through the centuries of Spanish domination. The few important seaports, of which more is said later on, were entrepots for receiving the annual convoys from Seville, for outfitting the fleets of canoes and the trains of mules that carried the goods from the fortresses to the other parts of the Spanish dominions, for assembling the treasures to be sent to Spain, and for loading and outfitting the convoys for the voyage back across the Atlantic.

Of all the heavily fortified seaports Vera Cruz and Cartagena far outranked the others in importance. The former was the key in the supply of New Spain and the dispatch to Spain of the Aztec treasures; and the latter was long the greatest port in South America as well as the strongest fortress in the world. Cartagena's role as a center of commerce was enhanced by the prohibition of the transportation of goods across the Isthmus of Panama for reshipment to Pacific ports. (The routes to Valparaiso and Callao were via Cape Horn.) From it fleets of canoes left for the interior, and especially for Honda about 500 miles up the Magdalena River. This trip took about six months. There the cargoes were trans-

4 *Ibid.*, p. 119.

ferred to the backs of mules, and here the trains began the climb up the rough, steep, rocky, and slippery trail to Bogotá, capital of New Granada. Others set out on the much longer trip to the south, to Popayán first and then on to Quito. From Cartagena to Quito required from about 20 months to a full two years.[5] Obviously transportation being what it was, a thriving merchant class was not a prominent feature of Spanish American cities when the new places were established in the sixteenth century; and the same element was largely lacking when the various provinces began as independent countries during the first half of the nineteenth century.

Unusual interest should be attached, however, to the extent to which colonial Spanish American cities served, or failed to serve, as hubs in the important systems of transportation and communication. As has just been indicated since the vast portions of America involved were possessions of the Spanish Crown, it was inevitable that a few places in the New World would function importantly as seaports. Havana, Santo Domingo, Vera Cruz, Cartagena must be mentioned in this connection, and perhaps Buenos Aires, Montevideo, Valparaiso, Callao, Guayaquil, and Acapulco should be added. Definitely, though, this should not be taken as an endorsement of the widely held social and economic generalization which maintains that the location of cities is determined largely by breaks in transportation. Perhaps many of the data for the United States support such a proposition. But in Europe, where the origins of contemporary cities go back largely to the Middle Ages, such a thesis is untenable. These European cities (fortresses at first and later on fortresses with markets attached) sprang up along established trade routes at points where robber barons could most effectively interrupt travel and exact tribute from everyone who wished to pass. Still more interesting and important, however, in connection with this thesis are the locations of the Spanish American cities.

Suppose we examine this briefly by glancing over the list of the national capitals. Santo Domingo and Havana have already been mentioned, as have Buenos Aires and Monte-

5 *Ibid.*, p. 121.

video. Panama City should be added. They are the five in
a total of 18 that were favorably located from the standpoint
of transportation facilities. But if we consider Mexico City,
Guatemala City (or Antigua as well), San Salvador, Tegucigalpa, Managua, and San José we must conclude that a favorable location for the purposes of transportation was least in
the thoughts of those selecting the sites for such major places.
Mexico City was even established on an island in a lake! Much
the same is true of the South American capitals: Bogotá,
Caracas, Quito, Lima, La Paz (Sucre, too,) and Santiago certainly owed little of their importance in colonial times to the
transportation factor. Moreover, the vast majority of all the
other cities and towns founded by the Spaniards during the
colonial era were fully as limited in functions performed, if
not more so, than the national capitals just enumerated. They
were merely strong points, garrison towns and administrative
and religious centers (these two functions had hardly been differentiated in the colonial period) from which the Spaniards
exercised overlordship over the vassals they had conquered,
the slaves they had imported, and the choicest expanses of
the land they had seized and transformed into pastures.

The cities of colonial Brazil differed from those in the Spanish dominions in several significant ways which can be summarized briefly. In the first place they were built to no standard plan, such as that prescribed by the Laws of the Indies
for the new Spanish settlements. Hence the former lack prominent features of the latter such as the central plaza, the
solares or house lots all uniform in size and shape, and the
grid work of streets all intersecting at right angles. Second,
unlike the Spaniards who were granted immense holdings of
land, but who chose to live in the cities, the owners of the
large estates in Brazil resided in the country, each in the
mansion which served as the center for the small barony over
which he reigned. His vassals included slaves, often in large
numbers, free retainers of many kinds, a small private army,
and so on. Among his many retainers was the priest, frequently one of his less opulent kinsmen. Third, largely because
the city served to a limited extent only as a residence for the
affluent families of colonial Brazil, those that did exist were
extremely limited in functions. Throughout the sixteenth,

seventeenth, and eighteenth centuries the finest of harbors were closed to the ships of all nations except Portugal. Imports in any case were small; and the exports were limited largely to sugar, fine timber (much of this illicitly and from little-frequented anchorages), and precious metals and stones. Even such splendid natural facilities as those at Santos, Rio de Janeiro, Bahia, and Recife were not sufficient to make any of them into a great seaport. The cities that did exist, other than Rio de Janeiro which eventually became the seat of colonial government, and Bahia, once seat of both religious and administrative powers, and later on of ecclesiastical affairs only, were few in number and weak in importance. Trade and commerce, shipping, and the terminus of mule trains radiating into the interior were their chief features.

The Functions of Latin American Cities in the Period 1825 to 1945

Remarkably little change took place in the cities of Latin America during the first century of existence as independent nations of the various Spanish American countries and Brazil. With a few exceptions, of which Buenos Aires and Montevideo are the most prominent examples, the social and economic roles of these cities were about the same at the close of the First World War as they had been at the termination of the struggle for independence. Between 1918 and 1940 more fundamental changes got underway, but the effects of most of the new factors influencing the situation did not become fully apparent until after the Second World War.

Throughout the nineteenth century and well along into the twentieth, government and administration and residence for the best families, their numerous servants, and for the craftsmen and artisans required to meet their needs, continued to be the bases of urban life. Consider, for example, the fact that the era of canal building, which determined largely the location and basic functions of many important cities in the United States, in the "opening of the West," never fired the imaginations of those responsible for the policies of Latin American countries. Similarly, the river steamboats, a transportation factor which determined many of the important features of dozens of other important cities of the United States (Cincinnati, Louisville, St. Louis, Memphis, and New Orleans to mention a few of the major ones), played virtually no role in the development of Latin American cities. In this case there was interest involved, and as Spanish domination crumbled emissaries from the United States were among the first on the scene in the various capitals seeking, among other things, concessions for the operation of steamboats on such rivers as the Magdalena and the Orinoco. Some lines were actually established on these, on the Paraná-Paraguay system, on the São Francisco (Brazil), and other lesser streams. In fact the services on a few still linger. Steam navigation on the greatest of all river systems (Amazon), however, was via ocean-going vessels, including those from Liverpool and other European ports and Brazilian coastal ships operating out of Rio de Janeiro and Santos. With a few possible exceptions, though, the role of the steamboat was practically nil in the transformation of Latin American cities into centers specializing in the transportation and commercial functions.

Due to the reciprocal relationship between transportation facilities, on the one hand, and trade and commerce, on the other, in the vast majority of Latin American cities and towns trade and commerce were slow in developing. However, in Argentina the heavy flow of immigrants of European origin, the settlement of new lands, and the development of farms and farming to go along with the traditional pastoral activities, brought forth huge amounts of wheat, flax, corn, and other products for sale and export. As a result, Buenos Aires and Rosário, to mention the two most important cities, grew with great rapidity, and greatly diversified their functions. Both emerged as great transportation centers in which the transfer from land to sea forms of transportation took place; both became bustling centers of trade and commerce; and both experienced a level of financial activities previously unknown in Latin America. Except for the lack of manufacturing and processing to furnish employment for large parts of their labor forces, by the close of the nineteenth century these Argentine cities had come to be multifunctional centers in the truest sense of the term.

Elsewhere in Latin America, the transformation got underway later and proceeded more slowly, so that most Latin American cities in the opening quarter of the twentieth century were strikingly like what they had been in the middle of the nineteenth. Argentina's cities, however, felt the full impact of the revolution in transportation on land brought about by the use of mobile steam engines to move trains of cars over railroads. Buenos Aires, particularly, became the hub of a great system of transportation.

On a much lesser scale during the years from 1850 on systems of railroads also were constructed in parts of some of the other countries. However, only São Paulo and Rio de Janeiro in Brazil, along with Santiago (and perhaps Valparaiso) in Chile, and Panama City actually were changed very much by the coming of the epoch of the railways. Mexico City, Bogotá, Caracas, Quito, Lima, La Paz, and Montevideo are among the capitals which felt only a minimum impact of the new revolutionary factor in transportation which elsewhere had a huge role in transforming the functions of cities.

Along other lines as well this particular aspect of social differentiation proceeded very slowly. The functions of most of the cities remained limited and comparatively little division of labor between various centers and specialization on the part of individual places took place. All of this set the stage that was to come in the middle of the twentieth century when the fever of modernization and development finally struck the Latin American countries in a vigorous form.

Current Metamorphosis of Latin American Cities

Following the close of the Second World War the functions of Latin American cities have changed and diversified almost as if accomplished by the wave of a magic wand. The populations of these urban centers have increased at a dizzy pace; at long last they quickly have become important commercial and transportation centers; many have developed substantial bases for their economies in the manufacturing and transforming industries; their financial roles have been modernized and greatly expanded; and their construction activities have doubled and redoubled time after time. Already the functions of most Latin American cities resemble much more closely those of important urban centers in Western Europe, the United States, and Canada, than they do the ones they themselves were performing in 1900 and in large numbers of cases as late as 1940. This metamorphosis deserves thorough-going consideration and study.

Before we focus our attention upon some of the details of the radical transformation that is underway, however, it is well to re-emphasize that the exact timing of the revolutionary developments differed considerably from country to country and city to city. As indicated above, the progress began earliest of all in Argentina, probably due largely to the immigration of large numbers of Europeans. These newcomers were thoroughly imbued with a venturesome commercial spirit, and they were not dominated largely by a feudalistic and pastoral outlook on life. In any case the promotion of agriculture by D. F. Sarmiento and others, the building of a web of railways with Buenos Aires as the hub, the construction of docks and storage facilities, the establishment of essential financial institutions, and so on, all were accomplished before the close of the nineteenth century.

In other countries Montevideo, São Paulo-Santos, and Rio de Janeiro, to a limited extent, were among the first places to experience some of the impact of the modern stream of urban development. Before the opening of the Panama Canal, however, all the West Coast cities were virtually shut off from effective means of promoting trade and commerce; and the extreme cost in time and money in bringing centers such as La Paz, Quito, Bogotá, Caracas, San José, Guatemala City, and Mexico City into the circulatory system of international trade meant that they would be among the last to feel the impulse of modern urban transformations. Moreover, in some cases, of which Mexico's cities are prime examples, bloody revolutions and protracted civil wars were to delay for decades any substantial start on overwhelming the basic functions performed by the cities.

TRADE AND COMMERCE. Perhaps the change, almost a societal mutation, in trade and commerce has best claim to primacy in the fundamental transformation of the basic functions of Latin American cities. Perhaps, too, the commercial outlook on life of a few Europeans who established residences in Latin American cities, sometimes as representatives of foreign companies and often as immigrants, was the factor which set the wheels in motion. Refugees from the Hitlerized Central Europe of the 1930's probably played a role inordinately out of proportion to their number. By ship and train the present writer travelled with hundreds of these people as they were seeking new locations in the Latin American countries; and only a few years afterward friends were indicating to him large sections of the shopping centers of city after city in which they were reputed to own and control every store in block after block of the commercial districts. Be this as it may, suddenly in the 1940's and 1950's great department stores, highly specialized retail outlets, and all the appurtenances of modern commerce sprang up as though by magic. Simultaneously, in city and country alike, the handicrafts began to become more standardized, it became obvious many things were being made for a specific market, barter became less prevalent, the practice of selling at established and marked prices became the rule in the stores, the metric system of weights and measures became of importance functionally, and in brief the commercial spirit waxed in importance in the cities themselves and even throughout their hinterlands. By 1968 it is likely that commercial enterprises lead all others in furnishing employment to those living in Latin American cities and towns, and probably the same is true in a majority of all the places if each were considered separately.

TRANSPORTATION. From what has already been said it should be evident that in the great nineteenth century transformation of urban functions, in a figurative sense and also in a very literal one, most Latin American cities "missed the boat" and they also "missed the train." In the present century, though, as the motor vehicle worked its revolutionary effect upon urban places, Latin American centers did not entirely "miss the bus," even though they were somewhat late in catching it. Specifically, as Latin American cities took on important roles as transportation centers, neither river steamboats nor rail facilities played any very great parts in the transformation. The former continues to be vital in a few cases, such as that of Asunción; but interestingly enough in places such as Belém, Manaus, Iquitos, and Pulcalpa, to mention only four of those in the great Amazon Basin, transportation by means of motor launches and canoes propelled by outboard motors have been of major importance in the development of transportation. With respect to railroads, some extension of lines is still taking place, and there also are some efforts to modernize facilities for commuters within the metropolitan communities. On the relative basis, though, the lines and rolling stock get more and more inadequate every year, for the additions fail by huge margins to keep pace with the tremendous annual increase in the urban and suburban populations.

The automobile, the motor truck, and improved roads are the great agents now swelling the importance of the Latin American cities as transportation centers. One must stress, however, the recency with which the impact of these factors has been felt and the fact that they by no means have lost their force in making for change. When I travelled extensively through Mexico, Brazil, and Colombia during the years 1935–1945, I relived in thousands of respects the early days of automobiling which I had experienced during my youth in Colorado and New Mexico in the period 1910–1915. "Roads" which consisted of the ruts worn by vehicles previously passing that way, the fording of streams, the practice of carrying along extra cans of gasoline and oil, extra tires and tubes, frequent sojourns in mudholes, gates by the hundreds to open and close, frequent blowouts and other tire troubles, encounters with herds of cattle and sheep, stops for conversations with natives along the wayside, unceasing alertness to keep on the trail and take the correct road at the fork, these were only a few of the joys of motoring in the mountainous sections of the United States when I was a boy. They also were features of motoring which I experienced 25 years later in the three countries named.

The important point of all this in relation to the present topic is that as late as 1940 the role of the motor vehicle in moving goods and people in and out of Latin American cities was a very limited one. If all of the automobiles and trucks I encountered in an entire month of travel in Mexico, Brazil, and Colombia had converged on Mexico City, Rio de Janeiro or São Paulo, or Bogotá, respectively, their volume of traffic would not have equalled that which now moves into each of those cities daily, during half a day, and perhaps even hourly. More and more paved highways and superhighways choked with motor traffic, radiating out from the capitals are indicative of the high degree in which those large cities have greatly enhanced their function as centers of land transport. But the revolution involved goes far beyond the limits of the metropolitan centers. Its impact is great in cities of all sizes, towns in the most remote recesses of the various countries, and even in almost 100 per cent of the villages.

The principal Latin American cities also have become great centers of air transportation. The very same places which missed the boat, missed the train, and almost missed the bus, were among the first in the world to take to the plane. Again, though, almost all of this development has taken place since 1940. That year one who had the temerity to travel by plane or even took the trouble to drive out to an airport encountered no huge, scrambling masses of humanity, and no extensive depot for the reception and shipment of goods such as now must be contended against in hundreds of teeming terminals. In 1968, air transport competes with motor transportation for the place of primary importance in moving people, produce, and manufactured goods to and from the city. Much of this, of course, involves tremendous sleek jets which link the Latin American cities to others in all parts of the world. Shipments between the Unitel States and many places, particularly the once remote cities such as Bogotá, Quito, and La Paz, cost less if the goods are moved by air freight than if they are sent via surface transportation. The international traveler, though, is likely to be most impressed by the hordes of people with whom he competes for breathing space in various greatly over-crowded passenger terminals. The people move between various parts of their nation in fleets of older, smaller and slower planes. Finally, one who himself undertakes to go to many still remote places in the various countries may find himself in a "mixed" carrier along with a motley array of fellow passengers, crates of livestock and poultry, boxes and bales of merchandise, and sacks of various kinds of produce. In short, the emergence, perfection, and proliferation of the

means of moving people and things by air has been a powerful factor in bringing the transportation function to the fore
in Latin American cities and, simultaneously, of altering substantially the basic forms of life and labor in the Latin American countries.

MANUFACTURING AND PROCESSING. The rapid development
of light and heavy industry and urban locations for most
of the greatly expanded numbers of processing plants constitutes the third of the major features of the recent and
current diversification of the functions of Latin American
cities. These trends, although getting well underway only in
the recent past, are hemisphere-wide. Before World War II
the Latin American countries were almost exclusively dependent upon imports for manufactured goods, and most of
the processing of their own products (the making of sugar,
the cleaning and drying of coffee, the milling of rice, the
preparation of flour and meal, the slaughter of livestock and
the chilling of meat, and so on) were carried out on the
plantations and other estates. Moreover, except in connection
with products for export, the processing of products was min-
imal: most of the foodstuffs for domestic consumption showed
up in the large, open air, public market in about the same
form as they were when dug, cut, pulled, or picked as the
case might be. Now all this has changed to a radical degree.
Almost to a man those who succeed one another at the helms
of national policies seem to regard industrialization as the
cure-all for each nation's host of chronic and acute social
and economic problems. Immense amounts of public and
private funds from at home and abroad are being expended
for the purpose of promoting the industrial plants which
are springing up by the thousands. The processing and marketing of food and other products for domestic consumption
are being modernized at a rapid pace.

As a result, manufacturing and processing industries are
now significant functions in hundreds of Latin American
cities in which only 25 years ago they were conspicuous by
their absence. All of the great cities, such as Buenos Aires,
Rio de Janeiro, São Paulo, Mexico City, Lima, Bogotá, and
Santiago, now include substantial industrial activity as impor-

tant items in their highly diversified set of functions, and one of them (São Paulo) is rather highly specialized along this line. Moreover, on the basis of the high proportion of all those in the labor force who are engaged in manufacturing, it now is possible to characterize a few important Latin American cities as being rather highly specialized in the industrial function. The list of these could take on an impressive length if the smaller industrial centers such as Volta Redonda (Brazil), Oroya (Peru), and Paz del Rio (Colombia) were included. For our purposes, though, it probably is best to limit it to the few great cities which properly belong in a category of places specializing in manufacturing, all places that were in existence in the colonial period and once were primarily governmental and administrative centers. Even so at least São Paulo, Monterrey, Cali, and Medellín must be specified.

OTHER DIVERSIFICATION OF URBAN FUNCTIONS. It is hoped that enough has been said to call attention to the rapid change and diversification in the functions of Latin American cities which is going on during the second half of the twentieth century. The vast majority of these cities entered the twentieth century performing functions that had changed very little since the sixteenth and seventeenth centuries when they were founded by the Spaniards and the Portuguese. For well over 300 years they continued to be largely governmental and administrative centers. Since 1900 in many cases, and since 1940 in almost all, they have rapidly diversified by taking on important roles as commercial, transportation, and, in many cases, industrial centers. This growth has been covered in our analysis.

It also would be possible to discuss in some detail the important changes in other functions such as communication, construction, repair and service work (which mounts by leaps and bounds in an age of automobiles and electric equipment), commercialized recreation, professional and cultural activities, and so on. There has even been the establishment of Brasília, another purely governmental and administrative center (where the haste with which banks in all parts of the Republic established their branches in the new city is an object lesson in the close interdependence of government and finance in the modern state). It is believed, though, that enough has been presented to demonstrate adequately the thesis of this paper that the functions of Latin American cities are rapidly undergoing a complete metamorphosis.

Selected Bibliography

◆

THIS BIBLIOGRAPHY is highly selected. Most of the titles are those used in the reading lists prepared for the students in the author's courses and seminars on Latin American societies. Only works in English are included, and those wishing to consult studies published in other languages are referred to two excellent bibliographies, namely, the *Handbook of Latin American Studies* prepared in the Hispanic Foundation of the Library of Congress and published annually by Harvard University Press from 1938 to 1950 and by the University of Florida Press from 1951 on; and a *Bibliografía Sistemática* compiled by Orlando Sepulveda and Francisco Fernandez and published as Volume I of the three-volume *Anuario de Sociología de los Pueblos Ibéricos,* Madrid: Instituto de Estudios Sindicales, Sociales y Cooperativas, 1967.

ADAMS, DALE W., and SAM SCHULMAN, "Minifundia in Agrarian Reform: A Colombian Example." *Land Economics,* Vol. XLIII, No. 3 (August, 1967), pp. 274–283.

ADAMS, RICHARD N., "A Change from Caste to Class in a Peruvian Sierra Town." *Social Forces,* Vol. 31, No. 3 (March, 1953), pp. 238–244.

ALERS, J. OSCAR, "Population and Development in a Peruvian Community." *Journal of Inter-American Studies,* Vol. VII, No. 4 (October, 1965) pp. 423–448.

ANDRESKI, STANISLAV, *Parasitism and Subversion: The Case of Latin America.* New York: Pantheon Books, 1966.

ARRIAGA, EDUARDO E., "Components of City Growth in Selected Latin American Countries." *Milbank Memorial Fund Quarterly,* Vol. 46, No. 2, Part 1 (April, 1968), pp. 237–252.

AZEVEDO, THALES DE, *Social Change in Brazil,* Latin American Monographs No. 22. Gainesville: University of Florida Press, 1962.

BASTIDE, ROGER, "Religion and the Church in Brazil." In T. Lynn Smith and Alexander Marchant, editors, *Brazil:*

Portrait of Half a Continent, New York: The Dryden Press, Inc., 1951, pp. 334–355.

BENDIX, REINHARD, and SEYMOUR M. LIPSET, editors, *Class, Status, and Power: Social Stratification in International Perspective.* New York: The Free Press, 1966.

BIESANZ, JOHN, and MARVIS BIESANZ, *Costa Rican Life.* New York: Columbia University Press, 1944.

———— and ————, *The People of Panama.* New York: Columbia University Press, 1955.

BLACKMAR, FRANK W. *Spanish Institutions of the Southwest.* Baltimore: The Johns Hopkins University Press, 1891.

BORAH, WOODROW, and SHERBURNE F. COOK, "Marriage and Legitimacy in Mexican Culture: Mexico and California." *California Law Review,* Vol. LIV, No. 2 (May, 1966), pp. 946–1008.

BORGES SCHMIDT, CARLOS, "Rural Life in Brazil." In T. Lynn Smith and Alexander Marchant, editors, *Brazil: Portrait of Half a Continent,* New York: The Dryden Press, Inc., 1951, pp. 165–187.

CANDIDO, ANTONIO, "The Brazilian Family." In T. Lynn Smith and Alexander Marchant, editors, *Brazil: Portrait of Half a Continent,* New York: The Dryden Press, 1951, pp. 291–312.

CAPLOW, THEODORE, "The Social Ecology of Guatemala City." *Social Forces,* Vol. 28, No. 2 (December, 1949), pp. 113–133.

CARTER, WILLIAM E., *Aymara Communities and the Bolivian Agrarian Reform,* Social Sciences Monographs No. 24. Gainesville: University of Florida Press, 1964.

DAVIS, KINGSLEY, and ANA CASIS, "Urbanization in Latin America." *Milbank Memorial Fund Quarterly,* Vol. 24 (April, 1946), pp. 186–207.

DE YOUNG, MAURICE, *Man and Land in the Haitian Economy,* Latin American Monographs No. 3. Gainesville: University of Florida Press, 1958.

DOBYNS, HENRY F. *The Social Matrix of Peruvian Indigenous Communities.* Ithaca, N.Y.: Department of Anthropology, Cornell University, 1964.

DOTSON, FLOYD, and LILLIAN OTA DOTSON, "Ecological Trends in the City of Guadalajara, Mexico." *Social Forces,* Vol. 32, No. 3 (March, 1954), pp. 367–374.

———— and ————, "Urban Centralization and Decentralization in Mexico." *Rural Sociology,* Vol. 21, No. 1 (March, 1956), pp. 41–49.

ELIZAGA, JUAN C., "A Study of Migration to Greater Santiago." *Demography* Vol. 3, No. 2 (1966), pp. 352–377.

FALS BORDA, ORLANDO, "Bases for a Sociological Interpretation of Education in Colombia." In A. Curtis Wilgus, editor, *The Caribbean: Contemporary Colombia,* Gainesville: University of Florida Press, 1962, pp. 183–213.

————, *Facts and Theory of Sociocultural Change in a Rural Social System,* Monografias Sociológicas, No. 2. Bogotá: Universidad Nacional de Colombia, 1960.

————, "Fragmentation of Holdings in Boyacá." *Rural Sociology,* Vol. 21, No. 2 (June, 1956), pp. 158–163.

————, *Peasant Society in the Colombian Andes: A Sociological Study of Saucio.* Gainesville: University of Florida Press, 1955.

————, "Violence and Break-Up of Tradition." In Claudio Veliz, editor, *Obstacles to Change in Latin America,* London, Oxford, and New York: Oxford University Press, 1965, pp. 188–205.

FLIEGEL, FREDERICK C., "Differences in Prestige Standards and Orientation to Change in a Traditional Agricultural Setting." *Rural Sociology,* Vol. 30, No. 3 (September, 1965), pp. 278–290.

FORD, THOMAS R., *Man and Land in Peru.* Gainesville: University of Florida Press, 1955.

FORM, WILLIAM H., and ALBERT A. BLUM, editors, *Industrial Relations and Social Change in Latin America.* Gainesville: University of Florida Press, 1965.

FREITAS MARCONDES, J. V., *First Brazilian Legislation Relating to Rural Labor Unions,* Latin American Monographs No. 20. Gainesville: University of Florida Press, 1962.

————, and T. LYNN SMITH, "The Caipira of the Paraitinga Valley, Brazil." *Social Forces,* Vol. 31, No. 1 (October, 1952), pp. 47–53.

FRETZ, JOSEPH WINFIELD, *Immigrant Group Settlements in Paraguay.* North Newton, Kansas: Bethel College, 1962.

————, *Pilgrims in Paraguay.* Scottdale, Pennsylvania: Herold Press, 1953.

FREYRE, GILBERTO, *The Masters and the Slaves,* translated by Samuel Putnam. New York: Alfred A. Knopf, Inc., 1946.

FUJII, YUKIO, and T. LYNN SMITH, *The Acculturation of Japanese Immigrants in Brazil,* Latin American Monographs No. 8. Gainesville: University of Florida Press, 1959.

GOLDRICH, DANIEL, *Sons of the Establishment: Elite Youth in Panama and Costa Rica.* Chicago: Rand and McNally Company, 1966.

HANSEN, ASAEL T., "The Ecology of a Latin American City." In Edward B. Reuter, editor, *Race and Culture Contacts,* New York: McGraw-Hill Book Company, 1934, pp. 124–152.

HARRIS, MARVIN, *Town and Country in Brazil.* New York: Columbia University Press, 1956.

HAUSER, PHILIP M., editor, *Urbanization in Latin America.* Paris: United Nations Educational, Scientific and Cultural Organization, 1961.

HAWTHORN, HARRY B., and AUDREY HAWTHORN, "The Shape of a City: Some Observations on Sucre, Bolivia." *Sociology and Social Research,* Vol. 33 (1948), pp. 87–91.

HAYNER, NORMAN S., "Mexico City: Its Growth and Configuration." *American Journal of Sociology,* Vol. 50, No. 1 (January, 1945), pp. 295–304.

——, and UNA MIDDLETON HAYNER, *New Patterns in Old Mexico.* New Haven, Connecticut: College and University Press, 1966.

HEATH, DWIGHT B., and RICHARD N. ADAMS, editors, *Contemporary Cultures and Societies of Latin America.* New York: Random House, 1965.

HUTCHINSON, HARRY WILLIAM, *Village and Plantation Life in Northeastern Brazil.* Seattle: University of Washington Press, 1957.

IUTAKA, SUGIYAMA, "Social Mobility and Differential Occupational Opportunity in Brazil." *Human Organization,* Vol. 25, No. 2 (Summer, 1966), pp. 126–130.

——, "Social Stratification Research in Latin America." *Latin American Research Review,* Vol. I, No. 1 (Fall, 1965), pp. 7–37.

LAMBERT, JACQUES, *Latin America*. Berkeley: University of California Press, 1967.

LEONARD, OLEN E., *Bolivia: Land, People and Institutions*. Washington, D.C.: The Scarecrow Press, 1952.

————, *Canton Chullpas: A Socioeconomic Study of an Area in the Cochabamba Valley of Bolivia*. Washington: U. S. Department of Agriculture, 1948.

LEONARD, OLEN E., and CHARLES P. LOOMIS, editors, *Readings in Latin American Social Organization and Institutions*. East Lansing: Michigan State College Bookstore, 1953.

LEWIS, OSCAR, *The Children of Sanchez: Autobiography of a Mexican Family*. New York: Random House, 1961.

————, *Pedro Martinez: A Mexican Peasant and His Family*. New York: Random House, 1964.

————, *Tepoztlán, Village in Mexico*. New York: Henry Holt & Co., 1960.

LEYBURN, JAMES G., *The Haitian People*. New Haven, Connecticut: Yale University Press, 1941.

LIPMAN, AARON, "Social Backgrounds of the Bogotá Entrepreneur." *Journal of Inter-American Studies,* Vol. VII, No. 2 (April, 1965), pp. 227–235.

LIPSET, SEYMOUR M., and ALDO SOLARI, editors, *Elites in Latin America*. New York: Oxford University Press, 1967.

LOOMIS, CHARLES P., and JOHN C. MCKINNEY, "Systematic Differences between Latin American Communities of Family Farms and Large Estates." *American Journal of Sociology,* Vol. LXI, No. 5 (March, 1956).

LOOMIS, CHARLES P., JULIO O. MORALES, ROY A. CLIFFORD, and OLEN E. LEONARD, editors, *Turrialba: Social Systems and the Introduction of Change*. Glencoe, Illinois: The Free Press, 1953.

MCBRIDE, GEORGE M., *Chile: Land and Society,* New York: American Geographical Society, 1936.

MORSE, RICHARD M., *From Community to Metropolis*. Gainesville: University of Florida Press, 1958.

NELSON, LOWRY, "Cuban Paradoxes." In A. Curtis Wilgus, editor, *The Caribbean at Mid-Century,* Gainesville: University of Florida Press, 1951, pp. 136–148.

———, *Rural Cuba.* Minneapolis: University of Minnesota Press, 1950.

———, "Rural Sociology: Some Inter-American Aspects." *Journal of Inter-American Studies,* Vol. IX, No. 3 (July, 1967), pp. 323–338.

PIERSON, DONALD, *Cruz das Almas: A Brazilian Village.* Washington, D.C.: The Smithsonian Institution, 1951.

———, *Negroes in Brazil.* Chicago: University of Chicago Press, 1942. (Re-issued by the Southern Illinois University Press, Carbondale, 1967.)

RIOS, JOSÉ ARTHUR, "Assimilation of Emigrants from the Old South in Brazil." *Social Forces,* Vol. 26, No. 2 (December, 1947), pp. 145–152.

———, "The Cities of Brazil." In T. Lynn Smith and Alexander Marchant, editors, *Brazil: Portrait of Half a Continent,* New York: The Dryden Press, 1951, pp. 188–208.

ROSS, EDWARD A., *South of Panama.* New York: The Century Company, 1915.

SAUNDERS, JOHN VAN DYKE, "The Brazilian Negro." *The Americas,* Vol. XV, No. 3 (January, 1959), pp. 271–290.

———, *Differential Fertility in Brazil.* Gainesville: University of Florida Press, 1958.

———, "Man-Land Relations in Ecuador." *Rural Sociology,* Vol. XXVI, No. 1 (March, 1961), pp. 57–69.

———, *The Population of Ecuador: A Demographic Analysis,* Latin American Monographs No. 14. Gainesville: University of Florida Press, 1960.

———, *Social Factors in Latin American Modernization,* Occasional Paper No. 5. Nashville: Vanderbilt University, Graduate Center for Latin American Studies, 1965.

SCHNORE, LEO F., "On the Spatial Structure of Cities in the Two Americas." In Philip M. Hauser and Leo F. Schnore, editors, *The Study of Urbanization,* New York: John Wiley and Sons, Inc., 1965, pp. 347–398.

SCHULMAN, SAM, "The Colono System in Latin America." *Rural Sociology,* Vol. 20, No. 1 (March, 1955), pp. 34–40.

SENIOR, CLARENCE, *Land Reform and Democracy.* Gainesville: University of Florida Press, 1958.

SILVERT, KALMAN H., *The Conflict Society: Reaction and*

Revolution in Latin America. New York: American Universities Field Staff, 1966.

SIMPSON, EYLER N., *The Ejido: Mexico's Way Out.* Chapel Hill: University of North Carolina Press, 1937.

SMITH, T. LYNN, "Agrarian Reform in Brazil." *Luso-Brazilian Review,* Vol. I., No. 2 (December, 1964), pp. 3–20.

————, editor, *Agrarian Reform in Latin America.* New York: Alfred A. Knopf, Inc., 1965.

————, "Agricultural Systems and Standards of Living." *Inter-American Economic Review,* Vol. III, No. 3 (Winter, 1949), pp. 15–28.

————, *Brazil: People and Institutions,* third edition. Baton Rouge: Louisiana State University Press, 1963.

————, "Colonization and Settlement in Colombia." *Rural Sociology,* Vol. XII, No. 2 (June, 1947), pp. 128–139.

————, *Colombia: Social Structure and the Process of Development.* Gainesville: University of Florida Press, 1967.

————, "Current Population Trends in Latin America." *American Journal of Sociology,* Vol. LXII, No. 4 (January, 1957), pp. 399–406.

————, *Current Social Trends and Problems in Latin America,* Latin American Monographs No. 1. Gainesville: University of Florida Press, 1957.

————, "The Cultural Setting of Agricultural Extension Work in Colombia." *Rural Sociology,* Vol. X, No. 3 (September, 1945), pp. 235–246.

————, "The Giant Awakes: Brazil." *The Annals of the American Academy of Political and Social Science,* No. 334 (March, 1961), pp. 95–102.

————, "The Growth of Population in Central and South America." In U. S. House of Representatives, Committee on the Judiciary, *Study of Population and Immigration Problems,* Special Series No. 6, Washington: U. S. Government Printing Office, 1963, pp. 151–176.

————, "Land Tenure and Soil Erosion in Colombia." *Proceedings of the Inter-American Conference on the Conservation of Renewable Natural Resources,* Washington: U. S. Department of State, 1949, pp. 155–160.

————, "Land Tenure in Brazil." *The Journal of Land and Public Utility Economics,* Vol. XX, No. 3 (August, 1944), pp. 194–201.

————, *Latin American Population Studies,* Social Sciences Monographs No. 8. Gainesville: University of Florida Press, 1961.

————, "The Locality Group Structure of Brazil." *American Sociological Review,* Vol. IX, No. 2 (June, 1944), pp. 103–115.

————, "Notes on Population and Rural Social Organization in El Salvador." *Rural Sociology,* Vol. X, No. 4 (December, 1945), pp. 359–370.

————, "Notes on Population and Social Organization in the Central Portion of the São Francisco Valley." *Inter-American Economic Affairs,* Vol. I, No. 3 (December, 1947), pp. 45–54.

————, "Patterns of Living in the United States and Brazil: A Comparison." *Journal of Inter-American Studies,* Vol. III, No. 2 (April, 1961), pp. 187–200.

————, "The Population of the Central American Countries." In A. Curtis Wilgus, editor, *The Caribbean: The Central American Area,* Gainesville: University of Florida Press, 1961, pp. 38–47.

————, *The Process of Rural Development in Latin America,* Social Sciences Monographs No. 33. Gainesville: University of Florida Press, 1967.

————, "The Population of Latin America." In Ronald Freedman, editor, *Population: The Vital Revolution,* New York: Doubleday & Company, 1964, pp. 178–190.

————, "The Racial Composition of the Population of Colombia." *Journal of Inter-American Studies,* Vol. VIII, No. 2 (April, 1966), pp. 212–235.

————, "The Reproduction Rate in Latin America." *Population Studies,* Vol. XII, No. 1 (July, 1955), pp. 3–17.

————, "The Rural Community with Special Reference to Latin America." *Rural Sociology,* Vol. 23, No. 1 (March, 1958), pp. 52–67.

————, "Salient Features of Agrarian Reform in Latin America." *International Labour Review,* Vol. 91, No. 4 (April, 1965), pp. 321–331.

————, "Some Observations on Land Tenure in Colombia." *Foreign Agriculture,* Vol. XVI, No. 6 (June, 1952), pp. 119–124.

————, "Urbanization in Latin America." *International*

Journal of Comparative Sociology, Vol. IV, No. 2 (September, 1963), pp. 227–242.

————, "Values Held by People in Latin America which Affect Technical Cooperation." *Rural Sociology*, Vol. 21, No. 1 (March, 1956), pp. 68–75.

————, "Why the Cities? Observations on Urbanization in Latin America." In Philip L. Astuto and Ralph A. Leal, editors, *Latin American Problems*, Thought Patterns No. 12, Jamaica, N.Y.: St. John's University Press, 1964, pp. 17–33.

————, Justo Díaz Rodríguez, and Luis Roberto Garcia, *Tabio: A Study in Rural Social Organization*, Washington: U. S. Department of Agriculture, 1944.

STYCOS, J. MAYONE, "Survey Research and Population Control in Latin America." *The Public Opinion Quarterly*, Vol. 28 (Fall, 1964), pp. 367–372.

————, *Human Fertility in Latin America*. Ithaca, N.Y.: Cornell University Press, 1968.

TAYLOR, CARL C., *Rural Life in Argentina*. Baton Rouge: Louisiana State University Press, 1948.

————, "Some Land Situations and Problems in Caribbean Countries." In A. Curtis Wilgus, editor, *The Caribbean: Contemporary Trends*, Gainesville: University of Florida Press, 1953, pp. 59–73.

TUMIN, MELVIN M., *Caste in Peasant Society*. Princeton, N.J.: Princeton University Press, 1952.

VAN DEN BERGHE, PIERRE L., "Ethnic Membership and Cultural Change in Guatemala." *Social Forces*, Vol. 46, No. 4 (June, 1968), pp. 514–522.

WAGLEY, CHARLES, *An Introduction to Brazil*. New York: Columbia University Press, 1963.

————, *Amazon Town: A Study of Man in the Tropics*. New York: The Macmillan Company, 1953.

————, "The Brazilian Revolution: Social Changes Since 1930." In Council on Foreign Relations, *Social Change in Latin America Today*, New York: Random House, 1960, pp. 177–230.

————, *Economics of a Guatemalan Village*, Menasha, Wisconsin: American Anthropological Association, 1941.

————, editor, *Race and Class in Rural Brazil*, Paris: UNESCO, 1952.

WHETTEN, NATHAN L., *Guatemala: Land and People*. New Haven, Connecticut: Yale University Press, 1961.

———, *Rural Mexico*. Chicago: University of Chicago Press, 1948.

———, and ROBERT G. BURNIGHT, "Internal Migration in Mexico." *Rural Sociology*, Vol. 21, No. 2 (June, 1956), pp. 140–151.

WHITEFORD, ANDREW H., *Two Cities of Latin America*. Beloit, Wisconsin: Logan Museum of Beloit College, 1960.

WHITTEN, NORMAN E., JR., "Power Structure and Sociocultural Change in Latin American Communities." *Social Forces*, Vol. 43, No. 3 (March, 1965), pp. 320–329.

WILLEMS, EMILIO, *Followers of the Faith: Culture Change and the Rise of Protestantism in Brazil and Chile*. Nashville, Tennessee: Vanderbilt University Press, 1967.

WILLIAMSON, ROBERT C., "Some Variables of Middle and Lower Class in Two Central American Cities." *Social Forces*, Vol. 41, No. 2 (December, 1962), pp. 195–207.

WINNIE, WILLIAM W., JR., *Latin American Development*. Los Angeles: University of California, 1967.

WOOD, JAMES R., and EUGENE A. WEINSTEIN, "Industrialization, Values, and Occupational Evaluation in Uruguay." *American Journal of Sociology*, Vol. 72, No. 1 (July, 1966), pp. 47–57.

ZIMMERMAN, CARLE C., "Family Organization and Standards of Living." In Foreign Policy Association, Commission on Cuban Affairs, *Problems of the New Cuba*, New York: Foreign Policy Association, 1935, pp. 68–94.

INDEXES

SUBJECT INDEX

INDEX OF AUTHORS

ANCHOR BOOKS

THE NAVAHO—Clyde Kluckhohn and Dorothea Leighton; revised by Richard Kluckhohn and Lucy Wales, N28

THE NEGRO AND THE AMERICAN LABOR MOVEMENT—Julius Jacobson, ed., A495

THE NEWCOMERS—Oscar Handlin, A283

THE NEW MEDIA AND EDUCATION: Their Impact on Society—Peter H. Rossi and Bruce J. Biddle, eds., A604

OF TIME, WORK AND LEISURE: A Twentieth-Century Fund Study—Sebastian de Grazia, A380

ON INTELLECTUALS—Philip Rieff, ed., A733

THE ORGANIZATION MAN—William H. Whyte, Jr., A117

POLITICAL MAN: The Social Bases of Politics—Seymour Martin Lipset, A330

POPULATION: The Vital Revolution—Ronald Freedman, ed., A423

THE PRESENTATION OF SELF IN EVERYDAY LIFE—Erving Goffman, A174

PRISON WITHIN SOCIETY: A Reader in Penology—Lawrence Hazelrigg, ed., A620

PROTESTANT-CATHOLIC-JEW: An Essay in American Religious Sociology—Will Herberg, revised edition, A195

PSYCHEDELICS: The Uses and Implications of Hallucinogenic Drugs—Bernard Aaronson and Humphry Osmond, A736

RACE AND NATIONALITY IN AMERICAN LIFE—Oscar Handlin, A110

THE RADICAL RIGHT—Daniel Bell, ed., A376

REALITIES OF THE URBAN CLASSROOM: Observations in Elementary Schools—G. Alexander Moore, Jr., A568

THE REFORMING OF GENERAL EDUCATION: The Columbia College Experience in Its National Setting—Daniel Bell, A616

THE RELIGIOUS FACTOR—Gerhard Lenski, A337

REVOLUTION AND COUNTERREVOLUTION: Change and Persistence in Social Structures—Seymour Martin Lipset, A764

A RUMOR OF ANGELS: Modern Society and the Rediscovery of the Supernatural—Peter L. Berger, A715

THE SACRED CANOPY: Elements of a Sociological Theory of Religion—Peter L. Berger, A658

SOCIAL AND POLITICAL PHILOSOPHY: Readings from Plato to Gandhi—John Somerville and Ronald Santoni, eds., A370

THE SOCIAL CONSTRUCTION OF REALITY: A Treatise in the Sociology of Knowledge—Peter L. Berger and Thomas Luckmass, A589

SOCIALIST HUMANISM: An International Symposium—Erich Fromm, ed., A529

SOCIETY AND DEMOCRACY IN GERMANY—Ralf Dahrendorf, A684

SOCIOLOGISTS AT WORK: The Craft of Social Research—Phillip E. Hamond, ed., A598

STRUCTURAL ANTHROPOLOGY—Claude Lévi-Strauss, A599

STUDIES OF LATIN AMERICAN SOCIETIES—T. Lynn Smith, A702

TAMING MEGALOPOLIS, Volume I: What Is and What Could Be, 16Cb

SOCIOLOGY *(cont'd)*